# BLINDNESS AND WRITING

In this innovative and important study, Heather Tilley examines the huge shifts that took place in the experience and conceptualisation of blindness during the nineteenth century, and demonstrates how new writing technologies for blind people had transformative effects on literary culture. Considering the ways in which visually impaired people used textual means to shape their own identities, the book argues that blindness was also a significant trope through which writers reflected on the act of crafting literary form. Supported by an illuminating range of archival material (including unpublished letters from Wordsworth's circle, early ophthalmologic texts, embossed books and autobiographies), this is a rich account of blind people's experience, and reveals the close, and often surprising, personal engagement that canonical writers had with visual impairment. Drawing on the insights of disability studies and cultural phenomenology, Tilley highlights the importance of attending to embodied experience in the production and consumption of texts.

Heather Tilley is a Birkbeck Wellcome Trust ISSF Fellow at Birkbeck College, University of London.

CAMBRIDGE STUDIES IN NINETEENTH-CENTURY LITERATURE AND CULTURE



Nineteenth-century British literature and culture have been rich fields for interdisciplinary studies. Since the turn of the twentieth century, scholars and critics have tracked the intersections and tensions between Victorian literature and the visual arts, politics, social organization, economic life, technical innovations, scientific thought – in short, culture in its broadest sense. In recent years, theoretical challenges and historiographical shifts have unsettled the assumptions of previous scholarly synthesis and called into question the terms of older debates. Whereas the tendency in much past literary critical interpretation was to use the metaphor of culture as 'background', feminist, Foucauldian, and other analyses have employed more dynamic models that raise questions of power and of circulation. Such developments have reanimated the field. This series aims to accommodate and promote the most interesting work being undertaken on the frontiers of the field of nineteenth-century literary studies: work which intersects fruitfully with other fields of study such as history, or literary theory, or the history of science. Comparative as well as interdisciplinary approaches are welcomed.

*For a complete list of titles published see end of book.*

# BLINDNESS AND WRITING

## *From Wordsworth to Gissing*

HEATHER TILLEY

To Mike

With best wishes.

[illegible]

**CAMBRIDGE**
**UNIVERSITY PRESS**

University Printing House, Cambridge CB2 8BS, United Kingdom

One Liberty Plaza, 20th Floor, New York, NY 10006, USA

477 Williamstown Road, Port Melbourne, VIC 3207, Australia

314–321, 3rd Floor, Plot 3, Splendor Forum, Jasola District Centre, New Delhi – 110025, India

79 Anson Road, #06-04/06, Singapore 079906

Cambridge University Press is part of the University of Cambridge.

It furthers the University's mission by disseminating knowledge in the pursuit of education, learning, and research at the highest international levels of excellence.

www.cambridge.org
Information on this title: www.cambridge.org/9781107194212
DOI: 10.1017/9781108151863



First published 2018

Printed in the United Kingdom by Clays, St Ives plc

*A catalogue record for this publication is available from the British Library.*

ISBN 978-1-107-19421-2 Hardback

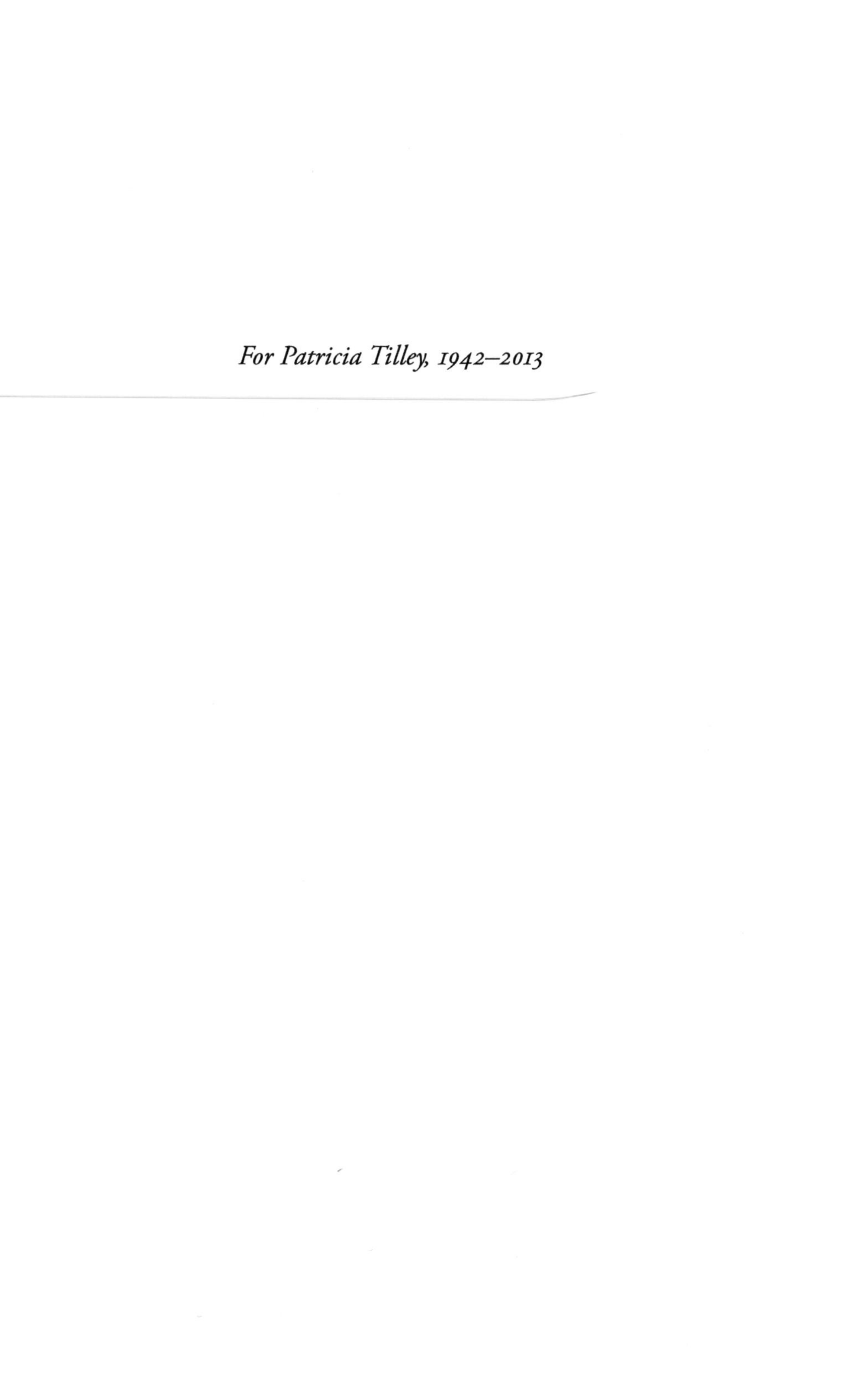

*For Patricia Tilley, 1942–2013*

# *Contents*


*List of Figures* — *page* ix
*Acknowledgements* — x

Introduction: Embodying Nineteenth-Century Blindness — 1

PART I BLIND PEOPLE'S WRITING PRACTICES — 19

1 Writing Blindness, from Vision to Touch — 21

2 The Materiality of Blindness in Wordsworth's Imagination — 41

3 'A Literature for the Blind': The Development of Raised Print Systems — 70

4 Memoirs of the Blind: The Genre of Blind Biographical Writing — 97

PART II LITERARY BLINDNESS — 121

5 Blindness, Gender and Autobiography: Reading and Writing the Self in *Jane Eyre*, *Aurora Leigh* and *The Life of Charlotte Brontë* — 123

6 Writing Blindness: Dickens — 152

7 Embodying Blindness in the Victorian Novel: Frances Browne's *My Share of the World* and Wilkie Collins's *Poor Miss Finch* — 182

8 Blindness, Writing, and the Failure of the Imagination in Gissing's *New Grub Street* 208

*Epilogue* 215
*Notes* 220
*Bibliography* 255
*Index* 271

# Figures


1 John Thomas Smith, *A Blind Beggar*, etching (1815–16). © Trustees of the British Museum. *page* 2

2 Ford Madox Brown, *Henry Fawcett; Dame Millicent Garrett Fawcett (née Garrett)*, oil on canvas (1872). © National Portrait Gallery, London. 39

3 Plate from John Vetch, *A Practical Treatise on the Diseases of the Eye* (London, 1820). © The British Library Board (shelfmark 7611.bb.19). 44

4 Margaret Gillies, *William and Mary Wordsworth*, watercolour (1839). The Wordsworth Trust, GRMDC.A4. By permission of the Wordsworth Trust, Grasmere. 54

5 W. Ridgeway, after George Smith, *A blind girl reads the bible by touch to her illiterate family in the dark*, engraving (1871). Wellcome Library, London (ref. L0073758). 83

6 James Gall's typhlograph in use. From Gall, *A Historical Sketch of the Origin and Progress of Literature for the Blind* (Edinburgh, 1834), p. 383. © The British Library Board (shelfmark 1031.k.15.2.) 95

7 W. Sharp after A. Fisher, *Oliver Caswell and Laura Bridgman*, lithograph (1844). Wellcome Library, London (ref. V0015876). 159

# *Acknowledgements*

This book has been the product of many years of thinking, writing and crafting. As such, my debts and thanks are many, and I only hope that I acknowledge duly the many wonderful friends and colleagues who have helped to bring this project into being, and whose advice and support have strengthened it (and me) along the way. *Blindness and Writing* started life as a PhD project, and I am grateful to the AHRC for a doctoral funding award that allowed me to begin my research. I was fortunate to benefit from the lively research culture of both the University of Cambridge and Birkbeck, University of London, during my PhD and I am especially grateful to John Harvey and Heather Glen for their expert early supervision of the project. Reaching back further to my first undergraduate forays, I also owe both John and Heather thanks for instilling a passion and curiosity for Victorian literature and visual culture that remain unabated. At Birkbeck, I had the privilege of working with Hilary Fraser as my graduate supervisor, with support from Luisa Calè, and their insights and questioning both sharpened and challenged my early research. Both Luisa and Hilary have continued to read and comment on portions of the project as it has evolved beyond the thesis. I am especially grateful to Hilary for many years of mentoring, friendship and inspiring advice, given always with much kindness – it has been invaluable. Thanks are owed also to my thesis examiners, David Trotter and Isobel Armstrong, for helping me to develop the project beyond the confines of a PhD. I also owe great thanks to the two anonymous readers of the manuscript, who took such care to engage with the book's themes and contents, and whose astute feedback has immeasurably improved my project.

At Birkbeck, I also owe thanks to the Centre for Nineteenth-Century Studies which has proved to be an excellent home for developing the interdisciplinary scope for the project; I have benefited greatly from friendships and connections established there. Notable were the advice and enthusiasm I received from the wonderful, generous Sally Ledger, still so-much missed. Her reading of portions of my research on Dickens, in particular, helped to strengthen the literary framework of my research. I am also grateful to my colleagues Carolyn Burdett, Patrizia di Bello, David McAllister, Vicky Mills and Ana Parejo Vadillo for their support over the years discussing my project, and also for their time and expertise in reading portions of the manuscript in various formats. I have also gained much from the insights of Birkbeck's remarkable students, particularly those involved in fascinating projects on disability and Victorian culture over the past few years – notably Alison Moulds, Peter Molloy and Simon Jarrett. Thanks are also due to Ben Winyard for providing such close and careful reading of draft chapters – over numerous cups of coffee, he helped me to make connections previously missed and gave me courage when mine was ebbing. I am also very thankful to the British Academy for a three-year postdoctoral research fellowship award that allowed me the space and time to rework the manuscript in its later phases. I am also immensely grateful to colleagues in the Department of English Literature, Language and Linguistics at Newcastle University, who supported me in my postdoctoral application to the British Academy: Kate Chedgzoy, Jenny Richards, Ella Dzelzainis and Matthew Grenby. Their insights helped shaped a new phase of research on Victorian tactile culture, which strengthened the focus of *Blindness and Writing* in unexpected and important ways. Latterly, I have been fortunate to receive funding from Birkbeck and the Wellcome Trust as an ISSF early career research fellow, and through this role I have been enriched by new colleagues as the book neared completion. Many thanks to Jo Winning, Suzannah Biernoff and Peter Fifield, and to colleagues involved in Birkbeck's Medical Humanities Reading Group, who have provided such fascinating opportunities to think newly about the body, illness and disability.

Numerous other friends and colleagues have generously shared their thoughts and insights about this project. Many thanks to Sean Ryder, not only for reading drafts of the project, but also for such perceptive and inspiring discussion over the years as it has evolved. Colleagues in the material texts network here at Birkbeck have also helped me to develop my research on embossed writing: notably Dennis Duncan and Gill Partington. The opportunity to discuss the project with Naomi Hetherington, Reina van der Wiel, John Chu and Mary Wills has also been much appreciated, as has the friendship of all. Many thanks also to Gavin Edwards and Holly Furneaux for their careful reading of sections of my manuscript, and generous engagement with the project. I have also benefited enormously from the rich and growing field of research into blindness and its cultural traditions, which is generating exciting new forums for discussion. I was fortunate to meet Hannah Thompson and Selina Mills at a conference on blindness in Paris in 2013, and ongoing conversation and friendship with them both have strengthened the framework of my project. Thanks to Georgina Kleege and David Bolt, who were excellent early readers of my research into Frances Browne and the autobiographical writings of other nineteenth-century blind spokespeople. Thanks also to Jan-Eric Olsén for many fascinating discussions of our shared research interests in nineteenth-century blindness, and for an important introduction to the archival holdings of the Medical Museion, Copenhagen. Matt Rubery has likewise provided invaluable advice and support over the past few years, and proved to be an astute reader of sections of the manuscript. Finally here, I am very grateful to Vanessa Warne, for many years now of invigorating conversation, friendship and generosity as we have developed our projects on nineteenth-century blindness and literary culture. Scholarship in this field is marked by openness, and primarily motivated by a desire to understand the agents, objects and modes of thinking and feeling at stake, and Vanessa's work is exemplary of how this is producing important new readings of nineteenth-century culture.

I am also grateful to the many archivists and librarians who have helped to identify objects and materials relating to the historical experience of blindness, including staff at the Rare Books room in the British Library. I spent a productive couple of weeks exploring the rich and extensive research collections of the Perkins School, Boston – aided most generously by Jan Seymour-Ford. Huge thanks are also due to the heritage team at RNIB, who have granted me most generous access to their important and diverse collections and provided expert advice on holdings. Thanks especially to Phillip Jeffries, Robert Saggers, Sarah Haylett and Sean Wilcox. Thanks to the National Portrait Gallery – both to the archive team and to former colleagues from the curatorial department for many helpful and inspiring opportunities to discuss my project: in particular, Peter Funnell, Ruth Brimacombe, Lizzie Heath, Carol Blackett-Ord and Jan Marsh. I am immensely grateful to Linda Bree and Emily Hockley at Cambridge University Press, who have helped steer the project editorially (often it feels like with great patience); thanks also to Tim Mason for editorial support. And thanks to the series editor, Gillian Beer, for supporting the project at an early stage.

Finally, the crafting of this book has been interwoven with the complex fabric of life and family. Notably, work on the project stopped with the illness and death of my much-loved mother, Patricia, to whom I owe possibly the greatest debt of all for encouraging, protecting and supporting a love of literature and writing: she was a wonderful teacher to me, and many others, and has been a brilliant, beautiful inspiration. There are innumerable thanks to the friends and family who nurtured me and helped me recover from grief, many of whom are already noted above. But I must also extend thanks to Jackie, Elaine, Lea, Dani, Zoe and Bear for food, shelter, pub quizzes and laughter. And to my wonderful and intelligent sister, Elizabeth, with whom I've discussed this project probably more than anyone else, and whose insight and knowledge of disability studies, and whose great empathy and sensitivity, have enhanced my work beyond measure. Her family, Ralph and little James and Beatrice, and our dad, Allan, have helped me in countless ways to continue to feel motivated and happy. Ian, who has brought such love into my life in the past few years, and provided so much support – thank you, with all my heart; and thank you to Millie, Meg, Dot and Pete for all your love, support and friendship. And lastly, thanks to Pip, whose coming into being has given me impetus to finish the book with such enthusiasm, and whose arrival we joyfully and eagerly await.

Sections of Chapter 2 have previously been published as 'Wordsworth's Glasses: The Materiality of Blindness in the Romantic Imagination' in Luisa Calè and Patrizia Di Bello, eds., *Illustrations, Optics and Objects in Nineteenth-Century Literary and Visual Culture* (Basingstoke: Palgrave Macmillan, 2010), pp. 44–64, and are reproduced with permission of Palgrave Macmillan.

Sections of Chapter 7 have previously been published as 'Frances Browne, the "Blind Poetess": Towards a Poetics of Blind Writing' in the *Journal of Literary & Cultural Disability Studies*, 3:2 (2009), 147–61, and are reproduced with permission of the journal and Liverpool University Press.

# Introduction
## *Embodying Nineteenth-Century Blindness*

An image of a blind man by the illustrator, antiquarian and curator John Thomas Smith, etched in 1816 and published the following year, introduces the main themes of this book (Figure 1).[1] The man's clothes are tattered and ill-fitting, emphasising his poverty. He is depicted as static, still: propped up against a wall, his long cane functions not so much as a guiding tool but as an object that pins him in place. Smith's representation of sensory modes underscores further a sense of helplessness and passivity in his subject. The man's eyes are turned downward, as if anticipating and rejecting his visual apprehension by the artist and, in turn, the viewer. The image is silent: the beggar's mouth is closed, and rather than speaking, he wears a placard which is inscribed in ink print, bearing perhaps his story, a plea for charity or advertisement for his wares – which he himself cannot read. Contributing further to the impression of stillness, both his hands clutch his hat, which is turned outwards to await alms, or meagre payment for the tracts he sells.

Smith's etching perpetuates an image of the blind person as helpless and dependent. It underscores the way in which this man's blindness disables him on several fronts: it (seems to) render him immobile, restricted from moving easily through the new spaces opening up in London; and it renders him poor, as he is unable to participate in an economy that was becoming increasingly dependent upon the labour of healthy, non-disabled individuals. In particular, wealth potential is associated here with visual literacy: the man's income derives from the sale of ink print tracts, and whilst the man cannot read either the tracts or the advert he wears around his chest, he directs it towards a passerby who can. This man's story, and indeed his status as a subject of the engraving, is rendered in a visual medium, to which he, as a blind person, has no direct access. Distanced from his story, he suffers a loss of voice: a palpably common recurrence in blind people's experiences of this period, and which *Blindness and Writing* seeks to redress.

Figure 1 John Thomas Smith, *A Blind Beggar*, etching (1815–16).
© Trustees of the British Museum.

The portrait introduces us to an important factor that structured both the cultural perception *and* experience of visual impairment in the nineteenth century: its increasing identification with the issue of literacy. Produced at a moment of heightened anxiety over the growing numbers of itinerant poor people in urban spaces, Smith's print reinscribes a long-held association between blindness and poverty.[2] Here, however (and in other of Smith's depictions of visually impaired people), the presence of the written word is freshly troubling. Etched on the eve of the introduction of embossed reading and writing technologies for blind people to Britain, Smith's representation of blindness opens up key questions for my study: in what ways does this man's exclusion from a literate culture – on which he seemingly depends above an oral culture to elicit alms and income – disable him beyond his blindness? Crucially both this man's blindness *and* his (il)literacy are placed under the scrutiny of a sighted, literate observer. Smith's portrait exemplifies how the blind person was newly identified with the act of reading, their ability to communicate and interpret text becoming a point of anxious social concern. So whilst Mara Mills argues that 'blindness and reading began to be co-constructed in the twentieth century', she in fact describes a twinning that began in the late eighteenth, and was consolidated in the nineteenth century.[3]

This twinning also permeated wider cultural representations of blindness, particularly in literary texts, investigation of which forms a large focus of my study. William Paulson has pinpointed the emergence of a 'new kind of social and cultural status for blindness' to this period, and he, along with scholars including Kate Flint, Martha Stoddard Holmes and Mary Klages, have impressed how material, as well as spiritual, concerns came to shape its meaning.[4] Yet less attention has been paid towards the central ways in which attitudes towards literacy, and the written word, began to shape the status of blindness in Victorian Britain. One of the key aspects to my argument is that blindness assumed new meanings through its relationship to literacy in the nineteenth century, which in turn produced new forms of experience for people living with or alongside sight loss. These new associations in turn had important implications for the ways in which "sighted" writers invoked blindness in their texts (I use scare quotes here as the binary between sighted and blind cannot always be so rigorously defined). Blindness revealed the arbitrary relationship between the phenomenal creation and appearance of the literary sign and its apprehension by an embodied reader. It thus functioned as a key device through which writers explored the material constraints of text. In this argument, *Blindness and Writing* resonates with Jennifer Esmail's recently published account of the changing status of signed languages for deaf communities in Victorian Britain. She details how 'thinking *through* deafness was a consistent rhetorical practice that spanned a wide range of Victorian discursive fields interested in human language and use'.[5] Similarly, my project demonstrates the ways in which debates concerning blind people's reading and writing practices were both shaped by, and in turn shaped, Victorian ideas around language and communication in the wider culture. Yet whereas Esmail emphasises the privileging of speech in the shift from signed languages to oralism in deaf communication, this book considers how blind people's literacy contributed to a suspicion about accessing textual materials via solely aural methods, and raised new anxieties concerning the visual and material status of writing.[6]

*Blindness and Writing* is concerned then with the extent to which literature was understood by nineteenth-century audiences to be a visual medium, both at the level of content and form. In this respect, my approach towards literary inscriptions of blindness clearly builds upon those critics who have considered blindness in relation to visual culture.[7] In his influential account of the relationship between drawing and blindness, *Memoirs of the Blind: The Self-Portrait and Other Ruins*, the philosopher Jacques Derrida writes that 'every time a draftsman lets himself be fascinated by the blind, every time he makes the blind a *theme* of his drawing, he projects, dreams, or hallucinates a figure of a draftsman, or sometimes, ... some draftswoman'.[8] This is because to draw involves an act of blindness, a turning away from observation of the object at the moment of inscription. The trace of drawing proceeds 'in the night', outside the field of vision; the draughtsperson's hand a haptic echo of a blind person's.[9] Extending the *trait* of the pencil on paper to the line of writing, we can identify a shared concern with literary writers in the nineteenth century who portray blindness in their texts. To inscribe a figure of blindness is a self-reflexive action by writers: an acknowledgement of the limits to the privileged nature of vision in the construction of writing. Derrida's account of blindness stresses its lack – as a type of non-seeing – but also describes how a compensatory discourse of touch adhered to it. Such a compensatory discourse became all the more sharply defined with the development of raised print and finger reading from the 1820s onwards in Britain. In nineteenth-century culture, blindness cohered debates concerning the (multi)sensory regimes of text, as the tactile abilities of blind people were set in complex and contradictory ways against the widespread conception of reading and writing as visual acts.

*Blindness and Writing* proposes that this contradictory treatment of blindness within the nineteenth-century literary imagination was shaped by three distinct but interrelated themes. Firstly, blindness was subject to a changing status within shifting sensory hierarchies. The expansion of blind people's writing practices – embossed literature, biographical writing, fictional writing – developed within a culture that tended to privilege vision as the best sensory mode for accessing knowledge about the world and communicating it in language. This had several important effects. It initially circumscribed the possibilities for blind people's writing practices, which were at first governed by visual prejudices. For example, experiments in embossed literature were accompanied by anxiety as to whether the finger could be an equal substitute for the eye – debates which continued to marginalise blind people. At a representational level, sighted writers frequently framed blind people and blindness as objects of suspicion and fear. Contrarily, the evidence of blind people's intellectual and tactile abilities helped to challenge this emphasis on vision's superiority, in turn opening out a wider sensory environment for literary culture, both imaginatively and materially.

Secondly, blindness came to occupy a prominent place in cultural debates concerning the relationship between reading and the material form of the book. Blindness drew attention to the ways in which the material form of the page and book, as well as the ways in which text is perceived, shaped the creation and interpretation of textual meaning. Experiments with embossed literature, which received a significant amount of public attention and scrutiny in the period, exposed writing as a technology compatible with particular users, rather than an essential, spiritual medium. Blindness posed a challenge to idealist and referential systems of language, and suggested how language was contingent upon the interrelation of two material entities: the text and the human body.

Thirdly, the lived, embodied experience of blindness and visual impairments became arguably more pervasive, as warfare and industrialisation aggravated the spread of infectious diseases and eye injuries. A rise in incidences of visual impairment had certain important effects, not least encouraging the development of ophthalmology as a medical discipline in the nineteenth century, which was supported by an expanding textual reference base. Ophthalmological discourse both conceptualised blindness as a problem in need of medical intervention, and supplied writers with a new set of images and associations developed from a more precise symptomology, which I elaborate throughout *Blindness and Writing*. Ophthalmology tended, however, to divorce the individual from the body, reducing a person to his or her symptoms. In order to counter the reductiveness of medical models of blindness, I seek to recuperate aspects of the lived experience of blind and visually impaired people. This includes the introduction of testimonies by both prominent blind spokespeople who are now largely forgotten from the historical record, alongside a re-evaluation of more popular and canonical figures. I thus demonstrate how blindness had a strong bodily, as well as symbolic, currency for Victorian writers. Moreover, the relationship between blindness and writing was gendered, as the material practices of literary production and reception (such as the roles of originator of literature vs transcriber or amanuensis) were coded variously as masculine and feminine.

So whilst this book, interdisciplinary in focus, explores a range of discourses about blindness produced by diverse writers, what unites my discussion is that the majority of writings about blindness I investigate emerge from a lived, embodied experience of impaired vision and sight loss. In the literary texts I discuss, blindness is not simply metaphorically deployed (although there is not always a clear disjuncture between embodied and metaphorical conceptions of visual impairment, a point I return to at the end of this introduction). Rather, it frequently has a specific experiential referent for writers: for example, those who were subject to persistent eye disease (Wordsworth), and those who acted as carers for family members with eye conditions (Charlotte Brontë). It is with this focus on lived experiences of blindness that *Blindness and Writing* differs most significantly from recent studies that have investigated the relationship between blindness and literary form.[10] Notably, it departs from David Bolt's important study of the relationship between blindness and Anglophone literature of the twentieth century, in which he argues for the recurrence of situations in which 'the person who does not have a visual impairment assumes a kind of authorship, indeed authority, as the person who has a visual impairment is told rather than asked about her or his own life'.[11] The examples I discuss challenge this framework by considering the ways in which writers identify with blind and visually impaired people, and incorporate such identifications in their literary works. Yet I also attend to the ways in which the lived experience of blindness was itself shaped by social and cultural conditions and prejudices, a theme resonant with Bolt's notion of the 'metanarrative of blindness'. This concept articulates how literary representations of blindness have power to define people with visual impairments, displacing agency.[12] Let me briefly expand upon this point by outlining the relation of my project to the field of disability studies.

Disability studies significantly reveals how the experience of impairment is situated within particular social and cultural milieu. Following on from the disability rights movement of the 1960s to 1970s, disability studies emerged as an academic discipline in the 1980s, shaped by research and thinking from the sciences, social sciences and humanities, and motivated by a concern to trace the social (rather than just medical) meanings of disability.[13] Early disability studies was characterised by a neo-Marxist critical stance, which emphasised how disability came into being with the growth of capitalist economies in the nineteenth century. One of the most important theorisations of disability studies is the social model of disability. This model understands 'disability' to be a socially produced phenomenon, by which individuals are disabled by institutions and environment, rather than by their physical, cognitive or sensory impairments. Bodily impairments, or differences, become disabilities in relation to the qualities and values that are valorised by dominant communities at particular moments.[14] The social model roots the tightening identification between impairment and disability in the nineteenth century, as capitalist forms of production changed the relationship between people with and without impairments. The construction of blindness as a *disability* is, in many ways, a nineteenth-century phenomenon, arising from concern about the role that people with visual impairments could play in a newly industrialised society, and shaped by its increasing medicalisation. Indeed, as Smith's portrait worries about the itinerant identity of this blind man, so more typically the material wants and needs of blind people came under the purview of an emerging capitalist society anxious about charitable giving, as it increasingly linked individual value with ability.

One materialisation of the difficulties blind people faced in adjusting to increasingly mechanised modes of work and labour can be found in the growth of asylums during the nineteenth century. Martha Stoddard Holmes notes that in the context of anxiety over the New Poor Law (1834), the number of institutions and societies for blind people rose from 4 to 154 between 1799 and 1899.[15] John Thomas Smith's concern to document London beggars – many of whom were blind or visually impaired – in the 1810s was explicitly tied to a call for reform of the poor laws to remove beggars to workhouses and thus make such people invisible.[16] Martha Stoddard Holmes describes the anxieties concerning the 'deserving poor' that structure representations and understandings of blind people in social and educational texts, as well as the ways in which blind people resisted being cast as dependents to either the state or charities. Whilst I do not wish to repeat Holmes's careful study of the representation of blind people in these texts, what does emerge in these discourses is a prejudice that blind people cannot compete in a society which privileges the visual. I use this point to argue that the privileging of the visual nature of language systems in nineteenth-century culture meant that blindness was experienced as a disability in a print economy. And moreover the anxiety that blindness was an *obstruction* towards print culture – because it closes down the possibility of reading or writing ink print texts – permeates its representation in literary texts, helping to shore up prejudices against visual impairment.

Thus, the disablement of people with visual impairments in the nineteenth century's print economy also found expression within the popular representational modes circulated by that economy. As Douglas Baynton argues, the concept of normality that emerged in the nineteenth century became deployed in all aspects of modern life as a means of measuring, categorising and managing populations, co-opting the natural in order to legitimate discriminatory practices against subjects who did not fit the norm.[17] Cultural representations contributed towards a process of naturalising disability, whilst fixing the idea of a normal, able body.[18] Lennard J. Davis argues that disability emerges as a problem in relation to the construction of normalcy in the nineteenth century. He shows how the concept of the norm, and normal body, entered European culture in this period, evidencing this through the development of statistics as a branch of knowledge, and traces how the novel as a form 'promotes and symbolically produces normative structures'.[19] Cultural forms played a powerful role in the management of subjects with physical difference, for example by entrenching attitudes of fear and pity in their intended nondisabled user; or presenting people with impairments as outside certain social institutions, such as marriage and family life.[20] Recent literary and cultural disability studies have done much to further our understanding by theorising the powerful and widespread ways in which representational modes have effected the cultural understanding and embodied experience of disability.[21] David Mitchell and Sharon L. Snyder were among early critics advocating for closer analysis of the relationship between literary form and disability. They have been particularly influential in their theorisation of 'narrative prosthesis', a concept that outlines how disability has been deployed by literary writers to help consolidate cultural ideas of the normal body. Importantly, they identify the ways in which literary strategies of representing disability have had a 'visceral effect on the lives of disabled people', arguing: 'Literature serves up disability as a repressed deviation from cultural imperatives of normativity, while disabled populations suffer the consequences of representational association with deviance and recalcitrant corporeal difference.'[22] Mitchell and Snyder stress that unlike other identities such as race, sexuality and ethnicity which are notable for their absence from historical forms of representation, there has been a 'plethora' of representations of disability in visual and discursive works.[23] Yet the ubiquitous nature of this imagery has served to further marginalise disabled people and has contributed to their social erasure. Mitchell and Snyder describe how, rather than acting as a realist marker of disability experience, the widespread tendency of disability representation in literature acts as a narrative prosthesis that helps to shore up the normal; either by serving as stock characters, or as a metaphor for deviance.[24] In this analysis, disability is 'foundational to both cultural definition and to the literary narratives that challenge normalizing prescriptive ideals'.[25]

Mitchell and Snyder are concerned with the ideological work that literature does in the management of bodily difference, and note the stages in which critical approaches to disability studies have progressed from its initial theorisation of negative imagery.[26] Whilst their study is alert to the inherent problems of universalising disability representation, and calls attention to its 'variegated historical patterning', they identify modern and postmodern renderings of disability as most likely to disrupt 'normalcy narratives'.[27] More recent analyses have complicated this rendering of the nineteenth-century novel as inherently denigrating of disability by illustrating the complex and multilayered meanings – material and symbolic – that bodily impairment connoted to both writers and readers.[28] Certainly my interpretative approach, which also draws upon phenomenology, tracks the multiple ways in which blind and partially sighted people resisted – as well as conformed to – their society's ocularcentric narratives. I show how blind people recognised the potential for literary form to be a tool for resistance as well as an instrument of control. In so doing, they both articulated their own identity as blind people and helped to reconceptualise reading and writing as a multimedia experience. Significantly, unlike Mitchell and Snyder, I also consider how the representation of blindness in literary texts by sighted authors is frequently underpinned by experience of visual impairment, a point I return to below. These different modes of engagement between blindness and literary form are sometimes recognisable as forms of narrative prosthesis; but at other moments more clearly disrupt notions of the normal, ideal body.

So whilst my project shares with those critics who have identified the intersections of social and cultural constructions of disability, I am less beholden to a social constructionist position, to borrow Rosemarie Garland-Thomson's terminology. Rather, I adopt a phenomenological approach to the material I bring forward.[29] This is partly because the changing forms of literary media, alongside the construction of blindness as disability, share focus in my investigation. A phenomenological approach allows me to track the multiple intersections of blindness and literary media, whilst mapping more fluid encounters between 'sighted' and 'blind' people. Such an approach opens out the surprising ways in which seemingly sighted authors identified as blind, both negatively and positively.[30]

If the field of disability studies more widely has provided literary and cultural studies with tools to analyse and interrogate the production and circulation of disability representations, specific projects have also focused attention on the relationship between visual disability and literary and cultural form. These studies have drawn attention to the significant binary not only between vision/blindness, but also language/knowledge. In her introduction to a special issue on blindness and literature for the *Journal of Literary & Cultural Disability Studies*, Georgina Kleege notes both the fascination that blindness has held for cultures 'since the beginning of time' and the fact that blindness is often synonymous with 'prejudice, obliviousness and ineptitude'.[31] Contributions to this special issue trace manifestations of both of these observations, examining the role of language in shaping popular conceptions of and associations with blindness; as well as the formation of these ideas in literary texts from the medieval to contemporary periods. These analyses reveal the complex side effects that blindness induces in literary texts. Tory Vandeventer Perman, for example, considers how the blinding of the adulterous Queen Gwenore in Thomas Chestre's fourteenth-century Middle English *Sir Launfal* is both representative of a narrative drive to control her sexual deviancy, yet also produces 'alternative narratives to common medieval assumptions about courtly masculinity, womanhood, and disability'.[32] And more recently, a special issue of the interdisciplinary journal *Mosaic* took blindness as its theme, with contributions focused largely on the representation of blindness in modern and contemporary literature and culture. As editor Dawne McCance noted, the essays collectively posed 'challenges to Western modernity's idealizing of sight' by repositioning vision as a mode prone to obscurity, as well as the embodied nature of perception.[33] H. Peter Steeves, for example, uses the condition scotoma – a partial loss of vision or visual migraine, which he has been affected by since 2000 – to meditate on the ways in which vision is always already enfolded by blindness. He considers how sighted people often do not see much more than what is in front of them: 'not-seeing is the norm'.[34] And valuably, Mark Paterson re-orientates the enduring fascination with 'what the blind see' to examine instead how blind people feel. Dispelling the common imaginary of blindness as a form of darkness, Paterson draws on writings by blind and visually impaired people, including James Holman, Jorge Luis

Borges and John Hull, to construct a 'non-normate sensorium' replete with diverse textures, tastes and smells.[35]

In a similar vein, *Blindness and Writing* stresses that whilst literary depictions of blindness frequently construct it as vision's other through language and naming, literature also acts as a space in which the overlapping, proximate nature of vision and blindness is explored, by both sighted and blind authors. This dialectical relationship is reflected in the two-part structure and interdisciplinary range of the book, which brings ophthalmologic discourse, autobiographical writings by blind people, and blind people's changing access to literary form into dialogue with sighted writers' literary depictions of blindness. The first part, comprised of four chapters, is concerned largely with the changes that took place in blind people's writing practices over the course of the nineteenth century, and the philosophical, technological and social factors that shaped them.

Chapter 1 details the theoretical framework of the book. It examines the central role played by the figure of the blind person in Enlightenment philosophy, whereby philosophers including John Locke and George Berkeley analysed the experience of blindness in order to prove what vision, and consciousness, was. These discourses stressed that the figure of the blind posed particular problems for how perception, experience and language related, by firstly challenging the representational systems of language, and, as the nineteenth century progressed, demonstrating how language might be accessed outside of vision. Yet to challenge the potential reductiveness of these philosophic debates (in that they reduced the blind person to an Other against which to test normal vision), I set out my framework for re-reading blindness phenomenologically. In particular, I draw on the work of the French twentieth-century phenomenologist Maurice Merleau-Ponty. As I have touched upon already, a phenomenology of blindness invites us to attend to the experience of visually impaired subjects who have long been defined against sighted subjects by their different relations to the senses and perceptual faculties. Moreover, phenomenology's insistence on attending to the way in which the material world manifests itself has productive implications for the questions we will ask about the materiality of writing in this book: how is writing perceived? How does it come into being as phenomenon?

The tension between ideal and embodied interpretations of blindness that I trace in Chapter 1 forms the basis of a reappraisal of the poet William Wordsworth as a *blind* poet, and a critical examination of his own textual invocations of blindness as materially grounded. Chapter 2 considers Wordsworth's experience of ophthalmia, an eye disease brought over to

Britain by soldiers returning from the Napoleonic war, which Wordsworth first contracted in 1805 and experienced recurring bouts of throughout the rest of his life. I show how Wordsworth's experience of visual impairment was shaped by both the development of ophthalmology, which provided increasingly specialised diagnosis and treatment of eye diseases as the century progressed; and the problematic relationship blind people posed towards literacy. Blindness is a recurrent trope in Wordsworth's writing, yet it has scarcely been analysed in relation to the poet's own experience of visual impairment. I focus on three episodes of blindness in his literary writing, including his encounter with a blind beggar in his autobiographical poem *The Prelude*.

The next two chapters focus largely on blind and visually impaired people's changing access to and use of textual material. Chapter 3 examines the development of embossed writing systems for blind people, focusing on the roles played by technological advancements, evangelical desire and shifting ideas concerning literacy and the education of people with sensory impairments. This discussion shares with Vanessa Warne's recent insistence that the relationship between visual impairment and literacy is 'shaped by, if not founded upon, a radical reconsideration of not only the relative value of touch and sight but also the ways in which bodies and books interact and what it means to read'.[36] Chapter 4 examines a number of memoirs written by blind people, including James Wilson, who published the first biography of blind people in 1821, Edmund White, a railway guard who published poetry after losing his sight in the early 1850s, and Hippolyte van Landeghem, who published two narratives in the 1860s focusing particularly on her experience of segregated schooling. By seeking to understand how blindness may have been experienced by blind people themselves through the evidence of biography, I identify, to borrow G. Thomas Couser's term, a 'category of life stories' produced by blind people which, rather than being relatively new (as Couser's examples are), are over 150 years old. By turning to narratives produced by people with disabilities, we can begin to recover a fuller sense of the ways in which people felt about their own perceived difference, rather than relying on the dominant accounts of disability found in medical, pedagogical and social texts, and canonical literature. Yet they are still, in the main, inscribed within visual form, produced as ink print books, signalling the limited possibilities for embossed literature during the middle of the century.

The second part of *Blindness and Writing* examines more sustainedly blindness as theme and method in nineteenth-century literature. Whilst Maren Linett has recently argued that Victorian novels could only depict blindness as tragedy, suggesting that by contrast a variety of early twentieth-century Irish and British texts 'demonstrate an interest in exploring life *with* blindness', *Blindness and Writing* argues that nineteenth-century representations of blindness are frequently grounded in a concern for the ways in which visual impairment shapes lived experience.[37] Here, I investigate the relationship between writers' own experiences of blindness and depictions of blindness in literary texts that share attributes of the Bildungsroman and the Künstlerroman. This part of the book opens in Chapter 5 with a reassessment of two of the most famous blind characters in Victorian literature, Edward Rochester in Charlotte Brontë's *Jane Eyre: An Autobiography* (1847) and Romney Leigh in Elizabeth Barrett Browning's *Aurora Leigh* (1856), via an examination of the writers' experience of blindness in personal relationships. I also argue that blindness is deployed as a structural device via which three women writers – Brontë, Barrett Browning and Elizabeth Gaskell in her biography of Charlotte Brontë (1857) – critically and creatively read each other.

The author Charles Dickens took an extensive interest in blindness throughout his career. Chapter 6 examines this interest through three key episodes: his encounter with the blind, deaf and mute Laura Bridgman, recounted in *American Notes* (1842); the description of David Copperfield as 'blind' in the eponymous novel (1849–50); and Esther Summerson's near-blinding in *Bleak House* (1851–2). I analyse the educational and medical contexts to Dickens's literary constructions of blindness, tracing thus their shifts from metaphoric to material registers. As blindness is intimately bound up with the production and interpretation of writing in these contexts, I demonstrate the connection between the figure of the blind and the figure of the writer in Dickens's imagination.

I next examine two distinct constructions of blindness in works by a blind writer, Frances Browne, and the sensation novelist Wilkie Collins. Frances Browne was a well-known writer of the mid-nineteenth century whose fame arose in part from the fact that she was effectively born blind (she was known contemporarily as 'The Blind Poetess of Ulster'). In her novel *My Share of the World* (1861), the female love interest, Lucy, experiences sight loss and commits suicide. Conversely, Wilkie Collins's *Poor Miss Finch* explores the negative impact of sight restoration to a person born blind, recognising the anxiety this would cause. Chapter 7 therefore explores questions around the realistic representation of blindness in both texts, and the way that gender continues to determine its representation.

The final chapter details how George Gissing's novel *New Grub Street* (1891) deploys blindness as a key trope through which the end of the writing self is interrogated. In his novel, Gissing blinds the man of letters, Alfred Yule, to question whether there can be writing without material vision. Coding blindness as tragedy, Gissing returns us to the issues raised in this introduction concerning the power of literary form to inscribe, or re-inscribe, limiting models of visual impairment. Finally, an epilogue considers how Gissing's novel functions as a riposte to the episodes of blindness and writing detailed throughout the book, assessing again the key claims and central findings of *Blindness and Writing*.

Throughout the book, I demonstrate how a phenomenological approach helps to avoid reinforcing cultural interpretations of blindness that frame it in hypothetical and/or metaphorical terms: that is, interpretations in which blindness is co-opted in order to explain or describe something else – such as normal sight (idealist philosophy) or the anxiety of influence (psychoanalytic theory). Let me make some final comments concerning the distinction between metaphorical and material registers of blindness, a division that is not at all straightforward. As the anthropologist Christopher Tilley points out, both language and material culture are in part metaphorical constructions of the world.[38] He goes on to argue that the human body has long been recognised as a potent source of metaphors for understanding and ordering the social world:

> The human body is the most accessible and ready-to-hand image of the social system, providing a potent source of metaphors for society as a whole. Cultural conceptualisations of the body are intimately linked with bodily experience and perception and thus appear natural and basic.[39]

Disability studies scholars have analysed the complex relationship between the body and metaphor that shapes disability representation, in which physical and cognitive anomalies lend a "tangible" body to textual abstractions; a strategy which Mitchell and Snyder call the 'materiality of metaphor'.[40] In their formulation, literary narratives have historically invoked disability as part of an associative relationship between bodily form and character.[41] Significantly for my argument, the lived experience of visual impairment is also shaped by its various cultural conceptions. David Bolt emphasises this when he critiques the 'profoundly disturbing and disabling influence' which cultural representations have upon people with visual impairments, asking whether it is not the 'idea rather than the lived reality of acquiring such an impairment that has the greatest pejorative impact on the person'.[42] Nineteenth-century commentators articulated a similar notion to Bolt's concept of the metanarrative of blindness, which outlines how cultural representations impact on the lives of people with visual impairment. Blind writers such as John Bird expressed their frustration about the ways in which sentimental portrayals of blindness in literature (including Milton's legacy) created limited expectations of blind people in the wider society, a point to which I return in my discussion of Wilkie Collins's construction of a blind character in *Poor Miss Finch* (1872).[43] And in a slight reversal, cultural conceptions could also be reframed through bodily experiences: Rochester's blinding in *Jane Eyre*, for example, is shaped by Charlotte Brontë's experience of shortsightedness, her role as carer for her father, Patrick, as he was treated for cataracts, and her concern for how weak eyesight affected artistic practice. Rochester's blinding is invested with Brontë's concern for the way in which her text is written and read by bodies and selves at risk of impairment and fracture – but in turn it also became a powerful metaphoric symbol of curtailing the patriarchal system for subsequent feminist readers.

Blindness has the troubling feature of slipping between literal and metaphoric states in nineteenth-century texts. Indeed, the sheer variety of forms and conceptualisations that the term takes is striking.[44] As William Paulson states, 'writings on blindness are simply too disparate, too different from one another, to lend themselves to general interpretations or sweeping conclusions'.[45] Dickens voices some of the disparate meanings of the term through the blind villain, Stagg, in *Barnaby Rudge* (1841), who tells Barnaby's mother:

> 'there are various degrees and kinds of blindness, widow. There is the connubial blindness, ma'am, which perhaps you may have observed in the course of your own experience, and which is a kind of wilful and self-damaging blindness. There is the blindness of party, ma'am, and public men, which is the blindness of a mad bull in the midst of a regiment of soldiers clothed in red. There is the blind confidence of youth, which is the blindness of young kittens, whose eyes have not yet opened on the world; and there is that physical blindness, ma'am, of which I am, contrairy to my own desire, a most illustrious example. Added to these, ma'am, is that blindness of the intellect, of which we have a specimen in your interesting son, and which, having sometimes glimmerings and dawnings of the light, is scarcely to be trusted as a total darkness.'[46]

Here Stagg lists various examples of metaphoric blindness, such as 'connubial blindness' (the refusal to acknowledge the abuses of one's partner); as well as states of physical blindness (that of 'young kittens'); and cognitive impairment (Barnaby Rudge's 'blindness of the intellect'). As John Bowen persuasively shows, Stagg's speech – the discourse of a blind man on blindness – importantly makes explicit the concern in Dickens's novel to explore patterns of norm and deviancy. This is achieved through contrasting the clear, lucid gaze of Varden with the 'various deviant, distorted, and perverse gazes and blindnesses, both literal and metaphoric' that populate the text. In particular, Bowen lucidly explores the metaphoric potential of blindness in his discussion. He points to the thematic cluster of sight, blindness, keys and locks as evidence of the Oedipus complex, developing a psychoanalytic reading of the text that is strengthened by the novel's obsession with relationships of fathers and sons.[47] Importantly, Stagg's list also distinguishes between metaphoric and 'physical' blindness. It is this relationship – more so than the metaphoric structures of blindness that have been amply charted elsewhere – that my study is concerned with. I am interested not so much on the way in which blindness is used to describe something else (usually negative), not least injustice, ignorance, sexual and familial anxiety. Rather, I examine more closely the discourses concerned with the actual experience of blind and visually impaired people and the traces of its physical manifestation as it intersects with the nineteenth-century's burgeoning textual environment and economy. However, as Bowen's study disrupts the binaries he identifies through the introduction of Derridean difference, I also want to argue – prompted by the observations of blind and partially sighted commentators – that a clear binary cannot be drawn between metaphoric and physical blindness in the texts I analyse. The cultural conceptions of blindness underpinning their metaphoric meanings in the nineteenth century did have material ramifications upon the lives of blind and visually impaired people, constructing them variously as objects of pity, fear and scorn.

Stagg omits the blindness which structures writing, and with which Dickens's own writing is deeply preoccupied in this period. Such a preoccupation is the corollary to the visio-centric drive in nineteenth-century society. Thinking about the relationship between 'physical' blindness and writing in the nineteenth century illuminates various ways in which writers grappled with ideas about sight, knowledge and truth, and their relation to language. Yet as Bowen also argues, *Barnaby Rudge* 'repeatedly emphasises the difficulty or impossibility of relying upon the evidence of one's senses, in particular the authority of visual knowledge' and that this manifests in a frequent recoil 'from language to dumb show': blindness is thus part of a framework that tests the limits to knowledge and language.[48] Here then, as in the literary texts I examine throughout this book, the blind man of empiricist philosophy transmutes into a spectre of the writer's own authorial self, haunting the edges of the nineteenth-century literary text. Yet blindness was also re-formulating the material conditions of writing and language, as developments in raised type and finger reading began to ascribe new associations to the figure of the blind. Blindness might mark the closure of writing and reading the traditional ink print book in the nineteenth-century literary imagination; but it also opened up new, and intriguing, alternative ways of imagining the book's material form. To borrow Nicholas Mirzoeff's discussion of the function of blindness in Western visual art, blindness functions not just as a metaphor but also as a *condition* of the nineteenth-century literary subject.[49]

This is not to deny the powerful ways in which cultural representations contributed to a process of naturalising visual disability by fixing the idea of a normal and able perceiving subject. Such constructions can be identified at even the simplest levels of language, which, as David Bolt argues, is frequently institutionally ableist, leading to an important point here about the terminology I adopt throughout the book.[50] When describing nineteenth-century people who were fully or, by today's definition, legally blind, I mainly use the term blind people; when describing people with partial vision, I predominantly use the term visually impaired, and occasionally partially sighted, people. When citing directly from nineteenth-century sources, I follow original terminology. Nineteenth-century commentators (both sighted and blind) tended to describe people with visual impairments using the collective noun 'the Blind'. As my research has progressed, the repetition of this collective noun has come to rub and jar, signalling as it does the way in which a diverse group of people came to be defined purely by the physiological functioning of their eyes and optic health. 'The Blind' is a term which flattens and suppresses subjectivity by reducing the people it signals to their difference from the sighted: it erects and polices a binary between the two groups, spatially suggesting that 'the Blind' are somehow *over there*: a group which must always be kept at a distance from the normally sighted. Scrutinised by the gaze of the sighted, 'the Blind' function as the negative other against which normative vision is tested.[51]

The seeming simplicity of the collective noun 'the Blind' belies the ideological work it does to naturalise a separation between a supposed normative vision and its other. Tanya Titchkosky notes Ludwig Wittgenstein's discussion on how attending to the outer edges of legal blindness can bring to consciousness the ambiguity that lies between sight and blindness. She states:

> Of all the things that sight can see, it often does not observe the intimate relation between sightedness and blindness as ways of being in the world ... attending to sight usually only occurs in relation to blindness and what we

> have to say about blindness. Between all the different ways that sight and blindness appear lies something much more meaningful and much more complex: the sheer opposition. Ten per cent of normal vision is not simply the outer limit of blindness, it is also the outer limit of sightedness and it is both at the same time.[52]

Titchkosky stresses how 'blindness' is a conceptual marker – or perhaps a linguistic placeholder – *needed* by sightedness in order to define itself. Yet she also draws attention to the ways in which the boundary between some people's experience of (medically defined) normal vision and blindness – both of which exist on a continuum – might in reality be much more blurred. Looking again at Smith's etching, the thick cross-hatching renders the man's placard illegible to the viewer, an uncanny reminder that to participate in print culture is often arbitrary, reliant as much upon the material form of the text as it is upon the body parts (eyes, fingers, ears) of the user. The distinction between the blind subject and the sighted viewer breaks down here, as writing, as a visual form, cannot be brought into being. It is in this mode of blurring and fogging, where the separation between blindness and sight breaks down, that I situate my book.

# PART I

# *Blind People's Writing Practices*

CHAPTER 1

# *Writing Blindness, from Vision to Touch*

Writing in 1827, the printer James Gall (who produced the first embossed books for blind people in Britain) expressed doubts about whether blind people were capable of accurately reading and writing. Arguing that language is a visual medium, he suggested that without visual experience, an individual may not be able to grasp fully the concepts used in linguistic systems:

> Language is almost the only means by which information is conveyed to the Blind. But as a large portion of every language is figurative, and the large majority of figures used in language is derived from objects of sight, of which the blind can form no idea, it follows, that these terms and figures, though they may be used, can never be fully or very clearly understood by them.[1]

Gall argues that people born blind can form no idea of visual concepts such as light, and therefore that they have no referential basis to the common language, saturated as it is with figurative symbols drawn from sight. Blind people, Gall suggests, will always struggle to accurately interpret the content of language, and, by extension, literary discourse. Gall's account here certainly resonates with a pattern Jan Eric Olsén identifies in other nineteenth-century European educational institutions for blind people, in his discussion of the development of writing devices for blind people. Olsén argues that debates amongst school directors concerning the appropriate educability of blind people were underpinned by the central concept of *Sinnesvikariat*, a German term meaning vicariate of the senses, which referred to the senses that act as substitutes for a non-functioning sense organ (typically touch and hearing for blind and visually impaired people). Yet as Olsén also points out, *Sinnesvikariat* 'expressed the widely held view that blind people have an incomplete access to exterior reality', and that the vicariate sense therefore needed to perform 'double work'.[2] This prejudice underpinned early discourses on blind people's educability.

This also produced an anxiety concerning the relationship of blind people to language, a point stressed by William Paulson in his study of blindness in Enlightenment France. Paulson describes how blindness posed the problem of an opposition or connection between two properties and ways of understanding language: the externally referential (or representational), where a linguistic sign refers to an object directly apprehended; and the internally referential (or systematic), where signs and signifiers are ordered in a system of hierarchical interrelations (what would later be described as the synchronic system in Ferdinand de Saussure's structural linguistics).[3] The blind person, without visual reference, thus called into question the structure of Western representation and the relationship between thought, language and perception on which it depended.[4] As disability scholar Julia Miele Rodas has noted more recently, Western culture's emphasis on sight has also had the effect of engendering feelings of inferiority in blind people. She argues that whilst a blind person 'may not experience her own blindness as a loss or absence on a personal level (since perception and the integration of knowledge do not necessarily require sight)', the sharing of language based on 'sighted culture and experience' may subject her 'to the powerful affect of symbolic blindness'.[5] Significantly then, the symbolic work of language, saturated with visual references, *creates*, rather than names, a sense of difference and lack.

But it was not simply blind people's presumed inability to associate a linguistic sign with an object directly (that is, visually) apprehended that positioned them outside of the common language. As an inventor of a raised print format, Gall was also aware that blind people were challenged by the fact that inscription systems for language took a predominantly visual form. Experiments for embossed literature, as Chapter 3 examines in more detail, took place within a culture in which the visual nature of the linguistic sign was privileged. In his hugely popular lecture series, *Sesame and Lilies* (1865), the leading art and social critic John Ruskin considered the nature of good and bad literature. He emphasised:

> First of all, I tell you earnestly and authoritatively (I *know* I am right in this), you must get into the habit of *looking* intensely at words, and assuring yourself of their meaning, syllable by syllable – nay, letter by letter. For it is only by reason of the opposition of letters in the function of signs, to sounds in the functions of signs, that the study of books is called 'literature'.[6]

Ruskin articulates here the dominant cultural conception that reading is a visual act, as he privileges the organ of the eye at the moment of interpretation. Whilst Gall urged that processing linguistic information is culturally and cognitively bound up with vision, Ruskin reminds us here that reading as a sensory act also belongs to sight, as it is via the habitual act of 'looking intensely' at letters as signs that one garners the meaning of a text. As Walter Ong argued powerfully in his seminal 1982 investigation into the relationship between orality and literacy, the emergence of print culture privileged sight, rather than hearing, and indeed marked the transition from hearing-dominance to sight-dominance in mental processes.[7] More recently, Gerard Curtis has examined the notion of 'visual literacy' in his 1999 study *Visual Words: Art and the Material Book in Victorian England*, which explores the growing graphic presence of text, the role of the graphic trace, and the competition between image and word as systems of communication.[8] Arguing that 'nineteenth-century literary culture … drew on a partnership between the textual and visual', Curtis develops a foundational and structural analysis of the 'objectness' of the image–word relationship, taking as his main theme the 'representation of writing and the written word as object'.[9] Curtis notes how the content of writing became related to its visual appearance, as writers – from sign writers to literary authors – became increasingly aware of how visual elements such as typographic style and illustrations shaped readers' interpretation of text.[10]

If both reading and writing were coded as predominantly visual acts, what happened if one could not see: could reading and writing still take place? A large part of my book is concerned with both addressing this question and exposing its limits. I re-orientate its terms to present the multiple ways in which blind and visually impaired people were active in nineteenth-century literary culture. Blind people's entry into formal literacy through experimentation with raised print formats both denaturalised the roman alphabetic system, and challenged the sight-dominance of literary exchange. In this chapter, I propose a phenomenological approach towards reading blind culture that also challenges recent critical analyses of nineteenth-century literary culture as visio-centric. Firstly, though, I will outline some important background to this discussion, by considering the close relationship that existed between concepts of blindness, experience and language in idealist philosophy in order to detail how blindness came to challenge representational systems of language in the nineteenth century, as William Paulson states. I show how the blind person was deployed as an Other against whom to test the workings of "normal" sight, and consider how this emerged in concepts of language. Yet as a counter to this othering, some philosophers, including Denis Diderot and Edmund Burke, also began to focus attention on the blind person's perceptual abilities and actual experience. Their evidencing of blind people's participation in an active intellectual and imaginative life helped to challenge assumptions that language depended upon vision.

## Vision, Experience, Language: The Hypothetical Blind Man

From the Enlightenment period onwards, hypothetical constructions of blindness were used to test the relationship between vision, experience and language that underpinned epistemological debates in empiricist and idealist philosophy. Conceptually, blindness allowed philosophers to test the ways in which knowledge of the world was gained from sensory (specifically visual) experience rather than innate ideas. The empiricist philosopher John Locke reconfigured Cartesian optics via the deployment of a blind man hypothetically restored to sight in the second edition of *An Essay Concerning Human Understanding* (1690). Here, Locke responded to the question posed by the scientist and philosopher William Molyneux, now known as 'Molyneux's problem': could a blind man restored to sight distinguish through vision between a cube and globe what he had previously known by touch alone? Refuting René Descartes' analogical model of representation (in which the stick used by a blind man is a direct analogue for the rays of light that strike the eye), Locke used Molyneux's problem to refocus questions of understanding on the nature of experience. He proposed that the blind man, when presented with two objects, would not be able immediately to tell which was a cube and which was a globe, because this distinction was the result of habitual judgement, the interrelation of touch and sight.[11] This hypothetical example also illustrated for Locke a new relationship between language and perception: we can form no idea of words without once having seen the objects they stand in for.

George Berkeley drew upon Locke's and Molyneux's intuitions about the blind man restored to sight in *An Essay Towards a New Theory of Vision* (1709), in which he proposed a radical way of understanding the faculty of sight that further challenged Cartesian geometric optics and contributed to the development of his idealist philosophy. In *Vision*, Berkeley argued that sight is experiential, and that one cannot form an idea of distance or magnitude by sight alone, refuting the claim that we perceive the same spatial properties by sight and touch.[12] Again, Berkeley's invocation of the blind man restored to sight turned also on the relationship between vision, experience and language. Soon after publication of Berkeley's text, the hypothesis became a reality, with William Cheselden's successful cataract surgery in 1728, as I discuss in more detail in Chapter 7. Speculating on whether the blind man restored to sight can perceive if a man stands erect or not, Berkeley notes:

> It's evident, in that Case, he wou'd neither judge the Man he sees, to be *Erect* nor *Inverted*; for he never having known those Terms applied to any other, save Tangible Things, or which existed in the space without him, and what he sees neither being Tangible, nor perceived as existing without, he cou'd not know that in propriety of language, they were applicable to it.[13]

The example of the blind man demonstrates that the process of naming is inherently unstable, the restoration of his sight illuminating the arbitrary nature of the relationship between referent and object. Without vision we cannot know 'in propriety of language' the terms applicable to what we 'behold' before us; therefore it is vision itself that brings into being the structure of these relations between perceiving subject and the referential world. The blind man restored to sight will learn to name things through experience, as touch and vision do not immediately correlate.

Indeed, Berkeley later argued in *The Theory of Vision Vindicated* (1733) that vision functions like a language: in the case of language we call the mark by the same name as the thing it stands for, because the mark, as a visual shape, has no intrinsic value. As Margaret Atherton argues, Berkeley makes the point that vision, like any other language, has a significatory function: 'What vision is for is to stand for nonvisible objects'.[14] Visible extension and visible shapes share the same name as tangible extension and tangible shapes even though they are not the same sort of thing, because the visible name stands in for the tangible. Likewise, *writing* itself is a system of visual shapes which stand in for things, yet writing itself has no intrinsic value: its sole value, argues Berkeley, lies in what it refers to.

Berkeley's account of vision continued to predominate into the nineteenth century, until its displacement by physiological and psychological models in the latter half of the century. In 1842, Samuel Bailey was prompted to publish a *Review of Berkeley's Theory of Vision, Designed to Show the Unsoundness of that Celebrated Speculation* in light of the continued acceptance of Berkeley's theorem, some 120 years after it was first published.[15] The main points of Bailey's critique of *Vision* turn on Berkeley's emphasis on the experiential nature of sight (Bailey wants to return the value of sensation to sight), and Berkeley's use of language. Bailey's work prompted a fierce rebuke from John Stuart Mill, in a response published in the *London and Westminster Review*.[16] Mill argued that leading thinkers of the analytical school of mental philosophy and of the school of common sense philosophy had proven Berkeley's theory to be beyond doubt.

He stressed that the eye was capable only of perceiving sensations which are 'merely colour variously arranged, and changes of colour', and that all else is inference, obtained by the eye as 'an acquired power' – Berkeley had proven conclusively, Mill argued, that distance from the eye is 'not seen, but inferred'.[17]

The debate between these two philosophers illustrates the way in which the relationship between vision, experience and language continued to problematise logical responses to Berkeley's theory into the nineteenth century. Moreover, it points to the continued significance of the hypothetical (and real) blind person restored to sight in proving or disproving theories about the way in which vision worked, with Bailey arguing that 'we have now to examine how far [Cheselden] and the subsequent accounts confirm or invalidate [Berkeley's] theory'.[18] Mill criticises in particular Bailey's attack on 'the primitive phraseology' that he ascribes to Berkeley and his successors, accusing them of failing to communicate their ideas logically and unambiguously.[19] Mill is wary of the notion that language might conceal or hinder universal ideas and is reluctant to accept that language constitutes ideas as well as mediates them.[20] Thus Mill's response to Berkeley derives from the assumption that there is a recoverable universal truth in vision, and further, that language can constitute that truth. Bailey, however, suggests that as language is the way in which we experience those ideas, language is capable of constituting its own truth. He examines how the narratives published by cataract surgeons – which seemingly prove Berkeley's theory – are problematised by the arbitrary nature of language. By beginning to deconstruct these narrative accounts (through increased attention to what the blind person is recorded as saying), Bailey demonstrates that not only is the relationship between sight and experience complex, so too is the relationship between language and experience. Language, it seems, can never be a pure form of expression; instead, it is based on one's *experience* of the world – which, circuitously, is also based on what you see.

Bailey's interest in the language used by blind people is derived from a desire to understand the nature of visual experience: in this way, through deploying blindness to describe the relationship between the senses and their cognitive functioning, he continues to construct blind people as other. Writing from a disability studies perspective, Georgina Kleege has recently reflected on the disempowering function of the 'Hypothetical Blind Man' in the Western philosophical tradition. She argues that 'Hypothetical' has 'long played a useful, though thankless role, as a prop for theories of consciousness', outlining how 'his primary function' is to 'highlight the importance of sight and to elicit a frisson of awe and pity which promotes gratitude among the sighted theorists for the vision they possess'. She concludes her commentary by calling for philosophy to let go of him: 'if the Hypothetical Blind Man once helped thinkers form ideas about human consciousness surely his day is done. He does too much damage hanging around. It is time to let him go. Rest in peace.'[21]

The figure of the hypothetical blind man continued to permeate accounts of vision in the nineteenth century. However, an interesting landscape opens up if we put him to one side (even if it is difficult to let him fully rest in peace). The types of evidence I bring forward in this book – the development of embossed literature and finger-reading practices, the tradition of autobiographical and biographical writing by blind people, and documentation of people's experiences of eye disease and accidents – invite a shift from idealist models of blindness (that is, concerned with what it reveals about the functioning of mental processes) to phenomenological analyses of its material culture. I am, in other words, more critically concerned to trace people's actual experience of blindness and visual impairment. Here, I am partly following the lead of the eighteenth-century philosopher Denis Diderot who, in a radical contemporary attack, argued that speaking to blind people about their actual experiences dismantled the premise of idealist philosophy.

Diderot's *An Essay on Blindness, in a Letter to a Person of Distinction* (published clandestinely in France in 1749 and in 1750 in Britain) was one of the first texts to interrogate the experience of being blind. He included narrative accounts of real blind individuals, such as the mathematician Professor Saunderson, who stressed that his blindness set him at an intellectual advantage.[22] Dominated by the sense of touch, Diderot's account insists that a blind person could discern not only objects, but also the relations between them (such as symmetry and beauty), an affirmation of 'one index of the positivity of [his] blind universe', as Jeffrey Mehlman points out.[23] Diderot refuted the common belief that simultaneous perception could only be achieved by the eye. In response to 'Molyneux's problem', he answered that a blind man restored to sight would be able to distinguish and identify at a distance the cube and sphere that he formerly knew only from touch. Moreover, he anticipated the systematisation of a tactile alphabet that took place in the nineteenth century, predicting that such a language for the blind would be fixed in a 'grammar' and a 'dictionary'.[24] Rather than approaching blindness simply from the question of what it revealed about vision, Diderot sought to map and understand the world and the experience of blind people.[25] Diderot also suggested that in order to do this, we would need to reorient discussion of the senses away from the visual, in this way challenging the dominant paradigms that were emerging in Western philosophical discussion.

As Diderot realised in his dream of a tactile grammar, blindness opens out the media forms and sensory environments of language and writing beyond the visual. Notably, Edmund Burke, writing a few years later, drew on the experiences of blind people to impress how words and language belonged to sound, as well as vision. The final part of Burke's influential treatise on aesthetics, *A Philosophical Enquiry into the Origin of Our Ideas of the Sublime and Beautiful* (1757; 1759) considers the adequacy of words and language as a representational system to convey sublime experience. Burke is particularly interested in the effect of poetry in raising ideas in the mind of 'those things for which custom has appointed them to stand'.[26] Comprehension of words is – like much of his wider aesthetic project – a sensory activity. Words have all their possible extent of power, Burke states, by stimulating three effects in the mind of the 'hearer': firstly, the *sound*; secondly, the *picture*, or representation of the thing signified by the sound; thirdly, the *affectation* of the soul produced by one or both of the above. According to Burke, the pictorial dimension of words is in fact the weakest, as compounded abstract words such as honour and justice do not produce an image in the hearer's mind. Moreover, an examination of his own and others' minds suggests that even simple abstract words, including colour – as well as aggregate words of nouns such as 'horse', likewise do not stimulate the formation of pictures unless as a result of 'a particular effort of the imagination for that purpose'.[27] Burke acknowledges how the visual predominates in theories of imagination and ideas, and frustratingly he records how he has found it 'very hard to persuade several that their passions are affected by words from whence they have no ideas; and yet harder to convince them, that in the ordinary course of conversation we are sufficiently understood without raising any images of the things concerning which we speak'.[28] And significantly he also turns, like Diderot, to the experiences of blind people to dispel what he identifies as an over-privileging of the visual.

Burke details in the second edition of the *Enquiry* how he came across two 'striking instances' in the blind poet Thomas Blacklock and blind mathematician Nicholas Saunderson that seemed to prove his conviction that the pictorial dimension of words is not necessary to their comprehension and re-articulation by the hearer. Burke challenges Blacklock's editor, Mr Spence, who identifies improprieties in the poet's language, which Spence attributes to the blind poet's 'imperfect conception of visual objects'.[29] Instead Burke insists that 'few men blessed with the most perfect sight can describe visual objects with more spirit and justness than this blind man'. Likewise, whilst acknowledging that Saunderson, in his celebrated lectures on light and colours, taught others 'the theory of those ideas which they had, and which he himself undoubtedly had not', Burke stresses that the words 'red, blue, green' answered to him as well as the colours themselves. That is, the image that a word might effect in the mind of a reader is only a secondary adjunct to its comprehension in common discourse, and as such a blind person is perfectly capable of grasping through the application of 'reason' the ways in which ideas are constructed and exchanged amongst sighted people. In terms Ruskin might take issue with a century later, Burke points to the shared ground of sighted and blind people in language usage by downplaying the role of vision in the creation and interpretation of text. Explicitly drawing attention to his own embodied writing self, he notes that 'when I wrote this last sentence, and used the words *every day* and *common discourse*, I had no images in my mind of any succession of time; nor of men in conference with each other; nor do I imagine that the reader will have any such ideas on reading it'.[30]

Whilst occupying only a brief section of the *Enquiry*, Burke's evidencing of these two blind people's language usage offers an important alternative to the classical *ut pictura poesis* regime and, as Edward Larrissy argues, set the scene for the musical preoccupation of nineteenth-century poetry. Larrissy's recent analysis of the topos of the blind poet and seer in the Romantic period attentively shows how 'writing about blindness or the blind is to be found in one of the most prominent theories of the age: namely, that the blind possessed a compensatory sensitivity to sounds and music, and a concomitant facility at musical performance'.[31] Catherine Maxwell's study on blindness and the female sublime also develops a compelling account of how blindness was figured as a form of lyric compensation in nineteenth-century poetic traditions. Burke's ambitions were not, however, wholly realised in nineteenth-century literary discourse. I return to the concerns he raised in the *Enquiry* in my discussion of the blind poet and novelist Frances Browne in Chapter 7, and trace how responses to her poetry continued to perpetuate the emphasis on the pictorial nature of poetry that Burke aimed to dispel. This produced, I argue, an anxiety in Browne's literary identity (despite her own success), which leads to a particularly tragic outcome for the blinded heroine of her first novel, *My Share of the World* (1861).

An analysis of blind people's literacy practices in the nineteenth century does, however, demand a more nuanced account of material culture that also interrelates sensory modes, media and embodied experience. This methodology resonates with the work of social and visual anthropologists such as David Howes, Elizabeth Edwards and Christopher Tilley, who all insist on the multisensory nature of material experiences.[32] For Tilley, a phenomenological approach considers 'material forms as encountered through the multiple sensuous and socialised subjective apparatus of our bodies (sight, sound, touch, smell, taste)'.[33] Similarly, I take the sensory qualities of language to be active agents in shaping the interpretative possibilities of text within particular social and cultural encounters. The different effects produced by oral and visual components of language systems have been documented. Walter Ong, for example, considers how the phenomenological qualities of sound (its evanescence and immersiveness) influenced the psychodynamics of oral culture. This orality encouraged a verbal economy consonant with 'aggregative (harmonizing) tendencies' rather than the 'analytic, dissecting tendencies' that came with the inscribed, visualised word.[34] My focus here, though, is less on sound, and more on touch. The notable shift in blind people's literacy in the nineteenth century was in fact away from the auditory (as subjects who were read aloud to) to the tactile (as subjects who directly consumed text through the finger).[35] It is my aim to present the ways in which the tactile and haptic qualities of text associated with blind people's reading practices unsettled relationships between textual subjects.

So whilst Ruskin sought to reify reading as a *visual* act, embossed literature for blind people dramatically revealed how books were objects that were not just visually apprehended, but were also touched, held and exchanged. This speaks to current critical debates in media and book history. Driven partly by recent transformations in digital technology, media historians have given urgency to the question of what constitutes a text. By asking whether or not a text can be dematerialised, thinkers such as N. Katherine Hayles have focused our attention on the importance played by the substrate via which readers encounter textual material.[36] Relatedly, book history scholars have shone new light on the book as a medium and as a thing endowed with agency that both instigates and is shaped by the relations between text, reader and its own material properties.[37] Drawing on a critical discourse that encompasses network and thing theory, critics including Christopher Flint and Christina Lupton have shown the pervasiveness of writing that was reflexive about the economic and material production of literature in the eighteenth and nineteenth centuries. As they argue, this knowingness about the format of writing by communities of authors and readers determined how the book was used, and the type of actions the reading subject performed.[38]

There has also been a growing body of scholarly work focused on the material history of the book and readership in the nineteenth century, as well as the material cultures of literature in the period.[39] Leah Price has called compellingly for greater critical analysis of the way in which the book's material form can generate meanings and relationships beyond the influential scope of reader response theory, using the nineteenth-century literary environment as her key example. Rather than focusing on the ways in which ideal ('platform-independent') readers absorb the verbal content of a book, Price develops a concept of 'rejection theory', concerned with the act of 'nonreading' which instead traces the social relationship between 'readers' and the book as physical object.[40] She aims to reconstruct:

> The often contentious relation among three operations: reading (doing something with the words), handling (doing something with the object), and circulating (doing something to, or with, other persons by means of the book – whether cementing or severing relationships, whether by giving and receiving books or by withholding and rejecting them).[41]

Whilst Price focuses on fictional descriptions of such events, the first two operations converge in the history of embossed literature for blind people in the nineteenth century, as perception of words becomes a manual act in the shift from eye to hand.

Experiments with embossed literature exposed the material construction of the book, and in turn the way in which the book's material form determined the relationship between writer, reader and the text. Indeed, as Andrew Piper has so eloquently illuminated, the book has always, from its inception, been a particularly tactile object, which all readers grasp, hold on to, and whose pages they stroke and turn.[42] Yet by unsettling the boundaries between book and body, blindness implicitly and explicitly cohered debates concerning the relationship between sensory perception and interpretation of the text. In the next section, I examine how blindness was not simply an object of idealist philosophic discussion that tested the workings of normal sight. It was also a condition that revealed the interactions between different sensory modes and the material world. Concomitantly, I trace how blindness draws our attention to the complex and overlapping relationship between vision and touch that took hold in the nineteenth-century cultural imagination.

## *Towards a Phenomenology of Blindness and Writing*

Phenomenology helps illuminate the slippage between blindness and sight, and invites us to assess the manifold ways in which textual meaning is shaped by the embodied and material act of reading and writing. As a philosophical practice, phenomenology is concerned with how phenomena manifest themselves, and the mental acts concerned with experiencing them. In its distinction from 'the idealist return to consciousness', early twentieth-century phenomenologists including Edmund Husserl, Martin Heidegger and Maurice Merleau-Ponty placed particular emphasis on knowledge as embodied and experiential and investigation into its mediation through the senses.[43] In the past two decades, critics have turned increasingly to phenomenology as a way to re-interpret nineteenth-century cultural form. Frustrated with the dependence of contemporary cultural studies on Foucauldian critical frameworks, cultural phenomenology sprang in the 1990s from an attempt to understand the materials of culture in themselves. Whilst acknowledging the 'huge variation in phenomenological thought' amongst phenomenologists including Martin Heidegger, Maurice Merleau-Ponty and Gilles Deleuze, Isobel Armstrong suggests that phenomenologists collectively 'dissolve the dualism of subject and object at the same time as they keep a relational structure between the two subjects in play'.[44] Cultural phenomenologists seek a kind of permeability to the object of study; to open up a range of experience for thought, from sensorial and affect to the forgotten objects of a culture.[45] More explicitly still in relation to literary studies, a phenomenological approach can denaturalise our assumptions about what it means to write and read as embodied acts.

I argue that Merleau-Ponty's work is particularly valuable for understanding and analysing the relationship between blindness and writing for two reasons. Firstly, his phenomenological project drew upon – and reframed – empirical investigations into sight disorders. Secondly, his model of haptic visuality, in which sight must also be considered on the model of touch, illuminates how nineteenth-century writers incorporated cultural debates on blind people's tactile experience in their works. Both these facets, as I will show, have a tangible connection to the philosophic and cultural lineages of blindness with which this book is concerned. Visual disorders and blindness occupy an important role in Merleau-Ponty's reconceptualisation of vision: both in the understanding of its limits and in the exploration of its relation to a tactile field. Martin Jay writes that Merleau-Ponty's phenomenological project sought to reaffirm and redeem the visual through challenging the assumptions made about vision. As I discuss in relation to case studies of sight restoration to people with long-term blindness in Chapter 7, Merleau-Ponty returned to empiricist investigations into perceptual disorders. However, he re-orientated the debate to address questions of being through perception, rather than perception as an object in itself:

> Although his own philosophical tools were inevitably reflective, Merleau-Ponty sought to explore the pre-reflexive phenomenal field he called 'being in the world'. He did so by drawing on the psychological examinations of perceptive disorders, which revealed the suppressed assumptions of 'normal' perceptions.[46]

Merleau-Ponty evidences late nineteenth- and early twentieth-century case studies of blind people restored to sight following cataract operations in a discussion of the relationship between sense experience and perception. This engagement with case studies of blind people's perceptive experience does not serve simply to entrench what normal sight is (as in the case of empiricist investigations into the hypothetical blind man). Rather, it forms part of a critique that there might be any such thing as 'normal' perception. Merleau-Ponty is critical of the way in which empiricist philosophy takes for granted that the 'pure tactile data' taken from investigations of blindness can inform theories of the perception of space from a visual, sighted perspective. A blind person's tactility is instead 'a highly particularised kind of experience, which has nothing in common with the functioning of touch in its wholeness, and which cannot give any help in analysis of integrated experience'.[47] In addressing the particular sensory conditions of the perceiving subject, phenomenology invites investigation into visual impairment that does not turn upon the blind person's otherness.[48]

In his later writings on art and visuality, notably his posthumous essay 'The Intertwining – the Chiasm', Merleau-Ponty reframed the relationship between subject and object by revoking the qualities of distance and detachment usually associated with visual perception. His model of 'haptic visuality' outlined a way of being in the world that was based on tactile qualities of proximity and contact, transforming vision into, as William A. Cohen describes it, a 'corporeally grounded and reciprocal one'.[49] Sight takes on the tactile qualities of proximity, and the hand, rather than the eye, becomes the new marker of the self, as the awareness of one's hands touching, and being touched, reveals how the roles of perceiving and being perceived can be reversed:

> there is a circle of the touched and the touching, the touched takes hold of the touching; there is a circle of the visible and the seeing, the seeing is not without visible existence; there is even an inscription of the touching in the visible, of the seeing in the tangible.[50]

In this essay, Merleau-Ponty develops an idea of the reversibility of perception, in which the human is not only subject of perception (the one who perceives), but also perception's object. It is the case of one's hands touching, and being touched, that most clearly illustrates how the roles of perception can be reversed. Rejecting the delimitation of the senses as 'crude', Merleau-Ponty points not only to the diversity of experiences which make up seemingly individual senses, but also to the overlap between different senses.[51] Vision is articulated in terms of touch, privileging a haptic perception as the mode through which to understand self and others.

'Haptic' today can be glossed broadly as the notion of an active, whole-body touch as well as referring to the interoperability of touch and sight. The *Oxford English Dictionary* also defines the term 'haptic' as 'having a greater dependence on sensations of touch than on sight, esp. as a means of psychological orientation'.[52] As I have traced elsewhere, understanding of the haptic sense developed as part of a nineteenth-century scientific investigation into the workings of touch, which placed a strong emphasis on the perceptual faculties of blind people.[53] For example, the mid-nineteenth century psychophysiologist Alexander Bain, whose work influenced later psychologists including Henry Maudsley and William James, argued that 'in order to represent to ourselves the acquisitions of touch in their highest form, we must refer to the experience of the blind'.[54] By the 1850s, scientific treatises on the senses were beginning to evidence blind people's finger-reading skills in analyses of touch.[55]

This haptic perception also enfolds the literary imagination of the nineteenth century, as writers traced the exchanges between the visual and tactile in the interpretation of text. This collocation of sight and touch redresses some of the dominant paradigms that have shaped nineteenth-century cultural studies in the past two decades, notably Jonathan Crary's work on optical technologies and the figure of the observer. Crary's study marked a significant intervention into nineteenth-century cultural studies by placing vision at the centre of changing ideas of human subjectivity, innovatively re-reading the relationship between the observer, visual technologies and art discourse in the period. Drawing on Michel Foucault's *Discipline and Punish* (1977), Crary argues that the 1820s to 1830s witnessed a reordering of vision and the observing subject, with vision the interface of a wider reorganisation of knowledge and social practices. Crary claims that the construction of this new observer is predicated on a separation of the senses in the nineteenth century. In his discussion he evidences changing responses to Molyneux's problem to show that whereas vision had been conceived in terms of analogies to the sense of touch in Enlightenment philosophy, by the nineteenth century it increasingly meant 'an interrogation of the physiological makeup of the human subject'.[56] For artists and art writers such as Cezanne, Ruskin and Monet the blind man restored to sight signals the possibility of conceiving of a vision uncontaminated by historical codes and conventions of seeing – that privileged a pure opticality above other sensory and social associations.[57] Yet, as I have detailed, interest in Molyneux's problem extended long into the nineteenth century, and its transmutations continued to turn on the relation of touch and sight.

In the field of literary studies, Crary's work has been particularly influential in reifying the primacy of the visual in Victorian fiction and poetry.[58] This is exemplified by Nancy Armstrong's 1999 work on the relationship between photography and realism, in which she states that Victorian fiction 'equated seeing with knowing and made visual information the basis for the intelligibility of a verbal narrative', arguing via Crary that 'photographic technology increased exponentially the separation of the senses that privileged seeing'.[59] We can, however, find alternatives to this account. Gerard Curtis, for example, briefly acknowledges how Victorian artists, writers and educators called attention to the importance of training both the hand and eye, suggesting the interoperability of touch and sight in the production of text.[60] Critics have also begun to challenge these accounts via more integrated readings of the nineteenth-century sensorium and the embodied subject, frequently drawing upon phenomenological theories to do so. They impress how the embodied subject cannot simply be reduced to a set of eyes and their neurological appurtenances but is shaped rather by gender, sexuality and health.[61] Hilary Fraser describes how Crary's project of delineating the emergence of a new corporealised observer requires him to 'slough off the tactile'.[62] And as William A. Cohen notes, whilst Crary's and Armstrong's studies have made important contributions in their placement of the visual imagination at the centre of changing ideas of human subjectivity in the nineteenth century, both 'demonstrate the cost to other sensory modalities that an exclusive preoccupation with vision exacts'.[63]

A study of blindness contributes towards these recent critical debates concerning the sensory hierarchies of nineteenth-century literary culture. Victorian writers frequently framed debates about sensory experience and its relationship to writing through discourses on blindness. George Eliot notably explores the tension between visual and tactile codes of writing in her portrayal of the blind scholar Bardo in *Romola* (1862–3), her historical novel set in Renaissance Florence. In the novel, Bardo mourns no longer being able to see or author his '"fine Roman letters; and the Greek character"', which his daughter Romola describes as '"more beautiful than any of your bought manuscripts"'. He tells Romola:

> 'Assuredly, child,' said Bardo, passing his finger across the page, as if he hoped to discriminate line and margin. 'What hired amanuensis can be equal to the scribe who loves the words that grow under his hand, and to whom an error or indistinctness in the text is more painful than a sudden darkness or obstacle across his path? And even these mechanical printers who threaten to make learning a base and vulgar thing – even they must depend on the manuscripts over which we scholars have bent with that insight into the poet's meaning which is closely akin to the *mens divinior* of the poet himself'.[64]

Blindness throws Bardo's scholarship into disarray, severing his relationship with writing by making him dependent on the eyes of others to interpret text (which thus becomes open to corruption), and disrupting the synchronicity between mind and hand as the thinking subject brings writing and thought into being. Eliot's hermeneutics resonate here with Victorian commentators' fear of how the mechanical nature of typed print denigrates writing, a topic I explore further in connection with the development of embossed writing systems for blind people in Chapter 3. Yet the passage alerts us to the mechanistic processes which shape modern literature: Bardo's statement is clearly ironic, for how does Eliot's novel come into being if not through another set of 'mechanical printers'? Eliot also gestures here towards her own era's emerging writing and print cultures for visually impaired people: Bardo's finger passing across the page recalls the finger tracking of blind people discriminating between the symbols of raised type. Innovations in nineteenth-century printing presses and paper production enabled the widespread embossing of text, and facilitated a more direct relationship between paper, words and blind reader, although of course the script remains obscure to Bardo. Unpacking the resonances of this passage further then, these traces of tactile reading rescue somewhat the technological processes of book production feared by Bardo.

The passage from *Romola* quoted above illuminates how the relationship between blindness and writing is shaped by gender politics. The father, Bardo, is cast as a Miltonic figure, who makes meaning through his scholarship whilst his daughter Romola, as his amanuensis, can only bear meaning. Eliot recasts this myth, however, not least through Bardo's anxiety concerning the corruption inherent in transcription. Notably, Eliot returns to this issue with the husband and wife pairing of Dorothea Brooke and Edward Casaubon in *Middlemarch* (1872). Dorothea acts as amanuensis and secretary to Casaubon, whose eyesight is failing from excessive reading.

Indeed, Dorothea asks if she might not '"learn to read Latin and Greek aloud to you, as Milton's daughters did to their father, without understanding what they read?"'. Dorothea struggles to learn the Greek alphabet, and is dismayed at her 'own stupidity', leading her uncle, Mr Brooke, to reflect on the 'lightness' of the 'feminine mind'.[65] Yet even whilst Dorothea is attributed a metaphoric 'blindness' in her inability to accurately read social and familial situations, ultimately it is Casaubon – a literal and figurative Milton – who struggles to integrate knowledge and learning, as poignantly attested to by the failure of his *Key to all Mythologies*.[66]

Feminist literary historians have identified blindness as a leading trope through which to explore the contentious issue of whether women are cast either as bearers or makers of textual meaning in literary canons, as I explore in Chapter 5. However, I critique the ways in which blindness has tended to be interpreted through psychoanalytic frames in relation to gender identity, not least in Sandra Gilbert and Susan Gubar's analysis of blindness in their influential study *The Madwoman in the Attic: The Woman Writer and the Nineteenth-Century Literary Imagination* (1979). Such studies have tended to stress blindness as a negative metaphor that expresses anxiety about women's inability to claim parity with men, in both romantic and creative terms. These analyses demonstrate what David Mitchell and Sharon Snyder have identified as a problematic strategy of multicultural studies, noting that as feminist, race and sexuality studies sought to 'unmoor their identities from debilitating physical and cognitive associations', they repositioned disability as the '"real" limitation from which they must escape'.[67] Valuably, however, Catherine Maxwell has recently reoriented the discussion of writing and blindness from one of anxiety to creativity, as she argues that blindness and its ensuing feminisation is the condition for poetic creativity. She refutes Harold Bloom's classic analysis in which he reads the relationship between male poets and their literary forbears as predicated on masculine strength.[68] Blindness, according to Bloom, is symptomatic of an enervating anxiety, as 'a man's unconscious fear of castration manifests itself as an apparently physical trouble in his eyes; a poet's fear of ceasing to be a poet frequently manifests itself also as a trouble of his vision'.[69] Blindness has traditionally signalled a metaphoric end of writing: Maxwell instead argues that the identity of the lyric poet is in fact determined by their giving up their masculine status.[70]

Whilst this process of emasculation or feminisation is still part of the dynamic I trace in both male and female writers' invocations of blindness, I am concerned with the way in which this manifests materially, as well as metaphorically. The material practices of writing associated with blindness (for example, dictation, the role of the amanuensis) are variously gendered masculine and feminine and, as such, precipitate new sets of creative concerns (and freedom) for both the male and female writer. Situating this discussion within a more phenomenologically grounded analysis of the relationship between blindness and writing opens up new enquiries: in what ways, for example, can we read Rochester's blinding in *Jane Eyre* not simply in disciplinary terms (i.e. Jane, and by extension, Charlotte Brontë, must destroy the male gaze as they appropriate the pen), but rather as a probing of the embodied conditions of writing and reading text? How does this disrupt the relationship between gender and writing that feminist historians have outlined?

The various strands I have been discussing in the latter part of this chapter come together in a fascinating portrait of the Liberal politician Henry Fawcett, who became blind in his mid-twenties, and his wife, the writer and suffragist Millicent Garrett Fawcett, painted by the Pre-Raphealite artist Ford Madox Brown in 1872 (see Figure 2). In the painting, Henry is depicted seated in an armchair, wearing academic dress. Millicent sits on his left, perched on the side of the chair, slightly raised above him and looking in his direction but not quite focused on him. Her right arm is wrapped across his right shoulder, and she holds a pen in this hand. Their left hands are touching, and she also clasps a piece of paper, to which Henry gestures with his right. His mouth is open, as if in speech.

The portrait is unusual in several respects, not least for so directly presenting Fawcett's blindness. Fawcett wears no obvious markers of blindness here: he is portrayed without the dark glasses that he wore and was usually depicted with. His eyes, which had been damaged by gun pellets, are also more frankly depicted, and whilst the viewer cannot connect with his gaze, the forceful command of his presence is impressed through the sense of sound and touch. This portrait has been painted within a culture in which touch and vision are connected: in order to invoke in the viewer a shared experience of blindness it appeals to the tactility of or beyond vision. Viewers are invited less to consider what Fawcett cannot see, and more to anticipate what he might say; to feel the pressure of touch and stroke the different textures of creamy skin, crisp paper, silk dress and woollen academic gown, vividly rendered in the painting. It is an invitation to *behold*, as Calè and di Bello put it, rather than to view.[71] In the intimacy of the Fawcetts' private touch made public, something of Maurice Merleau-Ponty's notion of the reversibility of the flesh and circularity of touch and vision discussed above plays out here, destabilising the boundaries of subject and object, blind man and woman transcriber, viewer and sitter.

Figure 2 Ford Madox Brown, *Henry Fawcett; Dame Millicent Garrett Fawcett (née Garrett)*, oil on canvas (1872).
© National Portrait Gallery, London.

The portrait also engages closely with text and literary form. The composition is quite literally centred around text and plays on language as the material forms of speech (Henry is represented with mouth open in speech), writing (Millicent holds a pen) and indeed as paper that is both touched and looked at. In his composition and arrangement of figures, Brown invokes, yet importantly re-frames, that famous scene of intrigue in the nineteenth century: Milton dictating to his daughters.[72] Millicent, holding a pen, is seemingly positioned like Milton's daughters in a transcribing role. Yet the paper Millicent holds is inscribed with both their names, and transcription of their signatures (which Henry could still be guided to make), 'Your obedient servants / M G Fawcett / Henry Fawcett'.[73] As 1872 was also the year in which their co-authored *Essays and Lectures on*

*Social and Political Subjects* was published, again, this seems to represent a moment of mutual authorship, rather than transcription. Furthermore, whilst Millicent is in the background, both her positioning above him and the circularity of their hands and reciprocity of touch reconfigure the relationship between Milton and his amanuenses, which traditionally stress their distance and division from the great male poet. Brown's painting presents a dialectic, rather than binary, image of gender that owes more, I suggest, to Charlotte Brontë's and Elizabeth Barrett Browning's recent portrayals of blindness. As I argue in my discussion of these two texts, the blinding of Rochester in *Jane Eyre* and Romney Leigh in *Aurora Leigh* not only creates a sense of shared equality with Jane and Aurora; it also creates the conditions for these female writers' narratives materially to proceed, in this way also challenging the Miltonic legacy that framed women as bearers, rather than makers, of meaning.

## Conclusion

The following chapters in this part of *Blindness and Writing* all consider the complex ways in which blindness intersected with material cultures of writing. They show the ways in which blind people accessed literary form, both materially with the development of raised print, and used the genre of autobiography to articulate both a poetics and politics of blindness. They expand upon the topics introduced here, and show how blind people's literacy contributed to a redefinition of the sensory regimes of writing. I firstly turn, however, to the poet William Wordsworth. I argue that Wordsworth's own experience of visual impairment manifested as an anxiety that blindness would disrupt his poetic project, at odds with a Romantic-era privileging of blindness as a space of creative inner vision. Building on the insights of this chapter, my discussion draws attention to a tension between idealised and embodied states of blindness in Wordsworth's literary representations of blindness.

CHAPTER 2

# *The Materiality of Blindness in Wordsworth's Imagination*

> The complaint in my eyes which gave occasion to this address to my daughter ... first shewed itself as a consequence of inflammation caught at the top of Kirkstone when I was over-heated by having carried up the ascent my eldest son a lusty infant. Frequently has the disease recurred since, leaving the eyes in a state which has often prevented my reading for months – & makes me at this day incapable of bearing without injury any strong light by day or night. My acquaintance with books has therefore been far short of my wishes; and on this account to acknowledge the services daily and hourly done me by my family and friends this note is written.[1]

This note to a poem Wordsworth addressed to his daughter Dora, in which he imagines himself in the guise of three literary and mythical blind figures – Oedipus, Samson Agonistes, and Milton – opens up a critically important, yet little-known, aspect of the poet's biography. From January 1805 until his death, Wordsworth experienced sustained attacks of chronic trachoma, known at the time as 'Egyptian ophthalmia'.[2] These attacks confined him to darkened rooms for days at a time, prevented his travelling, and left him sensitive to light and reliant upon wearing green eyeshades to relieve his photophobia. Reflecting on his experience of ophthalmia towards the end of his life, Wordsworth fixed upon the ways in which episodic visual impairment disrupted his relationship with literature. It prevented him from accessing textual material directly, and made him dependent upon others – friends and family – to assist his reading. Whilst ophthalmia facilitated and enriched communal bonds between Wordsworth and his group, ultimately he assessed the condition as limiting to his literary endeavours: 'My acquaintance with books has therefore been far short of my wishes.'

The figure of the blind also, of course, permeates Wordsworth's writing. Notable depictions of blindness in his oeuvre include Herbert in *The Borderers* (1797–9; published 1842), 'Lines Written a Few Miles Above Tintern Abbey' (1798), 'The Blind Highland Boy' (1806), the blind man of *The Excursion* (1814), and the blind Beggar of *The Prelude*. Yet discussion of Wordsworth's own experience of visual impairment has usually been relegated to scholarly footnotes, recognised if at all as an interesting fact, but one which has little bearing on our interpretation of his poetry.[3] Critical accounts of the topic of blindness in Wordsworth's writing have instead documented its potent symbolic value, as a trope that structures psychological relationships in his texts, as well as one which gives rise to important reflection on the nature and reality of mental images and the workings of the imagination.[4] In particular, the model of imagination as inner vision, independent of physical sight, has been central to the ways in which Romanticist scholars have interpreted blindness in Wordsworth's writing.[5] I argue, however, that reading Wordsworth's depictions of blindness through his experience of ophthalmia casts new light on his poetic project.

In its precariousness, Wordsworth's vision exemplifies what Merleau-Ponty defines as 'conditioned thought' occasioned 'by what happens in the body'.[6] In this chapter, I outline how trachoma affected Wordsworth's bodily eyes and the ophthalmologic treatments he sought to manage the condition. I also demonstrate how Wordsworth's visual impairment makes visible the gender politics that underpin his production of writing, as he frequently relied upon female members of his household and circle to act as amanuenses when he was experiencing symptoms, their hands transcribing his spoken poetry and correspondence when his eyes were failing. This biographically grounded discussion leads to a reassessment of three figures of blindness from Wordsworth's literary oeuvre: the blind figure of Herbert in Wordsworth's play *The Borderers*; his poem to Dora; and the blind Beggar of *The Prelude*. These figurations of blindness are rooted in the body of the writer, and can be analysed as important meditations on the disjuncture between a poetic idea and its physical manifestation as text. I also appraise the ways in which these figures are situated within Wordsworth's poetic project over time, and how they both respond to the ophthalmia directly or are revised following his experience of it.

Whilst it might seem odd to open a book largely concerned with blindness and Victorian fiction with a Romantic-era poet, Wordsworth's blindness is important to this study in several ways. Firstly, Wordsworth's experience of trachoma is situated in, and shaped by, a set of emerging medical and social discourses of blindness central to my larger study, and which I expand on throughout subsequent chapters. These include the development of ophthalmology, which provided increasingly specialised diagnosis and treatment of eye diseases as the century progressed; and the problematic relationship blind people posed towards literacy. Reading Wordsworth's poetry in its multiple versions also reminds us that he is a Victorian as well as a Romantic-era poet: *The Prelude* was of course first published in 1850. The trope of blindness as a condition of inner vision that I begin to trace in this chapter also recurs in the Victorian writers I analyse, and I demonstrate explicitly the intertextual resonances between Wordsworth's poetry and Dickens's fiction in Chapter 6. As my book makes clear, however, this trope comes under strain in both Wordsworth's poetic project and in those later writers who invoke it. For whilst blindness is, on the one hand, valorised as an ideal condition that promotes imaginative thinking, it also signals a physical state that disrupts the ability to produce and consume text. The embodied experience of blindness points to the fact that literature cannot exist independently of the perceptual and physiological processes of the human subject.[7] As Elizabeth Dolan argues in her analysis of eye disorders (including the ophthalmia) as metaphors for social justice in the Romantic era, subjective perception 'emerges as much from medical theories about the physiology of vision in individual bodies as from idealist philosophy'.[8] It is this tension between idealised and embodied states of blindness that I examine in Wordsworth's poetry.

## Romantic Ophthalmia: The Materiality of Blindness in Wordsworth's Imagination

Visual disorders were highly visible in the early nineteenth century. Industrialisation fuelled the rapid growth of insanitary urban centres and promoted infectious conditions; poor working conditions also contributed to an increase in eye-strain and accidents. Warfare was a major contributory factor to the high incidence of eye accidents and diseases, which included ophthalmia (known today as trachoma). Soldiers returning from the campaign in Egypt (1798–1801) in the war against France carried the disease back to Britain, and it rapidly spread from the naval and military forces to the civilian population, becoming endemic. Ophthalmia was soon one of the most common causes of blindness in early nineteenth-century Britain.[9] The condition caused the formation of pustules along the eyelashes and eyelid margins, which could lead to permanent loss of vision if it spread to the eyeball. Figure 3, a plate from John Vetch's extensive study of the ophthalmia in 1820, illustrates the effect of purulent ophthalmia on the eyelids. John Stevenson, one of the leading early ophthalmologists in Britain,

Figure 3 Plate from John Vetch, *A Practical Treatise on the Diseases of the Eye* (London, 1820).
© The British Library Board (shelfmark 7611.bb.19).

attributed part of the rapid growth of the field of eye medicine to the effect of the Egyptian ophthalmia. He wrote:

> Of late years, however, a dreadful Ophthalmia, before unknown amongst us, has been introduced into the country from Egypt, and has not only added greatly to the frequency of their occurrence, but also at the same time not a little increased the malignancy of their character.[10]

He went on to suggest that the seriousness of the disease attracted the attention of 'regular practitioners' of medicine to the eye. The historian

Luke Davidson describes how the 'cultural nature of the ophthalmic epidemics motivated practitioners to study the eye in earnest', with practitioners surmounting obstacles intrinsic to medical culture including the division between physicians and surgeons, and hostility to specialisms.[11] Thus despite ophthalmology having one of the worst reputations for quackery at the end of the eighteenth century, it became one of the first and most successful specialities, advancing rapidly in the first few decades of the nineteenth century. By the 1810s specialist hospitals were being built across Britain, including in London (1805), Exeter (1808), Bath (1811) and Manchester (1814), leading to the development of new surgical techniques.

Michel Foucault influentially drew attention to the special relationship that existed between vision and knowledge in modern medicine. He argued that modern medicine 'succeeded in striking a balance between *seeing* and *knowing* (*le voir et le savoir*) that protected it from error', as the clinic evolved into a space in which the doctor learned to 'see what he saw' when examining the human body – that is, give name to the new layers of the visible body emerging in medical investigation, in turn conferring disciplinary power on the clinic.[12] The visual organ at stake in these investigations was itself also subject to the clinical gaze and rational discourse of ophthalmology. The development of an ophthalmologic print culture shaped the field by beginning to construct a rational discourse around the diseased eye, and ideas and discoveries were disseminated across the country via textbooks and specialist journals. One of the earliest British ophthalmic texts and 'first major treatise on the eye's pathology',[13] James Wardrop's *Essays on the Morbid Anatomy of the Eye* (1808) stated that despite the publication of 'several excellent practical treatises and detached essays', as 'no attempt has yet been made in this country to treat of the pathology of the human eye, little apology seems necessary for the present undertaking'.[14] The building of new hospitals aided the development of the discipline still further, as the surgeons at these hospitals published their research, compiling complete textbooks of ophthalmology.[15] The leading medical journal, *The Edinburgh Medical and Surgical Journal* (1805–5), was also launched, as a vehicle for the latest and most important discoveries in medicine, surgery and pharmacy, publishing reviews of contemporary questions and disputes, critical evaluations of monographs and textbooks. Texts which dealt specifically with the ophthalmia include Sir William Adams, *Practical Observations on Ectropium, or Eversion of the Eyelids, with the Description of a New Operation for the Cure of that Disease; on the Modes of Forming An Artificial Pupil, and On Cataract* (1812) (Adams recommends operating on the diseased eyelid after inflammation has subsided, and cutting away part of the diseased tissue), and John Vetch, *A Practical Treatise on the Diseases of the Eye* (1820).

Janis Caldwell usefully terms the 'double vision' of leading doctors and writers in the early nineteenth century 'Romantic materialism', in their shared concern with consciousness and self-expression and their shared interrogation of what natural philosophy revealed about the material world. For Caldwell, 'Romantic materialism' was a dialectical hermeneutic, an interpretive method which 'tacked back and forth' between physical evidence and inner, imaginative understanding'.[16] This dialectical relationship is evident in the discursive construction of ophthalmia, which fuelled new investigation into the material structure and functioning of the eye, and had rich metaphoric potential for literary writers. In its contagious nature, for example, it signified a dangerous and unstable boundary between self and others which ran contrary to the period's expanding individualism. Elizabeth Dolan argues that the ophthalmia 'provided an embodied example of the fear that contact with alterity would destroy one's identity'. Mary Shelley invokes the disease in *Frankenstein; or, the Modern Prometheus* (1818) in Frankenstein's creature's dull yellow and watery eyes, to stress how fear of contagion might limit the viewer's ability to see both suffering and individual subjectivity in 'the other'.[17] In Wordsworth's poetry, the otherness of ophthalmia is experienced as a sense of dislocation in the poet's writing self. As a lived condition, and not simply a metaphor, troublingly it revealed how poetic creation was centred in a physiological body subject to damage and decay.

Wordsworth first experienced symptoms of the ophthalmia in January 1805, a few months after his sister Dorothy noted she had caught an eye infection.[18] Several unpublished letters in the Wordsworth Trust collection record that Wordsworth experienced several further bouts of the ophthalmia throughout the 1810s to 1840s, and those in Wordsworth's circle often commented on 'the inflammation' of his eyes.[19] The disease also left Wordsworth sensitive to light and reliant upon wearing green eyeshades when out walking in bright sunlight. These coloured eyeshades are now amongst the Wordsworth memorabilia on display at Dove Cottage, Grasmere, along with a blue stone thought to be the one used to relieve his eye inflammations, as well as the poet's spectacles. Wordsworth's experience of the ophthalmia prompted him to seek medical advice, which initially focused on altering his diet, whilst using a few restoratives. In 1820 he appeared to be using natural remedies, with his sister Dorothy detailing the changes made to his diet (given a slight improvement in his condition he was 'now … allowed to take a little light animal food, and a small portion of wine').[20] By 1825, Wordsworth was experimenting with other palliatives. In a fascinating letter, Sara Hutchinson, Wordsworth's sister-in-law, described some of the remedies Wordsworth had tried, and provided an account of him as a patient; the fact that both her correspondent, John Monkhouse, and one of their friends were suffering from the same disease highlights the widespread nature of the disease. She wrote:

> You give no particulars of the state of your eyes at present – therefore "I guess" they are not materially worse or better – William has been sadly teezed lately with inflammation on the Lids, & consequent heat & irritation of the eyeballs – Tillbrook had the same when he was here – and since his return to College he has been to Town consulting Alexander whose prescriptions would, we are sure, be of use to William – but he is a most refractory Patient – Alexander recommends nothing more than bathing in water (morning and Evg) as hot as the eye can bear till the water becomes nearly cool – to accustom the eye to the light, & variety of colours – not to stick to green – else nothing else in time would be endured – to eat & drink moderately no "condiments" to use Wms favourite word & an [?] abstinence in Tea.[21]

As in many ophthalmologic texts of the period, there is a direct link here between the effects of diet and vision. This arises from a conception of the body still based on the humouric model, in which illness in one location was understood to be the result of an imbalance of the body's more general constitution. This model demonstrates the tension between theory and practice in medicine in the period, as it neglects certain key developments beginning to take hold in medicine, not least the contribution of the French physician Marie François Xavier Bichat, whose work advanced the theory of general anatomy.

General anatomy is the study of the elementary parts of the body, independent of the organs which they concur to form. Elementary parts, or textures, by the diversity of their combinations, produce all the modifications of structure and functions which the different organs of animals exhibit. Bichat identified 21 elementary textures at work in the body, all differently organised, and hence he proved the dissimilarity of their properties both in health and disease. As Wardrop noted, 'this is the groundwork of the whole fabric, and to it we must ultimately recur in every attempt, to account either for the natural or morbid appearances which are to be met with among organised beings'.[22] Diseases occur in an organ in one part of elementary texture, but not others. This recognition led to an increasingly differentiated and specialised approach to the study of the diseased body. By structurally analysing the shape and texture of the eye, the more specific nature of its particular diseases and impairments could be more readily identified, and more focused treatments developed.

The treatments that Wordsworth's doctors advised evidence the widening split between folk and modern medicine. On the one hand, they did include the application of specific remedies to treat the site of the infection and inflammation, for example copper sulphate, also known as the blue stone. Frederic Reynolds, editor of the *Keepsake*, suggested to Wordsworth in 1826 that he touch his eyes with 'the blue stone', and Sara Hutchinson recorded that it 'acted like magic upon them – & I never saw him look so well & *bonny* as he did yesterday, upon his return from Keswick, for many years'.[23] A few months later, Dorothy reported that Wordsworth's eyes were much better and, 'thanks to touching the eyelids with the blue stone', his eyes 'are become useful again. He holds the pen himself, and even reads aloud to us by candlelight. This happy change, through God's blessing, has been brought about by touching the eyelids with blue stone. A very few applications were sufficient'.[24] This treatment was grounded, however, in ancient, rather than modern, therapeutic practice: the ancient Egyptians are believed to have used copper sulphate to treat ophthalmia.[25] Whilst some eye doctors, such as Sir William Adams, were advocating new surgical techniques to treat opthalmia, this met with resistance from others. Vetch advised that application of a blue stone or silver nitrate was more effective than Adams's operative cure, which required 'the complete eversion of the palpebrae'.[26] Despite using copper sulphate, however, Wordsworth's symptoms flared up again in 1829, and Sarah Coleridge wrote that 'Mr Wordsworth is suffering from an attack in his eyes – his left eye is very much affected; this is most vexatious as we all hoped the enemy was put to flight forever'.[27] Critically, the experiment with the blue stone demonstrates Wordsworth's use of supplements rather than surgical techniques to manage his impaired vision and to bring it back to normal functioning, as does his wearing of the green eyeshades – a further intervention advised by his doctors.

Wordsworth started to wear green eyeshades in 1820.[28] Green glass had been used in eyeshades to treat photophobia since at least the seventeenth century. In 1666 Samuel Pepys recorded that he bought a pair of green spectacles to help alleviate the pain he was experiencing in his eyes.[29] In Oliver Goldsmith's sentimental novel *The Vicar of Wakefield: A Tale Supposed to be Written by Himself* (1766), the vicar's son Moses famously exchanges the family's horse for 'a gross of green spectacles with silver rims and shagreen cases'.[30] Green eyeshades were also associated with distorted vision, a metaphor for the gap between reality and perception of the external world. In an early journalistic paper published in *Bentley's Miscellany* (1838), Dickens plays with the idea of coloured spectacles when Mr Tickle proudly displays his 'new-invented spectacles', at the 'Second Meeting of the Mudfog Association for the Advancement of Everything'. In a satirical swipe at scientific and philosophic societies, the narrator describes how the glasses 'enabled the wearer to discern, in very bright colours, objects at a great distance, and rendered him wholly blind to those immediately before him. It was, he said, a most valuable and useful invention, based strictly upon the principle of the human eye'.[31] Wordsworth's coloured glasses also invite a reimagining of the materiality of vision in his poetry, especially as they are not just objects to be looked *on*, but objects which, looked *through*, mediate and indeed disorder the subject's visual perception of the phenomenal world.

By the time Wordsworth began wearing green glasses, their function in managing ocular dysfunctions was coming under ophthalmologic scrutiny. Vetch, for example, advised against wearing eyeshades. His intervention in this matter ('the exclusion of light, so invariably enforced, is often more detrimental than useful') suggests the popularity of wearing shades to alleviate symptoms, whereas Vetch stipulated: 'I have never suffered a shade to be worn.'[32] The colour of glass was also understood to impact on the eye. In a populist ophthalmic treatise, Georg Beer noted that although most people of weak sight used spectacles to improve their vision, others went further and imagined 'that since green silk has such beneficial effects upon the eyes, so green glasses cannot fail to have the same influence'.[33] As this quote from Beer indicates, the fabric as well as the colour was understood to impact upon the eyes. Yet the benefits of wearing coloured glasses was challenged in a later guide to spectacles and glasses from 1824: 'green, or any coloured glasses' veil objects 'with a gloomy obscurity' and therefore are not to be recommended. Nor did it approve of 'other ridiculous refinements', such as 'thin *Green-Gauze* or *Crape*, instead of Green Glass', recommended 'under the pretence, that while it moderates the Light … it still admits the Air, and is, therefore, cooler to the Eyes'.[34] More worryingly, Stevenson argued: 'By using *green* spectacles, especially those of a *deep tint*, the eye is subjected to frequent, and not inconsiderable variations in respect to the degree of light; and every such sudden and violent change, must of necessity be detrimental to the organ of vision.'[35] The advice given to Wordsworth to use a 'variety of colours – not to stick to green' indicates that his physician was aware of ophthalmologic concern over the effects of green light on the eyes.

Early ophthalmologic treatises also stressed the ways in which the conditions of reading and writing put great strain upon the eyes. Stevenson noted:

> the instances of weakness of sight, which occurred in the early part of my ophthalmic practice, were marked with great constitutional delicacy, and the individuals had most clearly brought on the disease, either by excessive attention to fine dazzling work, or by inordinate indulgence in literary pursuits protracted frequently to late hours.[36]

Wordsworth's daughter Dora suggested that not only did the attacks of blindness disrupt the mechanical act of reading and writing, they also disrupted the metaphysics of writing (that is, the mental activities associated with composing poetry). In an important letter of 1829 she recorded:

> My greatest anxiety now is for my dear Father's eye, which I am grieved to say is almost worse this morning than it has ever been. The inflammation seems to have moved from the lid to the eye itself – though not being able to read or write is bad enough but this is the least disturbing consequence to him – he cannot amuse himself by any mental occupations – if he attempts to think or to compose the eye instantly suffers.[37]

The notion that mental disturbance aggravates the eyes is borne out further in a letter of 1833 in which Dora wrote, again to her cousin Christopher, that her father has been 'a prisoner in a dark room' because of a recurrence of the inflammation. She outlined:

> For my father is still a blind man – but thank god the inflammation has entirely subsided. Tonics were applied to his eyes and he has now permission to go into the garden; for the last ten days he has been a prisoner in a dark room & so very very patient but not very good; for compose sonnets he will in spite of all the dreadful threats of his medical attendant, nor will the recollection of blisters on blisters or leaches on leaches keep him quiet. Within the last few weeks he has composed upwards of 40 sonnets, I believe principally on subjects connected with his late tour … now that the inflammations in the eyes have taken so alarming a form we are all extremely anxious that he should consult Alexander or some oculist of note and we hope by & bye to persuade him to go to London for the purpose.[38]

Blindness was not only thought to be brought on by reading and writing, but by the act of thinking itself. The relationship between vision and writing is emphasised still further by the detail that the sonnets he composed were 'on subjects connected with his late tour'. This instance records the reciprocal nature between composition and vision – composing poetry requires the perception of an original, real object (the tour) to stimulate mental activity – yet that activity is recognised as potentially destroying vision. Thus, in many respects, to those around him, Wordsworth's blindness seemed to uphold the blindness/insight paradigm, in which a withdrawal of physical vision opened up the potential for visionary, or imaginative seeing. A letter dated 29 December 1834 from William's nephew Chris to his father (William's brother) noted: 'My uncle's eyes are … much better, indeed they would be quite well, if he did not write verses: but this he will do; and therefore it is extremely difficult to prevent him from ruining his eyesight.'[39]

Withdrawing from the light seems to have been a regular way of dealing with the attacks; Dora noted again that in 1837, after a 'most severe' attack, her father had been compelled to sit in darkened rooms for ten days.[40] As Vetch pointed out in his 1820 treatise on the ophthalmia, the presence of light, although seemingly not injurious in itself, appeared 'to add so much to the irritation'.[41] This retreat into a dark room echoes the speaker's invocation of the Platonic 'blind cavern' towards the *Prelude*'s conclusion, figured as the birthplace of the imagination:

> This faculty [imagination] hath been the moving soul
> Of our long labour: we have traced the stream
> From darkness, and the very place of birth
> In its blind cavern, whence is faintly heard
> The sound of waters, follow'd it to light
> And open day, accompanied its course
> Among the ways of Nature, afterwards
> Lost sight of it, bewilder'd and engulph'd,
> Then given it greeting, as it rose once more
> With strength, reflecting in its solemn breast
> The works of man and face of human life.[42]

Here, the speaker names the faculty of imagination as the object of the poem, and emphasises that it is not a static force but rather a 'moving' soul of a long labour. Figured as a stream, the imagination has its origin in blindness, in the dark space of a cavern where the only sense noted is aural, 'the sound of waters'. As the imagination matures, the speaker and his interlocutor engage vision to trace its progress through the natural world, following it 'to light'. Bearing witness to the landscape of the natural world, embodied in the Lake District, strengthens the course of the imagination. Yet despite the speaker's attempt to keep the faculty in sight, the imagination precariously disappears from vision in the bewilderment of the speaker's experience in city spaces. Importantly, as I trace below, this bewilderment is encapsulated in the poem in an encounter with a blind beggar in London. The threat that blindness poses – it is figured as a space from which the imagination must leave in its journey towards the light – is mirrored also in Wordsworth's experience of visual impairment. His withdrawal into darkened rooms to ease the ophthalmia was marked by anxiety lest the mental, imaginative activity of composing poems should cause permanent damage to his eyes.

The physical experience of Wordsworth's blindness demonstrates the ways in which writing takes place through supplements and prosthetics, alerting us to the materials and technologies of writing as well as the hands that record Wordsworth's voice when he cannot see to write. Writing as a material act is here a feminine supplement to a masculine composition. The intersection of the biographical evidence of Wordsworth's blindness with the production of his poetry allows the voices which are silent, yet present in the text, to come forward and speak: the women who nursed Wordsworth in his blindness, communicated his blindness to their own friends, and acted as his amanuenses when he was unable to write. There is an explicitly gendered dimension to the material existence of these letters, which also signals the collective nature of writing. I will examine briefly Wordsworth's dependency upon the hands of others to inscribe his voice, before setting forward a reading of Wordsworth's poetic invocations of blindness analysed through his embodied experience. The condition of blindness coheres a set of anxieties concerning both the nature of the visible world, and the visible form of writing.

## Wordsworth's Amanuenses

In *The Prelude* Wordsworth describes his sister Dorothy as that 'beloved Woman' who, in the 'midst of all preserv'd me still / A Poet' (x, 908, 918–19). Yet his dependency on Dorothy's eyes (he said of her that 'she gave me eyes, she gave me ears') was not limited to her ideal vision, as he came also to rely upon her (and others) to assist him in the material production of writing when suffering the effects of the trachoma.[43] Dorothy wrote of an occasion when his eyes were so bad 'he was utterly unable to use a pen himself; and for many days suffered so much from inflammation in his eyes that it was injurious to him even to dictate to another person'.[44] As Wordsworth's sight disappeared, so too did his voice: he is doubly absent from us as we lose the trace of his writing, another hand standing in for his signature. Frequently Wordsworth's letters are transcribed by unknown hands, or introduced with such disclaimers as 'I hold the pen for Mr W., whose eyes, I grieve to say, do not serve him for this & scarcely any other purpose at present'.[45]

Judith Pascoe shows how representations of Wordsworth can be situated usefully within the context provided by romantic-era depictions of Milton, which highlight that poet's 'necessary composition practice of dictating to his daughters'.[46] Pascoe is not quite right, however, to read these depictions as evidence of Wordsworth's theatrical performance of his poetry writing, as whilst Milton might be 'exempt from accusations of exhibitionism by his blindness, Wordsworth was not; but in styling himself after Milton he perhaps hoped to benefit from the earlier poet's immunity in this regard'.[47] There is clearly a stronger identification made between both poets and their composition processes than Pascoe allows for, given Wordsworth's experience of the ophthalmia. These composition processes are, however, both constructed along a clearly gendered binary: the male voice speaks, the female hand transcribes.[48] A miniature double portrait of Wordsworth and his wife, Mary, made towards the end of his life by society portrait painter Margaret Gillies embodies this division of labour. Drawn during a period of several weeks when Gillies stayed with the Wordsworths at Rydal Mount in the autumn of 1839, the miniature depicts William and Mary seated at a desk, writing materials spread before them (Figure 4). Wordsworth's hand is poised resting on a book, his head turned to the left and the gaze focused outside of the frame. Mary is depicted in the act of transcribing. Her eyes rest on her husband, what was perhaps intended as an affectionate smile uncannily bordering on a grimace, repeating yet refiguring the resentful glances in paintings of Milton's daughters that Pascoe discusses (in none of which do Milton's daughters gaze directly at the poet).[49] Correspondence from around the time of the sitting literalises this visual allusion to Milton, as Dora transcribed a letter from William to his niece Susanna in which he dictated: 'Dora is so good to hold the pen for me tho' my eyes are so much improved I could write myself.'[50] Just a few days before Gillies arrived then, Wordsworth was again beset by pain in his eyes, prompting him to employ Dora as an amanuensis. The traces that exist of Wordsworth's amanuenses – the eyes and hands of his writing – point to the silent acts of gender difference that underpin the production of his writing.

I turn now to Wordsworth's construction of blindness and blind figures in his poetry, tracing the uneasy position such episodes occupy within his literary project. By detailing the manifestation of his own visual impairment, I have foregrounded the particularly physical engagement with vision and its threatened loss which affected Wordsworth at critical stages in his later poetic career. It is through these episodes of blindness, centred in the experience of the physical eye, that the transcendence of the poetic word comes under renewed strain.

Figure 4 Margaret Gillies, *William and Mary Wordsworth*, watercolour (1839).
The Wordsworth Trust, GRMDC.A4.
By permission of the Wordsworth Trust, Grasmere.

## Figures of Wordsworth's 'own poetic self': Reading Blindness Biographically

Whilst 'figures of deprivation' – that is, 'maimed men, drowned corpses, blind beggars' – have been discussed in theoretical accounts as figures of Wordsworth's 'own poetic self', the tendency has been to interpret such figures metaphorically. Paul de Man stresses that Wordsworth's 'near-obsessive concern with mutilation, often in the form of a loss of one of the senses' in *The Excursion* and *The Prelude* reveals the autobiographical dimension that these texts have in common, signifying the threat of elision.[51] They also demonstrate the critical value of returning to the author's body. Although De Man claims that the question of whether the writer is himself blinded is 'somewhat irrelevant', Wordsworth's embodied experience of blindness reveals his anxiety that his language may indeed be 'blind to its own statement', as his experience of blindness is also an encounter with the gaps and absences that punctuate the material production of the text.[52]

A discussion of Wordsworth's play *The Borderers: A Tragedy* begins to open out some of these concerns. Although written in 1796–7, the play was only published in 1842, in Edward Moxon's seventh volume of *The Poetical Works of William Wordsworth*, titled *Poems: Chiefly of Early and Late Years.*[53] In his note to the 1842 publication, Wordsworth explains his decision to publish the play at this point. Noting how the play made 'impressions upon my mind which made me unwilling to destroy the MS., I determined to undertake the responsibility of publishing it during my own life, rather than impose upon my successors the task of deciding its fate'; he adds that it has now 'been revised with some care'.[54] The ageing Wordsworth seeks to determine the shape and fate of the play by taking responsibility for its publication. Further, the 'impressions upon my mind' which made him unwilling to destroy the manuscript alert us to the complex biographical factors that shaped the production and reception of Wordsworth's texts in this period, and invite us to look more closely at the experiences that guided publication of the later texts.

Blake Reeve argues in her recent examination of the play that reading the unstaged tragedy in its compositional, intertextual contexts (for example, Wordsworth's engagement with theatre culture in Paris in the 1790s and his anxieties over leaving his pregnant lover, Annette Vallon) reinstates the significance of the play within the poet's oeuvre. It prompts 'considerations of the relation of work to author, of the shaping influence of dramatic representation, and of the role tale-telling voices play in life and art'.[55] Reeve documents the play's fascination with tales and tale-telling and the construction of character. Drawing upon J. Hillis Miller's notion that the 'self' of the writer one encounters in reading a text is *made* by the work (rather than the work's originator), she convincingly argues that Rivers, in the early version, is 'the author of' Wordsworth.[56] However, Wordsworth's experience of chronic trachoma in the intervening years intriguingly refocuses our attention on the 'feeble, old and blind' Herbert as author of Wordsworth (1842, v, iii, 2221).

The play's central theme is abandonment: the villainous Rivers/Oswald character is compelled by an earlier crime (abandoning the captain of a ship he sailed on to certain death on a rocky outcrop near Syria) to deceive the borderer Mortimer/Marmaduke into abandoning Herbert (the blind father of his love Matilda/Idonea) to his death on a wild, storm-besieged moor. Herbert was blinded after rescuing the baby Idonea from a fire (both Charlotte Brontë's Rochester and Elizabeth Barrett Browning's Romney Leigh would later be blinded in similar circumstances). Herbert's blindness and his ageing, frail body, with their clear literary allusions to the figures of Shakespeare's character King Lear and the poet Milton, heighten the tragic pathos of the play. The emphasis on Herbert's blindness is strengthened in the revised version, with Herbert himself describing in the 1842 version how he had returned from the Holy Land 'sightless' (1842, II.iii.829) – most of the descriptions of him as blind are made by other characters. Moreover, the nature of the tragedy's spectacle shifts: it is no longer conceived as a staged play, but rather as text to be read in a more private and solitary mode. Whilst Herbert's blindness would assume a certain type of visible pathos before the audience in a staged performance, solitary reading encourages more interpersonal identifications. It also shifts the sensory focus from the aural and visual (listening and watching actors on stage) to the visual (reading print), a problematic shift for blind subjects such as Herbert, who is indeed deceived by Oswald and Marmaduke into signing a letter to Idonea in Oswald's hand, telling her: 'Be not surprised if you hear that some signal judgment has befallen the man who calls himself your father; he is now with me, as his signature will shew: abstain from conjecture till you see me' (1842, V, iii, 2188–90). Because Herbert cannot read the letter by sight, he cannot interpret the plot against him.

Like Herbert, Wordsworth himself relied upon (predominantly female) amanuenses and scribes to read to him or help edit his manuscripts when his own sight was affected. Indeed, many of the 1841 revisions to the 1799 fair copy are in his wife Mary's hand.[57] More poignantly, in between composing the first draft of *The Borderers* and its publication, Wordsworth wrote an untitled poem in which the speaker fears the loss of sight, and becoming dependent upon his daughter to guide him. The poem thus replays the scene imagined in *The Borderers*, whereby Idonea and 'blind' Herbert first come into view, the father led by his daughter and made breathless by the difficulty of walking hesitantly along 'that dismal Moor' (1842, I.i.108). Written in 1816, the poem opens with lines from Milton's *Samson Agonistes*, in which Samson asks 'a little onward lend thy guiding hand'.[58] Whilst enjoying the idea of walking with Dora in the English countryside, Wordsworth's mind is disturbed by Milton's voice as he spontaneously recalls the opening lines of *Samson Agonistes*, which also echoes the opening of Sophocles' *Oedipus at Colonus*, where the blind Oedipus is guided by his daughter Antigone. The poem reflects a certain anxiety then: the disturbance caused by Milton's and Sophocles' voices points to the exact reversal of the pleasure that Wordsworth contemplates, as it depicts no longer a father leading his child into the Lake District, and perhaps the Alps, but rather a blind man led by his daughter. Anticipating, and indeed engendering his own future blindness, the speaker foresees that 'Time' will enrol him 'among those who lean / Upon a living staff, with borrowed sight' (lines 4; 9–10). His anticipation of dependence upon his daughter – 'O my Antigone, my beloved child! / Should that day come', which inverts his role as 'for me thy natural leader' – strikes an uncanny note. It is a position he has already assumed through effects of the opthalmia (lines 11–12; 14). In the later published version this identification is made stronger as Antigone becomes 'my own Dora'.[59] Moreover, his fear over this reversal of role as 'natural leader' indicates the ways in which experience of blindness disrupts seemingly natural and established gender relations. The voice in the poem registers a real and traumatic tension between the activity of the mind, and the experience of the body. The topography of the Lake District which the father, as his daughter's 'happy guide' envisages travelling across, also doubles as a more disturbing metaphor for the limits of the mind as a physical object. The speaker registers the limits of their geographical excursion; he imagines them gaining the top of 'some smooth ridge, whose brink precipitous / Kindles intense desire for powers withheld / From this corporeal frame' (lines 26–8). The preceding vision of the speaker's future as blind man imbues this image with a foreboding, an anxiety that an absence of vision signals an absence of the sights from which writing springs.

Geoffrey Hartman offers an insightful reading of this poem. Drawing on psychoanalytic theory, he focuses on the similarity of the opening quotation to an inner voice, and explores the echoes and allusions to Sophocles, Milton and Lear (he does not connect it to Wordsworth's own blind character Herbert). Whilst Hartman briefly notes Wordsworth's own eye troubles, he analyses this invocation of blindness in more metaphoric terms. For him, the poem evinces a possible anxiety about Wordsworth's future relations with Dora, as the proleptic image of blindness that comes to him in the form of Milton's voice (whose daughters acted as his amanuenses) may 'indicate a guilt of the eyes, a fear for their punishment or "castration"'. However, the poem is most probably not a wish to 'avoid such a trial by an imaginary exclusion of the guilty organ, by its ideal "sheltering" or "immunization"', as Hartman puts it.[60] The speaker's physical blindness is anticipated and constructed through the dialogue with his literary predecessors and along masculine hierarchical lines; yet the feelings expressed towards his daughters indicate a fear of blindness that is not altogether unknown, nor unrealistic. Indeed, Wordsworth's own note to the poem, quoted at the opening of this chapter, makes this connection explicit. The poem acknowledges and plays out a traumatic response to the poet's physical experience of disordered vision which threatened permanent blindness. Reciprocally, the activity of composing the poem itself invokes further anxieties about perpetuating the state of blindness, as I detailed above. Situated in between his literary forebears and his young daughter, stripped of vision and dependent upon both, the speaker anticipates and fears not only this future blindness, but also his present absence.

Moreover, eye disease is a 'darksome bondage' with the power to shut down reading: the speaker describes his despair at being shut from the 'gates' of the 'holy writ' (lines 49–51). In revisions to the poem, this loss is emphasised still further:

> Now also shall the page of classic lore,
> To these glad eyes from bondage freed, again
> Lie open; and the book of Holy Writ,
> Again unfolded, passage clear shall yield
> To heights more glorious still.[61]

Here, Wordsworth stresses that not being able to read directly the Bible and other classical texts obfuscates their meaning: the return of good eyesight is figured as yielding the return to clarity of meaning. In the final section of this chapter I turn to one of Wordsworth's most important statements about the relationship between blindness and textual meaning, found in book VII of his autobiographical work *The Prelude*. His record of an encounter with a blind beggar on the streets of London bearing a written label of his life can be read as a moment of critical doubt regarding the transcendence of textual meaning beyond its material form. Blindness is invoked as a trope that calls into question the relationship between an embodied observer and the visual nature of language. Drafted shortly before he first contracted ophthalmia, the passage, like much of the poem, was later revised. Reading the encounter with the Beggar through its textual versions and in the light of Wordsworth's experience of impaired vision draws attention to the poet's anxiety that writing belongs to the material, rather than the ideal. The blind Beggar's paper relatedly stands for the difficulty of representing any life in words, and it throws into relief the anxieties that permeate the poet's attempt to write his own life.

## Blindness and Autobiography: The Blind Beggar's Written Paper

Published shortly after his death in 1850, *The Prelude* became a monument to Wordsworth, poet laureate and national literary hero, whose voice exhorted both romantic ideals and Victorian values.[62] However, the text's own publication history points to the problematic status of autobiography in realising the claims it makes about representing the self, as it was subject to heavy revision and change throughout the latter part of Wordsworth's life, and as such it exists in multiple forms.[63] Its early drafting was interrupted by the traumatic news of the death of the poet's brother John in a shipping accident off the coast of Portland in February 1805. The period in between the completion of the first major draft of the poem, in 1805, and its publication in 1850 following Wordsworth's death is marked by further absences: the death of Coleridge (the poem's already-absent addressee), the death of close members of Wordsworth's family (including his daughter Dora) and, finally, the poet's own death.

Across its different versions, the poem stands for the problem of representing reality, which is shown to be tragically contingent upon an observing self destabilised by both the distorting tendencies of the material world and the forces of history. In conclusion to this chapter, I will focus on the experience which throws this contingency into the sharpest relief for Wordsworth: his residence in London, recounted in book VII. The distress the speaker records in response to the overwhelming and seemingly denaturalised environment of the city is articulated primarily as an assault on his senses, which struggle to compute with accuracy the meaning of the scenes he beholds. This also manifests as a self-reflexive anxiety regarding the nature of the written sign and character, and it is in this context that I analyse the blind Beggar who strikes Wordsworth with such force towards the book's close. In a poem concerned with the sensory nature of language, and its transition from speech to writing, the Beggar poses a particularly fraught obstacle to the interpretation of language as a visible form.

The speaker of *The Prelude* figures the imagination as a sensory faculty that opens up a new visual world:

> Yet the mind is to herself
> Witness and judge, and I remember well
> That in life's every-day appearances
> I seem'd about this period to have sight
> Of a new world, a world, too, that was fit
> To be transmitted and made visible

To other eyes, as having for its base
That whence our dignity originates,
That which both gives it being and maintains
A balance, an ennobling interchange
Of action from within and from without,
The excellence, pure spirit, and best power,
Both of the object seen, and eye that sees.
(*Prelude*, XII, 367–79)

This 'new world' in being 'fit / To be transmitted', is not a passive visual spectacle; rather, it makes itself visible to other eyes. Yet subjective viewing is privileged as it is the 'mind', figured effeminately as 'witness and judge' to 'herself' and the embodied 'eye that sees', that brings the world forward as representation. This tension in whether to locate the perceiving subject in the phenomenal or the noumenal world informs much of the treatment of vision in *The Prelude*, and is further complicated by the act of revision. Blindness, if we follow the internalist model, absents the speaker from the phenomenal world and heightens access to the noumenal in the text. However, the imagined and corporeal episodes of blindness, which structure the poem's composition, revision and publication process, collapse distinctions between the imaginary and the real. Explicitly, they point to the arbitrariness of ideas as they are mediated through the material form of writing. This use of blindness as a bridging device is also explicit in Coleridge, who figures his soul as 'a blind man', and himself as a writer who must see through his own hieroglyphic 'with his protended Staff dimly thro' the medium of the act & instrument by which it pushes off, & in the act of impulsion'.[64]

We can see further how this model comes under strain in Romantic-era discourses of Milton, whose influence on Wordsworth's self-fashioning as poet has already been noted above. Harold Bloom attributes the 'implicit distrust of the visible' in Wordsworth to Milton's blindness, as Milton is the poet who yearns 'most movingly, for the visible' but who 'does not need it'. In his blindness, Milton seems to affirm the primacy of the relationship between poetry and inner vision.[65] Bloom's observation emerges from a long tradition of using Milton's blindness as a marker between the sister arts of poetry and painting. As Luisa Calè summarises, eighteenth-century theorists of the arts used Milton's blindness to test differences between visual and verbal media. Philosophers – notably Burke in *Enquiry* (1757, 1759) and Gotthold Ephraim Lessing in his *Laocoön* (1766) – defended Milton against charges that his blindness had created a paucity of visual images in his poetry. Rather, Burke used *Paradise Lost* to argue against the visual as a criterion of the verbal. He insisted that rhythmic demands of the poem meant the perceiver was unable to keep pace with the act of conjoining words with images, and stressed that verbal texts act on the reader through sound instead.[66] Lessing built upon Burke's insight to argue that verbal media have a distinct visuality that may not necessarily translate into the media of painting. As Calè shows, his attempt to 'save Milton from the allegation of pictorial barrenness' led Lessing to formulate his theory of the difference between poetry and painting as the difference between temporal and spatial sequencing of actions.[67] Milton's blindness was thus pivotal to the ways in which the imagination was conceived in Romantic-era aesthetic discourse, and provided a model for examining the relationship between the senses and the production of the poetic sign which privileged the absence of physical sight.

Yet interest in Milton's blindness was not so de-materialised as this discussion might imply to early nineteenth-century commentators. Rather, in certain contexts it took on distinctly corporeal forms. As ophthalmologic discourse and the classification of eye diseases expanded, eye doctors turned to Milton's poetry and biography as an important source of information about the experience of blindness. Ophthalmologists also examined quotations from his poetry that described states of blindness and visual experience, and offered diagnostic assessments as to the nature of his visual impairment.[68] This practice demonstrates a cultural concern with the embodied nature of Milton's blindness, a concern Wordsworth certainly must have shared as the medical advice he sought raised the possibility that he himself might lose his sight permanently.[69] Milton's blindness signified not simply an ideal state for writing poetry; it also suggested a real experience rooted in the body.

The connection between blindness and the speaker's own bodily experience in *The Prelude* turns on a collapse of distinctions between the imaginary and the real. This phenomenological approach (looking also at the objects that shape writing) signals that *The Prelude* cannot be closed off as one privileged text: reading the poem demonstrates the way in which the self's history is shaped by time; its relation to the objective world; and the body of the speaker. Drawing upon Wordsworth's own experience of blindness, and a textual analysis of the moments of vision and visionary moments in *The Prelude*, a phenomenological model of reading begins to emerge which challenges the internalisation model privileged by the Romantic literary canon. That is, the moments of blindness are as embodied as they are metaphoric, a thickness due in part to the revisioning process.

Book VII opens by foregrounding the body of the poet at work on his text. Observing that it is now five years since 'I first pour'd out ... a glad preamble to this Verse' (VII, 1–4), the speaker alludes to the techniques of poetic language, framed initially in terms of sound – 'I sang / Aloud in Dythyrambic fervour' (4–5). A dithyramb is an ancient Greek choric hymn sung to Dionysus, which connects the poet to a longstanding tradition of poetry as an aural text.[70] The exuberance of words pouring out in a 'short-liv'd transport, like a torrent', and the emphasis on 'aloud' at the start of the line, draw attention to the physicality of the poet's voice. For Wordsworth, these traditions are also identified with nature, and with his immersion in the Lake District, as the uproar of his song is figured 'like a torrent' of rain showering down 'Scafell or Blencathra's rugged sides' (6, 7). Words exchanged through speech and songs belong to a bardic tradition that has a particularly strong association with blindness, from Homer to Ossian. Indeed, Wordsworth carefully details how his poetry is a vocal performance and takes inspiration from things heard, disassociating poetic activity from physical sight. The 'work' itself advances 'slowly' – both referring to a dwindling of the poet's voice whilst at Cambridge as well as a possible allusion to its transcription as a written text (16). With an immediacy of presence, the poet draws attention to the situation of his body once again, 'sitting' frustrated 'within doors betwixt light and dark' (22). In this state between sight and blindness, he recalls how 'a Voice ... stirr'd me' – a band of robins whose song brings him back to his own dithyrambic chorus and, 'listening' he half whispers how he and the birds 'will chaunt together' (23, 34, 37). Yet as a caution to the aurality the passage has set up, immediately 'thereafter' he sees whilst out walking in the 'dusky shade' of twilight a 'clear-shining' glow-worm (37, 40). The speaker suggests that 'silence touch'd me here / No less than sounds had done before' and that the 'voiceless Worm' seemed 'sent on the same errand with the Quire', by providing 'genial feeling' – matter to the imagination – that 'fits me for the Poet's task' (41–8). In its ability to touch the poet, silence has shape, and body.

I linger over these episodes, as they help to establish the primacy of physical experience for the material of the poem – both as content (things observed) and as medium (a communicable text). The passage seeks to construct a favourable environment in which the imagination can savour both the sonorous and visual quality of poetic words, in its incorporation of the 'sweetness' of birdsong as well as the 'shining' of the glow-worm. Arguably, however, the poem itself can neither transcend the body of either its speaker or listener/reader, which must act as receptors for these stimuli, nor can it equivocate so neatly between the senses. Book VII as a whole inscribes a much greater doubt as to the relative imperfections of the eye and ear as organs of perception, and registers in particular an anxiety about writing as a transcript of experience. The experiences recorded in the book call into question the sensory nature of text, and whether Wordsworth's performance of poetry can renounce the physical eye outside of visual signs, and in particular print culture (which is identified with the city).

Soon after this excursion, the speaker leaves Cambridge and, unsettled on 'what plan of life' he should fix on, moves to London (Wordsworth had left Cambridge in 1791 moving to London soon after, the first of several brief residences there throughout his life). London is figured firstly a place of the imagination, to which the speaker describes being held by a 'chain / Less strong of wonder and obscure delight' (VII, 89–90), and of which his 'fancy' had 'shaped' full of 'marvellous things' (108–9). The actual experience of London overturns his fancy, however, and in so doing his senses challenge the 'wondrous power of words' (121) that had shaped his preconceived mental images of the city. Instead, words are shown to be arbitrary and 'sweet … according to the meaning which they bring' (122). London presents a chaotic, disordered reality that cannot be reconciled with its imagined counterpart, and much of the speaker's account turns on the struggle to draw meaning from the city's sensory data. The speaker no longer has space to linger over the phenomenality of the objects and spaces he encounters, or to explore the slippage between the poetic self and external world.[71] Rather, the poetic diction becomes cramped with the need to list an 'endless stream of men, and moving things', with the lines proliferated by nouns reducing things observed to mere objects, such as 'Stalls, Barrows, Porters; midway in the Street / The Scavenger, that begs with hat in hand' (163–4).

Next a questioning unfolds of what it means to have sight in the visual spectacles of the rapidly expanding urban spaces. In the city's visual spectacle, seeing becomes equated with the interpretative act of reading within the city space, as stimuli are not things-in-themselves, but rather signs that can only give access to 'the absolute presence of reality' (VII, 249). Neil Hertz argues that the descriptions of London, with their plethora of prefabricated items such as tradesmen's signs and statuary, 'are intended to be legible, not merely visible'.[72] Moreover the speaker is disturbed by the way in which written language comes to structure relations between people and things in the city space. He notes:

> Here files of ballads dangle from dead walls,
> Advertisements, of giant-size! from high
> Press forward in all colours on the sight;

These bold in conscious merit; lower down
That, fronted with a most imposing word,
Is peradventure one in masquerade.
(209–14)

This lettering is monstrous: the ballads flutter in the graveyard space of the wider streets separated from the throng of the city, whilst the advertisements are not texts that elicit contemplative reading, but rather, in their 'giant-size' 'press forward' on the eyes, the written character figured as 'a most imposing word'. Immediately after this, the speaker notes the sight of a 'travelling Cripple' on the pavement, with 'another' lying beside him (219, 221). They lie 'beside a range / Of written characters, with chalk inscribed / Upon the smooth flat stones' (221–3). Whilst the speaker does not transcribe these written characters, they are likely a plea for financial help. By the time the poem was written in 1804–5, wounded veterans returning from the Napoleonic wars were becoming increasingly visible on London's streets and reduced to street-begging as a source of income, an issue that when the war ended a decade later would register as a chronic problem to middle-class observers, as John Thomas Smith noted.[73] Foreshadowing the description of the blind Beggar, this brief episode connects the crippled sailor's chalk inscription with the advertisements, pointing to their use within an economy in which both goods and social good (as charitable giving) are transacted through the written word. Importantly, though, the texts are presented to the reader as blank, and therefore illegible.

It is in this context of anxious questioning around written letters and what it means to be literate that the encounter with a blind Beggar bearing a written label takes place, and is presented as a particularly significant crisis for the speaker.[74] The speaker is abruptly smitten 'with the view' of the blind Beggar, whom we are told:

… with upright face,
Stood propp'd against a Wall; upon his Chest
Wearing a written paper, to explain
The Story of the Man and who he was;
My mind did at this spectacle turn round
As with the might of waters, and it seem'd
To me that in this Label was a type,
Or emblem, of the utmost that we know,
Both of ourselves and of the universe;
And on the shape of this unmoving Man,
His fixed face and sightless eyes, I look'd
As if admonish'd from another world.
(VII, 612–23)

The encounter with the Beggar is singled out as critically powerful, in the face of which the speaker's mind turns round 'as with the might of waters'. Yet in contrast to the tumult and urgency of the other spectacles the speaker records, the blind Beggar stands in stillness, his body 'unmoving'. Presented as a different type of 'spectacle', the blind Beggar nonetheless calls into question the nature of both sight and visual representation: what it means to see and also to interpret visual signs. Yet what provokes this sense of crisis is not solely the Beggar's blindness, but also the label that he wears, which, written in visible type, cannot be read by the Beggar himself. Like the hypothetical blind man, the blind Beggar's wearing of the label invokes reflection on the workings of consciousness. He is the negative image of the hypothetical blind man, however, as he signals the blank space of self-consciousness: his inability to read his own story reveals 'the utmost that we know / Both of ourselves and of the universe'. In a denial of the blind man's subjective agency, communication between the blind man and the sighted is reduced to a system of visible signs (writing), and as such, the blind man cannot have unmediated access either to his own history or representation in Wordsworth's poem.

The blind man and his label function as objects which disturb the speaker's subjectivity, signalling the limits to vision and the arbitrary association of knowledge, language and sight. My reading differs here from Neil Hertz's, who argues that in the play between the Beggar's blank face and the minimally informative text on his chest, 'the difference between what Wordsworth can see and what he can read is hardly re-established in any plenitude'. The minimal difference between seeing and reading that Hertz identifies prompts him to argue that the encounter with the Beggar has served to keep 'the poet-impresario from tumbling into his text'.[75] However, the power of the label resides not so much in its minimalism (which we cannot establish in any case, as the speaker does not transcribe it for us), but in the prophetic registering of the blind man's inability to read the text. I want to argue here that the blind man *is* a reflection of the speaker's own poetic self. As he wears his 'story' on a written paper, so the speaker also produces his story through written papers. Yet, ironically, the poet also struggles with bringing his story before the reading public as a material text of words imprinted on paper, which I will briefly address in conclusion.

Wordsworth first drafted the episode in spring 1804, shortly before contracting ophthalmia.[76] The passage, like much of the poem, has a complex manuscript status and there are difficulties in establishing an authoritative version. Importantly, however, for our discussion, the revisions made to this passage in the ensuing years suggest that the encounter prompted continued speculation on a particular set of issues concerning the difficulty of textual interpretation. These included the problem of making sense of the biographical narrative content of the Beggar's paper, as well as the physical act of reading it. The passage's first iteration is as an inscription in William's hand, entered on the recto of leaf 28 of the early MS. X, dating from 1804.[77] Here, the poet recognises his meeting with the Beggar as an otherworldly encounter that signals the limits of human knowledge, at which the mind turns 'as if / It were [?admonishment] of other worlds'. The draft also shows how the poet was concerned to understand and articulate the relationship between self-knowledge and the Beggar's written label:

> ... and I thought
> That even the very best of what we know
> Both of ourselves & of the universe,
> [as insertion above next line: Was there set forth by symbol, that in fine]
> The whole of what was written to our view,
> Is but a lable on a blind man's chest.[78]

The sense of this passage wasn't quite right, though, and it is marked by a deletion from 'It were' through to 'chest'. These lines, revised, are then re-entered in William's hand towards the close of MS. x, on the verso of leaf 33.[79] Here, the poet's deletions and insertions show his attempts to settle on the most appropriate way to articulate the power of the encounter. Crucially, to do so, he draws upon a material discourse of literary production that shares with his own struggle to set his poem down as written text. The Beggar's paper is described as 'writing' in the opening base lines of this verso; this is, however, scored through and replaced by 'label'. Trying to describe the import of this paper, Wordsworth first enters that in this label was a 'symbol' of 'what we know'; symbol is subsequently deleted and replaced by 'type', and a further qualifier, 'emblem'. On the verso of leaf 33, Wordsworth draws a line under the first set of revisions and writes out the lines again, presumably to make clear his intended copy: the repeated text also bears some revisions in his account of the 'label'. We also see the poet hesitate about drawing further on printers' terminology to describe the 'writing' and 'type' as being 'set' – but this is scored through on both occasions. This revision also sees the blind man's 'fixed face' and 'sightless eyes' emphasised as the otherworldly force which now admonishes the speaker.

Two fair copies of the early *Prelude* were produced between 1805 and 1806: MS. A, transcribed by Dorothy Wordsworth; and MS. B, transcribed by Mary Wordsworth. These copies draw upon MS. X in their transcription of the blind Beggar passage, and Mark Reed draws upon the base

AB texts in his constructed reading text of the poem, from which I have quoted extensively above. In the first printed edition of *The Prelude* – and the version Victorian readers would have been familiar with – the passage bears subtle, but telling, changes:

> Amid the moving pageant, I was smitten
> Abruptly, with the view (a sight not rare)
> Of a blind Beggar, who, with upright face,
> Stood, propped against a wall, upon his chest
> Wearing a written paper, to explain
> His story, whence he came, and who he was.
> Caught by the spectacle my mind turned round
> As with the might of waters; an apt type
> This label seemed of the utmost we can know,
> Both of ourselves and of the universe;
> And, on the shape of that unmoving man,
> His steadfast face and sightless eyes, I gazed,
> As if admonished from another world.

The poem's first printer, Edward Moxon, drew upon MS. E, which in turn, as W. J. B. Owen points out, used revised MS. D (dated between 1838 and 1839) as a base text.[80] The revisions concerning the verbal content of the man's written paper in MS. D and MS. E provide a stronger sense of a linear narrative, as the story, we are now told, reveals 'whence he came, and who he was'.[81] The matter with which the man's story is composed is also subject to continued alteration, with changes made to what the label is; what it stands for; and its accessibility. In its AB iteration, the speaker describes how 'in this label was a type', drawing attention to how it both represents a certain class of knowledge, as well as, perhaps, the type of writing. D stage revisions, in William's hand (and entered on the preceding verso of p. 166 of MS. A), slightly alter this sense, by adding stress that the label itself seems 'an apt type'.[82] The Beggar's material text stands now for 'the utmost we *can* know'. The italicised text represents a further D stage revision, again entered onto 166v, which subtly, but profoundly, alters what the episode reveals about knowledge. The addition of 'can' inscribes a future limit to our knowledge, implying this boundary cannot be transcended.

Stephen Gill, commenting on Wordsworth's difficulty at settling on a final form for his poems, observes that his manuscripts show 'just how hard he struggled throughout his life to bring poems into being', marked as they are by deletions and marginalia.[83] Certainly, it is difficult to identify with certainty the chronology of changes in this passage of book VII, although the revisions made to MS. A in both Mary's and William's hands, are accepted to be D stage and date from around 1831–2, recognised as the last major reworking of the poem authorised by Wordsworth.[84] The revisionary history of this passage serves as a model for the palimpsest nature of the poem as a whole, in which years of deletions, additions, and transferences of inscription have made it impossible to establish an authorised text, and, by extension, a definitive 'life' in writing.[85] Here, Wordsworth's visual impairment throws into relief the complex working of his writing practice, which moved between direct transcription, dictation, direct revision, and dictated revision. As a sensory text then, the *Prelude*, as it comes into being, turns not simply on vision, but on the touch of hands inscribing words and shaping and arranging leaves of paper, and on the sound of voices dictating and recalling lines, passages and events. Yet to come into being as a reading text, we desire to return it to vision, as inked words on the page. This passage, so worried about the relationship between a blind man and the written account of the life he advertises, becomes a metonym for Wordsworth's own poetic project, which will require such intense visual scrutiny from future editors to reconstruct, but still resist being held fully in view, slipping from the gaze as readers sift through the many layers of selves it represents. As these accretions gathered pace, so Wordsworth's own identification with the figure of the Beggar grew. Indeed progress towards the poet's own 'paper' was interrupted by the opthalmia, which re-surfaced particularly acutely during the first period of major revisioning of MSS. A and B, the production of MS. C in 1818–20.[86] Wordsworth, acutely aware of the challenges that impaired vision presented to the production and interpretation of writing after his first drafting of this poem, continued to explore and shape the meaning of this encounter in the ensuing years.

## Conclusion

The blind man's 'written paper' stands as an uncanny reminder that Wordsworth's life, itself materialised in the text, has no real transcendental existence. Rather, the self is haunted by blindness, materially wrought, at both the subjective and objective edges of its existence; it can neither see nor read itself; as a result, the boundaries between self and others begin to blur. Wordsworth's different selves coalesce; the young Romantic poet's idealising of blindness merges with the mature writer suffering from prolonged and protracted pain in his eyes, whilst revising his autobiographic project. Disappearing from the visual field, the text loses its semblance of autonomy and authority and is revealed to be an object threaded through different eyes, voices, hands and experiences, constructed in and through impermanent and shifting material conditions.

Finally, though, the addition made to MS. D as part of the final revisions towards preparing a manuscript for the printers returns this episode to the social and cultural body. A bracketed note tells us that this view of the blind Beggar was, at this time, 'a sight not rare'. As Edward Larrissy observes, the blind Beggar is an 'overdetermined hieroglyph of social damage', a signifier for the multitude of blind beggars found in London who were casualties of war.[87] Indeed, Wordsworth's blind Beggar might be read as a linguistic counterpart to the blind beggars depicted by John Thomas Smith in his series of engravings, discussed in the introductory chapter. The blind beggar remained a subject of interest throughout the nineteenth century and into the twentieth, continuing to reify the relationship between blindness and poverty. Two of the most famous visual depictions from blindness in this period, John Everett Millais's *The Blind Girl* (1856) and Paul Strand's photograph *The Blind* (1916), also portray their subjects bearing labels identifying them as blind. The labelling of these representations posits the sitters not only in opposition to sight, but also to writing. Yet directly between the first drafting of *The Prelude* and its publication in 1850, this association began to be challenged through the development of alternative printing methods by which blind people could access text directly through touch. The next chapter traces the history of embossed writing for blind people in this period, and assesses in particular the contested relationship between touch and vision that characterised it. Blind people's reading and writing practices came under intense public scrutiny, evidencing just how strongly the relationship between blindness and literacy was in the cultural and social imagination of the nineteenth century. At stake in the extensive debates concerning the format of raised print was its potential to denaturalise the relationship between body and text. The possibility of reading by touch emphasised how central the material form of writing was to textual meaning.

CHAPTER 3

# 'A Literature for the Blind'
## The Development of Raised Print Systems

Joseph Paxton's Crystal Palace, a ferro-vitreous construction revolutionary in its prefabricated design measuring 1851 ft long and 450 ft wide, stressed the importance of light, vision and viewing in the visitor's experience at the Great Exhibition of 1851. Yet amongst the 100,000 exhibitions sent in by almost 14,000 individual and corporate exhibitors was a small set of objects that disturbed the scopic regime of the exhibition by alerting viewers to a perception based on touch, rather than sight.[1] These items were early examples of writing apparatuses and embossed texts for blind people.

A charity for blind people noted the interest these objects aroused in other visitors. Separating the aesthetic from practical value of the materials submitted by blind people at its school, the 1851 *Annual Report for the London Society for Teaching the Blind to Read* states:

> Specimens of the different kinds of apparatus used in the School, together with some articles of work done by the pupils, have been deposited for exhibition in the great building in Hyde Park; and though they cannot compete in outward appearance with the beautiful and showy objects with which they will be surrounded, the Committee trust that their practical utility, and the illustration they afford of the successful adaptation of educational means to the wants of an especial class, will render them, in the eyes of the Christian philanthropist, not the least interesting objects in that great collection.[2]

The report for the following year touches again upon the interest aroused by the exhibition, as many 'noble persons', including the younger members of the Royal Family, visited the specimens. The report's author notes that the visit of the Prince of Wales was followed a couple of days later by the Royal Princes and Princesses, and that 'shortly before the closing of the Exhibition W. Levy [who was blind] had the honour of reading before her Majesty the Queen'.[3] In this display, Levy's body became testimony to the ability to access text outside of vision – both the perception of letter characters through the finger, and the cognitive activities that translated those perceptions into meaningful information.

The location of these objects and texts within the space of the Crystal Palace illuminates the intimate and fluctuating relationship between the material and visual at stake in this history, and also emphasises how blind people's reading practices came under the scrutiny of a seeing public in the period. At the exhibition, embossed books for the blind fell into the 'Paper, Printing, and Bookbinding' class. They were part of a wider collection of items and objects that demonstrated 'social purposes', industrial projects aimed at improving the lives of marginalised groups.[4] Turning on the relationship between books and the social economy, the *Official Catalogue* to the Exhibition noted that 'books ... carry the productions of the human mind over the whole world, and may be truly called the raw materials of every kind of science and art, and of all social improvement'.[5] This discourse of book production works on a dialectic of mind and matter: mind charges matter, yet matter is also necessary for the advancement of mind.

The Great Exhibition both stimulated further interest in the status of tactile print systems and exposed problems that were hindering their future development. Edmund C. Johnson, a mid-century educationalist who was himself blind, noted that the report of the Great Exhibition had 'awakened considerable attention among all who are interested in ... [the] welfare and education' of 'the blind'.[6] Despite early proposals to have a competition amongst blind readers as to which type of alphabet was most suitable it was only after the Great Exhibition that serious discussion began about selecting a standardised alphabet. In his *Cyclopaedia of Useful Arts and Manufactures* published after the Great Exhibition, the science lecturer and writer Charles Tomlinson (who later became visually impaired) argued for a greater degree of consultation between different schools and systems:

> The greatest kindness which could possibly be shown to the blind, as it respects their intellectual progress, would be for those inventors and heads of institutions who are now pursuing separate and independent paths, to meet together and consult on a common alphabet, and a universal system of typography which should be adopted at all their establishments, so that the printing press of one establishment should be a source of instruction not to the few who use the same character, but to all who speak the same language.[7]

Tomlinson introduces us here to the tension that marked the development of tactile alphabetic systems in Britain throughout much of the nineteenth century, prior to the more universal acceptance of braille by the century's end. His note that both inventors and educational directors were pursuing 'separate and independent paths' signals the proliferation of alphabetic types that were in circulation, and the competition between them.

As I will show in this chapter, the struggle for ownership over embossed literature was most fiercely played out at the level of the alphabet, and particularly whether writing for blind people should be based on the Roman alphabet or use an alternative symbolic system (termed 'arbitrary' by contemporary commentators). Initially, there was a clear desire to privilege visual design, and to assimilate the reading practices of blind people with those of the sighted. This threatened to shape the outcome of embossed reading and writing systems for blind people, as Vanessa Warne has recently argued.[8] Yet in his urging for a 'common alphabet' governed by a 'universal' system of typography, Tomlinson rejects the terms of debate which had overshadowed the discussion of embossed literature since its introduction to Britain some 25 years previously. As Tomlinson argues here, the best alphabet will not be one which is the most popular 'with the seeing public', but rather that which 'the blind can understand the most readily by the means of their fingers'.[9] Further, Tomlinson's recommendation of two dotted systems devised by two blind men – G. A. Hughes and Louis Braille – was a recognition that the format of tactile literature would best be understood and developed by those with the greatest investment in it.

The final sections of my discussion here will consider the evidence and testimonies available from blind readers and writers as to the relative success of the different systems that proliferated. These testimonies indicate how the proclaimed progressiveness of early systems tended to serve the agendas of sighted educational and religious directors. The role of advocacy became increasingly important in debates over the format of embossed literature, and my concluding section shows how blind people, including John Bird, William Hanks Levy and Thomas Rhodes Armitage, became increasingly insistent on having control themselves over raised print formats, an act which is coterminous with the spread of autobiographical and biographical texts by blind and visually impaired people, the focus of the next chapter.

## Tangible Typography

Although ad hoc tactile communication methods had been deployed by blind people for many centuries in Europe, the first systematic attempts to produce embossed books and educational programmes for blind people date from the end of the eighteenth century. Valentin Haüy invented the process of embossing letters from the standard Roman alphabet on paper in 1784, founding the (later Royal) Institute for Blind Youth in Paris the following year. Contextually, Haüy's experiments emerged from changing attitudes towards both visual impairment and touch, not least Denis Diderot's argument in *Essay on Blindness* (1749) that blind people's tactual perception should be understood on equivalent terms to sighted people's visual perception, as I discussed in the first chapter. His experiments also emerged from a new promotion of the value of literacy and private reading. Haüy stressed:

> Reading is the only method of adorning the memory, so that it may command the stores which it has imbibed, with facility, promptitude, and method. It is, as it were, the channel through which every different kind of knowledge is communicated to us. Without this medium, literary productions could form nothing in the human mind but a confused heap of disarranged and fluctuating ideas. To teach the blind therefore to read, and to form a library proper for their use, must constitute the object of our first care.[10]

Haüy's remarks point to the increasing weight that was placed on private, individual reading as a disciplinary aid to knowledge and indeed civilisation. Reading is the *sole* methodical tool that allows each reader's 'memory' to retain and make sense of the potentially 'confused heap of disarranged and fluctuating ideas' that inhere in improperly processed textual data, and indeed helps to constitute the human mind.

Haüy's call for a library of embossed books was taken up slowly, as printing presses for embossing books were established on a small scale in other parts of Europe (such as Vienna, with the invention of Klein type in 1807). Embossing inventions and techniques were certainly known of contemporaneously in Britain: indeed, Haüy's *Essay on the Education of the Blind* – 'an explication of the different means, confirmed by successful experiments, to render them capable of reading by the assistance of touch, and of printing books' – was translated and published in the third edition of the blind poet Thomas Blacklock's works in 1790. However, the war with France hindered the advancement of raised literature in Britain: Blacklock's translation was prefixed by an advertisement asking subscribers to excuse 'their being disappointed of the specimen of printing by the blind children of the charitable seminary at Paris, which the Editor hoped to have been able to subjoin to this volume, but which the present distracted state of France, has made it impossible to procure'.[11]

Some 40 years after Haüy's press was established, and a decade after the Napoleonic wars had ceased, embossing practices began in earnest in

Britain with James Gall's publication of a class book for blind people in 1827. The text of this book followed Haüy's lead by using an embossed font based on the Roman alphabet. The publication of Gall's book prompted intense competition between inventors and educationalists, who introduced and promoted a range of different systems from the 1830s onwards. In both Britain and abroad in North America and Europe embossed systems most usually emerged from specific institutions and schools for blind people. Alongside Gall, the main competitors, who I will discuss in the following sections, included: John Alston (from the Glasgow Asylum, whose system was developed in 1836 and based on the Roman alphabet); James Hatley Frere (whose arbitrary system was developed in 1838 and based on phonetic principles); T. M. Lucas (from the Bristol asylum, whose arbitrary system was developed in 1837 and based on shorthand); William Moon (from Brighton, whose adapted version of the Roman alphabet was created in 1845).

Setting out his initial advancements in printing embossed books and the attainability of 'the art of *Writing by the Blind*', Gall acknowledged the material, economic and semantic difficulties facing those working on tactile alphabets. However, he also argued that such difficulties related largely not to 'the principles of its operation – for these are now beyond question' – but rather to 'matters of ultimate economy and expense'.[12] He anticipated the imminent possibility of 'correspondence between the Blind themselves' with the power to 'assist greatly in producing and maturing in the Blind, both the desire and the capacity to read'.[13] Yet whilst Gall wrote of the imminence of a 'literature for the blind' in his first accounts of the developments in embossed printing, the material history of tactile writing and reading systems resists a straightforward linear narrative of progress. Rather, it developed in line with contested notions concerning the relationship between body and text and the universality of the linguistic sign, articulated in terms of a more profound struggle for blind people's ownership of language.

Certain key factors were identified in early discourses that would facilitate the progress of tactile writing: as well as a simplicity of form and paucity of characters, the ability of an alphabet to be 'readily deciphered and perused by ordinary readers' was identified as important.[14] This desire for raised print to conform to sighted people's reading material governed initial experiments and investment. Fry type, an alphabet modelled on the Roman letter, won the Gold medal in a competition for the best writing system for blind people held by the Edinburgh Society of Arts in 1832, along with a prize of 20 sovereigns, despite the fact that more arbitrary than Roman alphabets were put forward. One of the leading early inventors, John Alston, noted that 'the Society of Arts deservedly awarded their medal to Dr Fry's alphabet, as the simplest and most practical scheme that had hitherto been suggested'.[15] Alston himself modelled his own raised alphabet on Fry's: it consisted of upper-case, sans serif Roman letters. In 1839, Alston was awarded a £400 government grant to print the Bible in relief, indicating the initial preference for touch alphabets based on the Roman letter.

Whilst educationalists noted the potential (but as yet untapped) cognitive abilities of blind people, they frequently failed to account for the sensory requirements of touch. Alston also stressed that 'the more closely the alphabet for the Blind could be assimilated to the alphabet of the seeing, so much a greater boon would be conferred upon them'.[16] Indeed, early examples of raised script were frequently supported by an array of visual description and coding intended to aid the (presumed) sighted teacher. This was partly because, as Charles Baker argued, it would facilitate a far greater number of teachers.[17] Yet this was not simply a case of protecting a scarcity of resources: it also emerged from a clear prejudice against promoting systems of writing for blind people grounded on difference. This bears out Jennifer Esmail's astute observation in relation to debates around sign language that 'language was an overdetermined category for the Victorians, who used it to define notions of Britishness, normalcy, and the human'.[18] As Vanessa Warne notes with regards to raised print, the anxiety that sighted commentators felt towards the introduction of arbitrary scripts – dismissing them as 'bewildering, unnatural and uncivilized' – arose from a perceived threat to the status of the Roman alphabet 'as natural and logical'. She continues: 'what, in simple terms, the existence of non-Roman systems advertised was that, instead of blind people adapting to written language, written language was adapting to blind people'.[19] Indeed, Warne's point is borne out in the discussion surrounding Frere type, one of the most popular arbitrary systems, invented by James Frere and modelled on a combination of elementary sound consisting of vowel-sounds and the pure sounds of consonants, derived from Walker's *Pronouncing Dictionary*.[20] Frere's system demonstrated the importance of hearing and speech in educating blind people, and he described it as 'a scientific representation of speech'.[21] Frere rejected criticisms that focused on his system's move away from the Roman alphabet, which he recognised as arbitrary anyway. Indeed, he suggested that experiments in writing systems for blind people might provide an opportunity to correct the limits and imperfections of the Roman alphabet.[22]

Ferdinand de Saussure described 'the alphabet of deaf-mutes' as merely one example of a system of writing.[23] However, the history of alphabets for blind people touches on and illuminates the ideological construction of language more generally in nineteenth-century Britain. It both shares with and shapes the trajectory in which Saussure developed his linguistic theory, turning on the relationship between not only language and the speaking subject, but also between language and the perceiving subject. Saussure distinguished between language (speech) and writing, denigrating the latter: 'they are two distinct systems of signs; the second exists for the sole purpose of representing the first'.[24] Saussure further denigrates writing when he argues that 'writing obscures language; it is not a guise for language but a disguise'.[25] Gall similarly claimed that 'writing … is merely a substitute for speaking'.[26] Yet the prejudices inherent in the battles over embossed scripts show how important the form and appearance of the linguistic system was to both the educationalists and readers directly engaged in their invention and promotion, as well as the wider public who commented on their development.

Arbitrary scripts were developed in recognition of the difficulty of distinguishing by finger the shapes of the Roman letter characters, as well as the length of word strings in that script. T. M. Lucas, of the Bristol Asylum for the Blind, developed one of the first popular arbitrary systems. Based on stenography, it consisted of three basic signs of a circle, a straight line and a point, divided then into four straight lines, four semicircles and four curves. It owed its initial popularity to the establishment of the London Society for Teaching the Blind to Read, set up in 1838 with the aim of its promotion. Blind schools in Exeter, Bath and Nottingham, amongst others, also adopted this system. Physiological reasons guided Lucas's decision to simplify the characters, which would be easier to decipher than the Roman alphabet. Cautious of the capacities of touch compared to the privileged sense of sight, Lucas outlined 'the inferiority of the tactual compared with visual reading', as the finger can 'comprehend far less at one touch than the eye can receive at one glance'. For Lucas, the difference between touch and sight demanded an alternative structure of writing: simplifying and abbreviating words in their embossed form converted 'laborious spelling into facile reading'.[27] Lucas put forward the idea of the 'feeling' and 'seeing' reader, and his analogy of 'finger reading' with railway travelling (the greater the number of obstacles or complicated characters in the way of the finger, the more retarded its progress) incorporates the kinetic energy at stake in tactual reading. An arbitrary system allowed movement with minimal loss of energy, speeding the reading process, 'for the fingers of the blind reader must both move as fast as the letter, syllable, or word can be properly pronounced'.[28] Notably, Lucas challenged John Alston to test their relative systems before a public assembly in 1837, but Alston declined.[29]

As this discussion shows, developments for a 'tangible typography' took place within an anxious questioning as to the relative values of touch and sight, a subject which had greatly occupied philosophical discussion in the Enlightenment period (as I detailed in Chapter 1). Indeed, the early experiments of embossed printing in Paris were influenced by Diderot's insistence upon the possibility of equivalence between visual and tactual perception (and intelligence) of the sighted and blind person. In the nineteenth century, tactual perception also became the subject of significant interest from the newly emerging disciplines of neuroanatomy and physiology. As Vanessa Warne has detailed, nineteenth-century science was 'profoundly interested in the physiological mechanisms of touch, a fact that complicates predominant conceptions of Victorian sensorial science, and Victorian culture in general, as visually oriented'. Developments for embossed writing in Britain coincided with investigations into tactual perception in the wake of Enlightenment debates on the relationship between touch and vision, including Ernst Heinrich Weber's experiments on sensation (published in 1834) which 'laid the groundwork not only for haptic studies but also for modern experimental psychology'.[30] Weber's research helped redefine the role of touch in nineteenth-century hierarchies of the senses by pointing to the complex function of its organs and detailing how the workings of the primary apparatus for tactile perception, the skin, connected to the nervous system. As Warne suggests, discussions around the education of blind people were influenced by these discussions. Moreover, finger-reading techniques came to be cited as examples of tactual acuity in early physiological manuals. William Benjamin Carpenter, who helped to consolidate the disciplines of physiology, anatomy and neurology in the first part of the nineteenth century, expanded his textbook on physiology in 1844 to include a survey of the sensory functions and their apparatus (notably, his section on touch opens with details of Weber's experiments). He also turns to the recent experiments of blind people reading by touch as examples of how the sense of touch may be improved (or the tactile organs themselves developed) with the loss of other senses, stating that 'the process of the acquirement of the power of recognising elevated characters by the touch, is a remarkable example of this improveability'. He explains:

> When a blind person first commences learning to read in this manner, it is necessary to use a large type; and every individual letter must be felt for some time, before a distinct idea of its form is acquired. After a short

> period of diligent application, the individual becomes able to recognise the combination of letters in words, without forming a separate conception of each letter; and can read line after line, by passing the finger over each, with considerable rapidity. When this power is once thoroughly acquired, the size of the type may be gradually diminished; and thus blind persons may bring themselves, by sufficient practice, to read a type not much larger than that of an ordinary large-print Bible.[31]

Enlightenment debates on vision had called attention to visual perception as a habitual action, with judgement of distance and mass learned by supplementing sight with touch. Here Carpenter stresses that touch itself is a skill that must be learned, through a process of enlarging then diminishing tactile data to enable the hand and body to recognise its form. Whilst Carpenter's citing of pedagogic techniques for finger reading accounts for the need to develop tactual sensitivity, it also assumes a stable, universal reader, who is able to read text resembling – that is, conforming to – an 'ordinary, large-print Bible' (the presumption is of course that their reading matter will be spiritual).

However, some blind people were uneasy with the ways in which presumptions about their enhanced tactile skills overshadowed discussion on how to meet the in-reality diverse needs of visually impaired readers. William Hanks Levy, the young teacher selected to read for Queen Victoria at the Great Exhibition, went on to become an important spokesperson for blind education and welfare issues through his work with Elizabeth Gilbert, founder of the General Association for the Welfare of the Blind. Levy published an impressive compendium on blindness in 1872, which covered subjects ranging from the causes of blindness and its therapeutic cures to the training of poor blind children and education of upper-class blind people, alongside an extensive range of biographies of blind people. It also included a survey of 'Printing for the Blind'. Whilst published in ink print format, the preface noted how it had been the author's constant practice over the past 25 years 'to make embossed notes of whatever appeared worthy of preservation, his motto being that a thought unrecorded was a thought lost', stressing his agency as both a reader and a writer.[32]

Levy insisted that the education of tactile techniques must be tailored according to the ability of the pupil. Arguing against the belief that blind people possess equivalent compensatory powers of touch, he notes:

> In considering the means best adapted for enabling the blind to read, it is not only desirable to understand the nature of the sense of feeling as it exists generally in the human race, but it is also necessary fully to comprehend the powers of touch, as enjoyed by the persons for whom the means of reading

> are especially intended. It is generally supposed that to be blind necessarily involves the possession of superior powers of touch. This is incorrect, for the tactual power of many blind persons is inferior to that enjoyed by the average sighted man.[33]

Distinguishing between 'the Keen Touch', the 'Medium Touch' and the 'Dull, or Obtuse Touch', Levy states that 'a full investigation of the subject will indicate that greater extremes could scarcely be shown than those existing in the powers of touch, as possessed by different blind persons' and that the 'greatest error that has prevailed ever since the invention of raised letters is the supposition that the sense of touch exists with equal intensity in all blind persons'.[34] For Levy, this naturally raised the question of whether it is possible to conceive of a system of embossed reading that will provide for all three degrees of touch. Whilst a select few people with a keen touch might be able to discern raised Roman letters, Levy dismissively notes that 'the books of the blind being printed so as to be read by the sighted is not of the slightest importance, for it must be admitted that whatever is intended to be perceived by a given sense should be suited to the peculiar requirements of that sense'.[35] Indeed, the failure to get this right – to associate clarity with sharp lines, for example – could have disturbing consequences: Levy describes his own experience of reading Frere type, which produced a 'stinging sensation in the point of the finger, which gradually extends itself up the hand until it reaches the wrist'. He also reports how children reading Boston Line type (the leading American system based on the Roman alphabet, which converted rounded shapes to angular) 'have been known to read … until their fingers bled'.[36] Indeed, social factors may have mitigated against finger reading altogether. James Gall noted how a poor blind woman had to read books with her lips due to the obtuseness of her touch. He stressed that 'this was not an uncommon occurrence with blind people, when great delicacy of touch is requisite. They find it much easier, after a little practice, to distinguish forms, or to trace a fine line by their lips, and sometimes by the tongue, than by the fingers.'[37] This woman's hands, coarsened by work and manual labour, cannot distinguish and differentiate letters; only by consuming the text through her mouth and tongue can she bring the words to bear.

Commentators were not only concerned about the perceptiveness of raised scripts to the finger; they were also anxious about the weight of books in the hand. The development of embossed literature was shaped – and hindered – by numerous economic and material concerns. James Gall early recognised that books for the blind must 'both in regard to their size and convenience … always labour under many disadvantages'. He therefore paid great attention to the processes of printing, inventor and educationalist sharing the same space in his accounts.[38] Lucas boasted that his stenographic system employed 'the most simple characters that can be invented for letters' and 'no more letters in spelling words than will sound them … by making every letter represent some syllable or word'.[39] This reduction in characters was designed not only to ease reading (as I detail above), but also to reduce the size and material cost of the embossed books, Lucas declaring that 'the blind are now taught to read in as short a space of time, and as fluently, as those who can see' and 'their books are reduced more than one half, both in size and in price'.[40] The need to 'materially diminish quantity' of text was of paramount concern to early publishers.[41]

Embossed literature occupied an uneasy position in the market place. Its practical development was tied to several material and economic conditions, not least the fluctuating cost of paper.[42] As James Gall observed early on, 'the voluminous form of their books, and the weight and quantity of paper necessarily consumed in their production, will be great obstacles, for some time at least, to their being generally purchased by that class of individuals, whose distinguishing characteristics among their fellow-men, tends to beget and to perpetuate an almost hopeless poverty'.[43] Blindness was associated with economic disadvantages; yet the technologies to industrialise materials for blind people were initially costly. Significantly, the expensive technologies of embossed writing received a large portion of their funding from nineteenth-century evangelical bodies (via subscription appeals), which sought to translate and disseminate the word of God to previously occluded communities and individuals. Some societies were also supported by the British and Foreign Bible Society (BFBS), which had been established in 1804.[44]

Evangelical culture shaped the development of embossed literature for the blind ideologically, economically and materially. Of course, evangelical principles were well-suited to the exigencies of an increasingly complex industrial society, within which they were therefore widely accepted, and evangelicalism conferred identity and authority more widely on an emerging bourgeois class.[45] Evangelical culture also blurred discourses of religious faith and reason. Doreen M. Rosman, reappraising the diversity of evangelicals against Matthew Arnold's reduction of them as 'philistines' in *Culture and Anarchy* (1869), draws attention to the overlap between evangelical beliefs about creation and man with eighteenth-century Enlightenment ideals.[46] This is apparent in narratives detailing embossed writing programmes, in which concerns about civilising and educating blind people coincide with the desire for their salvation. For example, the rhetoric used in the briefly published *Magazine for the Blind* (one of the first embossed journals printed in Britain) moves between spiritual and Enlightenment registers, the editor claiming that 'though it has pleased the Supreme Being to seal their eyes to the natural light, He has not incapacitated them from the enjoyment of the light of reason'.[47]

Blind people were also identified as more susceptible to states of moral despair than the sighted, and in especial need of salvation, which embossed print would help facilitate. This anxiety is articulated by James Gall:

> there has hitherto been no literature for them; not even one single source of knowledge, nor any other way of expressing or recording their thoughts, except the living voice. Shut out from the visible world, of which they can form no idea beyond the extent of their arm … the *most wretched* of our fellow men.[48]

Here, the word is recognised as a thing materially mediated; grace and salvation are not innate but arrived at through an embodied engagement with the Bible, an attitude that shares with Valentin's Haüy's insistence upon the act of private reading, but modulates it to a more fervent spiritual register. This concern is illuminated by the changing methods of the Indigent Blind Visiting Society (IBVS), founded by Lord Shaftesbury in 1834 to send out sighted readers to narrate the Bible to poor blind Londoners in their own homes. Within just five years, however, a report by the London Society for Teaching the Blind to Read suggested that this act would soon become redundant with the expansion of embossed literature. The report's author predicted that as a result of the London Society's plan to teach embossed type, blind people would be 'not only independent of such assistance, but moreover, capable themselves of employing the many hours which otherwise might be spent in idleness, both to their own spiritual instruction and the benefit of other individuals'.[49]

The desire expressed in the London Society's report to replace physical readers with embossed books, facilitating a direct relationship between blind people and the Word, was given dramatic treatment in a painting entitled *Light and Darkness* by the genre painter George Smith. It depicts a young blind girl seeking to convert her dissolute family by reading the Bible aloud from touch. Smith's composition stresses the ways in which embossed literature may transform blind readers from passive listeners of scripture into evangelical agents (even if the results, from the limited attention span of her audience, are mixed). The painting (now lost) was exhibited at the Royal Academy in 1865 and later enjoyed a wide circulation as an engraving, following its publication as a gift to subscribers by the

Art Union of London in 1871 (Figure 5). Contemporary reviewers noted that the more domestic subject of Smith's work marked a change from the historical and literary scenes usually chosen for the Art Union of London's engraving, testifying to the strength of public fascination with embossed reading systems. Smith's image also embodies the ideal blind reader: feminine, domestic and spiritual.

The trend for printing multi-volume editions of Bibles, which most schools and systems issued throughout the 1840s, signifies how these books, to borrow Leslie Howsam's insights into the transactions of the BFBS more broadly, function interchangeably as social and cultural objects.[50] The Glasgow Asylum for the Blind had printed 15 volumes of the Old Testament by 1840. The description of the printing procedure reveals the expense that this clearly would have entailed:

> The work consists of nine volumes of 200 copies each, and six volumes of 250 copies each – in all 3300 volumes. There are 3300 pages, each page containing thirty-seven lines; 1272 reams of paper, weighing 8.5lbs each ream – 10,812lbs. The paper was made on purpose, strongly sized, to retain the impression. In order to account for the great size of the work, it must be borne in mind that it can only be printed on one side of the paper, and that the letters require to be of a considerable size, in order to suit the touch.[51]

Moreover, the printing was effected by a copperplate printing press which Alston noted frequently gave way under the heavy pressure required, needing to be recast four times during the progress of the work. The operative department consisted of one man and one boy as compositors (taught at the institution), one pressman, and one teacher who acted as corrector of the press.[52] The high costs resulting from competition amongst types, alongside their reliance upon charitable subscription, had one important consequence for the first generations of finger readers: a limited reading list and over-investment in spiritual texts. Haüy's dream of a library of books for blind readers was far from realised in mid-nineteenth-century Britain, as even the most successful embossed system of the 1870s, Moon type, still only produced a limited range of approximately 300 books (including dozens of short pamphlets). Its list was dominated by guides to learning Moon, religious works, basic scientific textbooks and biographies. Literary offerings were notably in short supply, the poetry section predictably containing works by Milton, but dominated by hymnal works, whilst the 'Tales and Anecdotes' section was limited to a number of sentimental titles, including 'Blind Beggar' and 'I'm Never Unhappy'. Censorship limited the expansion of embossed literature at both the level of the alphabet,

Figure 5 W. Ridgeway, after George Smith, *A blind girl reads the bible by touch to her illiterate family in the dark*, engraving (1871). Wellcome Library, London (ref. L0073758).

and in the range of reading material made available to blind and visually impaired users.

Given that both its format and content were circumscribed, how did blind and visually impaired people respond to embossed literature, framed in such optimistic terms by so many of its sighted printers? The next section assesses the available evidence for determining the relative success with which early raised print formats engaged blind and visually impaired readers, as intellectual, spiritual and leisure pursuits. Whilst the historical record is poor in recording the responses of the first communities of blind readers, the available evidence does suggest antipathy, anxiety and frustration at the way in which literacy opportunities were being hindered.

## Blind Readers, or, Who is Harriet Curry?

Subjects produce language; but language also produces subjects. This mutual relation is voiced by Edmund C. Johnson when he writes in 1853 that the blind are capable of education, but they still need '*a literature of their own*, of a peculiar kind, which at present does not exist'.[53] How greatly, though, did tactile literature expand the reading experience of blind people in the nineteenth century? Much of the information we have about the development of embossed printing systems comes from official accounts, usually published in ink print format. This includes the (usually laudatory) outlines of systems inserted into embossed books by inventors; annual reports of institutions and societies who had endorsed a particular system; and the archived correspondence of institutional directors and teachers. Rarely, though, are we given names or details of the everyday readers towards whom embossed literature was directed. Instead, blind and partially sighted people are frequently framed anonymously or with scanty details: 'an old lady of 69 years'; a 'young boy'.[54] Accounts of their reading responses tend to stress their positivity towards the utility and impact of these new technologies. William Moon provides this quote from a teacher in one of his annual reports: 'I despaired of his ever doing any thing at the reading, when, to my amazement, *one lesson* on Moon's system was sufficient, and now he says he is *quite independent, adding that none but those situated like himself, can tell the pleasure of being able to take up a portion of Scripture whenever he* likes'.[55]

How far, though, do such reported instances reflect the reality of the experience of blind and partially sighted people's entry, or their re-entry if they had acquired visual disabilities, into literacy?[56] Blind people from higher socio-economic groups with access to resources and education might have been able to benefit by selecting from amongst the different types to suit their needs. This was the experience of Bessie Gilbert, co-founder with William Hanks Levy of the General Association for the Welfare of the Blind. Her first biographer notes how her parents (her father was Ashurst Turner Gilbert, principal of Brasenose College, Oxford, and afterwards bishop of Chichester) made contact with the Scottish asylums producing embossed books in the 1830s, securing for her a stock of texts including the Bible, and continued to keep up with developments in printing techniques throughout the 1840s, so that by 1852 she could read 'every kind of embossed printing', including Gall, Moon and several of the 'shorthand types'. Bessie, whose 'keenness of touch was marvellous' due to 'careful training', advocated 'Roman capitals' as she observed that adults who lost their sight in later life developed their sense of touch 'slowly'.[57]

What evidence is there, however, to explain how more ordinary readers contended with embossed systems? If, as Cathy Kudlick has lucidly contended, recent disability studies scholarship has 'not only aimed to give agency to groups previously excluded but has also sought to show how the interplay between the actors and the acted-upon has blurred the boundaries between them and therefore complicated our approaches to historical process', how might we animate some of the voices of early finger readers and so complicate the official record of nineteenth-century blind literacy?[58] In this section, I discuss some of the traces we can find of individual readers in archives, and question whether they might bring us closer to understanding readers' responses, or create further distance from these early communities of finger readers.

Inscribed in ink at the front of the Royal National Institute of Blind People's 1837 copy of St John's Gospel embossed in Lucas type is the name 'Harriet Curry'. Towards the back of the book, a further handwritten note details the circumstances of the presentation of flowers and the bible to Harriet Curry. The poem at the back of Harriet Curry's bible reads:

> On Presenting Mrs Harriet Curry with a Flower
> I here bring a flower
> To the Queen of the bower
> And all my best wishes attend her.
> May she live long and happy
> In peace and in plenty
> And see cheerfulness smiling around her.
> –
> 2
> –
> And may the great teacher

Her savior and Lord,
Who has given her tho' Blind
His own Holy Word
As she reads for herself
The most sacred pages
Illumine her heart
And bless her in ages.

The poem emphasises attitudes towards embossed reading that have been highlighted throughout this chapter, endorsing finger reading as a private, sanctified act ('she reads for herself / The most sacred pages'). The poem is further inscribed 'Norton Cottage, August 9 [?1841]', and initialled MHM.

I haven't been able to determine further details about Harriet Curry, or Norton Cottage, but an inscription on the following page of the bible, which details the public reading of embossed scriptural text by five blind pensioners in Greenwich, suggests that its bequeather was associated with a London institution: most probably the London Society for Teaching the Blind to Read (later Royal Society for the Blind, London) which had been established in 1837 by Thomas Lucas to teach his system. This book tells us something about the status of embossed scriptural texts for institutions, which, as presentation copies or as prompts for staged reading, were a public-facing symbol of the evangelical work of these institutions.[59]

How did Harriet Curry feel about the gift of this bible; how easy was it for her to read Lucas's newly invented embossed system, and what pleasure or instruction did she gain from it? Was she satisfied with the reading matter available to her, or did she perhaps crave other types of text, both for learning and pleasure? We may have a name, and a reader, of the book, but another hand inscribes the desires attached to this gift of literacy for Harriet Curry. The inscription of Harriet's name prompted me to look at the collection of nineteenth-century embossed books held in the archives of the Royal National Institute of Blind People, the organisation which evolved from the British and Foreign Society for Improving the Embossed Literature of the Blind, which I discuss in the next section. The archive comprises examples of the main British and European systems (Gall, Alston, Moon, Frere, Lucas, Braille, Worcester, Haüy) and American (Boston Line type, New York type). Looking at some of the paratextual information they bear, we can begin to identify early locations for these books (through institutional or library labels) and indeed particular readers or owners (names inscribed or embossed at the front of books include Sarah Thomas, Edward Davis, David Lindsay Johnson, H. Llewellyn). This information also gives us some sense of the networks and communities through which these books were passed and handled: for example, Yorkshire School for the Blind, where A. Robinson was presented with a gift of *Samson Agonistes* in braille in 1896; and the Bangor House Teaching Society for the Blind, which evolved into the North Wales Home Teaching Society for the Blind, who continued to loan books in Moon type in the 1910s even after braille had superseded it.

Several more of the Lucas type books in RNIB's collection are also inscribed with names. One name which recurs is 'Emma Mollard'. A copy of *The Book of the Prophet Ezekiel*, published in 1852, is inscribed 'E. Mollard' – there are no further inscriptions or annotations in the book. All other books inscribed with her name are also dated: a copy of *An Inquirer and the Bible: a Tract*, 1861; *The Gospel of St Luke*, 1863; *The Gospel of St Mark*, which bears a crossed-out name, 'Richard Hodgkins', and below that '1868, Emma Mollard'; *The First Book of Moses*, 1871; and finally, *The Prophecies of Jeremiah*, 1875. We have here then a small library of scriptural texts, all seemingly the property of one reader. The chronology of dates suggests Emma Mollard's persistence with Lucas's system, and also her investment in religious material: possibly a devout middle-class woman with the financial means to purchase the expensive embossed volumes for private use?

Emma Mollard can, I believe, be identified on census records. From 1851, the category of 'whether blind; or deaf and dumb' was added to the seven categories of information recorded about each citizen, broadened to 'imbecile or idiot' and 'lunatic' in 1861. This information suggests both the official concern invested in sensory impairments above other physical conditions in the period, and also constructs blindness, deafness and muteness as problematic categories that needed to be statistically mapped (indicating how they became *disabilities* in this period, as touched upon in my earlier discussion of the social model of disability). Mollard is a fairly unusual surname, and not many 'Emma Mollards' are listed on the 1871 census. One record locates an Emma Mollard in the civil parish of Edgbaston, in the municipal borough of Birmingham. The Emma Mollard listed here is aged 23. She was born in Birmingham in 1848. What is striking about this page is that the far right-hand column, which denotes a person's impairment, is almost full: Emma Mollard is listed as a pupil at the Birmingham Institution for the Blind. It is likely then that, rather than reflecting the active purchases of one reader, these books were given to Emma, firstly as a pupil aged 13 and then in her continuing relationship with the Institution which lasted beyond the age of 17, when pupils officially ceased contact with the Institution.[60]

Two rows below Emma Mollard's name is listed 'Sarah Thomas', a name inscribed in RNIB's copy of *Geography in Four Volumes* in Lucas type, dated 1873, suggesting – if this is the same Sarah Thomas – that pupils were provided with personal copies of embossed books. Indeed, the first annual report from the Institution – which opened the same year as Emma's birth in 1848, details how pupils were already learning 'that most important object, the reading of Holy Scriptures', aided by a 'handsome grant of books from the London Society in Queen's Square', and that a second grant had been received, 'kindly presented as gifts to those Pupils who are able to derive benefit from possessing a portion of the Sacred volume'.[61] Again, it is difficult to establish further material which indicates Emma's attitude (or indeed Sarah's) towards this reading matter, positive or negative, although we might assume she was a proficient learner: other female pupils were dismissed if they showed unwillingness or were unable to learn.

This case study reflects the wider problem facing researchers of blind literacy in the nineteenth century in that there seems to have been little attempt made to record or preserve responses from individuals in the numerous institutions and societies that sprang up in the nineteenth century to, as the London Society was so named, 'Teach the Blind to Read'. Although devices enabling blind people to write text were scarce, technologies were available in Britain from the early 1830s to produce embossed text, and from the mid- to late-century braille writing devices were increasingly used for communication and notation – both public and private, as I detail below. In the 1880s, the chaplain of the St. George's Fields school for blind people noted how students learned braille quickly and with dexterity, and that 'they like it because they can talk to each other in a cryptograph which nobody else can read'.[62] Yet – as far as I and other researchers are aware – this material seems rarely to have survived, so we have few letters or diaries, for example, to draw upon.

Why, though, are these instances important? Contemporary surveys of relief scripts indicate the need to search beyond the rhetoric of those with stakes in both individual systems and the promotion of literacy more widely. John Bird was part of a group of blind men and women who in the mid-nineteenth century publicly criticised educational and welfare policies for blind people on the basis they served more the interest of the sighted. Responding to a review of his book on blind education which had been published in the *Social Science Review*, he wrote:

> The more intelligent [blind], who have to struggle for mental health and to avert social degradation, soon discover how little can possibly be gained during the rest of their lives from Relief Type, and therefore give it up, and

> lay it aside altogether, regarding it only as one of those inventions, to be kept alive in its present state … as the germ of a brighter future which they will not live to see.[63]

Bird's frustration at the 'antagonism of the sighted partisans of different types' had led him to reject the prospect of tactile literature altogether, and advocate for the ear instead of the finger as instrument of reading.[64] He also insisted upon greater self-determination by blind people over matters of education and literacy, arguing that as 'the "sighted" have all their own way in society, on the platform and in their printed reports, it is very seldom that the voice of the independent blind … is ever heard'.[65] Bird was not alone in his critique of the state of blind education at this time. A report published in the *City Press* in 1862, and reproduced by Alfred Payne in the published account of a lecture he delivered on the education of blind and deaf people, attacked books produced in Roman letters, emphasising that they:

> *constitute one of the grievances of the blind.* They are admirable for people with eyes, but abominable for people who have only fingers to read by. The effort of manipulating a long word is such, that the mind is wearied and the sense lost in the mere act of spelling it out; and the blind exhibit almost universally an aversion to reading, because the types are quite unfit for apprehension by the fingers.[66]

Adherence to the Roman letter was clearly prohibiting blind people from using raised print formats.

It has been estimated that by the time of the Royal Commission into blindness of 1885, only one in two blind people could read a relief system.[67] Yet arguments over the best relief system to use hindered both the production of wider reading lists by keeping costs prohibitively high and the effectiveness of teaching methods for much of the nineteenth century. The boredom and apathy that may, in reality, have more commonly characterised early tactile readers is suggested in a telling quote by Edmund C. Johnson in his 1853 book, *Tangible Typography: or, how the Blind Read*, as he worries that in schools where portions of the Bible are used as the only class-book, 'consequently, monotony, begetting indifference, and indifference disrespect, the reading of the word of God is apt to be regarded as a *task*, instead of a pleasure and a privilege'.[68] Here, then, is the suggestion that it was not so much technical difficulty, but more frustration at being patronised and boredom with the limited reading material, that made blind and partially sighted people reluctant to invest in the new media of embossed books.

G. A. Hughes, whose punctiuncular system of writing resembled braille in its use of the dotted system, recognised the importance of the type of characters used in embossed type. Difference in form and structure was necessary to communicate information visually and tactually; the visible linguistic sign did not translate easily to the tactual. Hughes, blind himself, experimented extensively with different systems and types of writing, eventually endorsing a system based on stenography due to its simplicity. He rejected the Roman alphabet on the grounds that it 'is both tedious and expensive': his system of writing would, he claimed, enable the blind to 'imprint their thoughts with as much accuracy and facility as those who see'.[69] Hughes was also explicit about the reason some sighted people may have wanted to retain embossed print based on the Roman alphabet, noting how many reject 'symbolical writing' because 'they do not comprehend it at a glance'. Because the sighted cannot understand arbitrary systems, they are 'sure the blind cannot; either because the symbolic characters in relief appear confusing to them at the first view, or *that of the selfish feeling of not wishing the blind to have the power of writing in characters unknown to themselves*'.[70] Maintaining control over blind people's language was a way of allowing the sighted directors of blind institutions to retain control and discipline: allowing them to create a literature of their own was feared as transgressive. In this final section, I draw attention to the ways in which blind people sought to appropriate control over not simply the shape of raised characters, but also to win back 'a power of writing', and the means of producing as well as consuming text.

## A Power of Writing: Blind Leaders of the Blind

Writing in 1862, John Bird argued that 'the permanent form of relief type ... for the Blind will not be invented till the earnest and inquiring educated Blind of matured years shall be consulted, and their opinions, reasons, and objections shall be delivered, and submitted to the judgment of a competent body of educated and disinterested philanthropists'.[71] This call was reiterated in an article published in Dickens's journal, *All the Year Round*, in May 1870. Titled 'Blind Leaders of the Blind', the author defended the integrity of the blind person's subjectivity, arguing that they should be treated as equal and 'useful' members of society. The author also criticised the 'antagonism' that existed between various systems for educating the blind and suggested that it was one of the reasons why Britain lagged behind the Continent in its service to blind people. However, the central focus of the piece is on the question of raised print, with the author making recourse to Milton to stress the fundamental importance of literacy to the self: 'if the ability to read be essential to the welfare of a human being who can *see*, how much more so is it to all who have "wisdom at one entrance quite shut out"!' The piece repeats the now-familiar arguments in favour of adopting a more universal system, both in terms of improving pedagogic training and cheapening costs of production.[72] In the widely read forum of Dickens's journal, the author strongly impresses that decisions about embossed literature should be made by blind people: 'the sightless should take this matter into their own hands, being not only the best judges of what the blind really require, but, if in an independent position, being above all people the most fitted to assist their fellow-sufferers'. A shift in the power dynamic is required, as the author argues:

> For the blind to lead the blind has hitherto been considered unwise policy, but it is likely to prove the reverse in these material points; for, a council has been formed, the members of which are either totally blind, or so nearly so as to make it necessary for them to use the finger and not the eye for the purpose of reading; and around this nucleus a society is in course of establishment, which is taking into consideration all matters connected with the education and general welfare of the sightless.[73]

This committee, the British and Foreign Society for Improving the Embossed Literature of the Blind, later the British and Foreign Blind Association (BFBA) was one of the first organised movements for blind people in Britain. Significantly, it focused its energies on the question of raised print formats and 'sweeping away the confusion they create and establishing one universal embossed alphabet'. Founded in 1868 by Thomas Rhodes Armitage, in collaboration with other blind men including James Gale, W. Fenn and Daniel Connolly, it had set about two years previously to research the different systems in use.[74] The Association still operated on a structure of marginalisation, as all members were men, and only the views of the 'intelligent' were counted – one assumes that intelligence would have been conditioned by class factors given the poor state provision of education for blind people.[75] However, the Association was predicated on the understanding that differences between the visual and tactual in writing systems meant that the sighted were not well suited to develop an embossed writing system, and indeed was founded on the axiom that 'the relative merits of the various methods of education through the sense of touch should be decided by those, and those only, who have to rely upon this sense'.[76]

Armitage published the results of the findings in 1871, in which he described literature for blind people being in 'utter confusion', scathingly criticising a 'Babel' of systems.[77] In this book, Armitage set out the advantages and disadvantages of the different systems, with one arbitrary system taking the lead – braille. This dotted script had been developed by Louis Braille, a pupil and later teacher at the Royal Institution for the Young Blind in Paris.[78] Between 1821 and 1837, he converted an early military code of 'night writing' into a raised alphabetic system comprising of cells in which six raised dots could be variously arranged. The orthographic conventions of braille differ from those of print in its use of a dot matrix system and logographs (single characters that represent whole words), contracted forms, and mandatory rules for using these contractions as words and within words.

By 1871 Armitage and the BFBA were actively promoting braille, despite its hitherto relative unpopularity in Britain. An indication in the shift towards braille can be seen in the annual reports of the IBVS.[79] Although the Society's rules stated in 1868 (the year Armitage joined the board) that blind beneficiaries would be taught in Frere's system, the rule was altered two years later to 'instruction in reading by means of embossed characters'.[80] A year later, the Society was discussing and praising the 'French dotted system', describing it as 'extremely useful as the children can now be practised in writing from dictation, and they write exercises at home which can be read and corrected by their teachers'.[81] The first edition of Edmund C. Johnson's 1871 *Report on the Methods of Teaching the Blind* noted only one institution teaching braille; the next edition in 1883 reported that it was being taught in 21 institutions.[82]

The adoption of braille was far from a consensus, however. William Hanks Levy argued that the best systems for embossed reading and writing should be kept distinct, and whilst he noted that Braille's system has 'many advantages' for writing, he also cautioned that its 'greatest defect' arises from 'all the characters being formed by the multiplication of one kind of dot, which fails to present the touch with the requisite amount of variety of surface'.[83] Indeed, Armitage's 1871 report indicated how the selection of a standard script was far from straightforward. Moon type, the most popular alphabet in British institutions in the 1870s, was praised for its qualities 'which make it very generally useful', particularly as a tool for primary education. Further, its large letter characters 'can be felt by the dull, the aged and by those whose touch has been impaired by rough work'. These advantages were also its defects, however, rendering it too simplistic to be used for more advanced and compressed textual material as the letters 'are too clumsy to bear any material reduction in size without impairing their tangibility.'[84] Whilst William Moon had celebrated the global reach of his alphabet in his 1873 biography, noting how it had been translated into over

80 languages, he had notably failed to engineer a cheap and effective means of allowing people to write Moon type themselves.[85] And as Jan Eric Olsén points out, competition between different alphabets continued to mark European conventions on the topic of blind people's education. An 1876 meeting at Dresden was illustrative of both the variety of tactile alphabets still in circulation and 'the underlying tension between the subculture of touch and the hegemonic culture of vision'.[86]

One of the advantages of braille, along with the ease with which it lent itself to musical notation, was 'the extreme facility with which it is *written*', as well as read, and indeed Armitage's 1871 report instructs at length on how to use a braille writing frame.[87] These frames were also much cheaper to produce than other technologies for embossing letters, such as William Hughes's typograph, which Levy ruefully observed cost between one and five shillings.[88] Braille provided blind people with a cheap and reliable means of becoming active literary agents. This desire to author experiences, and thus establish a firmer control over their individual and collective representation and identity, emerges in the coterminous flourishing of autobiographical writings by blind people, the subject of my next chapter. Before turning to that genre, I will briefly consider how the concern to enable blind people to *write* text, as well as read it, influenced not only the selection of braille. Experiments with writing technologies for blind people also shaped ideas around the production of language in the wider culture.

In his investigation into the relationship between spirit and the letter in nineteenth-century German literary culture and the development of hermeneutic practice, the media theorist Friedrich Kittler is concerned with the distinction between the 'discourse networks' of 1800 and 1900. Kittler juxtaposes the late eighteenth-century investment in the alphabet, which universalises the material units of writing, against the late nineteenth-century media technologies of the gramophone and typewriter which emerge more from a 'psychophysical' conceptualisation of language. Kittler's work shares with phenomenology an insistence on corporeality: he sees hermeneutics as a discipline of the body rather than a natural condition. However, he also recognises the body as the site upon which the various technologies of culture inscribe themselves. He thus differs from the more dialectical relationship between body, world and technology conceived by phenomenology, declaring that the body is radically historical in the sense that it is shaped and reshaped by the networks to which it is conjoined.[89] As the gramophone was invented by a near-deaf man, Thomas Edison, and typewriters emerged from the very experiments in embossed writing for blind people this chapter is concerned with, Kittler claims that 'media, like psychophysical experiments, begin with a physiological deficiency'.[90] He continues: 'blindness and deafness, precisely when they affect either speech or writing, yield what would otherwise be beyond reach: information on the human information machine'.[91]

Certainly, there are significant connections between the history of writing for blind people and the emergence of technologies that reshaped the experience of writing for the "normative" body. Attempts to produce prosthetic writing devices for disabled people, especially for blind and deaf communities, were crucial to the development of typewriting in the nineteenth century. Darren Wershler-Henry points to William Hughes's typograph, exhibited at the Great Exhibition (and which won a gold medal), and Hansen's Writing Ball, as two examples of inventions for blind and deaf people which contributed to the development of the typewriter.[92] Another example, Gall's typhlograph, comprised a set of keys representing each character of the alphabet, which were stamped onto specially prepared paper supported in a frame, aided by the guidelines of a matrix system (see Figure 6).[93] Kittler claims that the typewriter frees writing from the control of the eye and that it uses a 'blind, tactile power', specifically acknowledging the typewriter's relationship with embossed writing systems for blind people,[94] although a note of caution should be exercised here. Early typewriter models were predicated on embossed writing systems that initially continued the disciplinary regime of the eye, with blind writing practices held as inferior to sighted.

A treatise published in 1837 by the director of the Edinburgh Asylum for the Blind, Thomas Anderson, clearly differentiates blind writing practices from sighted. In his descriptions of the experiments he has witnessed in providing literacy for the blind, Anderson claims that what he has seen did not resemble writing. He argues, that, apart from a facsimile of the writing of three blind girls from Boston (where blind pupils were taught to write by hand), 'I have never seen anything that approached to what we usually call *writing*'. He continues:

> In that term, *facility* ought, in my opinion, to be included as well as the mere fact of certain letters being formed. Thus stamping *letter* after *letter* by means of stamps, each having a letter of the alphabet upon it, has been gravely talked of as "writing".[95]

Blind people are capable, it would seem, only of mechanical copying; there is a suggestion that they lack the intellectual ability to truly grasp and form new concepts in language.

Figure 6 James Gall's typhlograph in use. From Gall, *A Historical Sketch of the Origin and Progress of Literature for the Blind* (Edinburgh, 1834), p. 383. © The British Library Board (shelfmark 1031.k.15.2.)

Anderson's anxiety about blind people's writing – the discrete imprinting of letter characters rather than the continuous flow of hand writing – chimes with Heidegger's denigration of the typewriter, which, he argues, 'tears writing from the essential realm of the hand'.[96] Do expanding forms of writing technologies denigrate the inspirational nature of writing, as both Anderson and Heidegger feared, mechanising language in a way that an embodied form of writing (such as handwriting) does not? These anxieties emerged as a set of tensions in nineteenth-century literary representations of blindness, as I trace in the second part of this book. Blindness pointed to an expanding set of possibilities for writing as a material form which also, ironically, suggested the arbitrariness of the sign system underpinning linguistic production and reception. Textual meaning was shown to be contingent upon the bodily faculties of the writer and reader.

## Conclusion

As this chapter has traced, a wide range of attitudes towards the linguistic sign and the nature of its mediation, both pedagogic and spiritual, coexist within the discursive realm of embossed reading and writing systems. The adherence to the visual in early embossed texts perpetuates their exclusive nature as historical documents. Strangely beautiful objects, they yield their histories from an intimate unfolding of the visual and material, as the eye traces writing from the shadows of the raised letters. Calling into play light and shadow, the visible comes into being as a condition of the material. If many of these script systems were obscure to the touch in nineteenth-century blind culture, they are even more so today. Similar issues of exclusion trouble their status as heritage items, as blind and visually impaired people require assistance to interpret and translate these documents and engage with them as historical sources. This is an ethical point which I, as a sighted researcher, continue to address.[97]

The early discourses on raised print formats were, however, concerned with the idea of their own history, with printers drawing upon historiographical rhetoric in order to articulate their own sense of progress and advancement. This is witnessed in James Gall's *A Historical Sketch of the Origin and Progress of Literature for the Blind* (1834) and John Alston's *Narrative of the Progress of Printing for the Blind at the Glasgow Institution* (1838). By the 1840s, discourses focused more on comparative studies and descriptions of relative systems. The initial concern with origins apparent in the accounts signals an attempt to circumscribe the discourses and confer authority. However, the history of printed books for blind people coexists with other important cultural and social narratives, which collectively reinscribe and reinstate the blind subject across the nineteenth century. The next chapter tracks these ideas through the form of the individual life history, considering the ways in which the genre of autobiography became a space of both poetic creation, and political resistance.

## CHAPTER 4

# *Memoirs of the Blind*
## *The Genre of Blind Biographical Writing*

James Wilson published what he claimed to be the first 'biography of the blind' in 1821. This publication marked a significant move towards documenting the experience and nature of blindness from the perspective of blind and visually impaired people. Connected to the politicisation of the blind community, autobiographies were produced in part to articulate blind people's experiences of sightlessness in their own terms. Mary Klages found shared conventions with slave narratives in the autobiographies of two blind writers she examined (Mrs S. Helen deKroyft, *A Place in the Memory* (1849)), and Mary L. Day, *Incidents in the Life of a Blind Girl* (1859)):

> as authorial subjects, blind authors, like women writers and authors of slave narratives, could claim equality to 'normal' (white, male, sighted) authors on the basis of linguistic skill, without regard to their bodily configurations; like slave narratives, blind autobiographies provided a forum for authors to assert, in their own terms and words, their existence as recognisable selves, rather than as silenced nonselves, as objects.[1]

As Klages recognises, access to language is a crucial aspect of whether disabled people can become speaking and writing subjects. Klages discusses a few examples of these writings found 'by chance', welcoming further reflection on this 'as-yet unexplored genre'. I extend Klages preliminary exploration of what she believes 'may well be an undiscovered genre of nineteenth-century American literature: the autobiographical writings of disabled people'.[2] In this chapter I explore the literary constructions of self and identity by four blind people, in both prose and poetry, published in Britain: James Wilson, whose *Biography of the Blind* was first published in 1821; John Bird, who edited Wilson's autobiography in 1856; Edmund White, a former railway guard who turned to poetry to supplement his income following loss of sight in 1856; and Mrs Hippolyte van Landeghem, who privately published two attacks in the 1860s on the 'exile' system of education, one of which used biography to support her argument. In conclusion, I will consider the role that biography and autobiography played in the constitution of public and private identities, by examining the first authorised biography of the blind campaigner Bessie Gilbert, and a frank autobiographical fragment by the visually impaired politician Robert Lowe.

This chapter reveals a networked community of blind and visually impaired people using life writing for therapeutic, financial and political means in nineteenth-century Britain. Yet I stress that certain tensions remained in blind people's biographic projects, as they were marked by an anxiety that writing – and selfhood – remained contingent upon vision. Public attitudes towards the appropriate discourse and behaviour of blind people, an increasingly visible community in nineteenth-century Britain, also shaped the way in which biographers and autobiographers constructed their subjects.

## The Genre of Blind Autobiography

> It is obvious upon reflection (though most of us rarely reflect upon it) that we have our being in the world, and act upon it, through our bodies. Yet, although our selves and our lives are fundamentally somatic, the body has not until recently figured prominently in life writing.[3]

According to some scholars, blind people's ability to tell their own stories and experiences was limited until the relatively recent politicisation of the Disability Rights movement from the 1960s onwards. Ronald J. Ferguson claims that 'the histories that exist to date on the blind … are not from the perspective of the blind'; rather, they are written 'primarily by people who worked within the blindness system and were sympathetic to its interests. Their approach focused on the rationalisation of the blindness system and the work of social and educational agencies on behalf of the blind.'[4] Further, Ferguson argues that 'like other marginalised groups, the blind were viewed as less than human, and this justified the actions taken to assume control over them … because they were perceived to be defective, their opinions [on educational policy] were not sought'.[5] Furthermore, G. Thomas Couser claims that whilst 'a comprehensive history of disability life writing has yet to be written … it is safe to say that not much of such literature was published before World War II'.[6] He also argues that, in America, 'the rise in personal narratives of disability has roughly coincided with the disability rights movement, whose major legal manifestation [in the United States] is the Americans with Disabilities Act, which was passed in 1990'.[7] Couser thus frames a causalist account of the relationship between the state, disabled subjects, and literature (in which the state creates the conditions for autobiographical writing), whereas the examples of life writing by blind people in nineteenth-century Britain suggest a more complex network of influence. Whilst Couser's and Ferguson's studies are of the situation in America, and policy is obviously determined along national lines, various blind people in nineteenth-century Britain did seek both to make their viewpoints heard and to intervene in policy-making decisions. Autobiographical and biographical form was used to communicate different and diverse experiences from 'marginalised groups' long before the advent of 'a cultural manifestation of a human rights movement'. In Britain, Victorian examples of life writing from the blind and visually impaired community were shaped as much by the cultural world they inhabited as by the social, political or economic worlds.

There is, however, an important note to make in terms of the material production of these narratives. Nineteenth-century autobiographical writings by blind people were usually mediated at inception, their authors reliant upon sighted assistants to bring them into being (as we saw with Wordsworth's reliance upon amanuenses during his periodic episodes of blindness). Couser alerts us to a similar issue in his account of deaf/Deaf autobiographies, arguing that until the development of adaptive technologies, the notion was a misnomer, as there was no equivalent writing system for sign language; it always had to be translated and transcribed by a hearing person.[8] Indeed, this was a problem recognised by nineteenth-century commentators. John Bird, quoting another blind man, Isaac D'Israeli, described how the 'dependence on the eye and hand of another to trace the thought ere it vanish in the thinking' and to 'retrace the written line that continuity may be sustained' was the 'greatest difficulty in composition' and constituted an impediment to authorship.[9] However, as articulations of both blind people's personal identity and their shared communities, which collectively voice resistance to their marginalisation, these texts clearly constitute a genre of autobiography.

James Wilson's *Biography of the Blind*, first published in 1821, presented positive and successful models of blindness as a counter to negative images circulating in culture.[10] Wilson identified three aims for his *Biography*: firstly, to answer the curiosity of the sighted about the processes by which blind people succeeded, in spite of their impairments; secondly, to provide a specialised account of the lives of blind people; and thirdly, to demonstrate the achievements of the blind in advancing both science and the arts. Although biographies of blind individuals had hitherto disparately appeared, Wilson argued that a biography of the blind 'has not until now been entered on as a distinct subject'. A specialised and differentiated account was needed:

> In all preceding works the lives of the blind have been classed, and confounded with those of others; and though individuals have been pointed out as objects of admiration and astonishment, yet, no work has appeared, in which they have been considered in a proper point of view, as a class of men seemingly separated from society, cut of [sic] as it were from the whole visible world, deprived of the most perceptive powers that man can possess; yet, in whom, perseverance, industry, and reflection, have in many instances overcome all those difficulties which would have been thought insurmountable had not experience proved the contrary.[11]

By identifying themselves as a group, and a community, Wilson believed that 'the blind' would have the best opportunity to understand the characteristics, nature of and challenges posed by the condition of blindness (as well as the diversity within it). Although this classification emphasises their blindness (it becomes *the* marker of their identity), it also allows for a lessening of the blind individual's isolation. This is indicated in Wilson's analysis of them as a 'class of men *seemingly* separated from society': the separation is arbitrary, not natural.

A number of blind people stressed the enabling role played by biography and history, when pitted against literary depictions of blindness that perpetuated the stereotype of them as pitiable, tragic, fearful and dependent. John Bird argued:

> The cause of the blind has been but little advanced, if at all, by poets, painters, or sculptors; their object generally in introducing a blind character is that of producing an affecting picture, by working up into misleading predominance helplessness, dependence, and incapacity. Romance writers have, for the most part, till of late, followed the same pernicious practice.[12]

For Wilson, his acquaintance with 'this useful branch of history', and discovery of a 'great number of eminent men, in all ages, and in every country, who had laboured under the same calamity as myself, and who had eminently distinguished themselves by their attainments in literature and science', is validating. In his autobiography, he described his hopes for the *Biography*, in that 'if these [stories] were collected together, and moulded into a new form', it might be 'useful' as well as 'amusing' and 'show what perseverance and industry could do, in enabling us to overcome difficulties apparently insurmountable'.[13] A community of blind people is addressed here: 'enabling *us*'. Wilson also recognises the constructed nature of disability, in which an individual's experience of his or her body predetermines social expectations of what he or she can achieve. Difficulties are only 'apparently' insurmountable. Wilson's biography is thus an intervention into such disabling constructions, as he states his 'chief object was to prove the power of the human mind, under one of the greatest privations to which we are liable in this life'.[14] The 'power of the human mind' exceeds the limits of the body. Yet Wilson's own memoir implicitly refutes the charges he lays against the physical privations of blindness.

In his autobiography, Wilson describes how he first went blind in early childhood from smallpox on a voyage from New York to England (in which his parents also died), only to recover partial sight 'contrary to all expectations'.[15] Later though, aged seven, Wilson was 'attacked and dreadfully mangled by an ill-natured cow' as he crossed the street. The accident destroyed his remaining sight, leaving Wilson doomed 'to perpetual blindness'.[16] Skill and ingenuity seem to have favoured Wilson, who adapted well to his altered condition. Settled in Belfast, he was soon working as a messenger boy carrying letters about his neighbourhood, and his punctuality and dispatch meant that he was 'generally employed in preference to those who enjoyed the use of all their senses'.[17] He describes how his 'local knowledge of the neighbourhood' facilitated these escapades, recounting how he could 'with great ease cross the country over hedge and ditch; nor do I at present recollect ever having lost my way, or met with an accident'.[18] He recounts an occasion on which he guided a stranger across Belfast, and took care 'to keep before him, that he should not discover I was blind'. Wilson recognises his own spatial advantage over the sighted, as the night would have been 'pitch black' without lights, yet this made no difference to Wilson's ability to navigate his way (a theme common to the *Biography*).[19]

The *Biography* itself includes the narratives of blind individuals from both the past and present, associated with a range of different industries and achievements: Samson, the 'blind hero of Israel'; John, the fourteenth-century blind King of Bohemia; Professor Saunderson, the seventeenth-century mathematician; Dr Nicholas Bacon; John Gonelli, the blind sculptor; John Metcalf, the engineer; and James Holman, the early nineteenth-century blind traveller. The first edition is dominated by male figures (the biography of one blind lady is included, notable for her skill and advancement in reading).[20] Later editions expanded to encompass more blind women, including Frances Browne's biography (whom I discuss in Chapter 7). Common themes and episodes that we find repeated throughout the *Biography* include the blind person's ability to navigate landscape; failure of the sighted to recognise blind individuals; the act of reading and responses to literature; and memory.

Poetry occupies a central place in the *Biography*. Alongside the inscription from *Paradise Lost* on the frontispiece, the first edition opens with two poems by Wilson that describe his experience of blindness from infancy ('To Memory' and 'A Dream'). Following the inclusion of Wilson's life story in the first edition, the *Biography* proper begins with comparative accounts of the lives of the poets Homer – recognised as the founder of epic poetic form and the Western literary canon – and Milton, thus claiming for them a leading role in the canon of blind figureheads. Evidence of Homer's blindness draws from a history that Wilson acknowledges is in a 'mutilated and imperfect state', more attributable to myth than verifiable facts.[21] Yet as Alexander Beecroft has more recently noted, his representation as a blind man has a long tradition: 'the biographical device of blindness is undoubtedly the single feature of Homeric biography most familiar to modern readers, and it seems to have been as central to ancient understandings of Homer as well'.[22] Whilst Wilson does indeed acknowledge that 'it has been doubted by some of Homer's Commentators, whether he was blind or not', he argues that as ancient culture tended to represent Homer as blind in portraits, busts and medals, his blindness can be interpreted as fact.[23] Wilson seeks to prove Homer's blindness, and draws on recent scholarship to detail how Homer lost his sight from an infection following the initial composition of *The Iliad* and the initial planning of *The Odyssey*.[24] Homer, Wilson stresses, wanted to travel after beginning the *Iliad* because he 'thought it of great consequence to see the places he should have occasion to mention', reinforcing the link between visual perception and literary writing. The observation that Homer was 'seized with a complaint in his eyes' after visiting Egypt, Africa and Spain echoes with the contemporary endemic of trachoma, the eye infection that soldiers returning from the Napoleonic wars had carried back to Britain and which also affected Wordsworth.[25] Wilson also turns to Homer's poetry as evidence for his blindness, citing Homer's dedication via the person of Demodocus in *The Odyssey* to the Muse who 'with clouds of darkness quenched his visual ray, / But gave him power to raise the lofty lay'.[26] However, Homer's blindness is not just associated with the content of his poetry: it also opens up fundamental questions regarding its material production.

Homer signifies the shift from an oral poetic tradition to one in which poetry is set down in writing; yet he continues to perpetuate the association of poet with voice, as his blindness necessitates amanuenses. Wilson draws attention to the relationship between Homer's blindness and the material production of his texts, noting how Homer began writing before losing his sight, but 'laboured under this privation' when he composed *The*

*Odyssey*: his literacy owes to his having once had sight. Indeed, as Alexander Beecroft observes, within his own culture 'a blind Homer must have been an illiterate Homer', whilst identifying a series of potentially contradictory goals concerning his literacy in Homeric biography. Beecroft points to the competing aims of Homer's early biographers, who stress or deny his blindness depending on whether they seek to endorse Homeric verbal media as either oral or literate. For example, the most detailed account of Homeric blindness, found in the Pseudo-Herodotean *Vita*, emphasises that Homer was well travelled and literate, and took written notes whilst travelling; yet insists that the composition and transmission of Homeric epic occurs only orally. Homer's life is thus divided into 'sighted/literate and blind/poetic halves'.[27] Significantly, the inclusion of Homer's biography in Wilson's book implicitly draws attentions to the relationship between blindness and textual production.

Wilson turns next to Milton, whose blindness can be attributed to more definite physiological causes, connected to the corporeal effects of his literary pursuits. The following commentary describes the period in which Milton composed *Paradise Lost*. Wilson notes of Milton's sight:

> Naturally weak, and impaired by incessant study … had for several years been sensibly declining; and when he was engaged in his last great work, had discovered symptoms of approaching extinction. In the course of that honourable labour he entirely lost the vision of one eye, and that of the other closing soon afterwards, he was resigned to total darkness.[28]

Wilson, like the ophthalmologists of the period, found evidence of Milton's experience of blindness in his poetry. Moreover, the poet's description in Book III of *Paradise Lost* is given a privileged position in *The Biography*'s schema, published as an inscription on the frontispiece:

> – Thus with the year,
> Seasons return, but not to me returns
> Day, or the sweet approach of Even or Morn,
> Or sight of vernal bloom, or Summer's rose,
> Or flocks or herds, or human face divine:
> But cloud instead, and ever-during dark
> Surrounds me, from the cheerful ways of men
> Cut off, and for the book of knowledge fair,
> Presented with a universal blank
> Of Nature's works to me expunged and razed,
> And wisdom at one entrance quite shut out.

The emphasis Wilson places on this passage is important, as the description of blindness as 'wisdom at one entrance quite shut out' is one of the most frequently repeated that we find in nineteenth-century sources, by both blind and sighted writers. For example, it was inscribed on the frontispiece portrait published in the first memoir by the celebrated blind traveller James Holman in 1822, and was quoted by the author of the article on 'Blind Leaders of the Blind' published in Dickens's journal *All the Year Round* in 1871, as I discussed in the previous chapter.[29] Yet its citation by blind people, as both a bathetic account of the emotional and intellectual loss that results from blindness and as evidence of the genius of the blind poet, often produces a tension in their accounts. Whilst blind people might want to stress what they *can* do without vision, the reiteration of this passage reinforces a link between acquiring blindness and losing knowledge.

In speaking of Homer's and Milton's shared 'genius' and 'misfortunes', and in trying to return Homer to the real via a factual account of his blindness, Wilson suggests that Homer, like Milton, wrote *in spite* of his blindness: their previous visual experience and memory enabled both to compose poetry, although they could not scribe their poems themselves. People with acquired visual disability are thus privileged above those born blind, as their having experienced a period of sight facilitates a visual memory. Having *seen* an object allows the poet to associate it with a word, and enables him or her to continue to access the visual metaphors and images that comprise poetic language systems. The inclusion of the poet Thomas Blacklock's biography – which Wilson copies verbatim without acknowledgement from Joseph Dennie's early nineteenth-century American series *The Port-folio* – complicates this issue.[30] Blacklock went blind from smallpox at birth, yet was read to at an early age, becoming familiar with the works of Milton, Spencer, Prior and Addison.[31] Through this process of being read aloud to, Blacklock was able to learn accurately the meaning and function of visual metaphors and images. This is an aspect of sensory knowledge that had deeply interested Edmund Burke, as we observed in an earlier discussion of his treatment of blindness in *A Philosophical Enquiry*, and indeed Wilson's source, Joseph Dennie, records how Burke turned to Blacklock's poetry for 'proof' of his doctrine that sight is not the only channel for information-gathering.[32] Dennie also drew upon the eighteenth-century Scottish common sense philosopher Thomas Reid's account of perception and knowledge to explain Blacklock's ability to construct mental images and communicate them through poetry:

> It has been observed, and I think very truly, by Dr Reid, that there is very little of the knowledge acquired by those who see, that may not be communicated to a man born blind; and he illustrates his remark by the example of the celebrated Saunderson.[33]

Reid's views on blindness, set out in his *Inquiry into the Human Mind*, were informed by his friendship with the famed blind mathematician Professor Saunderson. Reid stressed here that, despite 'what hath been said of the dignity and superior nature of this faculty, it is worthy of our observation, that there is very little of the knowledge acquired by sight, that may not be communicated to a man born blind'. Furthermore, he argues:

> One who never saw the light, may be learned and knowing in every science, even in optics; and may make discoveries in every branch of philosophy. He may understand as much as anyone else not only about the order, distances and motions of the heavenly bodies but about the nature of light and the laws of the reflection and refraction of its rays. He may understand distinctly, how those laws produce the phenomena of the rainbow, the prism, the camera obscura and the magic lantern, and all the powers of the microscope and telescope.[34]

This, Reid emphasises, is a fact 'sufficiently attested by experience'. Although a blind man may not directly perceive qualities such as colour, he can fully conceive of them, as well as come to know the appearance of things. Shifting theories of vision and perception redefine understanding of the blind person's ability and status; moreover, interrogation of the experience of blindness informs philosophic discussion.

However, Wilson continues to quote a passage from Dennie that remains cautious about the possibility of assimilating blind and sighted people. He maintains certain essential differences between them, including the construction of mental images. This leads to a different response and enjoyment from the experience of reading poetry, which Dennie understands – despite his referencing of Burke and Reid – to be a predominantly visual form.[35] He argues:

> But of the pleasures which Poetry excites, so great a proportion arises from allusion to visible objects, and from descriptions of the beauty and sublimity of nature; so much truth is there in the maxim *ut picture poesis*, that the word imagination, which in its primary sense, has a direct reference to the eye, is employed to express that power of the mind, which is considered so peculiarly characteristic of poetical genius; and therefore whatever be the degree of pleasure, which a blind Poet receives from the exercise of his art, the pleasure must, in general, be perfectly different in kind from that which he imparts to his readers.[36]

Dennie's reinforcement of the model '*ut pictura poesis*' – a poem should be understood analogically to painting and the visual arts – is exemplary of the tension that defines the relationship between blindness and writing in the nineteenth century. Whilst Dennie impresses that concepts in language can be understood and communicated through association with the non-visual senses, he re-inscribes the relationship between the imagination, poetic language and vision as one of dependency and necessity. Indeed, he clearly denotes that blind poetic practices are different from normative practices, as he distinguishes between the pleasure a 'blind man' derives from poetry, and that which 'we' – that is, the sighted – derive from it.[37] Wilson's biography, by including Dennie's biography without comment or note, implicitly condones his attitude that writing produced by blind people is somehow inferior, and other, to that produced by sighted people.

However, in a complex rejoinder to this, Wilson and other individuals included in his *Biography* do use poetry – seemingly a visual form – to shape responses to their experience of blindness. The range of responses includes both the initial, raw stage of grieving following sight loss, and the period of adjustment and renewal found in other senses and experiences. Wilson thus began to articulate a distinct poetics of blindness in which writing stands in for the loss of the visual.

## Towards a Poetics of Blindness

In spite of Wilson's underscoring of the difference in pleasure gained by the sighted and blind from reading poetry, he uses poetic form to express his emotional response to loss of vision in his 1825 autobiographical text, *The Life of James Wilson*.[38] Whilst his own prose memoir is optimistic – it is about moving forward, dealing with the challenges of sight loss, and acquiring new skills and ways of dealing with the world – he is more sombre in poetry. Indeed, given his belief that poetry belongs more to the visible and thus more to the sighted, the form itself perpetuates his sense of loss and absence; his grief increases as he struggles to articulate his self through a form which he understands to be conditioned by the visual, the very thing which points to his lack. In one untitled poem, he appeals to 'you, whom Heav'n has doubly bless'd / With light – Oh, gift divine!', and asks: 'did you know what others feel, / Beneath the shafts of woe'. Grief and despair increase as he mourns that 'from me the joys of life are fled, / Advancing fast in years … All I can give are tears'. Solace and comfort are found in 'religion', Wilson claiming that otherwise he would sink 'in grief's unlovely arms, / And willing cease to live'. The close of the poem marks the close of despair, as 'resignation bids me grieve / In language thus no more'.[39] Another poem, titled 'An Address to the Sun', calls out to the 'glorious orb' and celebrates how:

> … thy genial rays
> Promote and renovate my lays;

Though HE, who gave thee all thy charms,
Has folded me in darkness' arms.[40]

Although he cannot describe the experience of sight, objects and verbs of vision are scattered throughout the poem. The orb of the sun mirrors Wilson's own eyes in the poem's schema; whilst his eyes are 'now' enshrouded by a 'veil', that veil 'shall be withdrawn' and reflect both 'fulgent day' and the glory of God after death. The 'glorious orb' appealed to in the first line finds a figural counterpart in the speaker's 'eye-balls', referred to in the last line. The oscillation between the sighted and blind is emphasised here in the poem's sustained allusion to spiritual blindness, echoing the caution against earthly, physical sight found in Corinthians II, 4:18 ('whilst we look not at the things that are seen, but the things that are unseen, for the things that are seen are temporal, while the things that are not seen are eternal').

The final poem Wilson includes indicates his increasing robustness to his condition of blindness. Although it is unclear in what order he wrote the poems (authored when he was 17), 'From Memory' (a version of which also opens the 1821 *Biography*) is increasingly positive. It suggests that poetry offers a space in which to act out and through traumatic responses to events; the subject grows in self-awareness and as such gains strength. Wilson voices this when he notes that whilst the poems might not be of much literary merit, 'still … they were of service to me'.[41] In 'From Memory', the speaker reflects that when 'I backward turn my mind / I feel of sorrow's pain'. Although he at first weeps for 'joys I left behind', retrospective vision grants him 'intellectual eyes', through which he can gaze upon a 'happier shore … circled with eternal skies'. Although Wilson next turned his writing skills to prose writing, poetry had played an important part in his literary development.

As John Bird recognised in his attack on misleading fictional depictions of blind people, literature is a powerful medium, enabling both the creation and consolidation of dominant stereotypes. In his edited version of Wilson's *Life*, John Bird includes a poem from the New York *Literary World*, written by someone struck blind following an accident. The speaker relies on stock tropes to depict the alternating worlds of the sighted and of the blind; 'golden shores of sunshine' transform into a 'sea of night', 'black wings' flap through the air, and 'darkness, omnipresent' surrounds the speaker. The speaker identifies himself with 'chain'd and blinded Samson', questioning fearfully whether he is 'thus to languish, / In exile from the sun'. The speaker cannot generate new metaphors or descriptions of blindness; language does not move the speaker forward. Rather, he is caught in a cycle of repetition, as his language repeats and consolidates his preconceptions of blindness; he has not yet learned how to see, and speak, differently.[42]

A poetics of blindness is developed by another blind writer at the mid-century, Edmund White, who lost his sight later in life, and who published poetry drawing on his experience of blindness. His texts grapple with the gap between the experience of vision as seeing things in the present out there, and visual memory as a way of newly seeing things. His writing alerts us to the notion of the image as a representation predicated on absence – as something that marks the moment of disappearance. As his voice echoes other literary voices, his poetry also invites us to question both the nature of the image as it is first seen, and the originality of writing. Vision itself – the physiological act of seeing – is filtered and mediated through representations in a knitting-together of sensory perception and literary associations.

Edmund White's poetry proceeds from darkness, which he describes as 'deep and impenetrable as that of Chaos'.[43] White, a guard for the Great Western Railway, wrote poetry to supplement his income after losing his sight after he witnessed a traumatic accident. John Bird, who, in his edition of Wilson's memoir, included a poem from White's volume of poetry entitled 'Blindness', notes how White was dismissed by his company and given ten pounds, with the offer of another ten 'if he would sign an agreement never to apply for more'.[44] However, White turned to literature instead:

> Feeling he had a claim for long and active service, as well as good character, he declined it. He is self-educated, and contributes to the support of a numerous young family by his pen.[45]

Writing materially secures the body of this blind man; it is literally a way of feeding and clothing both him and his family. White explains:

> There are certain duties devolving upon us while we remain denizens of the earth, that neither blindness nor any other infirmity with which it may please Divine Providence to visit us, can entirely supersede, and it is in order to assist in providing the common necessaries of life for a young and numerous family, and if possible to attract the attention of the benevolent to the forlorn and destitute condition of many thousands of my poor afflicted brethren, that I have been induced to exert the humble talent with which it has pleased Almighty God to endow me.[46]

Alongside their economic necessity, White's literary pursuits also had the social aim of drawing attention to the 'forlorn and destitute' condition of other blind people.

John Kitto, in his study of deafness and blindness at the mid-century, observed differences in the poetry of those who had lost their sight and those born blind, 'who seldom or never allude to their blindness, because they are not really conscious of their privation' in their 'endeavour to express ideas of visual objects'.[47] Indeed, White's poem registers a way of seeing in which the visual memory projects images onto the seemingly blank landscape before it. The model of perception developed in White's poem echoes that set forth by Wordsworth in 'Lines Written a Few Miles Above Tintern Abbey', in which the 'eye and ear … half-create' the world before it.[48] As I trace more fully in discussion of Wordsworth's poem in Chapter 6, perception is not a passive function of the senses; rather, the mind has agency over what is perceived. Similarly, White proposes:

Hail! Roseate morn. What though my sightless eye,
No more beholds the bright cerulean sky;
The various tints, that gild the orient east
At early sunrise; still my mind can feast upon their beauties; can them all review,
And with bright fancy conjure scenes anew.[49]

Seeing is effected through time here. Day is marked by varying images of light, of the 'roseate morn' and 'bright cerulean sky' at early sunrise. Although the sightless eye can no longer 'behold' the sky and literally see what is before it, the 'mind' can 'feast upon their beauties', as the fancy allows the mind to 'review' images as well as 'conjure scenes anew'. White turns positively from the impact of sight loss ('though') to draw attention to the continuity of his inward vision ('still'). Memory and imagination perpetuate sight, which becomes purer through its selective nature. The speaker likens the power of this new vision to forms of technology, as he is able to suspend time and review 'the changes that each moment pass, / O'er Heaven, or Earth, or Air, as through a glass / Whose telescopic magnitude doth shrink / Newton's or Herschel's works'.[50] This vision also functions like narrative, as the sightless, dematerialised eye can freeze and separate into parts of a visual picture normally quickly grasped as a whole. Indeed, vision is hyper-realised, as 'I portray bright colours, far more vivid, than e'er lay / On Raffaell's canvass' (sic).[51]

The echo of 'Tintern Abbey' alerts us to the range of literary allusions and voices that are woven throughout White's writing, as he frequently draws on other voices to articulate his experience. In the preface to his poem, White aligns himself with Milton, recalling how he dictated his poetry to his young daughter:

> The composition of this little volume has therefore been to me a long, tedious, and protracted undertaking, having to instruct the writer, one of my

> daughters, who is only eleven years of age, how to spell almost every word as I dictated it, when it was afterwards corrected and copied by another of my daughters, thirteen years of age, in those hours that should have been devoted to rest, after the tedium of a long day's occupation.[52]

The description of this activity as 'long, tedious, and protracted' mirrors the popular image of Milton dictating *Paradise Lost* to his daughters, in paintings by Delacroix and Fuseli, and William Hayley's popular biography of Milton. The creative mind, gendered as masculine, overwhelms the feminine, capable only of copying.

There are further verbal echoes of Dickens's description of Laura Bridgman at the Perkins Institute in *American Notes* (1842). Note the terms with which the speaker in White's poem mourns the loss of his sight:

> No more the wonders that his Art creates;
> Enraptur'd view; for darkness dissipates
> A thousand glories, and ten thousand joys,
> And all the pleasures of this world alloys.
> There is in darkness an impervious gloom,
> Impenetrably deep; the marble tomb.[53]

The metaphor of the 'marble tomb' and description of the 'impervious gloom' resonate with Dickens's sentimentalised account of Laura (which I discuss further in Chapter 6), imprisoned because of her condition:

> There she was before me; built up, as it were, in a marble cell, impervious to any ray of light, or particle of sound; with her poor white hand peeping through a chink in the wall, beckoning me to some good man for help, that an Immortal soul might be awakened.[54]

Literary depictions of blindness shape White's poetic construction of sightlessness, his visual memory coinciding with his reading memory in the production of his poetry.

White also used his poem to raise awareness of the Indigent Blind Visiting Society, and he includes a passage from its annual report of 1854 to underscore and promote the work that it does to provide relief for 'some thousands of poor and aged blind'.[55] In this, he also recognises the social and political function of writing by drawing attention to the 'National evil' of the lack of provision for the poor and aged blind.[56] Not only was literature a means of gaining more economic independence, it also helped to politicise the blind community. Indeed, as already alluded to above, Wilson's *Life* and *Biography* proved to be a point around which resistance to the treatment of the blind could be organised in writing.

## The Politics of Life Writing

From a poetics of blindness to the politics of life writing: autobiographical writing by blind people was not simply concerned with individual selfhood, it was also used as an intervention in the social and political realm. John Bird and Mrs Hippolite van Landeghem both used biographical form to voice resistance to the dominant social models and educational treatment of blind people. John Bird, a surgeon at the Middlesex Asylum at Hanwell until he lost his sight in 1846, edited Wilson's autobiography for a Victorian audience. Bird outlined how, since he went blind, he had devoted 'my best energies to a serious enquiry into the mental condition of those who suffer from blindness and its consequent evils'. He argued that continued neglect impacted negatively on blind people's mental state.[57] Van Landeghem used autobiography to promote her manifesto calling for the end of exile schools. Both Bird and Van Landeghem spoke of blindness as a state of imprisonment and exile, an imprisonment constructed in large part by the social and educational conditions of the day.[58]

Biographical form was a way of communicating the experience and imparting knowledge of what it felt like to be blind, as Bird recognised when he argued that without such testimonies few people would attempt to 'form any conception of what must be the condition of that mind, chafing, stagnant or festering'.[59] Without intellectual stimulation, Bird argued, blind people faced serious challenges, for 'it stands to reason that, if the necessary amount of the means of health, growth, and exercise be not transmitted through the four remaining senses, the intellectual and moral faculties must wither, collapse, and decay'.[60] Bird suggested that intellectual and moral selfhood was not innate, but rather came from without, through social and educational structures: a dialectic exchange between an individual and the society in which they live. For blind people to gain independence, they must firstly be dependent upon the 'approach of enlightened humanity'.[61]

Moreover, Bird held that as writing and intellectual encouragement stimulate the memory, so the memory in turn stirs the intellectual powers. He noted:

> A blind man may feel fully convinced *that ideas do not fade away from the memory, but that when once clearly conceived they merge into, form a part of, and expand the insenescent and indestructible mind;* yet, if he be left too long in silence, isolation, and darkness, without the necessary refreshment, and repose, and hope from confidence in the sincerity of his friends, the accumulated effects of such treatment will, in a longer period, produce a degree

> of derangement or disease analogous to that which falls on the felon, whose silence and isolation *without darkness* has been more severe in a shorter time.[62]

James Wilson is a case in point; both his autobiography, as record of his life, and biography, as mark of his work, demonstrate the value and purposiveness of intellectual endeavour. Wilson's hopes for his biography were certainly felt by Bird. He emphasised the impact that Wilson's *Biography* had had on him:

> In the few pages of a preface it is impossible for me to do justice to the memory of James Wilson and the value of his writings, in any degree proportionate to the esteem and gratitude I myself, in common with other blind, feel for his character and labours. I would I had space and opportunity for that tribute of respect which is his due, and which could be no other than a careful analysis of the events of his life, his character, and the importance of the work he must have devoted so much of his time and of the energy of his intellect so successfully to accomplish.[63]

Here Bird stresses how Wilson's work, and his communication of blind people's biographies, served the important function of challenging the narrow stereotypes of blindness more typically available.[64] Indeed, Bird described how he regularly sought out editions of Wilson's *Biography* and circulated them to friends or families of blind people, and to libraries, to serve as alternative and inspiring models of blindness.[65]

Bird was convinced that Wilson was able to fulfil his intellectual potential because he was fortunate enough to have escaped 'imprisonment' in an 'exile school', uncompromisingly spoken of in terms of 'the evils of exile schools'.[66] By happily mixing with sighted friends, Wilson became 'fully established as a useful and valuable member of society'.[67] Advocating an integrated approach to schooling, Bird described a system practised in France, in which blind, deaf and dumb children 'receive the same instruction; they mingle with the other children in all the corporeal exercises which can allow it; and only during the intervals of school hours do they receive separate instruction in the branches for which their different deficiencies require a special mode of teaching'.[68] Whilst the blind children are still spoken of here in terms of 'deficiencies', Bird also posited that the binary between blind and sighted must be broken down, and that as blind and sighted 'mingle', the differences diminish.[69] He proposed that an experimental integrated system be established at King's College.

Education of blind people must start with blind people themselves, and Bird was scathing of the 'five-sensed amateurs, or officials insufficiently educated' who 'blast' the educational prospects of the blind.[70] He also argued that the opportunity for developing a more efficient embossed writing system would not be realised given the continued 'sighted partiality for the old alphabet'.[71] Bird's education proposal was conditioned along class lines, as the school would be 'for the middle classes' only – despite his later assertion that most blind people were from lower classes.[72] Yet Bird still provided a radical intervention into the repressive and restrictive treatment of the blind, concluding his introduction to Wilson's autobiography with the following question:

> I ask how it is possible for a blind man to enjoy either repose, confidence, or hope? … It is too often the blind man's fate; but would not be so if the sighted would discontinue to treat those blind in their power as their inferiors in intellectual capacity, social rights, and moral aspirations, by denying them those very means by which alone these inalienable privileges of every man's life, whether blind or sighted, can be secured.[73]

Similarly, Mrs Hippolyte van Landeghem attacked the isolation of blind children in exile schools, describing the system as an evil. She also wrote from a personal perspective – the full title of her 1864 treatise concluded with 'the question considered and answered. By Mrs Hippolite van Landeghem (blind, after 12 years' experience in an exile institution)'. In this pamphlet she argued that the problems faced by blind people were largely due to the misplaced attitudes of society. She was especially critical of the education system and endeavoured 'to prove that every scheme of mis-directed benevolence not only tends to perpetuate existing pauperism, but re-produces it under a new form'.[74] Not only was this system failing to benefit blind children intellectually, it further perpetuated an image of them as freakish, and nonhuman, with Van Landeghem likening the effects on pupils of visitors to these schools to those of animals in a zoo.[75] Like John Bird, she advocated the more integrated system of schooling practised in France. This call for integrated schooling was endorsed by the special report 'Training of the Blind' of 1876, which found that 'the Committee – commissioned by the Charity Organisation Society for a special investigation into blindness – think it highly desirable that blind children should be educated during a portion of their time with the sighted, and are of the opinion that efforts should therefore be made to provide in elementary public schools for those not in special schools'.[76]

Van Landeghem's treatise listed a series of famous blind individuals and pointed out that none of them had been educated in exile schools. Again, personal biographies and testimonies played an important role in

Van Landeghem's critique. In seeking inspiration she stressed: 'We are not limited to the blind of the past. There are many eminent living characters who, in spite of the manufacturers of shifting expedients for the evasion of duties, continually prove what the poor blind can do.'[77] Her next publication developed this argument, and she consolidated her attack against exile schools with the evidence of her own experience. She opens the treatise with one of her own poems, in which she represents the state of blindness as one of despair and imprisonment:

BLIND!
Dark is the House in which I dwell,
The shutter'd windows close and mute,
For never beam of heavenly light
Athwart their solemn bars may shoot.
Oh, blessing pour'd upon the air!
Oh, boundless light, so cheap and free!
To daily toil thou guids't a world,
Yet hast no single ray for me!
...
Counting the empty hours I sit—
How full might be each empty hour!
Not weak my hand nor dull my brain,
Nor spent the sun's meridian power;
But long the selfish world has laid
A ban upon hand, brain, and heart;
For all, the toil of healthy life;
For me, the Idiot's vacant part.[78]

The common trope of blindness as a darkened room and prison is subverted in Van Landeghem's poem. It is the 'selfish world', rather than the physical condition of blindness, which imprisons and isolates the speaker, and which frustrates the 'hand, brain, and heart' in their attempts to garner the fruits of a 'healthy life'. The speaker goes on to describe herself as being 'free, yet in bondage like a babe's': the subject's freedom is limited by its dependency on others. In the introduction to the biographies, Van Landeghem criticises how, if a blind person attempts to 'vary his lot by the exertions of powers mental or bodily, he is met by every conceivable difficulty'. She argues further that changes to the blind person's prospects must come from the outside as 'there can be no hope of an improved state of things until benevolent people awaken to the important truth, that every form of charity which tends to unsocialise is fundamentally false'.[79] It is not blindness itself, but rather the way in which the blind person is treated by the sighted, that is the most disabling. Significantly, Van Landeghem chose to evidence her point through the stories of blind individuals, and their successes and achievements. Grouping the biographies according to occupation, she emphasised that no field of knowledge or learning should be closed off to blind people.

William Hanks Levy, the blind educator and campaigner, also included a large range of biographies in his 1872 study of blindness (indeed, biographical information takes up nearly half of the volume). One such biography was James Wilson's *Life*, and Levy acknowledges the contribution the earlier biographer has made:

> [The *Biography*] has proved eminently useful in conveying an idea of the influence exerted on the world's affairs by persons without sight, and also in directing attention to the capabilities and requirements of the blind … In the list of the eminent blind there are many illustrious and distinguished men, but few could be pointed out who have proved as useful to their suffering brethren as James Wilson.[80]

Levy impresses here the *utility* of biography as a means of materially relieving suffering, by challenging limited and damaging stereotypes of blind people and providing them with aspirational role models – a point to which I will return shortly.

For Levy, editing biographies of blind people also provided an opportunity to consider historical sources afresh – to examine them for traces of other sensory modalities. So in the 'first case of blindness recorded in history', that of Isaac in the Old Testament, he described how 'we cannot do better than transcribe here the beautiful account given by the inspired historian of the conspiracy of Rebekah and Jacob to deceive their aged and sightless father; and we think the reader will be forcibly struck with the intelligent use made by Isaac of his hearing, touch, and smell', despite his acquisition of blindness in old age.[81] Autobiographical form clearly had an empowering role to play in the creation of blind communities in the nineteenth century, and they used it as a tool to challenge prejudicial and stereotyped attitudes towards them. The genres of autobiography and biography help to establish identities for blind people that are selected and promoted *by* them rather than conferred *on* them. However, I will conclude this point by offering a note of caution to the optimism which characterises blind people's deployment of autobiographical form in the period. The stress on proving their capabilities contributed towards an exclusionary focus on the lives of exceptional blind people, which perhaps did little to promote understanding of the lives or experiences of more ordinary blind people. More recently, Georgina Kleege has powerfully articulated the ways in which such examples help to inscribe the idea that 'disability is a personal tragedy to be overcome through an individual's fortitude and pluck, rather than a set of cultural practices and assumptions'.[82]

This prevalence for focusing on the lives of exceptional blind people is signalled by the first biographer of Bessie Gilbert, the campaigner who had established the General Association for Promoting the General Welfare of the Blind. Frances Martin wrote that 'the life of a blind person' 'is led apart from much of the ordinary work of the world'. She believed:

> such a life, with its inevitable restrictions and compulsory isolation, could offer little of public interest, and might well remain unchronicled. But in the rare cases where blindness, feeble health, and suffering form scarcely any bar to activity; where they are not only borne with patience, but by heroic effort are compelled to minister to great aims, we are eager to learn the secret of such a life.[83]

Martin notes her period's limited expectations of what people with visual disabilities might achieve by stressing that 'the life of a blind person is led apart from much of the ordinary work of the world'. Furthermore, both this passage and the biography itself suggest the Victorians' interest in the life of blind people who *overcome* adversity: 'we are eager to learn the secret of such a life'. For Frances Martin, such examples act as a pleasing morality tale that serves to stimulate, encourage and strengthen the reader.

Elsewhere in the biography, Martin seeks to distance Gilbert from the radical coterie of blind people who have been introduced throughout this and the last chapter, including John Bird (briefly Gilbert's tutor) and William Hanks Levy. She emphasises in Gilbert the qualities of meekness and piety, stressing that she had 'gradually learnt that blindness is a limitation which the most loving and tender care cannot entirely remove. To be blind, to be a woman, both imply considerable restrictions'.[84] This desire on the part of the Victorian sighted public that blind people should conform to correct notions of gratitude and propriety was given sharp comic treatment by one educationalist, Thomas Anderson (director of the Edinburgh Asylum for the Blind). Anderson resisted the tendency towards pitying and disabling attitudes to blind people, and rejected their denigration as 'melancholy' or 'pitiable'. Stating that he did not know where such views come from, he warned:

> I know nothing more erroneous, or more opposed to the feelings of by far the greater majority [of blind people]. They cannot endure such terms themselves, and strangers should be on their guard against using them in their presence.[85]

Thomas Anderson illustrates this caution with a story about an inspection of the school by a lady who, by 'half-articulated ejaculations', indicates her discomfort and pity of the pupils. Anderson goes on:

> but I believe none of us were prepared for the astounding climax which followed, when turning round to me she said, in the hearing of all – "Well! – poor things! – do they *ever speak!*" The effect was almost instantaneous, and I was glad to get her outside the room door, to allow vent to the burst of laughter which immediately followed her exit. "Poor things – do they ever speak", became quite a bye word among them afterwards.[86]

These blind children are bemused by this visitor's construction of them as meek, and their laughter destablises the patronising terms of pity with which this visitor seeks to both view and confine them. To use Rosemarie Garland-Thomson's theorisation of the relationship between starer and staree, this group refuse to be complicit in the power dynamics at work here, in their refusal to conform to the ideal disabled body that the visitor expects to see.[87] However, undoubtedly there was a wider cultural desire to reinforce more moderate and temperate representations of blindness. Indeed, many of the individuals mentioned in previous chapters such as John Bird and William Hanks Levy have been largely forgotten, whilst role models who more obviously met certain, sentimentalised ideals – such as Helen Keller – continue to be venerated.

Frances Martin attacked William Hanks Levy for his seemingly radical view that blind people should be autonomous and self-sufficient, and for his criticism of the impositions the sighted community placed on the blind:

> It is necessary to say so much at this time, because we shall see that in many points Bessie did yield to the judgment of one who took an extreme view; who, himself educated in an institution, surrounded only by blind people, often of a very feeble capacity, had learned to look upon himself more as a member of an oppressed and persecuted race than as an afflicted man.[88]

Martin's hostility towards Levy's 'extreme views' suggests we need to be careful in our interpretation of what a successful blind person might have said in public about the ways in which their sight loss affected them, and their private feelings. Before concluding, I will briefly explore this issue through a complex and challenging autobiographical fragment produced by Robert Lowe, Viscount Sherbrooke, who had experienced impaired vision since early childhood.

Robert Lowe entered Parliament in 1852, after returning from eight years spent in Australia, where he practised law and was elected a member of the New South Wales legislative council. Lowe's political career in the UK was controversial, particularly in his role of Chancellor of the Exchequer in Gladstone's 1868 government, as he was heavily rebuked for overspending and for financial irregularities involving the Post Office and the Zanzibar mail contract. Most notoriously, he attempted to implement a tax on matches, a policy that would have become a financial burden on the matchstick girls who sold them. Tellingly, his critics suggested that his shortsightedness (a result of albinism) made him liable to misread documents and figures. In an autobiographical fragment that Lowe composed in 1876 and typed using one of the early typewriting devices for blind people discussed in the previous chapter, he agrees that his visual impairment contributed to his difficulties and unpopularity.[89] However, he articulates this in somewhat more radical terms. His autobiography pulses with anger: at the inept medical treatment he had received, at the failure of others to understand and accept that his own visual cues and responses were different from those of the majority of his colleagues and friends, and at the isolation that ensued.

The fragment opens with a description of the chronic pain that his eye condition had caused him since childhood, as he states: 'I cannot even conceive the state of a person to whom sight is a function free from all pain and distress.'[90] He explains: 'my defect of sight is no slight disqualification; of its greatness those who have had no experience can form little idea'.[91] It structures all the events that Lowe recounts in his life: for example, making him a particularly ripe target for the bullying culture that was rife at his public school, Winchester. Although this ultimately aided him by forcing him to work harder at his studies, he does not exactly describe this experience in terms of gratitude. Moreover, he argues that the fact he has risen to so 'prominent a position [as Chancellor] prevented people from making allowances for physical deficiencies which, if better known, would doubtless have been more generally allowed for'.[92] Lowe acknowledges that in order to succeed he had to make his visual disability *invisible* – but it continued to affect and shape his interactions with others and, he suggests, required acknowledgement and understanding that was, more often than not, withheld. Lowe's reluctance to publish his autobiography during his lifetime is telling, as he represses a version of his visually impaired self that is angry and critical of the damaging prejudicial attitudes he experienced in an ocularcentric society.[93]

## Conclusion

This autobiographical survey has demonstrated how literature functions as a space in which to express and communicate the experience of bodies and selves at the edges of society and culture, who frustratingly have to prove their extraordinariness, not just in the actions of their lives, but in the very act of mediating their stories. It has shown how the desire to recuperate psychological, social and financial independence underscores the agendas of blind and visually impaired people who turned to life writing in the nineteenth century. Yet, certain tensions and ambiguities mark these projects. The texts sometimes endorse the same prejudicial attitudes they seek to challenge, for example by continuing to repeat debates and discussions from literature and philosophy on the nature of sensory experience that valorise the primacy of visual experience. Published within the same period in which relief systems to enable blind people to read and author textual matter directly were coming under debate and scrutiny, the production of these texts in ink print format also points to blind people's continued reliance on sighted assistants to both produce and read autobiographical material. They thus inscribe a mode of textual dependency at a material level which is at odds with the claims to independence made in their content.

The next part of this book extends the themes that I have established in the previous three chapters, but focuses more explicitly on sighted authors' engagement with the topic of blindness. It explores the ways in which anxiety and uncertainty over the sensory status of the linguistic sign – at both referential and material levels – finds particular expression in literary representations of blindness. Extending the concerns of this chapter, it examines in turn how blindness becomes therefore intimately connected with writers' self-conceptions. Frequently, the possibility of, or encounter with, blindness that a writer experienced in his or her own personal life prompted a questioning over the material production of writing. The tension that marks blind writers' attempts to employ literary form and genre to constitute their individual and collective identities thus also emerged in depictions of blind characters in the wider literary culture of the nineteenth century. On the one hand, blindness was equated with illiteracy, and the closing down of writing as a textual medium. On the other hand, its association with oral forms of narration (for example, in debates over Homer's blindness) and its association with newer technologies of tactile reading formats provided writers with rich imaginative material to think, and create, positively outside visual restraints.

# PART II

# *Literary Blindness*

CHAPTER 5

# *Blindness, Gender and Autobiography*

## *Reading and Writing the Self in* Jane Eyre, Aurora Leigh *and* The Life of Charlotte Brontë

*Jane Eyre: An Autobiography*, *Aurora Leigh* and *The Life of Charlotte Brontë* are three texts concerned with what it means to write a life. They are also haunted by an absence of vision, the trope of blindness connecting all three. Romney's blinding at the end of *Aurora Leigh* echoes that of Rochester's at the end of *Jane Eyre*. Elizabeth Gaskell, in framing her life of Charlotte Brontë with an epigraph from *Aurora Leigh*, not only alludes to the shared concerns of her texts with Elizabeth Barrett Browning's in charting the development of the woman writer, but also alerts us to the intertextual resonances between Barrett Browning and Brontë, which at a plot level clearly involve blindness. All three writers draw upon blindness as a way of structuring experience in their texts, and as a way of both creatively and critically reading each other.

These episodes of blindness have been interpreted largely symbolically, and most influentially via psychoanalytic readings that emphasise how a female linguistic subjectivity can only come into being through the destruction of the male gaze (and, by default, castration of the patriarchal figure). Here, though, I want to re-orientate discussion, and ask what happens if we read these episodes of blindness through their material, corporeal and biographical contexts. How might this bear further upon our understanding of the relationship between writing and gender being articulated in all three texts? I emphasise the importance of being more attentive to the experience of visual impairment and disability represented in these texts – approaching it as something which, as Lennard J. Davis has argued recently in a discussion of Brontë's novel, should precede rather than succeed the interpretative framework that we develop around blindness.[1] Here, I demonstrate Brontë's and Barrett Browning's personal understanding of two of the most pervasive forms of blindness in the period, cataracts and trachoma, and show how their representations of blindness were drawn through a more detailed knowledge and understanding of visual impairment than previously acknowledged. Brontë's father, Patrick, developed severe cataracts in the 1840s that were surgically removed in 1846. Brontë also experienced visual impairment, and Elizabeth Gaskell focused attention on the effect that Brontë's shortsightedness had on her artistic and literary practice in her biography of the novelist. Barrett Browning had an important intellectual relationship with the Greek scholar Hugh Stuart Boyd, who went blind after contracting trachoma in 1811 (they were friends from 1826 until his death in 1848).

The issue of disability has been most extensively considered in relation to *Jane Eyre*. As Julia Miele Rodas, Elizabeth J. Donaldson and David Bolt have recently insisted, 'disability is crucial to a critically engaged reading of *Jane Eyre*', and they draw attention to the range of physical, sensory and cognitive impairments that shape individual and social identity in Brontë's novel.[2] Their study critiques interpretations of disability in *Jane Eyre* that figure it variously as a 'tool for articulating spiritual values, as an expression of sexist oppression or imperialist complicity, or as a symbol of divine punishment', and they rightly stress that in such interpretative processes the 'embodied experiences of impairment and disability are erased'.[3] Yet despite this, their discussion overlooks Brontë's actual experience of visual impairment. As I suggest in my response to David Bolt's analysis of Brontë's novel as ocularcentric, this leads Bolt to argue that she writes from an ableist position. I show that experience of visual impairment in fact shaped Brontë's (and indeed Barrett Browning's) construction of blindness, and as such blurs the question of whether they spoke from an ableist or non-ableist position. This is not to say that these authors valorised a disabled position, particularly given the complex and sometimes contradictory attitudes towards visual impairment they articulated in their literary works and private correspondence. It does, however, make it more difficult to assume that their invocations of blindness are co-opted to shore up an ocularcentric agenda.

The embodied experience of blindness connects in these women's writings with its metaphoric potential, providing a complex array of tropes through which to explore the gendered conditions of writing. It is helpful here to turn to the twentieth-century French feminist philosopher Héléne Cixous, who in questioning what it means for her, as a female author to write, explains: 'I write without seeing that I write, what I write'.[4] Cixous, part of the wave of feminist writers who have explored most intensively the possibility of a feminine writing outside of the patriarchal symbolic order, visits the scene of blindness in her text, 'Writing Blind'. Cixous postulates that 'not seeing the world is the precondition for clairvoyance. But what does it mean, to see? Who sees? Who believes they know how to see'?[5] She privileges the category of blindness above the category of gender in her self-fashioning as writer:

> My nearsightedness is the secret of my clairvoyance … I owe a large part of my writing to my nearsightedness. I am a woman. But before being a woman I am a myope [une myope]. Myopia is my secret.[6]

Writing from this secret space of blindness, Cixous privileges myopia above gender in her understanding of herself as writer. 'I am a woman' is a seemingly emphatic pronouncement of identity that is then undone by the caution that follows: 'but before being a woman I am a myope'. To *not* see clearly through bodily eyes is to see as a woman; yet paradoxically this enhances the conditions for perceiving the world in its mystical, spiritual state. Cixous identifies with a disabled position not simply *as* a woman, but *before being* a woman; and it is this position, she stresses, that engenders writing. Significantly, Cixous's visual impairment is nearsightedness, in which distant objects in the field of vision appear blurred whereas those that are close and proximate are perceived with clarity. Those objects that are nearer to touch, then, are perceived with greater clarity, undoing a model of vision based on distance and deferral. Cixous's nearsightedness echoes with the nineteenth-century texts discussed here, in which new patterns of perception and understanding emerge for these women writers, who imagined states of blindness in order to consider how both the world and its narrative representation may be known and come into being through touch and sound as well as vision.

## The Embodiment of Blindness in *Jane Eyre* and *The Life of Charlotte Brontë*

Vision appears to be privileged throughout the narrative of *Jane Eyre*, as the reader frequently witnesses scenes, events, images and perceptions through Jane's eyes. Heather Glen argues that 'if all within Jane's narrative is seen from her point of view, that point of view is figured in emphatically visual terms. Again and again in the novel, the world that threatens and marginalizes the narrator appears as a series of "portraits" and "scenes", composed by her shaping eye'.[7] Yet the visual systems in the novel alert us to the blindness which pervades the narrative, composed as it is by a woman who has lived with her husband's near total blindness for two years, and partial blindness for further years, before setting out her autobiography, writing from the 'enclosed ground' of Ferndean, 'buried … in a heavy wood, where sounds fall dead, and dies unreverberating'.[8] Indeed, a metaphoric blindness permeates the text's representational system. This is apparent even in Jane's most seemingly scopic statement when, early on at Thornfield, she climbs to 'the top of the attic, looking out afar over sequestered field and hill, and along dim skyline', and expresses a longing 'for a power of vision which might overpass that limit, which might reach the busy worlds, towns, regions full of life I had heard but never seen … I believed in the existence of other and more vivid forms of goodness, and what I believed in I wished to behold' (*JE*, 109). Jane does not recall here the fullness of her gaze but rather its limit: she feels a sense of loss and lack for a world that has existed only in others' descriptions ('heard' but not 'seen') and which her 'power' to visualise is thus tempered. Jane articulates her own state of blindness, of not-yet-seeing, immersed as she is in a feminine space of enclosure and darkness, to which she returns at the novel's close – but with new perceptive and descriptive powers.

The more literal episode of blindness – Rochester's loss of sight following a fire caused by his mentally impaired wife, Bertha – has been read as an eruption of feminine anxiety, a symbolic castration, a punishment for his early transgressions and a sign that Jane/Charlotte Brontë can only imagine marriage as a union with a diminished Samson. Jane's narrative, and in turn Brontë's novel, can only begin with the symbolic castration of this literary patriarchal figure. Sandra Gilbert and Susan Gubar draw upon *Jane Eyre* in their seminal remodelling of Harold Bloom's paradigm of the anxiety of influence, when they argue that feminine writing evinces an anxiety as to its own creative origins, manifested as an even more primary 'anxiety of authorship'.[9] This construction is significantly informed by psychoanalytic theories, as the Oedipus complex – regarded as the nuclear complex of the neuroses in Freudian psychoanalysis – symbolically associates blinding with castration.[10] Gilbert and Gubar note that Rochester's blinding makes him Jane's equal, as Rochester, in the tradition of blinded Gloucester, is granted clearer vision.[11] Jane says to Rochester, 'I love you better now, when I can be useful to you, than I did in your proud state of independence' (*JE*, 445), and that it was his blindness that drew them close together 'for I was then his vision, as I am still his right hand' (*JE*, 451). Gilbert and Gubar's analysis of the function of blindness, whilst insightful, has been complicated, however, by more recent feminist and disability studies scholars. Usefully, Margaret Rose Torrell has shown how female empowerment in the novel occurs 'in concert with – not at the expense of – a progressive receconceptualisation of masculinity and embodiment'. She argues that patriarchal society male identity uses female embodiment to divert attention away from itself; but Jane rewrites this narrative through the deployment of disability to re-embody Rochester, thus permitting the performance of alternative gender identities.[12] And Essaka Joshua critiques the notion that Rochester's blindness is a form of divine punishment by paying particular attention to Brontë's selective approach to the Bible's representation of disability. Tracing the theological significance of sight and blindness, Joshua invites readers to interpret Rochester's disability not simply along the lines of Rochester's own view that it is a punishment, but within a schema that valorises more widely 'the benefits of disability for spiritual insight'.[13]

As Julia Miele Rodas, David Bolt and Elizabeth J. Donaldson collectively argue in an introduction to the edited volume in which Torrell and Joshua's essays appear, 'rather than occupying its own complex identity position, disability appears, for many readers, to exist as a kind of overlay, a caution against losing control or against defying social convention'.[14] They suggest that disabled subjects proliferate in the novel, including the cognitively and psychiatrically impaired Bertha Mason, the obsessive-compulsive Eliza Reed and even Jane herself as someone on the autistic spectrum. Yet their somewhat asymmetric reading of disability – using modern diagnostic categories to interpret Victorian structures of feeling and being – fails to acknowledge Brontë's own immersion in contemporary discourses of sight loss and restoration, despite their concern to illustrate how the novel is 'historically positioned at a time of radical transformation in the way Victorian bodies and minds were conceptualised, contained, and manipulated', a point I return to below.[15] In a connected essay, David Bolt, deploying a Derridean perspective of disability, complicates Gilbert and Gubar's analysis by arguing that 'Brontë's portrayals of alterity, castration and melancholia are patriarchal in so far as they are based on ocularcentric epistemology and thus unappreciative of the experience of people with a visual impairment'.[16] Bolt insists that 'the underpinning hierarchies of normativism over disability and "the sighted" over "the blind" remain intact' in the novel.[17] Bolt's analysis, whilst influential, has, however, been questioned by scholars: notably because of complications that they have identified in the relationship between ableist and disabled positions in the text.[18] In a nuanced discussion of the interpretative schema underpinning representations of both illness and disability in *Jane Eyre*, Susannah B. Mintz challenges those accounts of the novel as a genre that incepts an able/disabled binary, and which have contributed to critically suspicious readings of disability in Brontë's novel.[19] Whilst Mintz acknowledges that the force of interpretations that would argue the 'multiple instances of sickness and recovery' which haunt *Jane Eyre* are 'reminders of its complicity in the production of an ableist reality', she offers a counter-analysis by drawing on the psychoanalytic theory of recognition to show how Brontë instead models forms of interaction between characters which acknowledge the 'frailties of the body'.[20] She argues:

> In its emphasis on intersubjective regard as a means of disrupting hierarchical binaries of dis/ability ... the novel seems intriguingly forward thinking, reminding its readers of the need for more engaged ways of thinking about bodies, selves, illness and relationships.[21]

By pointing out that Rochester's bodily impairments towards the novel's close are part of a continuation, rather than reversal, of the protagonists' relationship (i.e. Rochester has always emphasised his ugliness and deformities), Mintz challenges the notion that 'disability marks a breach in the forward-motion of life'.[22]

My own critique of Bolt's argument arises from the fact of Brontë's experience of and engagement with visual impairment, which I argue both informs the representation of blindness in the text and works to disrupt the binary between sighted/blind identities represented in the novel. At a biographical level, this can be understood in terms of Brontë's role of carer to her father as he sought treatment for cataracts, which I will turn to shortly, as well as the effect that Brontë's own visual impairment had upon her artistic career. In Gaskell's biography, Brontë's turn away from art to literature was prompted by her weakening eyesight, as 'she had once hoped that she herself might become an artist, and so earn her livelihood; but her eyes failed her in the minute and useless labour which she had imposed upon herself with a view to this end'.[23] Gaskell suggests that Brontë wrote as a response to visual impairment: yet the anxiety that weak eyesight would impede her writing career continued to trouble her. Whilst I acknowledge the constructed act of any biographical writing, it is significant to note that Gaskell assigns Brontë's turn from the visual to the verbal arts to the condition of impaired vision, and in so doing associates her identity as writer with the figure of blindness.

Let me expand upon how this might shape new interpretations of impaired vision in Brontë's fictional work that privilege it as a condition for the generation of text and narrative. As William A. Cohen has recently argued, textual subjectivity in Brontë's fiction is distinctly embodied. For Cohen, this invites alternative – and more closely attentive – readings of the operations of sensory experience in her novels. Rather than reading the visual systems in Brontë's fiction in terms of disciplinary power, Cohen suggestively writes that 'we might instead consider how Brontë challenges the sensory hegemony of distanced looking by presenting vision as one among many bodily sensations'.[24] Importantly, Cohen's discussion points to the ambivalent role that vision occupies within Brontë's texts. Indeed, this is evidenced in the way Jane comes to learn of Rochester's blindness, which privileges the aural above the visual as Jane is called back to Thornfield after hearing a voice, seemingly materialising out of nowhere. It is a voice of 'unspeakable strangeness', trembling and vibrating on her 'startled ear' and in her 'quaking heart' and 'through her spirit', making her exult 'as if in joy over the success of one effort it had been privileged to make, independent of the cumbrous body' (*JE*, 421). As she approaches Thornfield Hall, Jane unfolds the events that have taken place there in her absence, learning from the innkeeper's narrative that Bertha Mason has started a fire, and Rochester has been injured attempting to save his servants and Bertha (who jumps to her death from the battlements). Rochester's injury represents a challenge to both the visual and tactile, as 'he is stone-blind'. A beam had fallen in such a way so as to knock one eye out, inflame the other, and crush his hand. 'He is now helpless, indeed – blind and a cripple' (*JE*, 429).

More specifically for the purposes of my discussion here, Rochester's blindness tests the way in which the literary word is produced and consumed through the senses. Firstly, as a textual device blindness merges the figure of the reader and narrator in relation to Rochester following Jane's first sight of him in Ferndean. Jane *reads* Rochester, who in his blindness is like a text, having no consciousness that he is looked at and interpreted: 'I stood to watch him – to examine him, myself unseen, and alas! To him invisible' (*JE*, 431). This initially grants Jane and the reader power, as, privileged with sight (the reader shares Jane's viewpoint here), they may look at Rochester whilst he cannot return their watchfulness (or even be aware he is the object of scrutiny).[25] It is helpful here to draw on Rosemarie Garland-Thomson's account of the generative, rather than oppressive, aspects of staring, in which starers and starees are yoked together in a mutually defining process that enables identity to emerge through interactive processes.[26] Jane's watching of Rochester initiates a series of new and productive encounters between the pair that redefines both of their identities, not least in terms of disability and caring. Christopher Gabbard, for example, highlights the subject-position shift that occurs at this point of the narrative as Rochester, former caregiver to Bertha, switches places to occupy the disabled position. Gabbard argues further that the story of disability at the conclusion signals a 'new beginning' and the 'hope of reform'.[27] As Martha Stoddard Holmes also observes, the novel distinctly and innovatively enacts a 'desire *for* disability', which doesn't simply mobilise gender power shifts or present an opportunity for service but is rather part of a 'sexual aesthetic', a point also emphasised by Margaret Rose Torrell.[28] In facilitating a renewed intimacy between the pair, Rochester's blindness is far from being an event that 'either ruin's one life or ends one text', as Maren Linett suggests.[29]

Indeed, Rochester's blindness also marks the *beginning* of Jane's narrative and text. Rochester, blinded, invites language and narration; he is the creative impetus for Jane's autobiography to proceed:

> Literally I was (what he often called me) the apple of his eye. He saw nature, he saw books through me; and never did I weary of gazing for his behalf, and of putting into words the effect of field, tree, town, river, cloud, sunbeam – of the landscape before us, of the weather round us – and impressing by sound on his ear what light could no longer stamp on his eye. (*JE*, 451)

In his blindness, Rochester prompts Jane to become an audible narrator as he is not only read, but also read *to*, eliciting description and narrative from Jane. Like Dickens's Bertha Plummer, whom I discuss in the next chapter, his blindness does not merely mark a feminised helplessness or passivity to the gaze. Instead, his sight loss signifies the conditions necessary for narration to begin and marks Jane's transition from portrait painter to writer, as words and language become the tools with which to appeal to the imagination. Through alternative modes of communication, Rochester is not a 'sightless block', as he initially fears he will be, incapable of authentic feeling outside of the visual. Rochester's blindness invites both Jane and the reader to participate in a wider sensorium beyond the visual. He develops a subjectivity through other senses, and through Jane's translation of visual experience for him: 'I described to him how brilliantly green [the fields] were; how the flowers and hedges looked refreshed; how sparklingly blue was the sky' (*JE*, 439). He tells her that 'all the melody on earth is concentrated in my Jane's tongue to my ear (I am glad it is not naturally a silent one): all the sunshine I can feel is in her presence' (*JE*, 439). The renewed relationship between Jane and Rochester, and the shifts in subject positions that it engenders in both, should not be seen at the expense of disability. Rather, as Torrell argues in her assessment of Rochester as 'an unusually progressive portrait of disabled masculinity', their new relations facilitate a 'significant rewriting of the terms of gender and ability'.[30]

Jane's voice is a more successful delineator of the phenomenal world than Rochester's hand, for although Jane records upon first sight of him that 'he seemed to wish by touch to gain an idea of what lay round him: he met but vacancy still' (*JE*, 431). This detail alerts us to contemporary debates concerning blind people's compensatory powers of touch. Indeed, textures of tactile literacy are discernible in Brontë's first novel, *The Professor*, in which, as William Cohen points out, the characters William and Frances, like Brontë, are nearsighted and 'figuratively ... like the blind, read with their hands'.[31] Rochester's manual dexterity and tactile acuity are, however, compromised by his accompanying physical impairment as an amputee, which makes him as a reader reliant upon audio description, rather than easily able to learn new techniques of finger reading. Jane describes to Rochester 'field, tree, town, river, cloud, sunbeam', seemingly faithfully delineating nature, offering to 'read to him' and be his 'eyes and hands' (*JE*, 435). Rochester is identified as a more passive reader, who must experience text through the sensory faculties of Jane, who both sees the world for him and translates it into sound. He is identified more with the practice of reading aloud for blind people which, as Chapter 3 traced, was treated with increasing unease by blind educators and evangelists keen to facilitate a more direct and active engagement between blind people and reading material through touch. Rochester's manual impairment through the loss of his left hand marks a certain counter to the optimism which characterised the first decades of embossed printing in Britain to renew blind people's spiritual salvation, which Rochester instead finds through Jane as interpreter. Yet the boundary between body and text is obscured in these final episodes, with Jane herself also figured as an embossed text, as Rochester reads her tactilely, seizing her with his 'muscular hand' and recognising her through her 'small, slight fingers' (*JE*, 433).

Rochester's blindness bears further layers of autobiographical inscription, allying him with Brontë's father, Patrick, who around the time *Jane Eyre* was published had undergone successful cataract surgery to reverse the steady loss of his eyesight. Rochester and Jane's trip to London to seek the advice of an 'eminent oculist' after Rochester begins to regain his sight (*JE*, 451) echoes Charlotte accompanying Patrick in his visits to ophthalmologists in Manchester, whilst his suitability for surgery was assessed and diagnosed. This complicates somewhat the binary between sighted and blind that David Bolt identifies in the novel, when he argues that 'Brontë portrays someone with a visual impairment but takes into account only the experience of people with unimpaired vision'.[32] Rather, her depiction of blindness is grounded by an intimate experience of caring for someone with sight loss, within a contemporary ophthalmologic discourse that laid emphasis on the hereditary nature of that particular form of visual impairment and thus blurred the distinction between father and daughter, patient and carer.

Patrick Brontë's operation was performed in August 1846. It lasted a quarter of an hour, was conducted without an anaesthetic and resulted in the complete extraction of the left lens. Charlotte was present in the room throughout. She described the event in a letter to her friend Ellen Nussey two days later. It had been Ellen's cousin's husband, William Carr – a physician and the 'Mr Carr' mentioned in the letter – who had advised Patrick to undergo surgery. Charlotte recorded:

> The affair lasted precisely a quarter of an hour; it was not the simple operation of couching Mr Carr described, but the more complicated one of extracting the cataract – Mr Wilson entirely disapproves of couching. Papa displayed the most extraordinary patience and firmness, the surgeons seemed surprised. I was in the room all the time, as it was his wish that I should be there – of course, I neither spoke nor moved till the thing was done.[33]

In the lead-up to the operation, Charlotte read medical texts around the nature of cataracts and the surgical procedures Patrick would undergo, learning the differences between the extraction and couching of the cataract.[34] Almost certainly she would have read the family's copy of Thomas John Graham's *Modern Domestic Medicine* (first published in 1826 and reissued several times throughout the first half of the century). Patrick Brontë annotated the family's copy with an in-depth description of the operation, noting the 'very acute pains' resulting from expansion of the pupil after the application of belladonna, a poisonous substance, and the 'not intolerable' burning sensation which lasted 15 minutes during the operation itself.[35]

Both Patrick's experience of the cataract and Charlotte's understanding of it as a medical condition influenced the representation of Rochester's blindness, perhaps not least by making it a condition which could be cured, rather than a new state of being for Rochester. Patrick and Rochester are both returned to some degree of sight (although not perfect vision; the extraction of Patrick's left lens would have left him, like Rochester, without visual focus). This experience also demonstrates further Sally Shuttleworth's compelling observation of the ways in which Charlotte Brontë's writing was part of a wider textual economy, which crucially encompassed medical tracts. Shuttleworth's study focuses on the absorption of and active engagement with contemporary psychological discourse in Brontë's writing, evidenced from an analysis of the reading patterns in the Haworth parsonage and surrounding community. In so doing, Shuttleworth explores how Brontë's fiction gave rise 'to new ways of expressing and conceptualising the embodied self'.[36] Patrick Brontë's being a vicar reminds us of the wealth of religious and spiritual metaphors of blindness available to Charlotte. Yet his acute interest in medicine, as well as his treatment as a medical patient, also opened up to Charlotte the increasingly scientific methods of interpreting the human body and curing its diseases, notably of the eye (as Shuttleworth observes, Haworth parsonage was a household 'where medical authority was constantly brought to bear').[37] As clergyman, Patrick Brontë would also have been expected to play a role in parish medical care. Moreover, his 'fascination with medical science, and with the inter-relations between the body and mind, went far beyond the bounds of professional duty ... Every symptom, whether of mental or physical ill-health, was closely scrutinised and checked against the near-infallible words of his secular Bible, Graham's *Domestic Medicine*, which was then checked against the wisdom of other medical texts'.[38]

Janis Caldwell notes how Charlotte, like her father, took a lay interest in medicine, demonstrating less faith in the kind of natural health promoted by domestic medical texts, and more in doctors and their interventions.[39] Charlotte was versed in the burgeoning textual construction of blindness and diseases of the eye in ophthalmologic discourses. The ophthalmologists whom Graham mentions in his section on 'Cataract', including Beer, Travers, Lawrence and Saunders, published increasingly detailed textbooks on the structure and function of the eye, and the diagnosis of different diseases and injuries which might beset it. By analysing early nineteenth-century ophthalmological treatises alongside Charlotte's literary texts, we can identify the cross-fertilisation of ideas concerning blindness across different disciplines. For example, cataracts were also understood to be caused by inflammation and structural aberrations to the eye resulting from accidents, and this understanding informs the description of Rochester's eye injuries. Graham's *Domestic Medicine* explicitly states that should a cataract result from a serious injury, 'the lens frequently recovers its transparency without any operation being necessary'.[40]

In many of the medical discourses, defects in vision were commonly associated with the engagement of literary pursuits – John Stevenson notes in one of the earliest ophthalmologic texts, published in 1810, *On the Morbid Sensibility of the Eye, Commonly Called Weakness of Sight*, that 'the instances of the weakness of sight, which occurred in the early part of my ophthalmic practice' were frequently brought on 'by inordinate indulgence in literary pursuits protracted frequently to late hours', often in dark spaces due to the expense of lighting.[41] The poet Milton was regularly invoked as a famous example of the dangers of literary pursuits upon the eyes.

Patrick clearly assumed the role of literary father to his daughters, exerting an important influence on their own taste and reading of texts, including Milton, as Elsie B. Michie notes.[42] His experience of the cataract identified him with Milton in other, more literal ways, as he became dependent upon others to be his eyes and hands in reading and writing. Charlotte described the impact of the cataract upon him:

> His sight diminishes weekly and can it be wondered at – that as he sees the most precious of his faculties leaving him, his spirits sometimes sink? It is so hard to feel that his few and scanty pleasures must all soon go – he now has the greatest difficulty in either reading or writing – and then he dreads the state of dependence to which blindness will inevitably reduce him.[43]

Having a cataract emphasises to Patrick Brontë that writing is a material act, centred in a body and mediated through supplementary technologies. This writing is also gendered; it is now borne by female hands, as Patrick comes to rely increasingly upon his daughters to act as his amanuenses.[44] It is easy to see how Charlotte would have identified with popular images and narratives of Milton circulating in the nineteenth century, in which his daughters reluctantly transcribe the speech of their blind father. Whilst Bolt argues that *Jane Eyre* is grounded in the same epistemology as Milton's *Samson Agonistes*, which is 'ocularcentric in the extreme', Brontë's engagement with Milton's biography opened up a rather different relationship between blindness and writing. Indeed, Brontë's novelistic project complexly repurposed the Miltonic myth and provided influential new ways to imagine the relationship between blindness and writing, as my discussion of Ford Madox Brown's portrait of Henry and Millicent Garrett Fawcett argued in Chapter 1.

This point returns us to critical interpretations of the symbolic resonances of blindness in Brontë's literary imagination. Gilbert and Gubar outline the 'many women writers who directly or indirectly recorded anxieties about [Milton's] paradigmatic patriarchal poetry', listing Charlotte and Emily Brontë, as well as Elizabeth Barrett Browning, whose 1843 poem *Upon Eden: A Drama of Exile* addressed her relationship to Milton.[45] More recent scholarship has, however, re-evaluated the model of anxiety that informs analysis of Milton's influence on nineteenth-century literary culture. Catherine Maxwell has recently shown how allied images of Miltonic blindness and the poet's inner illumination can be seen to ground the eighteenth-century sublime, with Milton's symbolic language co-identifying blindness, castration and feminisation as the necessary loss for the true compensatory vision – a particularly rich model for re-thinking

Milton's influence upon male poets of the nineteenth century.[46] Anna K. Nardo also challenges Gilbert and Gubar's study through a rehistoricised focus on Milton's influence, this time upon women writers of the nineteenth century, exploring how 'women writers in fact construct authorial selves-in-process out of already authorised language, the only language available'.[47] Nardo argues that George Eliot's inheritance of Milton's authoritative language and authoritative discourse about Milton offers a counter to the dictum that he had a debilitating effect on nineteenth-century women writers.[48] Gaskell's construction of Brontë as a blind writer also turned on this notion. For Brontë to achieve creative potency, Gaskell suggested she needed to impair her physical sight, mirroring her literal and poetic father's threatened castration. This marked a complex realignment of Brontë with Milton grounded in the real, for Brontë aligned the figure of Rochester with her father, Patrick, and Milton, whilst Gaskell looked to Brontë's own experiences of visual impairment as she attributed biographical meaning to her novels.

Eighteenth-century and early nineteenth-century readers were not merely interested in Milton's poetry; there was also a huge fascination with his life, marriage, blindness and his troubled relationship with his daughters. One significant example is William Hayley's biography of Milton, published in 1797, which offered a corrective view to Samuel Johnson's tyrannical account of him in his *Lives of the Poets* (1781). Hayley connects the ups and downs of Milton's romantic life to his political writings on the divorce laws, by tracing his separation from his unsuitable first wife, and his near-attachments to other women, including a Miss Davis, whilst still married. Nardo points out certain similarities between Hayley's biography and Brontë's novel – 'Hayley's dramatic account of Miss Davis's plight reads (at first) like the plot of *Jane Eyre*' – suggesting intriguingly how Brontë may have used Milton's *Life* to structure her fictional autobiography.[49] This is paralleled in Elizabeth Gaskell's use of blindness as a way to structure experience and events in her construction of Brontë as writer in the first official biography of Brontë, published two years after the novelist's death.

## Structuring Experience through Visual Impairment in *The Life of Charlotte Brontë*

Blindness structures *The Life of Charlotte Brontë*, as the second volume opens with Patrick Brontë facing blindness as a result of his worsening cataracts. This event marks a semi-crisis in Gaskell's narrative. The Brontës faced financial hardship should Patrick become blind; Charlotte's manuscript for *The Professor* had also just been rejected. Gaskell writes:

> During this summer of 1846, while her literary hopes were waning, an anxiety of another kind was increasing. Her father's eyesight had become seriously impaired by the progress of the cataract which was forming. He was nearly blind. (*LCB*, 229)

Patrick Brontë's impaired vision is figured tragically (he was 'driven inwards' by the cataracts), until the medical miracle of his restoration to sight occurs, which provides the narrative with a model of enlightenment and progress as the Brontë family are, momentarily at least, lifted from the darkness of the preceding volume, reinforcing a model of blindness as tragedy (*LCB*, 229). Gaskell's biography implicitly identifies Rochester with Brontë's father. The reviewer of the biography in *Blackwood's Edinburgh Magazine* noted that the eccentricities of character that Patrick Brontë stood accused of 'are but the evolution of the Rochester character, which as displayed in its entirety, women, at least, if not men, admire so much in the novel'.[50] As Brontë's narrator begins her narrative from a point of blindness, Gaskell directs the reader of her biography to see *Jane Eyre* itself proceeding from the experience of blindness. She writes that 'the brave genius', having received a rejection for *The Professor* on the very day her father underwent his operation, nevertheless persevered with her writing; and, 'in this time of care and inquietude', began *Jane Eyre*. Furthermore, Gaskell exhorts us to 'think of [Brontë's] home, and the black shadow of remorse lying over one in it … think of her father's sight hanging on a thread … and then admire as it deserves to be admired, the steady courage which could work away at *Jane Eyre*', all the time 'that the one-volume tale was plodding its weary round in London' (*LCB*, 233).

The trope of impaired vision helps give structure to the disparate threads and material traces of Brontë's life in Gaskell's biography. Attention is drawn repeatedly to Brontë's shortsightedness, and Gaskell, especially in the first volume, points to letters in which Brontë speaks of being inconvenienced by the loss of her spectacles and in which she jokes of employing an amanuensis. This also affected her composition process, as she would compose on bits of paper 'in a minute hand', a plan 'necessary for one so short-sighted', with her finished manuscripts being copied from these pencil scraps 'in clear, legible, delicate traced writing, almost as easy to read as print' (*LCB*, 234). Explicitly, Gaskell comments upon Brontë's fear of going blind herself, noting that one of her daily employments 'was to read to her father, and, that in secret, she, too dreaded a similar loss of vision for herself', having a 'dread of ultimate blindness' at this time (*LCB*, 207–8). The association between shortsightedness and cataracts in the medical discourses of the period also add weight to Brontë's fears, the ophthalmologist Wardrop commenting that 'near objects can be more distinctly seen that those which are remote; and thus a person affected with cataract appears short-sighted'. Moreover, Wardrop continues: 'in some cases, cataract appears to be hereditary'.[51]

Brontë articulates this anxiety that impaired vision will curtail her literary ambitions in a letter quoted by Gaskell to her French professor, Monsieur Heger (to whom she was romantically attached):

> *mais à prèsent, j'ai la vue trop faible; si j'écrivais beaucoup je deviendrai aveugle. Cette faiblesse de vue est pour moi une terrible privation; sans cela, savez-vous ce que je ferais, Monsieur? J'écrirais un livre et je le dédierais à mon maître de littérature.*
>
> (But, presently, my eyesight is very weak; if I write too much, I shall become blind. This weak vision is a terrible loss to me; for without it, do you know what I would do, Monsieur? I would write a book and I would dedicate it to my literature teacher.)[52]

Whilst weak eyesight prompted Brontë to turn from the visual to the verbal arts, she signals here how visual impairment also hindered her literary ambitions, and expresses her fears that writing itself will further damage her vision. This turns on an assumption that writing was a visual medium dependent upon the healthy functioning of the eyes which – mechanistically – might be compromised by over-use. And whilst Juliet Barker argues that 'the failing eyesight of which Brontë complained seems to have been a purely imaginary affliction, symptomatic of her depressed state of mind', medical treatises emphasising the relationship between shortsightedness and the hereditary nature of the cataract, may have added to her anxiety of going blind. However, Brontë's handwriting seems to suggest that, in reality, her sight was relatively stable. Barker observes:

> Her letters to Monsieur Heger and Ellen Nussey show no sign of any difficulty with her eyes: the writing is as tiny, neat and meticulous as ever and, on occasion, a long letter is packed into a half sheet of paper divided into four pages. This is in stark contrast to Patrick, whose approaching blindness is fully borne out by his increasingly large and untidy writing, uncharacteristically marked with blots and heavily punctuated as he paused, pen in hand, to peer at what he had written.[53]

The material production of writing is tied to the condition of the eyes, as Brontë observes her father's writing break down with the progression of his cataracts. Blindness threatens to quite literally blot out his ability to write and read. Brontë's preoccupation with her father's failing eyesight and the recurrent and repetitive nature of this anxiety in her imagination contributed to a general state of depression at this time. Circuitously, this manifested itself as a fear of the physical condition of blindness which might also prove a significant obstacle to her literary ambitions. Her neurotic construction of blindness emerged in part from her own struggle for self-identity in the 1840s, as she attempted to establish herself as a published author.

Literary theorist Paul de Man draws upon the trope of blindness to put forward a model of critical reading grounded upon simultaneous and reciprocal processes of blindness and insight. In his essay 'The Rhetoric of Blindness', he asks: 'what characteristic aspect of literary language causes blindness in those who come into close contact with it?'[54] Gaskell's text, as a reading of Brontë's fiction, is certainly reliant upon a certain conscious rhetoric of blindness in setting forward a life which is problematised by the nature of its evidence. De Man decentres the author from his account of rhetoric, arguing that 'the question as to whether the author himself is or is not blinded is to some extent irrelevant; it can only be asked heuristically, as a means to accede to the true question: whether his language is or is not blind to its own statement'.[55] Blindness remains metaphorical in De Man's theory, as a force or trope that prevents the author from seeing the object of his or her text truly as it is: it marks a certain failure of interpretative communication between writers and their readers at the ideational level of language. However, Gaskell's interest in Brontë's experience of blindness is shaped by her culture's wider investigation of the ways in which writing and reading are embodied acts, and as such must also be taken as a reflection on the material and corporeal conditions of writing and reading. The experience of blindness, then, facilitates a move back to the author's body. (As Naomi Schor argues, the full force of metaphor is not acknowledged in De Man's essay, because the body keeps returning, as disfigured.)[56] In Brontë's literary writing, the figures of blindness she inscribes are shaped by her own experience and anxiety of visual disorders which alert us to a pervasive concern in her texts with the ways in which books have a material existence, contingent upon an embodied reader and writer. Metaphors of blindness thus bear an uncanny force of real, literal presence in *Jane Eyre*. This re-emerges in Elizabeth Barrett Browning's epic poem of the growth of the woman writer, in which the text's figuration of blindness also brings us back to the body of its author.

## Blindness and Autobiography: *Aurora Leigh*

*Aurora Leigh* is as much a poem on what it means to see clearly as it is on the growth of the woman poet's mind. Whilst, as Deirdre David points out, *Aurora Leigh* is a poem pervaded by metaphors of writing,[57] eyes also pervade and populate the text; they are one of the most frequently referred to objects in the poem.[58] As well as examining what it means to write as a woman, *Aurora Leigh* is a complex interrogation of the potency of poetry as an intervention in contemporary political, social and moral debates. This is an interrogation which is often figured through the visual, as the speaker famously asserts:

> But poets should
> Exert a double vision; should have eyes
> To see near things as comprehensively
> As if afar they took their point of sight,
> And distant things, as intimately deep
> As if they touched them.[59]

This manifesto occurs at a point in the text when the speaker is exhorting poets to look to their own age for subject matter, arguing that in so doing the poet is in a unique position to intervene in contemporary social problems. This is part of a recurrent dialogue, in which Aurora compares the function and use of her role, and Art, to that of her cousin Romney, who seeks to effect social change through civic and political structures. Yet as we traced in Brontë's writing, the speaker inscribes here a certain ambivalence about distance vision. It is not enough to have a sweeping, masculine visual perspective – a 'power of vision', as Jane Eyre terms it. Rather, true understanding is understood to emerge from a vision that works together with the hand – that incorporates the more intimate, and feminine, mode of touch that is also intimately associated with the perceptual faculties of blind people.

The relationship between poetry and vision is a concern which pervaded much of Barrett Browning's writings. In her early poem from 1826, *An Essay on Mind*, the young Elizabeth Barrett outlined her views on the relationship between philosophy and poetry, defending the high intellectual position of poetry, frequently through its relation to the visual. In her preface to the poem, she defended poetry against the criticism that it is not a proper vehicle for abstract ideas. Rather, she argued that the example of Francis Bacon signalled the compatibility of the imaginative with the philosophic. It was, she stressed, Bacon's (and John Locke's) investigations into the relation between parts and whole that had 'assisted me in my trembling endeavour to trace the outline of these branches of knowledge'.[60] The speaker frequently appeals to 'light' to 'instruct her pen' to help cure the 'moral darkness' of the age (*EM*, I: 39, 106), as she invokes a theory of poetry which moves from the inner to outer (as Kate Flint also identifies in *Aurora Leigh*).[61] It is the poet, above the historian and scientist (recognised as potentially prejudiced), who, 'impartial', learns to 'trace the errors which her eyes discern; / View ev'ry side, investigate each part', using ink 'to write with – not to blot' (*EM*, I: 292–7). Sensory knowledge is important to Barrett, who takes issue with the idealist philosopher George Berkeley for trying to prove 'an old hypothesis! / "Out on the senses!" (he was out of his!)' (*EM*, II: 721–2). Mind is 'imprisoned in a lonesome tower', which, through gazing outward of its window, 'marks in outwards substance, inward sense'. Thus from the forming of 'first perceptions' we find the 'operations of the forming mind', which leads us to 'Reason', abstract 'Thought', and 'the faculties of Intellect' (*EM*, II: 739–58). Finally, the speaker concludes by emphasising the uniquely penetrating sight of the poet:

> And while Philosophy, in spirit, free,
> Reasons, believes, yet cannot plainly *see*,
> Poetic Rapture, to her dazzled sight,
> Pourtrays the shadows of the things of light;
> Delighting o'er the unseen worlds to roam,
> And waft the pictures of perfection home.
> (*EM*, II: 908–13)

In this early poem, Barrett Browning posits that as modes of thought, poetry, above philosophy, depends on seeing things clearly and thus as a process sets the mind free. By refuting Berkeley and upholding Locke, Barrett Browning suggests that the senses are fundamental to experience – not that experience gives meaning to our sensory perceptions.

Although Barrett Browning was later embarrassed by the poem, calling it a 'girl's exercise … nothing more, nothing less', what is interesting to note is her early development of a theory of poetry as a fullness of vision.[62] Moreover, its publication precipitated an important relationship with the blind poet and scholar, Hugh Stuart Boyd, who lived near the Barretts' home, Hope End, in Malvern. Boyd had contracted trachoma in 1811, and, unlike Wordsworth, he went totally blind, as he described in a poem published three years after the event, describing how 'gorgeous day with fervid beams / O'erpowers my dim, declining sight'.[63] Boyd had an exceptional verbal memory for Greek lines, which enabled him to continue his studies after going blind; however, he frequently sought out people who would read Greek to him. 'An Essay on Mind' caught his attention, and he wrote to its author in early 1827. An intense correspondence began, and Barrett quickly seems to have built Boyd up to be a romantic hero, his blindness very much a part of his attraction. Although they corresponded up to twice a day during 1827, they did not meet in person until 1828. Upon her first sight of him, Barrett described him as 'A rather young looking man than otherwise, moderately tall, and slightly formed. His features are good – his face very pale with an expression of placidity and mildness. He is totally blind – and from the quenched and deadened appearance of his eyes, hopelessly so!'[64] Boyd clearly appealed to a philosophic and Romantic interest in blindness in the young Barrett; soon after meeting, they began reading *Oedipus* together. Barrett addressed the nature of Boyd's blindness early on, imagining how she would be affected by blindness herself. She writes that she would 'suffer more deprivations' should she go blind, on account of her dislike of being read to, privileging a more direct relationship with text. She adds: 'The eyes of your memory however are both microscopic and telescopic – and will see further than any eyes physical or intellectual, that I know anything about.'[65] The eyes of Hugh Stuart Boyd, whilst physically blind, exert a double vision; not in terms of a transcendental vision, but in looking back through the past, suggesting the continuation of Boyd's sight through his visual memory.

In their early letters, Barrett and Boyd discuss intellectual topics covering the classics, philosophy and theology, and Boyd gradually assumes the role of her teacher. Barrett also acted as Boyd's amanuensis, although she was distressed when her father refused to allow her to do so in 1832, due to her ill health: she describes herself as 'turning into a shadow, thinner and thinner every day'. She also notes in this letter: 'how much pleasure it gives me to write to your dictation – to write even a letter'.[66] As their relationship faltered in the early 1830s, and Barrett faced the prospect of their separation (from when they first met in person they spent long periods of time together, with Barrett often staying for days at a time in his house), she wrote a letter describing her pain at losing him from her vision:

> Have I not asked again and again about going to see you, whenever there is a slightest chance of my receiving a favourable answer? ... Do you not think *in your heart* that I lost more pleasure, in not going to see you, than *you* did? – and that it gives me more pain at this moment to feel that I cannot see you, than it gives you?[67]

Barrett is rendered blind by this separation: she literally cannot see Boyd because of the propriety of social conventions.

Paradoxically, Barrett and Boyd grew close again when her relationship with Robert Browning started, and Boyd acted as a confidante during the pair's marriage plans.[68] He was also the first person she saw after the marriage took place. Her last letters to Boyd, written from Italy, feel different in tone and texture to her previous correspondence. Her writing is infused with a life that one senses comes from being freed of the interiority of writing to which she was confined in her sickroom, as she vividly describes the phenomenal world. Speaking to her blind interlocutor, her writing trips itself up with its urgency to recount things seen and experienced, not only through the visual; she makes reference to sound and touch, the heat of the sun, and coolness of stone. She documents the dazzling nature of this newly emergent world, describing joyfully how in Florence she has 'seen the Venus … seen the divine Raphaels … I have looked at the wonderful Duomo!' Describing Florence more fully she notes:

> I had neither seen nor imagined the like of it [the Duomo] in any way … Florence is beautiful as I have said before … The river rushes through the midst of its palaces like a crystal arrow; and it is hard to tell, when you see all by the clear sunset, whether those churches and houses and windows and bridges and people walking – in the water or out of the water – are the real walls and windows and bridges and people and churches. The only difference is that, down below, there is a double movement – the movement of the stream besides the movement of life. For the rest, the distinctness to the eye is as great in one as in the other.[69]

This honeymoon letter reminds us of another (fictional) bride in Italy, George Eliot's Dorothea Brookes. However, the exhilaration of vision Elizabeth Barrett Browning registers here is the opposite of Dorothea's visual bewilderment, in which the relics of Rome appear as a funeral, viewed from afar. Dorothea is metaphorically blind to the objects and the art she sees in Rome because, without experience (and love), she can neither make sense of nor interpret the visual data before her. Barrett Browning sees things too clearly – everything is distinct to the eye, and, in doubting the reality of the churches, houses, people, it is as though everything is hyperrealised, much like a pre-Raphaelite canvas. There is another similarity between Barrett Browning and Dorothea, as Casaubon's character echoes Boyd's. Both are antiquated scholars, one literally blind, the other figured as losing his sight, motivated by systems of learning and knowledge slipping into archaism. However, Barrett Browning writes from the vantage point of her honeymoon to Robert Browning, a younger poet and artist. One senses her own sexual freedom, allowing her to find her voice and self through the male other, as the object of love.

The importance of her relationship with Boyd was acknowledged in three poems she published after his death, which also commented on his blindness. In these poems, he is, like Rochester to Jane Eyre, represented as an idol, a towering figure: in the poem 'Hugh Stuart Boyd: His Blindness', she writes: 'God would not let the spheric Light accost / This God-loved man'.[70] Reflecting on his legacy, she remembers acting as his amanuensis, and is blinded by her own tears at his death:

> The books were those I used to read from, thus
> Assisting my dear teacher's soul to unlock
> The darkness of his eyes: now, mine they mock,
> Blinded in turn, by tears: now, murmurous
> Sad echoes of my young voice, years agone.[71]

One of the central roles Barrett assumed was as Boyd's literary assistant and reader. Boyd's blindness threatened his scholarly identity, closing books off to him without the intervention of another. Barrett's encounter with blindness raised profound questions about her intellectual, emotional and material vision that are in part reinscribed in the figure of Romney Leigh.

The special relationship between love and blindness in Barrett's imagination is also indicated in the terms in which she and Robert Browning presented themselves to each other in letters exchanged during their courtship. Figuring herself as blind in correspondence with Browning allowed her, by extension, to confirm herself as writer, an intellectual and visionary undisturbed by the limitations of physical vision. However, as she invokes this figuration she simultaneously resists it, longing for a different relationship between the body and the world. She affirms to Browning early on in their correspondence that she is 'a *blind poet*'; enclosed in her sick room, she is advantaged in that she has had 'much of the inner life – & from the habit of selfconsciousness & selfanalysis, I make great guesses at Human Nature in the main'. However, she also would 'willingly' exchange 'some of this lumbering, ponderous helpless knowledge of books, for some experience of life & man'.[72] She seems to have realised this new vision in her honeymoon letters, quoted above. These early courtship letters are permeated by a discourse of vision, which springs from their initial physical absence from each other's company. Reading their correspondence, one is struck by how intimate the relationship between love and vision is to them, in their anticipation of seeing each other, seeing through the eyes of the other, grasping at the initially few occasions when they might see each other, and be with each other. In one letter, written shortly before their marriage took place, Barrett reflects on how she might appear to Browning, in the eyes of others. Referring to Browning's shortsightedness, she continues:

> … & you draw crooked inferences for me, shutting *both* the eyes … the near-sighted eye & far-sighted eye. Or is it, in that strange sight of yours, that I walk between the far & near objects, in an invisible security? Or is it (which were best) that I am too near, to be seen even by the near-sighted eye, … like a hand brought close to the eyelashes, which, for over-closeness, nobody can see? *Let* me be too near to be seen – always too near … Never will I complain that you do not see me![73]

Here, Barrett draws upon Browning's eye condition to find this 'invisible security' for herself, voicing the hope that Browning will be fully in her presence, through being blind to the sight of her; that her proximity of self will overwhelm both his eyes and her visual appearance. Here, Barrett privileges the touch of a visually impaired person – 'a hand brought close to the eyelashes' – rather than the scrutiny of the gaze. She continues to write that, since knowing Browning, she has also understood how 'Love is better than Sight, & Love will do without Sight'. This intimacy engendered by blindness also shapes her treatment of it in her poem *Aurora Leigh*, in which Aurora – like Jane – gains her love object following his blindness. Aurora is, however, already a published author, but her inability to interpret Romney's blindness points to the limits both of her vision and the hermeneutics of the text.

Romney's blindness in *Aurora Leigh* is a central episode in the poem, with clear parallels to Rochester's blinding in *Jane Eyre*. In the extended dialogue between Romney and Aurora at the poem's end, it emerges that Romney has been blinded by an injury received in the fire that destroys his utopian socialist community, as Leigh Hall is burned down by a group of aggrieved poachers. As Rochester is blinded as a result of an injury received in a fire caused by Bertha, the similarities between the two events, both in nature and in their relative positions in the text appear to be clear enough. Yet when a friend noted this to Barrett Browning, she was surprised, and sent for a copy of *Jane Eyre* to compare the events (which she appears to have read between 1848 and 1850). Whilst acknowledging the similarities, she was also at pains to point out the differences between Romney's and Rochester's blinding:

> as far as I do recall the facts, the hero was monstrously disfigured and blinded in a fire the particulars of which escape me, and the circumstance of his being hideously scarred is the thing impressed chiefly on the reader's mind; certainly it remains innermost in mine.

For Barrett Browning, it is the *visibility* of Rochester's blinding that is the most striking, not the necessity of his punishment or the sensuality of invisibility that the episode precipitates. Moreover, she disputes similarity in the cause of their blindness, as Romney did '*not* lose his eyes in the fire'; thus he was still able to describe the ruin of his house 'as no blind man could. He was standing there, a spectator'. Indeed, Romney resembles Milton, not Rochester, for 'afterwards he had a fever, and the eyes, the visual nerve, perished, showing no external strain – perished as Milton's did'. Barrett Browning understands that this is physiologically plausible, believing that 'a great shock on the nerves might produce such an effect in certain constitutions'.[74] Barrett Browning defends the originality of Romney's blinding; yet her seemingly unconscious borrowing from the plot of *Jane Eyre* is perhaps indicative of the significance of Brontë's novel to her as reader, and woman writer.

At a symbolic level, Deirdre David argues that 'Romney's literal blinding seems to be a punishment for his political blindness ... If Brontë punishes Rochester for his vaunting masculinity, as some critics believe, then Barrett Browning certainly punishes Romney for his politics'.[75] The blinding of Romney also demonstrates, like Rochester's blindness, an anxiety about the female writer's relationship to the patriarchal order. Angela Leighton outlines the symbolic importance of the father figure in Barrett Browning's writing, arguing that 'it is the father who stands for that "Other" against which her poetry shapes itself and grows strong', arguing that the politics of her relation to him are essentially different to that of the male poet and his muse.[76] Barrett Browning dedicated her 1844 collection of poetry to her father, writing that 'it is my fancy thus to seem to return to a visible personal dependence on you, as if indeed I were a child again; to conjure your beloved image between myself and the public, so as to be sure of one smile'.[77] Elizabeth Barrett Browning describes a relationship in which she, as a daughter presenting herself as poet, stands visible before her father.

There is, however, another dynamic that structures the relationship between blindness and the female creative self in Barrett Browning's text: that of the maternal. Kathleen Blake, charting the similarities between *The Prelude* and *Aurora Leigh*, notes the importance of the absence of maternal figures in both texts. The death of the speaker's mother in both *Prelude* (after which the speaker seems to replace the child's babbling with full speech) and in *Aurora Leigh* seems to uphold a Lacanian reading, suggesting that access to the symbolic realm of language can only occur with the separation from the maternal. According to Freud, the absence of the maternal seems a necessary part of the Oedipus complex in relation to girls, as, although the mother is the original object (what Lacan would term 'desire') of the complex, girls abandon that object for their father. Freud attributes this – the way in which the feminine constitutes its sexual difference – to penis envy. It marks a sense of lack and it develops 'like a scar, a sense of inferiority'.[78] Although in boys the 'Oedipus complex is destroyed by the castration complex', in girls 'it is made possible and led up to by the castration complex'.[79] The fear of castration, and blindness as its substitute, which foregrounds the experience of sexual difference, are simultaneously aligned with the disappearance of the maternal. For Freud, this is more straightforwardly an 'intelligible consequence of the anatomical distinction between [the sexes'] genitals, and of the psychical situation involved in it'.[80] Yet these texts demonstrate a more fluid and performative construction of gender, as the bodies producing them, whilst still an important site for the expression and meaning of femininity and masculinity, do not necessarily determine those categories. More subtle invocations of maternal figures and metaphors, as well as the more complex relationship between vision and masculinity, signal the complexity of gender identities in these texts.

This is also evident in Dinah Craik's interesting reworking of *Jane Eyre* in her novel *Olive* (1850), in which the 'deformed' Olive's mother, Sybilla Rothesay, is blinded, seemingly as a caution against her girlish privileging of superficial beauty and initial rejection of her baby daughter for her one 'defect': 'an elevation of the shoulders' which shortened her neck, 'giving an appearance of a perpetual stoop'.[81] Craik's novel also interrogates the gender politics of cultural production, through the exchanges between the struggling artist, Mr Vanbrugh, and his would-be-protégée, Olive, who chooses art as a career because her bodily imperfection seemingly rules her out of the marriage market. Despite Mr Vanbrugh's prejudice that 'Genius, the mighty one, does not exist in weak female nature' (*Olive*, 123), Olive, who has 'almost a masculine power of mind' (*Olive*, 127), succeeds in selling her artwork, enabling her to pay off her dead father's debt to Harold Gwynne (whom she later marries). The narrator reminds us as well that there have been women painters, listing Angelica Kauffman and Properzia Rossi. Vanbrugh's sister Meliora tells Olive: 'if you read about the old Italian masters, you will find that many of them had wives, or daughters, or sisters, who helped them a great deal' (*Olive*, 118). Yet Sybilla's weak female gaze – which can only constitute itself through imagining what the male gaze would like to look upon – is checked by failing vision and ultimately blindness. The novel's representational system refuses to allow her to look upon Olive's paintings (which must then be mediated to her through the verbal):

> Gradually there had come over Mrs Rothesay the misfortune which she once feared. She was now quite blind … Her sight faded so gradually, that its deprivation caused no despondency; and the more helpless she grew, the closer she was clasped by those supporting arms of filial love, which softened all pain, supplied all need, and were to her instead of strength, youth, eyesight!
>
> Only one bitterness did she know – that she could not see Olive's pictures. Not that she understood Art at all; but everything that Olive did *must* be beautiful. (*Olive*, 140)

Sybilla's view of beauty shifts over the course of the novel; she understands here that beauty is something that springs from Olive's actions, and is not just attached to the woman as a passive object. Craik's novel proposes then a radically alternate mode of seeing, in which a visibly different female body is granted the role of artist and cultural producer. Although Olive's marriage to Harold conservativises the text's more radical vision, as the narrator accepts she 'should almost forget her own' fame in deference to her husband's, the novel suggestively allows a more powerful feminine gaze to play out.

Structurally, *Aurora Leigh* begins and ends with two figures of blindness; the last, Romney, is portrayed as a spiritual figure overlooking Florence as the new Jerusalem, gazing calmly, and feeding his 'blind majestic eyes / Upon the thought of perfect noon' (*AL*, 9: 960–1). The maternal is, however, the first figuration of blindness, as Aurora describes her mother's death in terms of blindness:

> I write. My mother was a Florentine,
> Whose rare blue eyes were shut from seeing me
> When scarcely I was four years old; my life
> A poor spark snatched up from a failing lamp,
> Which went out therefore …
> … As it was, indeed,
> I felt a mother-want about the world.
> (*AL*, 1: 29–33, 39–49)

Here, Aurora's assertion of poetic identity, 'I write' (which also marks the beginning of her self in writing), is metrically assimilated with her mother's identity. Aurora's 'mother-want' is a longing which comes from being outside of her mother's gaze, closed down by death. Alternatively, the harshness of her replacement-mother's gaze – her aunt's – recognises the anxiety of forming an identity within another's visual field. Her aunt's eyes are a 'burden', 'eyes that watched me, worried me … that dogged me up and down the hours and days, / A beaten, breathless, miserable soul' (*AL*, 2: 949, 945–6). Being the object of the gaze, Žižek writes, is akin to death; the voice vivifies, but the gaze mortifies.[82] Shut out from her mother's rare blue eyes, and freed from her aunt's harsh gaze, Aurora's poetic self unfurls.

However, children and pregnancy are a spectral presence in the text. The nine-book structure mirrors the nine months of pregnancy, and Marian Erle's rape and subsequent motherhood test the validity of social and moral attitudes towards proper womanhood, mirroring the challenges faced by Aurora in becoming a poet. Romney's blindness is coalescent in the poem with the book of revelations which signals genesis and so a pattern of renewal and beginnings, echoing the shut eyes of Aurora's mother. This echo suggests that Aurora's own life, and its interpretation in writing, is the creative act that will restore vision. Maternal, paternal and romantic love are collapsed in an attempt to realise what Marian yearns for as a child, a 'grand blind Love … This skyey father and mother both in one' (*AL*, 3: 987–8). Maternity is also implicated in one of the most important differences between Romney's and Rochester's blindness, which is of course that Rochester regains his sight, at least partially. This takes place around the same time as Jane becomes a mother; he can see that his newborn, legitimate son 'had inherited his own eyes, as they once were – large, brilliant, and black' (*JE*, 451). Tellingly, he recognises his son as his own, through the evidence of eyes: vision confirms his patriarchal authority. Aurora and Romney declare their love for each other, but there is no recovery of sight; and no bearing of literal, or legitimate, children.

Blindness has a complex relationship to creativity and gender in *Aurora Leigh* as the figure of the woman writer, or artist, is aligned with the figure of the blind man. In an important linguistic echo, Lady Waldemar says to Aurora:

> … You stand outside,
> You artist women, of the common sex;
> You share not with us, and exceed us so
> Perhaps by what you're mulcted in …
> (*AL*, 3: 406–9)

This resonates with Romney's description of himself when blind as 'turned out of nature, mulcted as a man' (*AL*, 9: 564). To mulct is to punish, or penalise; moreover, it is also to deprive, or to divest. Both Aurora as writer and Romney as blind stand accused of lacking that element which would make them integral woman, or man. However, the poem, in demonstrating that these categories of man, woman, writer and blind are all somehow co-dependent on each other, points to the supplementary nature of each. Aurora may strive to recover an essential selfhood; but that selfhood can only be negotiated through a series of constructed identities.

The fundamentally important association of love and blindness transforms both into a sublime experience; 'love' points to the limits of the aesthetic and social in recuperating self. As love is figured as blind, it is also portrayed as fundamentally unknoweable, or irrecoverable, and always outside the limits of experience. I am not thinking about the proverb 'love is blind' here (Naomi Schor offers an illuminating discussion of this), but rather being blind to love.[83] The final dialogue between Romney and Aurora reveals the failure of her poetic vision; she cannot claim to be all-seeing, and all-knowing, as at the poem's end she fails to recognise Romney's severance from Lady Waldemar, his intention to fulfil his duty to Marian, and his own love for her, Aurora.

Although they have been talking extensively, Aurora has not noticed Romney's blindness, despite his repeated allusions to it. He talks of the materialism of the age, invoking Christ, who gave sight to (the spiritually) 'still blind' (*AL*, 8: 647). He describes being in the dark and after telling Aurora about the burning of Leigh Hall, he cries: 'the sun is silent, but Aurora speaks' (*AL*, 8: 1024). By failing to read or interpret the signs Romney provides in this scene (in which Romney also tells Aurora that he has read her book, and understood her life), Aurora demonstrates, within her own written account, the gap between experience and judgement, and between signifier and signified, which comprises the ability to read accurately. By accepting that these moments of misreading are fundamental to experience, Aurora Leigh (and, through her, Elizabeth Barrett Browning), realises that sign and signified cannot converge; the human poet is by necessity incapable of absolute insight. Aurora's poem, standing in for her life, is ruptured by this necessary recognition that life proceeds from the gaps between what we perceive, and think we know.

Whereas 'hope' emerges at the end of *Jane Eyre* with Rochester's gradual regaining of sight, and the intervention of an oculist,[84] Romney sees 'hope' at the end of *Aurora Leigh* in his own self-enlightenment. Echoing Rochester, he 'thanks God who made me blind, to make me see' (*AL*, 9: 297). He invokes the medical terms of his blindness, only to reject the possibility of a physical cure, telling Aurora:

> … Yes, there's hope.
> Not hope of sight, – I could be learned, dear
> And tell you in what Greek and Latin name
> The visual nerve is withered to the root,

Though the outer eyes appear indifferent,
Unspotted in their crystals. But there's hope.
The spirit, from behind this dethroned sense,
Sees, waits in patience till the wall's break up
From which the bas-relief and fresco have dropt:
There's hope.

(*AL*, 9: 576–84)

Romney sees blindness as a release from the false materiality of modern life: with the breaking up of the walls in which his spirit has been caged, he can see clearly. Writing and the text are still figured as a material form that relies upon vision to bring it into being – to give it existence. Rochester's recovery of sight alternatively relocates Rochester in the phenomenal world, for although he can no longer 'read or write much', 'the sky is no longer a blank to him – the earth no longer a void' (*JE*, 451). These differing conclusions are suggestive of Barrett Browning's greater valorisation of a disabled position. Whereas experiences of blindness had clearly produced moments of anxiety in Brontë's personal life, borne out by its contradictory treatment in her text, Romney's celebration of his blindness echoes Barrett Browning's idealisation of it as a condition which helps grant intellectual and artistic insight.

Romney makes a final plea to Aurora's physical and poetical vision; calling her his 'morning-star' and 'my dear sight', he asks her:

Shine out for two … and fulfil
My falling-short that must be! Work for two,
As I, though thus restrained, for two, shall love!
Gaze on, with inscient vision toward the sun,
And from his visceral heat, pluck out the roots
Of light beyond him.

(*AL*, 9: 907–15)

Vision and love are interchangeable; Romney will love in compensation for his lack of sight. However, the appeal to Aurora to gaze on with 'inscient vision towards the sun' is interesting here. Whilst the *OED* records Barrett Browning's use as meaning to have 'inward knowledge or insight', it also lists a separate meaning: that of being unknowing, or ignorant.[85] As Romney's blindness has revealed the limits to what Aurora sees and knows, Romney's appeal to Aurora's vision as both insightful and unseeing opens up the text's sublimity.

## Conclusion

Elizabeth Barrett Browning, reading blindness in part through Charlotte Brontë, registers that reading is also, paradoxically, the expression of the desire to be blind, to summon forward a voice outside of the material limits of the visible word. The complexity of these figures' constructions, collocations of autobiographical inscription, imagined reader, imaginations of the act of writing itself, represent the coalescence of self and other in the writing subject that are bought into focus through the condition of blindness. Brontë's and Barrett Browning's contradictory responses to the experience of visual impairment in their own personal lives, alongside its inscription in their literary works, suggests the complex range of meanings which adhere to figures of blindness in contemporary discourses. For both, though, blindness raised questions about the nature of sensory experience that had particularly important implications for their own understanding of the function – and limits – of the verbal arts, and their own status as women writers.

The next chapter explores how an anxiety concerning the limits of empirical vision underpins Dickens's literary project, manifesting in repeated allusions to and figurations of blindness in his fictional and journalistic writing. Blindness functions as a trope through which Dickens examines the interpretative possibilities and limits to writing, and we frequently encounter episodes of impaired and failed vision at points in his fiction when narrative and textual identity are under intense pressure. David Copperfield and Esther Summerson – first-person narrators with a particularly intimate connection to Dickens as a speaking subject – are both marked by blindness, which, at a symbolic level, suggests that writing emerges from a subject who is impaired. Dickens's interest in blindness is also materially grounded, and evidences his engagement with some of the key public debates surrounding blind people's literacy, including the development of tactile alphabets. Blindness continues to inscribe a concern for the embodied conditions of writing and reading text.

CHAPTER 6

# *Writing Blindness*
## *Dickens*

'The first ray of light which illumines the gloom, and converts into a dazzling brilliancy that obscurity': thus opens Pickwick's history, and Dickens's meteoric launch into authorship.[1] Dickens pictures writing as an illumination, a bringing forth of the visible world. The narrative action of his first novel, *The Pickwick Papers* (1836–7), begins with Pickwick's desire to break free from the circumscribed space of Goswell-street, as he ponders:

> 'Such … are the narrow views of those philosophers who, content with examining things that lie before them, look not to the truths which are hidden beyond. As well might I be content to gaze on Goswell-street for ever, without one effort to penetrate to the hidden countries which on every side surround it'.[2]

This passage could read as a manifesto for Dickens's own writing project, which seeks to see the wider relations between people and things and be that 'good spirit who would take the house-tops off, … and show a Christian people what dark shapes issue from amidst their homes'.[3] Yet despite its intensely visual nature, we repeatedly encounter the spectre of blindness and failing vision in Dickens's writing, particularly in the earlier part of his career. As a ghost unsettles the sureties of the lived body, so blindness haunts Dickens's texts by unsettling the certainty of visual authority, its absence pointing to the end of writing. Blindness is part of the uncanny quality that John Bowen identifies in Dickens's books, in which unfamiliar events and presences turn out to be our most familiar and disturbing acquaintances, haunting Dickens's writing as an uncanny reminder of the limits to the vision that is so central to his literary project.[4] Yet, if a ghost is not wholly other to the self, but somehow a manifestation of its psyche as voice, breath or soul, so blindness is, paradoxically, part of visual experience in Dickens's fiction.[5]

We can locate some of Dickens's depictions of blindness within the literary and philosophic discourses of blindness considered in previous chapters. Traces of the hypothetical blind man, for example, are evident in *The Pickwick Papers*, as the innocent, childlike Pickwick must learn to see with greater accuracy. Pickwick's spectacles symbolise the limits of his empirical endeavours: it is his novelistic experience in the world that teaches him how to see afresh, beyond the boundaries of the Mudford scientific and philosophic society. Blindness does not function simply as a device to test the limits of empirical vision in Dickens's writing, however – it is also a condition that disrupts his own formation of identity as writer. As Gavin Edwards has recently shown, Dickens is intensely interested in the ways in which the material form of writing shapes literacy, and in the relationship between cognition and the visual signifiers of writing, as either script or printed text.[6] Whereas Edwards argues that this is a feature of Dickens's later career, and concomitant with his turn to public readings, I suggest that his recurrent interest in blindness indicates how it is also a feature of his earlier career. It is, however, more strongly connected at this earlier stage to the *production* of writing than to the consumption of text, and forms part of an anxious probing of the status and limits of authorship.

The episodes I discuss here attest to Dickens's sustained interest in blindness.[7] Structured chronologically in order to explore the continuities and changes in Dickens's treatment of blindness, the chapter begins with Dickens's encounter with blind, deaf and mute Laura Bridgman, recounted in *American Notes for General Circulation* (1842). Dickens's interest in Bridgman springs from how she acquired language without vision. Bridgman's education reminds the sighted writer of the visual nature of writing, and also suggests the possibility of language, communication and expression outside of visual signs. This encounter informs Dickens's fictional work in two important later invocations of blindness: the description of David Copperfield as 'blind' in the eponymous novel (1849–50) and Esther Summerson's near-blinding in *Bleak House* (1853). Crucially, these encounters with blindness, framed within first-person narratives, disturb the conventions of fictional narration. As I will show, both these novels are concerned with the gap between the appearance of evidence and its truth, with blindness functioning metaphorically within these texts to signal that disjuncture.

Blindness also has a distinctly material presence within the books, and I show how these episodes are informed by contemporary cultural discourses of blindness, including embossed writing practices and public health debates on smallpox. Importantly, the embodied, and experiential, dimensions to Dickens's depictions of visual impairment overlaps with its metaphoric deployment. In this overlapping, Dickens ties cultural debates and discussion about the nature and experience of blindness – with its strong contemporary association with the issue of literacy – to a self-reflexive probing of the nature of the material text and its limits.

The aligning of blindness (and its related sensory modality of touch) with the feminine also makes it a particularly potent trope through which to explore writing's constituent gender identities. This discussion builds on the insights of the previous chapter, in which Charlotte Brontë and Elizabeth Barrett Browning assumed blind identities as part of their critique of the gendered nature of writing. In Dickens's novels, blindness facilitates an erotics of writing, and allows expression of alternative gender identities. We will trace then the troubling nature of blindness in Dickens's writing, as a condition that unsettles subject and object boundaries in the text.

## Blind Writing: Dickens and Laura Bridgman, 1842

Amongst the first episodes Dickens recounts in *American Notes* is his visit to the Perkins Institution and Massachusetts Asylum for the Blind, run by Samuel Gridley Howe, which dominates the account of Boston in chapter 3 of the first volume. Within the context of his institutional tour of America, the visit is indicative of Dickens's interest in the management of those subjects at the borders of nineteenth-century society, and who indeed challenge the notion of the free, liberal subject – disabled people, prisoners, slaves. Their difference is doubled through the lens of Dickens's interrogation of the *foreignness* of the institutions at stake, as he constantly draws comparisons between the American 'them' and British 'us'. Furthermore, as Linda M. Shires argues, the trip to America prompted a larger self-crisis in Dickens, as he was confronted by the formation of a new kind of self, created by a shifting social authority in which the private life of the individual became increasingly public. Dickens feared becoming such a self, 'substanceless, un-critical, mass-produced, monotonous'.[8] Yet clearly Dickens was intrigued by the institutionalised selves he met, especially Bridgman and her fellow pupils, who seemingly had no private life, their lives constructed in and through public spectacle and discourse. More poignantly, these figures of blindness impressed upon Dickens the fragility and limitations of vision, at the start of a tour which was so centred around the observation of scenes, the interpretation of landscape and visual details, and the public observation and visual consumption of Dickens himself by his readers.

Indeed, the account of Laura Bridgman in *American Notes* begins with a verbal picture of the landscape surrounding the Perkins Institution. Dickens draws his own body into this scene as observer, reminding us that what is described is subject to his own vision:

> I went to see this place one very fine winter morning: an Italian sky above, and the air so clear and bright on every side, that even my eyes, which are none of the best, could follow the minute lines and scraps of tracery in distant buildings ... When I paused for a moment at the door, and marked how fresh and free the whole scene was – what sparkling bubbles glanced upon the waves, and welled up every moment to the surface, as though the world below, like that above, were radiant with the bright day, and gushing over in its fullness of light: when I gazed from sail to sail away upon a ship at sea, a tiny speck of shining white, the only cloud upon the still, deep, distant blue – and, turning, saw a blind boy with his sightless face addressed that way, as though he too had some sense within him of the glorious distance: I felt a kind of sorrow that the place should be so very light, and a strange wish that for his sake it were darker.[9]

Before entering the institution, then, Dickens is awed by the sight and 'scene' before him, which is imbued with a spiritual wonder in its expansive radiance and 'fullness of light'. Dickens sombrely plays with perspective here, as his power to gaze from 'sail to sail upon a ship at sea, a tiny speck of shining white' is emphasised by its juxtaposition with the blind boy's 'sightless face'. Blindness and vision meet in this encounter, and although Dickens registers that the blind boy may have had 'some sense within him of the glorious distance', he also feels 'a kind of sorrow' that he can see such beauty in the landscape, whereas the blind boy cannot. Blindness signals here a loss and absence for Dickens, an uneasy shadow moving across his consciousness. There is also, tellingly, a brief identification with the school's subjects, as Dickens draws attention to his own weak sight, describing how the intensity of light grants him clearer vision, even though his bodily eyes 'are none of the best'.

The first mention of Bridgman, as discussed in Chapter 4, describes her as a prisoner, enclosed within a 'marble cell ... beckoning to some good man for help, that an Immortal soul might be awakened' (*AN*, 40). However, Dickens's account of Laura quickly turns to focus on her as an intellectual being, with Howe in the role of that 'good man', figured explicitly as her rescuer, 'the one ... who has made her what she is' (*AN*, 41). The marvel she represents to Dickens is that, without any sensory faculty other than touch, she demonstrates intellectual capacity and is capable of acquiring language skills. He notes how her 'face was radiant with intelligence and pleasure' (*AN*, 40). Whilst Dickens sanitises Bridgman's environment, metaphors of prison punctuate the account, reminding us that she lives within clear disciplinary boundaries. Her dress is a 'pattern of neatness and simplicity', and she is pictured 'seated in a little enclosure … writing her daily journal' (*AN*, 40). Dickens encloses a 'few disjointed fragments of her history' from Howe's narrative of Bridgman's life; as a subject she is embedded and further enclosed within others' textual accounts and narratives, uneasily slipping between subject and object. Yet Dickens's account, and his selection of passages from Howe, indicates his interest in the ways in which Bridgman increasingly constitutes herself as subject by her grasp of a system of writing based on arbitrary (alphabetic) rather than natural signs.[10]

Indeed, much of what Dickens includes focuses on the mechanics of Laura's language acquisition. Before developing a fever that inflamed her eyes and ears aged two, Bridgman appeared to have displayed 'a considerable degree of intelligence' (*AN*, 41). Howe heard of Bridgman's case a few years later, and went to visit her at her family home in Hanover, noting: 'I found her with a well-formed figure; a strongly-marked, nervous-sanguine temperament; a large and beautifully-shaped head; and the whole system in healthy action' (*AN*, 42). When she was brought to Boston on 4 October 1837, two months before her eighth birthday, Bridgman already possessed a basic language based on natural signs. However, Howe wanted to give her 'knowledge of arbitrary signs, by which she could interchange thoughts with others'. He continues:

> There was one of two ways to be adopted: either to go on to build up a language of signs on the basis of the natural language which she had already commenced herself, or to teach her the purely arbitrary language in common use: that is, to give her a sign for every individual thing, or to give her a knowledge of letters by combination of which she might express her idea of the existence, and the mode and condition of existence, of any thing. The former would have been easy, but very ineffectual; the latter seemed very difficult, but, if accomplished, very effectual. (*AN*, 42–3)

Howe attempted the latter, experimenting by taking articles such as knives, spoons and keys, and pasting upon them their names in raised letters. Feeling these objects and labels carefully, Bridgman soon distinguished the raised lines of *s p o o n*, which differed as much from the raised lines of *k e y* as the spoon and key themselves differed in form. Soon she was able to match the detached labels with the objects, 'encouraged … by the natural sign of approbation, patting on the head' (*AN*, 43). At first, Howe notes that the 'process had been mechanical, and the success about as great as teaching a very knowing dog a variety of tricks'. However, following the next stage, in which Bridgman was given individual letters instead of labels, arranged side by side so as to spell *b o o k* etc., and which were then mixed up for her to arrange herself, 'the truth began to flash at her'. Dickens continues to quote Howe:

> Her intellect began to work: she perceived that here was a way by which she could herself make up a sign of any thing that was in her own mind; and at once her countenance lighted up with a human expression: it was no longer a dog, or parrot: it was an immortal spirit, eagerly seizing upon a new link of union with other spirits! I could almost fix upon the moment when this truth dawned upon her mind, and spread its light to her countenance; I saw that the great obstacle was overcome ... (*AN*, 43–4)

Troublingly, Bridgman in her pre-linguistic state is held to be non-human, and animalistic: it is her understanding of a language system that grants her a 'human expression'. The report also details how her language skills developed. Using a rudimentary typewriter (a board punctuated by small holes into which were inserted free-floating metal types with the letters of the alphabet cast upon them), Bridgman was able to spell out a range of objects given to her, and which she differentiated by touch. This was gradually replaced by the finger alphabet, as Bridgman was taught how to represent the different letters by the position of her fingers. Over the course of the year, she rapidly learned how to spell 'the names of every object which she could properly handle'.

As with Dickens, both Bridgman's public and private identities are strongly denoted by her relationship to language. She is most strikingly a textual figure, enmeshed in writing and narratives, both her own and others. She not only demonstrates an exceptional linguistic ability, but also seemingly delights in language, and the play and *jouissance* of language:

> When left alone, she occupies and apparently amuses herself, and seems quite contented; and so strong seems to be the natural tendency of thought to put on the garb of language, that she often soliloquizes in the *finger language*, slow and tedious as it is. But it is only when alone, that she is quiet: for if she becomes sensible of the presence of anyone near her, she is restless until she can sit close beside them, hold their hand, and converse with them by signs. (*AN*, 49)

Dickens concludes his account of Bridgman with a description of her dreaming, and a perusal of her diary. Dickens is fascinated to note that even though she cannot dream in 'words' (phonemes), Bridgman can still, like the sighted, 'carry on imaginary conversations, in which we speak both for ourselves and for the shadows who appear to us in those visions of the night'; only she dreams through touch, using her finger alphabet in her sleep (*AN*, 49–50). Turning over the leaves of her diary, Dickens finds that it is 'written in a fair legible square hand, and expressed in terms which were quite intelligible without any explanation'. Dickens asks if he can see her write again, and her teacher 'bade her, in their language, sign her name upon a slip of paper'. He observes that 'she kept her left hand always touching, and following up, her right, in which of course, she held the pen' (*AN*, 50). Peering into her diary, Dickens reminds us that Bridgman does not have a private self, mirroring his own fear of an entirely public self that the scrutiny of his American tour prompted. Her dreams and her handwriting are to be witnessed and made public, as a lithograph after a portrait by A. Fisher exemplifies (Figure 7). With her identity inextricably shaped by her ability to produce text, Bridgman acts as an uncanny spectre of Dickens's writing self, her identity opened to the public who gaze at her writing. Bridgman's writing and, by extension, her life, are made object.

Dickens's interest in the material form of blind writing persisted and I have written elsewhere on his important gift of 250 copies of *The Old Curiosity Shop* embossed in the Boston Line type to the Perkins School towards the end of his life. This event marked one of the first entries of contemporary literature into the Perkins's book catalogue (they were the foremost publishers of embossed books in nineteenth-century America). It also revealed certain contradictions in the emancipatory ethos governing the Perkins's publishing programme, as Howe heavily promoted an alphabet based on the Roman alphabet and which was more suited to reading by eye than by finger.[11] Dickens was certainly aware of the contentious debates concerning the correct system that raised print should follow, as both his journals *Household Words* and *All the Year Round* featured articles on the topic of embossed reading systems in 1853, as I discuss below in connection with *Bleak House*, as well as in 1870, which I discussed in Chapter 3. Importantly, his engagement with the issue of blind people's literacy through his editorial and philanthropic work involved him in debates concerning the ways in which the material format of the linguistic sign, and its arrangement in an alphabetic system, shaped its comprehension and meaning.

His engagement with the issue of blind people's literacy also influenced his fictional writing. Shortly after his American trip, Dickens drew upon meeting Bridgman in the construction of the blind character Bertha

Figure 7 W. Sharp after A. Fisher, *Oliver Caswell and Laura Bridgman*, lithograph (1844). Wellcome Library, London (ref. V0015876).


Plummer in one of his *Christmas Books*, making her the centre of a complex plot of narrative deception. Indeed, blindness is central to *The Cricket on the Hearth* (1845), both structurally and thematically, as it invites the imaginary reordering of the real world. The narrative is structured around a series of scenes, culminating in the Quilp-like Tackleton 'showing' John Peerybingle's wife, Dot, in an act of infidelity with Edward Plummer, and the spirits of the hearth showing John scenes from his marriage in Dot's defence. Bertha Plummer, the blind girl, is subject to her father Caleb's elaborate fantasy, as he seeks to protect her from the reality of their lives by pretending that his harsh and exacting master, Tackleton, is in fact kind and benevolent, and that they live in luxury rather than poverty. As Elisabeth Gitter notes, the plot is organised around seeing, watching and spying.[12] Bertha's blindness in turn has been read as a misogynistic portrayal which allows her father, Caleb, to project his fantasies onto her. Gitter suggests that the story's sentimental veneer barely conceals a punishing aggression directed towards the 'Blind Daughter', who, surrounded by eyes and games of seeing, is herself shrouded in sightlessness.[13] She goes on to argue that Bertha's blindness 'neutralises the old man's guilt; unable to return his gaze, she is pure object, incapable of subjectivity; she connotes, in Laura Mulvey's terms, pure "to-be-looked-at-ness"'.[14] In Mulvey's psychoanalytic formulation, pure 'to-be-looked-at-ness' functions as a lack, absence or castration onto which the active male can 'live out his fantasies and obsessions through linguistic command by imposing them on the silent image of woman still tied to her place as bearer, not of meaning, but of making'.[15] Here, however, Caleb's subjectivity is also confused as a result of his role as visual framer. Following on from the ways in which Laura Bridgman draws out Dickens's own anxieties concerning the uneasy relationship between his public and private self, Caleb's selfhood is radically undermined precisely by these attempts to control and reinscribe the visual and material world in which he and Bertha live. The narrative explicitly recognises the limits to both the male gaze and the fantasy it projects upon its female subject. Moreover, Bertha's blindness is not simply indicative of her status as woman in the text; it also alerts us to her narrative position. Her trust in the fantasy projected by her father as narrator figuratively aligns her with the reader, who must also trust in the detail and description provided by the authorial voice; although of course the reader is also shown the partiality of Caleb's narrative, placing him or her in a position of power over Bertha. Bertha's characterisation also resonates with Charlotte Brontë's and Elizabeth Barrett Browning's deployment of blindness in *Jane Eyre* and *Aurora Leigh*, by reminding us that to read is also, imaginatively, to give up one's own vision to the narrative one is immersed in.

We can also identify parallels between Bertha and David, narrator of Dickens's most autobiographical novel, *David Copperfield*, which began serialisation in 1848, shortly after *Jane Eyre* was published. In this book, Dickens draws upon cultural discourses of blindness to test the ways in which narrative truth and authority are produced. Blindness is invoked to suggest the limits of David's own knowledge and feeling, which in turn implicates us, as readers: for what happens if we exceed David's limited perception? Yet David's narrative also proceeds from the dark, a space of blindness. In this next section, I explore how Dickens's fictional autobiography of a writer utilises impaired vision as both a creative force that generates story and narration, and as a critical device via which David – and through him, Dickens – reflects on the limits to interpretation. Interpretation is shown to take place through a body revealed as bounded, and partial. Blindness, I argue, is not then simply an object of the narrative in *David Copperfield*: it is also a condition of the textual subject.

## *David Copperfield*: The Subject is Blind

*David Copperfield* is a haunted and haunting elegy for vision. In this text, which sits at the borders of fiction and autobiography, both in its use of first-person narrative and its theme of a writer's 'personal history', David's split self narrates the history of a subject who is blind and who struggles to overcome his empirical blindness and sees clearly only with retrospective vision. David shows how blindness is a condition of the writer, who speaks and writes of invisible things, and must learn to see what is truly at the heart of representation. My discussion will explore the ways in which some of the material and literary cultures of blindness that I have identified emerge as a metaphoric structuring device in Dickens's autobiographical novel, and are also invoked as part of a specific commentary on and concern with the craft and production of literary writing.

David presents himself as a visionary, who, born at midnight on Friday, is privileged 'to see ghosts and spirits'; his origin is identified with the gift of perceiving the invisible. He expounds this in the second chapter (titled 'I observe'), stepping outside of the narrative to account for the episodes he puts forward:

> It brings me to remark that I build these conclusions, in part upon my own experience of myself; and if it should appear from anything I may set down in this narrative that I was a child of close observation, or that as a man I have a strong memory of my childhood, I undoubtedly lay claim to both of these characteristics.
>
> Looking back, as I was saying, into the blank of my infancy, the first objects I can remember as standing out by themselves from a confusion of things, are my mother and Peggotty. What else do I remember? Let me see.[16]

This play between what is visible and invisible positions the reader seemingly within the narrator's perceptual faculty, as the reader can only see what is within the narrator's visual field. This has led some critics to argue that the narrative uses vision as a disciplinary force; for example, Gareth Cordery claims that David's 'panoptical position as central character and only narrator gives him total omniscience. All characters are subject to David's disciplinary gaze; he controls, observes, and allocates roles in the prison that is his novel within which his characters (and himself) are trapped.'[17] Yet whilst the manner in which David's history is told relies heavily upon the invocation of vision – visual images and verbs associated with seeing – sight is also subject to a radical doubt in the novel. For example, David instances the limits to his gaze early on, when Murdstone takes David to Lowestoft to visit his friends. The young David – perhaps nervous of the raucousness of Murdstone's friends – when directed to look at things through a telescope, feigns to see: 'I could make out nothing myself when it was put to my eye, but pretended I could' (*DC*, 35). As Audrey Jaffe suggests, the omniscient narrative that seems to see all is produced by a narrator who ironically as a subject 'is aware of and anxious about the possibility of becoming an object for others'.[18] David is also aware of and anxious about the acknowledged limits to his vision.

What does it mean then for David to present himself as blind? In chapter 35, David's aunt Betsey Trotwood unexpectedly arrives in London, where David has taken articles, with the news that she has lost her fortune. She conceals from the narrative what it will later reveal – that the loss is a result of her investment in Wickfield's firm, and that her capital has been mismanaged. Against a now destabilised domestic situation, Betsey Trotwood questions David's feelings for his fiancée, Dora, asking whether or not they are 'light-headed'. It is worth quoting this passage at length:

> 'Well, well!' said my aunt. 'I only ask. I don't depreciate her. Poor little couple! And so you think you were formed for one another, and are to go through a party-supper-table kind of life, like two pretty pieces of confectionery, do you Trot?'
>
> She asked me this so kindly, and with such a gentle air, half playful and half sorrowful, that I was quite touched.
>
> 'We are young and inexperienced, aunt, I know,' I replied; 'and I dare say we say and think a good deal that is rather foolish. But we love one another truly, I am sure. If I thought Dora could ever love anybody else, or cease to love me; or that I could ever love anybody else, or cease to love her; I don't know what I should do – go out of my mind, I think!'
>
> 'Ah, Trot!' said my aunt, shaking her head, and smiling gravely; 'blind, blind, blind!'
>
> 'Someone that I know, Trot,' my aunt pursued, after a pause, 'though of a very pliant disposition, has an earnestness of affection in him that reminds me of poor Baby. Earnestness is what that Somebody must look for, to sustain him and improve him, Trot. Deep, downright, faithful earnestness.'
>
> 'If only you knew the earnestness of Dora, aunt!' I cried.
>
> 'Oh Trot!' she said again; 'blind, blind!' and without knowing why, I felt a vague unhappy loss or want of something overshadow me like a cloud. (*DC*, 509–10)

This passage emphasises David's partial sight, as the reader, like Betsey Trotwood, sees far more than the David narrating at this moment. Here, David's alignment with the figure of the blind – who will shortly find a literal counterpart – suggests the conceptual work that blindness has to do in the novel. Betsey's use of 'blind' as an adjective to describe David works at a metonymic level, as David's inability to interpret his emotional landscape (his incompatibility with Dora, and Agnes's love for him) is figured as a failure of his physical sight. The reader is drawn into a complex obfuscation, in which the older narrator has to conceal from the reader what was later revealed to him through the illuminating light of the 'angel' Agnes, and narrate a seemingly pure memory, recalling his state of innocence and ignorance. The collapsing timeframes signal the impossibility of experiencing time as linear; and with this comes also the collapse of a Cartesian system of vision which posits a direct, linear relationship between what is seen and what is known.

Soon after David's encounter with his aunt in London, Agnes arrives with her father and Uriah Heep. They discuss Betsey Trotwood's fortunes, where she and Mr Dick are to live, and what David is to do. The older narrator notes:

> And how she spoke to me of Dora, sitting at the window in the dark; listened to my praises of her; praised again, and round the little fairy-figure shed some glimpses of her own pure light, that made it yet more precious and more innocent to me! Oh, Agnes, sister of my boyhood, if I had known then, what I knew long afterwards!
>
> There was a beggar in the street, when I went down; and as I turned my head towards the window, thinking of her calm, seraphic eyes, he made me start by muttering, as if he were an echo of the morning:
>
> 'Blind! Blind! Blind!' (*DC*, 525–6)

Whilst David thinks of Agnes's eyes, which, 'calm, seraphic', recall the glassy eye of a person with cataract, his own vision is punctured by the beggar's uncanny echoing of his aunt. These passages signal the limits of David's perceptual faculties: he must learn by experience the foolhardiness of his relationship with Dora and the strength of Agnes's love for him. The repetition of the warning 'blind' associates the limits of perceptual faculties with knowledge: not everything can be revealed to our perceptual faculties all at once; rather, we must learn by experience. In this emphasis on experiential knowledge above propositional knowledge, the novel seems indebted to a Lockean psychology. Yet the narrative goes beyond this empirical framework by suggesting that a certain force of emotional experience – sentiment, love, pity – mediates perceptual faculties. This implication resonates with the recent approach of critics including Michael Hollington and William A. Cohen, who emphasise how Dickens's interest in sight operates within a wider sensorium.[19]

This opening out of sensory perception beyond the visual also intriguingly identifies David further with blindness. This identification is discernible in David's childhood recollections of Peggotty, which are shaped primarily by tactile sensations:

> I believe I can remember these two at a little distance apart, dwarfed to my sight by stooping down or kneeling on the floor, and I going unsteadily from the one to the other. I have an impression on my mind which I cannot distinguish from actual remembrance, of the touch of Peggotty's fore-finger as she used to hold it out to me, and of its being roughened by needlework, like a pocket nutmeg-grater. (*DC*, 24)

Unable to visually perceive his mother and Peggotty clearly, David's memory shares with a blind person's, as the tactile detail of Peggotty's fore-finger, 'like a pocket nutmeg-grater', becomes a stronger marker of her identity than the visual portrait. Even the memory formation belongs to touch, framed as an 'impression' upon David's mind.

David's memory is, in part, Dickens's memory and early reviewers picked up on the novel's autobiographical resonances. An unsigned reviewer for *Fraser's Magazine* observed:

> We have several reasons for suspecting that, here and there, under the name of David Copperfield, we have been favoured with passages from the personal history, adventures, and experience, of Charles Dickens. Indeed, this conclusion is in a manner forced upon us by the peculiar professions selected for the ideal character, who is first a newspaper reporter and then a famous novelist.[20]

Furthermore, the reviewer senses a different tone in *David Copperfield*:

> There is, moreover, an air of reality pervading the whole book, to a degree never attained in any of his previous works, and which cannot be entirely attributed to the mere *form* of narration.[21]

What is this 'air of reality', or the 'wonderful reality' as John Forster describes it, that pervades the novel?[22] As *Fraser's* reviewer senses, it is something which slips beyond the form of writing; it is shaped by the uneasy overlap between the self writing the fiction, and the writer of fiction created in the work. The reviewer quotes the opening of chapter 48 as an example of this, in which David labours hard at his book, whilst adding a note of caution for the purpose of his autobiography:

> It is not my purpose, in this record, though in all other essentials it is my written memory, to pursue the history of my own fictions. They express themselves, and I leave them to themselves. When I refer to them, incidentally, it is only as a part of my progress. (*DC*, 696)

The events that shape the writer's imagination, his observations and experiences (the stuff of fiction) become the action and event of the novel. This is mirrored in David's own writing. Although David does not describe his own novels, he suggests they may have autobiographic aspects themselves. At the point at which he writes his own 'first work of fiction', he walks past the Steerforths' house whilst returning from a solitary walk, 'thinking of the book I was then writing'. His route seems to have been something of a compulsion, as he admits that he 'had often passed it before ... pretty often', as it was not easy to find another route when walking in Highgate (*DC*, 672). The frequency with which David takes this route is indicated in Rosa Dartle's observation of him, and she calls him in on this particular occasion (*DC*, 673). David's own mind is confused as to the attraction of the house for him at this present time, attributing it in part to the effect of writing fiction, which, with its 'blending of experience and imagination', makes the 'childish recollections and later fancies, the ghosts of half-formed hopes, the broken shadows of disappointments dimly seen and understood' that are embodied in the house seem 'more than commonly suggestive' (*DC*, 672). Imagination and the act of writing construct and determine both the space of the Steerforth's house and the space of the novels (both David Copperfield's novels and the novel *David Copperfield*). David, like Dickens, cannot keep his own self fully separate from his works.

This pattern of blindness and insight extends to the act of criticism: how do readers see and distinguish the blurred threads and traces of Dickens's own life, as recounted in his own autobiographical fragment, then retold by Forster, from the novel itself? As Paul de Man reminds us, we run into certain complications as critics when we see literary language from a perspective that is centred 'in the subjectivity of the author or author-reader relationship', as the category of that self turns out to be double-faced. The critic who uses such a category is compelled to 'retract implicitly what he affirms and to end up by offering the mystery of this paradoxical movement as his main insight'.[23] The novel itself invokes shifting perspectives of blindness and insight, in its construction of a textual subject that consistently recognises and misrecognises its merging with the body of the author (a pattern that is repeated with Esther Summerson). Blindness is a space in which narrator and author meet, without being fully reconciled.

As we have seen, early critics and reviewers of *David Copperfield* employed autobiographical approaches in their reading of the novel, frequently framing their identifications through visual tropes. Forster recounts the speculations made about the relationship between David Copperfield and Charles Dickens, noting that 'many guesses have been made since his death, connecting David's autobiography with his own; accounting, by means of such actual experiences'. Forster, in the first definitive biography of the author, claims that 'there is not only truth in all this, but it will very shortly be seen that the identity went deeper than any had supposed, and covered experiences not less startling in the reality than they appear to be in the fiction'.[24] Indeed, the first of Dickens's narrators that Forster invokes in *The Life* is David Copperfield; it is through Copperfield's heightened and uncanny powers of memory and observation, 'seeing so far back into the blank of his infancy', that we must see Dickens's biography. 'Applicable as it might be to David Copperfield, this was simply and unaffectedly true of Charles Dickens'.[25] *David Copperfield* partially uplifts 'the veil' surrounding Dickens's own shame of his childhood experiences in the blacking factory, acting thus as an event which partly reveals, and yet continues to hide, Dickens's own self; an event which had 'haunted him' up until and beyond the writing of the novel.[26] Forster also describes the decision, made by Dickens himself on 'the very eve of his death', to publish the autobiographical fragment and thus make explicit what his novel alluded to. Indeed, the novel has its origins in the fragment, Forster telling us that 'the fancy of *David Copperfield*' was 'itself suggested by what he had so written of his early troubles'.[27]

This process of the concealment and discovery of past selves is articulated within a pattern of blindness and insight that is also distinctly intertextual. Alan P. Barr, in a lucid discussion of mourning and melancholia in *David Copperfield*, insists that it is a novel 'that mourns and elegizes the loss of innocence and its enthusiasms'.[28] Drawing out Dickens's attentiveness to the 'surrounding literature of the nineteenth century, poetry as well as fiction', Barr notes the striking coincidence of the convergence of the publication of *David Copperfield* and Wordsworth's *The Prelude* in 1850, which connect in their exploration of the relationship between memory and self.[29] There is also a shared interest in the theme of blindness between

Wordsworth and Dickens's writing projects, a theme already explored in relation to Wordsworth in Chapter 2.

Jeremy Tambling notes how Dickens bought a copy of *The Prelude*, published in July 1850, within a month of its publication, quoting from it in the last double number of his novel.[30] Dickens's incorporation of Wordsworthian echoes illustrates the affinity between his novel and Wordsworth's autobiographical project.[31] By allowing Wordsworth's retrospective visions to shape his own memory and account of Switzerland, which marks a critical moment in David's self-recognition, Dickens alerts us to the difficulties of remembering and recalling the past. This is an anxiety that is once again focused through the figure of the blind person, with the narrative's interesting textual allusions to Wordsworth's 'Lines Written a Few Miles Above Tintern Abbey'. In the chapter 'Absence' David, newly struck by the realisation of his love for Agnes, resolves to stay in Switzerland, 'to resume my pen; to work'. David reveals: 'I sought out Nature, never sought in vain' (*DC*, 822). This echoes the speaker of 'Tintern Abbey', who after 'many wanderings' and 'many years, / Of absence', revisits the banks of the River Wye.[32] The speaker in Wordsworth's poem is animated by others, the 'sylvan Wye' herself, addressed as 'thee' throughout, and the speaker's 'dear, dear Sister!' ('Tintern Abbey', lines 57, 122). David also makes this transition from the subject formed in and through nature, to one shaped by his love for Agnes (who of course he refers to as his 'sister' throughout).

In 'Absence', David understands that his close powers of observation have failed him. Despite seeing closely, it is only when he receives Agnes's letter on his travels that he retrospectively remembers the nature of the love he has always felt towards her, and asserts its continued existence in both the past and the present. He puts her letter away and sees the 'quiet evening cloud grow dim, and all the colours in the valley fade, and the golden snow upon the mountain tops become a remote part of the pale night sky, yet felt that the night was passing from my mind, and all its shadows clearing, and there was no name for the love I bore, dearer to me, henceforward, than ever until then' (*DC*, 822). Dickens's narrative echoes Wordsworth's poem in drawing upon the analogy of a blind man, but does not straightforwardly repeat the relationship between blindness and memory inscribed there. The speaker in Wordsworth's poem recollects:

> ... though absent long,
> These forms of beauty have not been to me,
> As is a landscape to a blind man's eye'.
>
> ('Tintern Abbey', lines 23–5)

Wordsworth's speaker is not like the blind man, as his visual memory enables him to renew the landscape of the Wye, with its emotive past associations, both of 'thy voice' and 'from thy wild eyes these gleams / Of past existence' ('Tintern Abbey', lines 149–50). Dickens's narrator differs, and is aligned with the blind man, as he overlays these new scenes of nature with fresh interpretations of his own memories. Significantly, David recalls the incident when his aunt called him 'blind' just after he returned from his absence, in the chapter titled 'Agnes' (ch. 65), following on from the realisation of his love for her. Discussing Agnes with his aunt, he 'seemed to hear' her saying once more 'Blind, blind, blind' and believes that 'I understood her better now' (*DC*, 842). Here, Agnes is less the 'embodiment of surveillance' that some critics have claimed she is and more a force who disturbs the relationship between what is seen and what is known.[33] David understands that he has been blind as he reflects that 'in my wayward boyhood, I had thrown away the treasure of her love' (*DC*, 823). And David's moment of anagnorisis, of critical self-discovery through this identification of love for Agnes, is still partial, as his desire for Steerforth, the 'guiding star of my existence', remains hidden in darkness.

This darkness is, however, a space of privilege. The memory is crafted from the 'shadowy world' that Dickens describes in the preface to *David Copperfield*, a space creatively shaped from blindness. Darkness and shadows signify the start of writing, as the mind turns away from seeing the now, the present out-there, to look (or more precisely *feel*) back through past images, creating narratives from them as they mingle indeterminately. Indeed, David details how his storytelling career began in the 'dark' of the dormitory of Salem House, when James Steerforth conferred on him the role of narrator (*DC*, 105). Dickens's writing belongs to the visual, and yet at its origin it is also intimately conditioned by both what cannot be seen (the invisible, the unconscious) and the limits to the subject's vision. Blindness structures experience, rupturing the integrity of the self in time, as the subject recognises the absences that punctuate being. At the close of *David Copperfield*, David closes the leaves of his book, takes a final look back, and sees himself, Agnes at his side, and his children and friends around him. The retrospective narrative has shown us what happens to characters as they are held in David's gaze: expiration, as they exit the novel either through death or emigration. Although he calls to the 'dear presence' of Agnes to bear him company (*DC*, 878, 882), we sense instead that David becomes Ovid's Orpheus, fulfilling the text's tragic propensity as he seeks to hold in focus those who must disappear from view. As 'realities' melt from David, he shadows Orpheus (from whose gaze Eurydice disappears), in his necessary loss.

Metaphoric blindness is also linked with the material production of writing in the novel's schema. I will focus on one important episode before turning to a discussion of *Bleak House*. In *David Copperfield*, the attitude of the ageing scholar, Dr Strong, towards his wife, Annie, is spoken of in terms of blindness and self-deception, as, echoing the story of the Peerybingles in *Cricket on the Hearth*, he appears impervious to what everyone else believes they can see (his wife's infidelity with Jack Maldon). David worries that 'without looking at her cousin, she then addressed me, and asked me about Agnes, and whether she should see her, and whether she was not likely to come that day; and was so much disturbed, that I wondered how the Doctor, buttering his toast, could be blind to what was obvious' (*DC*, 531). The fact that 'what was obvious' has in fact been misread by David, Uriah (who calls Dr Strong as 'blind as a brick bat') and others further problematises the transparency of visible acts in the text. More than this, however, Dr Strong's compilation of the Dictionary connects both him and David to language in other, more material ways. Agnes suggests that David becomes Dr Strong's secretary on the Dictionary in chapter 36, in the midst of Betsey calling him 'blind'. David, as secretary (a copyist and administrator), cuts his literary teeth as a mechanised labourer of language, rather than as an originator of words.[34] Thus the novel's self-reflexive nature – what it means to be a writer – is also critically concerned with the material production of writing.

David expends labour on the Dictionary, 'up at five in the morning, and home at nine or ten at night' (*DC*, 532). This mechanisation of language continues as David seeks to become a parliamentary reporter, for which he must learn stenography. Traddles informs him that 'the mere mechanical acquisition necessary, except in rare cases, for thorough excellence in it, that is to say, a perfect and entire command of the mystery of short-hand writing and reading', will take many years to master (*DC*, 532). David resolves to 'buy a book' and learn the 'noble art and mystery of stenography' (*DC*, 533, 551). He later complains of the difficulty in interpreting these strange visual marks, dots and curves which metamorphose into 'flies' legs', impenetrable at first to the eye and mind. David has to learn this language, as a visual form, from scratch, and is troubled in both his waking hours and his sleep by the gap between the shape of symbols and their meaning. In his inability to read these symbols, distortions of the roman letter, he figures himself as blind:

> When I had groped my way, blindly, through these difficulties, and had mastered the alphabet, which was an Egyptian Temple in itself, there then appeared a procession of new horrors, called arbitrary characters; the most despotic characters I have ever known; who insisted, for instance, that a

> thing like the beginning of a cobweb, meant expectation, and that a pen and ink sky-rocket stood for disadvantageous. (*DC*, 551)

David (and, shadowing him, the young Dickens learning shorthand in his role as court reporter) is disturbed by the strange visuality of the words.[35] Dickens identifies the link between stenography and blind reading practices, introducing the tactile detail of 'blindly' groping to describe David's hesitant acquisition of both the alphabet and the 'arbitrary' characters (indeed, all reading systems for blind people that were not founded on the Roman letter were termed 'arbitrary'). This new language presents not only a 'procession' of 'horrors' in the difficulties of mastering it, but also a threat to civilisation in its despotic nature, which recalls the hieroglyphs of an Egyptian temple. This is not only in terms of the content of what David will write, capturing the rhetoric of politicians' speeches in his role as shorthand reporter in the Commons, as John Bowen notes.[36] It is also in terms of the material shape, form and expression of written language, which can be reduced, as Bowen continues in a reflection upon the character of Bumble in *Oliver Twist*, to a 'mere collection of arbitrary and despotic characters – six small squiggles, in short, absurd as a pen-and-ink skyrocket'.[37]

Bowen's observation that writing is not outside arbitrariness and despotism, but is another use of it, is reinforced by the association of David's learning shorthand with the efforts of blind people to read newly circulating embossed scripts.[38] Dickens touches on the debates already affecting their progress, as I traced in Chapter 3, about whether embossed literature should develop using a format best suited to the finger, or retain a shape visible to the eye. These arguments would preoccupy educators and commentators on blind people's education for several more decades. This passage evidences an anxiety about the strangeness of all written characters, which have the potential to resist or yield meaning, depending on the faculties and training of the reader. Dickens also distinguishes between learning 'arbitrary' characters and learning the regular alphabet, in whose form the eye is early disciplined. This is revealed in John Forster's account of Dickens's earliest memory of reading, which turns on the visual quality of letters and words. Forster asked Dickens in the early 1840s how he came to be taught reading by his mother, noting that he replied 'in almost exactly the words he placed five years later in the mouth of David Copperfield'. Dickens related:

> I faintly remember her teaching me the alphabet; and when I look upon the fat black letters in the primer, the puzzling novelty of their shapes, and the

> easy good nature of O and S, always seem to present themselves before me as they used to do.[39]

The young Dickens is first entranced by the visuality of writing, but also recalls here the 'puzzling novelty' of the shapes of the Roman alphabet. However, whilst so-called 'arbitrary' characters are despotic, letters from the regular alphabet are noted for their 'easy good nature'. Moreover, it is the maternal that here gives shape to both vision and the form of language. As I explored in my discussion of *Jane Eyre* and *Aurora Leigh*, the maternal occupies an uneasy position in relation to the symbolic system of language in psychoanalytic discourses. Yet here it is Dickens's mother who moves him from language as an oral system rooted in the body to a symbolic one, albeit one which remains couched in a strange, imaginative hinterland of play and personification. Dickens seeks to mitigate the strangeness of how he came to read by domesticating the letters of the Roman alphabet; but his own fiction continues to be troubled by its potentially arbitrary nature. As John Bowen suggestively notes, 'Dickens's work ... never escapes from the tyranny and absurdity of arbitrary and despotic character'.[40] Indeed, the potentially troubling relationship between language and vision continues to preoccupy Dickens in his next novel, *Bleak House*, and in the forum of his popular journal *Household Words*. Here, whilst blindness is associated with the breakdown of visible writing, it also invokes a way of knowing and reading the world outside of the visual. This strangeness is ultimately, however – like the O and the S to the young Dickens – brought back to the familiar, and to regimes of the eye.

## *Bleak House*: Feeling Sight

Whilst much attention has been paid to Esther Summerson's scarring as a result of an illness which shares many of the traits of smallpox, little attention has been paid to her temporary blindness as a result of this illness. In conclusion, I will consider briefly the ways in which this episode connects to the treatment of blindness in *David Copperfield*, in that it also alerts us to the limits of the interpretative schema of writing as a visual system. In this final section, I argue that a near-obsessive preoccupation with the material act of writing in *Bleak House* coincides with a sustained meditation on the limits, and partiality, of looking. Esther's experience of blindness is more somatic than David's. It impresses upon the narrative the texture of blind writing practices, in both her recourse to the tactile in the sickroom, and later in the surface of her scarred face, which is read like an embossed text.

The tension that marks Dickens's description of his visit to Boston comes full circle, as his own meditation about what it means to write is centred again in a feminine, blind body. David Copperfield is of course aligned not only with blindness but also the feminine, and his identity is implicitly bi-gendered: we recall how Betsey Trotwood initially desires a niece, whom she would name after herself; when told that Clara has given birth to a boy, she flees from Blunderstone Rookery, leaving Betsey Trotwood Copperfield in a space of blindness, 'forever in the land of dreams and shadows' (*DC*, 24). Steerforth also desires David's feminine self, calling him 'Daisy' in place of his imagined sister, and David never fully shakes off this sense of inhabiting two genders. The narrative of *Bleak House* is explicitly bi-gendered, alternating between an omniscient, male narrator and a first-person female narrator (Esther). It is in framing the latter narrative that Dickens draws upon a language of blindness and touch that, in its proximate nature, belongs to the feminine.

If *Bleak House*, as J. Hillis Miller famously asserts, is 'about the interpretation of documents', then the ability to perceive the linguistic sign assumes particular importance in the struggle to both interpret and generate text and to solve the novel's mysteries.[41] In a key passage which aligns blindness with illiteracy, the third-person narrator speculates on the 'connexion' between the Dedlock's Lincolnshire and London residences, the footman 'Mercury' and Jo the crossing sweeper, as well as 'between many people in the innumerable histories of this world, who, from opposite sides of great gulfs, have nevertheless, been very curiously brought together!' (*BH*, 256). Noting how Jo is unaware of such connections (Jo would sum up his mental condition as '"don't know nothink"'), the narrator reflects on the gap between the appearance of writing and its meaning:

> It must be a strange state to be like Jo! To shuffle through the streets, unfamiliar with the shapes, and in utter darkness as to the meaning, of those mysterious symbols, so abundant over the shops, and at the corners of the streets, and on the doors, and in the windows! To see people read, and to see people write, and to see the postmen deliver letters, and not, to have the least idea of all that language – to be, to every scrap of it, stone blind and dumb! (*BH*, 257)

Not only does Jo act as the origin of the disease that temporarily blinds and scars Esther, he is also figured, like Laura Bridgman, as 'stone blind and dumb', even though Dickens's meeting with Bridgman demonstrated how a person without sight or voice could be literate. This passage is, however, concerned with a subject's ability to engage with the communal alphabet – that is, the alphabet based on the Roman letter. Language requires both correct perceptual and cognitive functions. Jo, neglected and uneducated, cannot participate in society's textual economy, where commerce and communication turn on a shared system of visual writing.[42] There are echoes here also with David Copperfield learning shorthand, as language shifts from abstract visual symbols to a signifying system that, through discipline, can be known and interpreted. This passage revisits the questions that underpinned Dickens's encounter with Laura Bridgman: what does writing mean without an individual's ability to interpret it? The anxiety of how we visually map and interpret the connections between people shifts to the arbitrariness of how we consume text. Jo embodies – and connects – the novel's sustained meditation on the question of social and textual legibility.

Blindness and impaired vision are also central to the novel's unusual dual narrative structure, which attempts to knit together two different perspectives (that of the omniscient, unknown third-person narrator and Esther Summerson's first-person narrative) to form a holistic picture of the events and relations around the *Jarndyce vs Jarndyce* Chancery suit. Whilst the double narrative has been the source of much debate since the novel's first serial publication, I draw attention to two critical insights relevant to my discussion: Esther's narrative as a form of aut(h)o(r)biography and the authorial sight disorder produced by the double narrative, both of which illustrate how important blindness is to the conception of authorial identity.[43] Marcia Renee Goodman has argued persuasively that 'the characterization of Esther portrays many of Dickens's own psychological conflicts, particularly those related to issues of self-revelation and connection to an-other', and that she speaks of Dickens's wish for his 'own early feminine connection'.[44] If we can read Esther as a figuration of Dickens's authorial self, then her temporary blindness, followed by sight restoration, is a revealing portrait of the writer as blind. I argue that this act of authorial blindness makes explicit Dickens's anxiety that writing, as a material form, is an arbitrary system whose meaning is circumscribed by the limits of the bodies that produce and consume it.

These limits are impressed within the novel's own impaired vision, produced in part, as Hillis Miller has argued, by the triangulated relationship between the two narrators and the reader, as 'both narrators hide as much as they reveal', and the frequent failure of characters' interpretative quests (the novel is 'full of unsuccessful detectives').[45] We can understand this problematic hermeneutic in still more bodily terms. Noting how the dual narration of *Bleak House* replicates the nineteenth-century ideology of a male public and a female private sphere, Suzanne Graver comments that the double narrative produces a double vision, which is anatomically understood as 'a sight disorder created by inequality of tone in the muscles that yoke the two eyes together'.[46] Whilst for Graver, the double vision of *Bleak House* signifies 'social disorder', it also points to the limits of the authorial body that struggles to find a total vision in either its masculine or feminine guise even as it seeks a corrective vision.[47] The double narrative attempts, like the speaker in Barrett Browning's *Aurora Leigh*, to see things both near and far, but is disturbed by its own blind spots. These find a literal space in the novel's architecture in Tom all-Alone's, as Lady Dedlock's cold, dead body finally attests to the failure of the agents involved – narrators, characters, readers – to make sense of the (predominantly visual) clues given and to resolve the plot happily.

Notably, characters in the novel are consistently rendered with impaired vision in the fog that pervades London and its environs. The novel famously opens by creating a pictorial scene of London in November that resists interpretation by its confusion of the reader's visual sense. Smoke lowers down from chimney pots 'making a soft black drizzle'; dogs are 'indistinguishable in mire' and horses 'scarcely better'. Against the seeming 'death of the sun', we struggle to make sense of the social, and of the human agents in this scene, as 'foot passengers, jostling one another's umbrellas' slip and slide across street-corners, merging like the 'crust upon crust of mud' with the tens of thousands of other foot passengers who have performed this ritual in the past. More than by the wet and the mud, the visual order is disturbed by the encroaching spread of the fog. In a staccato tone, the narrator observes that there is 'Fog everywhere' (*BH*, 13). Short sentences, whereby places, things and effects are reduced to nouns and adjectives, such as 'London' and 'implacable November weather', contrast with longer ones describing the flowing and rolling movement of the fog which spreads up and down the river, along the marshes and amongst the meadows. The effect is a sensory confusion, whereby things are briefly glimpsed before being concealed again, aligning the reader (and indeed narrator) with the 'chance people on the bridges peeping over the parapets into a nether sky of fog, with fog all around them, as if they were up in a balloon, and hanging in the misty clouds'. Whilst Dickens in an earlier novel expressed the desire to imitate a good spirit 'who would take the house-tops off', and see the patterns and relationships between people more clearly, here the fog impairs the vision of all agents in the story.[48] The fog of *Bleak House* bespeaks the anxiety of how we visually map and interpret the connections between people, at eye level.

In her study of fog in nineteenth-century culture, Christine Corton has recently argued that the fog in *Bleak House* is not just a metaphor for the political obfuscation that emanates from Chancery: it also has a thickly material presence, corresponding to the real fog that blighted London at this time.[49] Moreover, Corton associates the fog with the images of blindness that dominate the novel, although her discussion focuses largely on metaphoric instances of this.[50] The fog also imitates the effect of two of the most well-known sight disorders in the period, cataract and glaucoma, particularly as we move from the fog that pervades London, to its particular concentration in the High Court of Chancery, which is 'at the very heart of the fog'. Here, we move from the fog as a phenomenon that people look *at*, to one that is looked *through*, and which mediates the process of sight itself. This mirrors the switch from the panoramic narrative lens that sweeps over indistinguishable crowds and the broadly outlined regions surrounding London to Temple Bar and the specific perspective of the Lord High Chancellor. Sitting in a 'foggy glory', he can 'see nothing but fog'. In the court, members are 'mistily engaged' in stages of an endless cause and the description of them 'groping knee-deep in technicalities' associates them with the cultural stereotype of the lecherous blind man, whose iconography has recently been traced by David Bolt.[51]

In its opacity, the court is figured as a cataractic lens, 'dim, with wasting candles here and there; may well the fog hang heavy in it, as if it would never get out; well may the stained glass windows lose their colour, and admit no light of day into the place' (*BH*, 14–15). As John Saunders described in 1811, the main diagnostic symptom of cataract was the 'opacity either of the lens or its capsule, or of both', frequently causing a milky screen to form across the surface of the eye.[52] Misting of the eye was also a symptom associated with amaurosis, or gutta serena as it was also termed. This condition, which sometimes combined with cataract, was pathologised as damage to the retina and optic nerve.[53] John Vetch described how, in a person experiencing amaurosis, 'this morbid sensation increases till it has the appearance of a dark net or crape, through which everything is seen indistinctly; sometimes the patient becomes myoptic, and at other times presbyoptic; diplopia, or double vision, when both eyes are employed on the same object'.[54] Not only does an amaurotic patient see things dimly and through a dark mist, they also have the propensity to experience double vision: a sight disorder which, as we have already traced, is embodied in *Bleak House*'s dual narrative. Moreover, it was a sight disorder that, according to some ophthalmologists in the first part of the century, might be exacerbated by physical and moral causes 'affecting the sensibility of the individual', leading to permanent blindness.[55] So whilst fog entrenches the metaphoric association of impaired vision with political failure in the novel, it also attests to the novel's concern with physical sight disorders in its metonymic association with amaurosis. The metaphor of fog pervades the body: the political authorities that should be able to see and judge clearly are instead depicted as damaged visual appurtenances.

Esther Summerson's experience of smallpox similarly inscribes doubt around the reliability of vision, through its effects upon both her sight and her skin. Whilst this episode has been analysed predominantly in terms of the production of feminine subjectivity via pain and scarring, I draw attention to the wider range of the illness's symptomology.[56] I am cautious of a pedantic medical mapping that ignores the novel's own efforts to fictionalise the condition: that is, a critical reading that confuses medical diagnosis with the medical imagination. That said, the political discourse around smallpox in the periods both in which the novel is set and written, as well as correspondences with its symptomology, progression and treatment suggest Dickens clearly had this disease in mind.

Smallpox was a viral disease that had inflicted high mortality rates on European populations in the Modern period.[57] Whilst a cure had been found at the end of the eighteenth century with Edward Jenner's innovations in vaccination, a lack of co-ordinated government response and investment of resources meant epidemics still persisted into the nineteenth century in Britain and the British Empire. For example, whilst a National Establishment for Vaccination founded in Britain in 1808 helped reduce death rates from smallpox through compulsory vaccination for children in London, it stopped short of the programme practised by other European countries and was not rigorously enforced. Contemporary reports indicate that, after the initial wave of public vaccinations following the founding of the National Vaccine Establishment in 1808, smallpox became a threat to public health again in the 1840s and 1850s. The public health commentator Alfred Collinson suggested this was due to the deterioration of the lymph charge supplied in the vaccine, as well as the lack of coercive measures by government.[58] Accounts of the British response in the first part of the nineteenth century suggest a tension between the need for government intervention to reduce the high mortality rates (particularly urgent in the context of the early nineteenth-century Napoleonic wars), and a concern to avoid over-intervention. It was in fact only in 1853, shortly after *Bleak House*'s publication, that vaccination was made compulsory, following several pandemics at home, and epidemics in colonial Britain.[59] Dickens was particularly anxious about debates over public health at this point. As well as speaking at meetings for the Metropolitan Sanitary Association, he also actively used his position as editor of *Household Words* to promote the campaign for sanitary reform.[60]

The specificity of smallpox is tied to the radical politics practised by the novel, which examines the material effects engendered by political ideology upon the most vulnerable members of society.[61] The progression of the disease from Jo to Charley to Esther emphasises quite literally how such sickness cannot conveniently be confined to the unparented and dispensable figures embodied by Jo. Rather, the model of contagion serves to illustrate how sickness spreads between classes, matching the symptomology of the smallpox disease. Smallpox could be transmitted via the respiratory system, by inhaling infected air breathed out by suffering victims, as well as via contact with its pustules and scabs.[62] Indeed, the miasmic nature of the disease is emphasised in the novel. Esther describes how the cottage in which Jenny and Liz nurse Jo 'was closer than before, and had an unhealthy, and a very peculiar smell' (*BH*, 489). Harold Skimpole, who has trained as a medical doctor, is anxious about the proximity of Jo's sick body when Esther and Charley bring him to Bleak House; smell and breath are coded as dangerous here.

Smallpox also performs a hermeneutic function in the novel, as Esther's experience of the disease tests and stretches the limits of realism and narrative. The experience upholds, to an extent, Lawrence Rothfield's argument that medicine is a constitutive element of the realist novel. Rothfield contrasts the difference between Mme de Merteuil's disfiguration by smallpox in Laclos's French novel *Les Liaisons Dangereuses* (1782) with Zola's description of the smallpox that kills the heroine in *Nana* (1880). Whilst the villainous Merteuil's scarring offers 'a legible figure of moral, social, and narrative closure', thus putting an end to interpretation, Nana's illness bears a sociological content, exposing the relationships between characters and disease. Moreover, in the microscopic detail with which its effects are described, Nana's disfigurement no longer makes her inner character visible, but rather reduces her to sheer flesh.[63] Yet *Bleak House* does not fall neatly into Rothfield's trajectory from Laclos to Zola, via which we might trace the disciplinary development of the clinic. This development, to borrow from Foucault's term, becomes increasingly *visible* in its level of description in the nineteenth century. In *Bleak House*, illness and disease are expressed not simply in terms of a visual semiotics, but through a wider sensorium, which Esther's temporary blindness crucially signals. Reading Esther's blindness and illness phenomenologically disrupts the relationship between vision and narrative, as the text inscribes different ways of knowing, feeling and recording the world. The novelist allows Esther to attempt – even if she falters – to describe her own experience, rather than making her the object of the novelist's diagnostic gaze.

Esther tells Charley she is blind at the end of chapter 31, 'Nurse and Patient', midway through the novel's tenth monthly instalment. This follows on closely from Lady Dedlock's realisation that the living Esther is her illegitimate child, whom she had been told was dead, which dramatically closes the novel's ninth instalment. After nursing Charley, Esther realises she has fallen ill herself. She hides the effect of the illness on her vision, only telling Charley as her narrative instalment closes:

> 'And now come and sit beside me for a little while, and touch me with your hand. For I cannot see you Charley, I am blind'. (*BH*, 504)

Illness and blindness produce a strange sense of embodiment in Esther, precipitating an altered sensory and spatial state which distorts her sense of size, rather like the effect on Alice of her adventures in Wonderland; for Esther, this loosens her from the confines of the text. In her fever, she wrestles with the impression of labouring up 'colossal staircases', never reaching the top, like 'a worm in a garden path'. Falling ill is like crossing 'a dark lake, and to have left all my experiences, mingled together by the great distance, on the healthy shore' (*BH*, 555). As her vision breaks down, her narrative falters – an effect both of the trauma of the experience and the sense that it is somehow beyond words. There is 'little or no separation between the various stages of my life which had really been divided by years' (*BH*, 555). Her narrative attempts to squeeze life back into a coherent experiential structure, in which her self progresses neatly from past to present. Instead, the illness throws up the anguish of multiple, ahistorical selves as she seems 'at once a child, an elder girl, and the little woman'. Esther verbalises the sensation of the pain and blindness caused by her illness: 'strung together somewhere in great black space, there was a flaming necklace, or ring, or starry circle of some kind, of which *I* was one of the beads!' (*BH*, 556). This inverts Molyneux's question of whether a blind man restored to sight would know through vision what he had known by touch alone. Without vision, Esther is strangely unanchored, but when she asks Charley to 'touch me with your hand' (*BH*, 504), Charley's voice and touch centre her in the sickroom.

Whilst the spiritual dimension to this is clear, the medical knowledge alluded to also impresses upon the text a more somatic meaning. The blindness Esther experiences is rather more literal than the metaphoric blindness ascribed to David Copperfield. By 1796 smallpox was also responsible for a third of all blindness and it remained one of the most significant causes of blindness in the early nineteenth century.[64] The viral rash in most forms of smallpox was usually densest on the face, affecting the eyes and causing damage through, most frequently, corneal ulceration; fever could also inflame the optic nerve. Pustules clustering around the eyes frequently caused the eyelids to swell and become sticky, leading to a more temporary blindness, as Esther experiences.

Esther's blindness impresses upon us the limits to the visual, an important counter to those interpretations of the novel which read visuality as power.[65] Why, though, is Esther's sight restored? She continues blind for several weeks, until the point comes whereby, shrinking from the light 'as it twinkled on me once more', she realises 'with a boundless joy for which no words are rapturous enough, that I should see again' (*BH*, 556). Of course, Esther's blindness might disrupt the romantic narrative and the possibility of her relationship with Allan Woodcourt by making her sexually unattractive, according to ocularnormative constructions.[66] Moreover, as this chapter details, although blindness provides the conditions for writing and the imagination to come into being, it also threatens the writer's identity by closing down established reading and writing systems which turn on the visible. The text cannot seam to bear an authorial subject who is blind. The first act that Esther recalls with her 'sight strengthening' is being able to read Ada's letters and to see the trace of her writing (rather than her actual self), figured in erotic terms as Esther 'could put them to my lips and lay my cheek upon them with no fear of hurting her' (*BH*, 556–7). Esther is 'afraid to hint at that time in my disorder', and – whilst still revealing to us something of her 'sick experiences' – worries that recounting the heat of the fever and darkness of blindness will make her narrative less 'intelligible' (*BH*, 556).

Whilst Esther's narrative breaks down as she attempts to describe the sensation of her illness, the experience remains legible in the scars on her face, which resemble the embossed writing surveyed in Chapter 3. As she begins to recover at Chesney Wold, and just before the moment of anagnorisis when Lady Dedlock reveals herself to her as her mother, a young child asks: 'why is the lady not a pretty lady now, like she used to be?' The violent severance from the visual world is counterbalanced here by a tender tactility drawn from the discourse of blindness as the child, 'no less fond of me', draws 'its soft hand over my face with a kind of pitying protection in its touch, that soon set me up again' (*BH*, 575). Her face, scarred, is read by the hand of this young child like an embossed text that yields momentarily a new knowledge of her identity that counters the visual, recalling images of Bridgman finger reading.

Yet this touch is cautionary, both in its 'pitying' nature and in its evocation of a mode of reading whose effectiveness was still uncertain in the wider public imagination. This uncertainty is evidenced in Harriet Martineau's 1854 article 'Blindness', published in *Household Words* a few months after the novel concluded. This article exemplifies the contradictory attitude towards blindness that we have charted already in the previous chapters. Whilst evaluating the relative advantages and disadvantages of deafness versus blindness (in which her own identity as a hearing-impaired person is very much suppressed), Martineau speculates on why blind people receive 'so much more compassion and sympathy' than 'any other class of sufferers from personal imperfection or infirmity'. This is, she continues, despite their potential to enjoy a 'full power of communication with other minds', noting that 'there is scarcely anything that some blind person or other has not excelled in, except painting and decoration'. She details further how a greater understanding of brain function in philosophy and medicine (citing Molyneux's problem) had opened up the possibilities for developing intellectual training for blind people.[67] Martineau also considers what type – as well as the type – of literature is appropriate for blind readers. Detailing the discomfort she and others have experienced at fundraising events for blind asylums, where children have to sing hymns and listen to addresses 'stuffed full of the very things the children know nothing about', she records a trial whereby new verse was produced 'without a single direct visual image in it – nothing but what some inmate or another of that very school had felt or thought'.[68] Here, the visio-centric nature of language is acknowledged, and an intriguing possibility set forth of a discourse that is organised instead around other sensory modalities, resonating with what blind children would feel or think. Martineau also makes recourse to 'their nice sense of touch', which will facilitate blind people's ability to share in the systems of visual description that characterise 'our literature'. Yet blind people are constructed as passive agents in the new tactile, textual world that Martineau envisages, as they must necessarily remain responsive to the innovations of 'us', the sighted:

> Their nice sense of touch, which used to be little more than an empty marvel to us, we have now learned to make use of in unbarring the doors which shut them out from literature. We now print books for them, in a type which they feel, instead of see.[69]

The diversity of embossed alphabetic systems is alluded to, but Martineau concludes that 'we feel no doubt about sticking to the ordinary alphabet'.[70]

In this article, whilst Martineau acknowledges that both the content and form of language and literature for blind and visually impaired people might be different to that enjoyed and used by the sighted, she proposes instead a process of normalisation that will erase traces of difference. Dickens's journal firmly entrenches the ocularcentric desire that the blind person's finger must follow and replicate the movement of the sighted person's eye as it tracks text. This contradictory logic, tacitly endorsed by Dickens as editor of *Household Words*, is also discernible in his own accounts and imaginings of blindness, as he explores the possibilities of narrators who experience the world with impaired vision, but returns them to sight.[71]

## Conclusion

In this chapter, I have explored how blindness occupies an important, but by no means straightforward, role in Dickens's journalistic and fictional writing, as it is invoked as both a metaphor and theme through which to explore the meaningful production and reception of literary language. I have traced the imprint of the material cultures of reading and writing for blind people on his thought, as well as his interest in its medical symptomology, suggesting that discourses which are explicitly addressed in his role as journalist and editor also inform his more imaginative constructions of blindness. I argue that these discourses lend new impetus to blindness as a trope that tests the limits to empirical vision and the representational systems of narrative in Dickens's fiction. Both the condition of blindness and mode of touch have strong cultural identifications with the feminine. These encounters are also queer in the way they destabilise, and disrupt, the affective bond between biological families.[72] The tactile mode of knowing on which both episodes turn is figured through children touching women who are motherly, but not their biological mothers; whereas Dickens recounts his own entry into visual language taking place through his mother's instruction. If Dickens hesitates about the endings open to David and Esther as blind characters, the next chapter amplifies the problematic limitations within which writers could imagine a blind identity. Whilst Frances Browne, a well-known poet and novelist who was also blind, chooses suicide for her blinded female heroine in her novel *My Share of the World* (1861), Wilkie Collins – in one of the nineteenth century's most radical novelistic treatments of visual impairment – restores his heroine to blindness to grant her a happy ending.

CHAPTER 7

# *Embodying Blindness in the Victorian Novel*
## *Frances Browne's* My Share of the World *and Wilkie Collins's* Poor Miss Finch

Frances Browne was a well-known writer of the London literary circuit at the mid-nineteenth century. Her poetry and prose pieces appeared regularly in popular journals such as the *Athenaeum* (she was a leading poetry contributor to the magazine throughout the 1840s), *Tait's Magazine* and *Ainsworth's Magazine*. During a career spanning 20 years, her works included a volume of poetry in 1844, a fictional autobiography, *My Share of the World*, in 1861 and a second novel, *The Castleford Case*, in 1862.[1] Significantly, Browne's fame also derived from the fact that she was effectively born blind: an attack of small pox at the age of 18 months led to the loss of her sight, and she was known contemporarily as 'The Blind Poetess of Ulster'.[2]

In *My Share of the World*, the female love interest, Lucy, experiences sight loss as the result, it is suggested, of anxiety, and subsequently commits suicide. In Browne's fictional account, sight loss metaphorically signifies feminine lack and is tragically presented, despite Browne's own career being testimony to the fact that blindness need not be a barrier to success. Lucy's loss of vision and death metaphorically associates blindness with the end of writing, an association that emerges, I argue, from the novel's investment in an externally referential system of language that privileges the relationship between vision and knowledge, and which Browne's own embodied self cannot experience. Conversely, Wilkie Collins's *Poor Miss Finch* (1872) explores the negative impact of sight restoration to a person born blind, recognising the anxiety this would cause. The novel attempts to create an accurate and realistic depiction of blindness and restore integrity to a blind identity, crucially through emphasising the blind protagonist Lucilla Finch's skill and pleasure in reading the world through the sense of touch. The plot is complex and sensational: Lucilla, a beautiful young blind woman with abhorrence for dark colours, falls in love with an identical twin, Oscar Dubourg. Oscar's skin is dyed blue by his taking silver nitrate to treat his epilepsy; fearing Lucilla's rejection of him, he swaps identity with his twin, Nugent (who has fallen in love himself with Lucilla). Nugent introduces Herr Grosse, an ophthalmologist, to Lucilla, who reveals he can operate on her cataracts and restore her sight.

Collins claims in his preface to the novel that this is the first example in literature of 'exhibiting blindness as it really is', and that Lucilla (one of the only central blind protagonists in Victorian fiction) is a tapestry of real voices, unlike the 'sentimental and ideal' representations of blindness which, Collins argues, precede her.[3] Whilst Collins draws on the real, via narratives of blindness from wider cultural sources, he does not write from a position of direct experience. Yet in returning Lucilla to blindness, Collins rewrites the paradigm connecting blindness and writing in literary tradition in a way that Frances Browne, as a blind female author, does not – or perhaps cannot.

Reading these two authors' presentations of blindness alongside one another invites reflection on the ways in which the nineteenth-century novel variously accommodates visual impairment. Whilst we should be careful not to absorb wholesale Nancy Armstrong's proposition that nineteenth-century fiction 'equated seeing with knowing and made visual information the basis for the intelligibility of a verbal narrative', Browne constructs a realist fantasy in her novel that seems to do just this, with tragic consequences for the blind identity it inscribes.[4] The sensation genre within which Collins writes offers a different model, and a caution to Armstrong's proposition. Although criticised for its 'implausible plot' that tempers its investigation into blind people's development of senses other than sight, Collins's realist claims and sensationalist style are not, I argue, completely at odds with one another.[5] Sensation fiction's interest in the way in which events are inscribed on and experienced through the body make it a particularly rich genre through which to investigate the condition of blindness and, by extension, the faculty of touch.

Briefly analysing Collins's novel within a discussion of the ways in which embodiment and sensation are embedded within nineteenth-century literary form, William A. Cohen has recently described how *Poor Miss Finch* is 'unusually acute in articulating a relation between inner self and outer form by emphasising both the surface elements of the body and the incorporative capacities of sensory perception'.[6] Cohen posits his discussion alongside analysis of twentieth-century French philosophical writing on the nature of embodiment, including Maurice Merleau-Ponty, who 'supplies phenomenological tools for conceiving of human encounters with the world in perceptual terms and of perception itself as fundamentally corporeal'. Victorian writers 'anticipate' such theoretical texts in Cohen's thesis.[7] We can take Cohen's investigations further here, though, as an analysis of Collins's sources connects his novel in unexpected other ways with Merleau-Ponty, who drew extensively on an early twentieth-century cognitive psychological investigation into examples of sight restoration in his chapter 'Sense Experience' in *Phenomenology of Perception* (1945).[8] Collins's effort to understand and describe Victorian blindness and touch through philosophical and cognitive psychological discourses places him within a phenomenological lineage.

## Frances Browne: The Blind Poetess

Frances Browne's work was published consistently throughout the 1840s and 1850s and she was well known enough in 1861 to top the list of her publisher Hurst & Blackett's notices of new novels in the *Athenaeum*.[9] Browne's historical and national style of poetry appealed to the taste of her readership, and one of her early reviewers drew attention to her 'beautiful verses'.[10] However, this same reviewer also focused on Browne's presenting 'us with the new and interesting phenomenon of a poetess who, although not born blind, was deprived of sight at an age when she could have acquired none of the ideas which are communicated to the soul by the organ of vision'.[11] The Countess of Blessington, editor of the *Keepsake*, added a footnote to Browne's poem, 'The First', drawing attention to Browne's blindness:

> The authoress is her country-woman, resident in a small town in a remote part of Ireland; one of a numerous family of humble fortune; and further, suffering under the heavy infliction of total loss of sight. Under circumstances like these, the genius which creates, and the energy which provides self-cultivation, surely acquires a double value, especially when accompanied, as in the case of the writer, by a modest and unrepining spirit.[12]

Elizabeth Barrett Browning was also a contributor to the *Athenaeum* during the 1840s. She was struck by Browne, discussing her poetry in a letter to John Kenyon:

> Think of her being quite blind since she was eighteen months old, & with no recollections of light & form – & poor, & in humble life, – the daughter of an Irish postmaster. The energy of a mind that could struggle through difficulty & darkness, & attain enough to produce those graceful poems, is a noble example, & will, I hope, be extensively considered & respected.[13]

The idea of blindness fascinates Barrett Browning as she reflects on how Browne can write poetry with no recollections of light or form, noting the 'energy of a mind' that could write without vision.

The reviewer of *The Star of Atteghei, The Vision of Schwartz, and other Poems* in the *Dublin Review* devoted a large section to the tracing of visual references in Browne's poetry, noting that 'we have marked in italics the images which are taken from light and colours'.[14] And in Browne's short poem 'Streams', the reviewer has 'marked in italics the touching allusion of the authoress to her blindness':

How is it that ye waken still
The young heart's happy dreams;
*And shed your light on darkened eyes,*
O bright and blessed streams?[15]

These examples place Browne within nineteenth-century debates concerning the structure and meaning of writing, particularly around its relation to sensory (and especially visual) experience. As I noted in the introductory chapter, William Paulson has described how, in the nineteenth century, blindness posed the problem of an opposition or connection between two properties and ways of understanding language: the externally referential (or representational), where a linguistic sign refers to an object directly apprehended, and the internally referential (or systematic), where signs and signifiers are ordered in a system of hierarchical interrelations.[16]

Browne's interest to critics emerged largely from what she revealed about the acquisition and employment of language without vision. One reviewer likened her to Laura Bridgman, and drew attention to Browne's own account of her education and the processes whereby she learned how to read and write, which takes the form of a long letter to the editor of her volume of poetry.[17] She detailed how, aged seven, upon hearing her pastor and wanting to understand the words he used, she devised a plan for her own learning:

> When a word unintelligible to me happened to reach my ear, I was careful to ask its meaning from any person whom I thought likely to inform me – a habit which was, probably, troublesome enough to the friends and acquaintances of my childhood: but by this method I soon acquired a considerable stock of words; and, when further advanced in life, enlarged it still more by listening attentively to my young brothers and sisters reading over the tasks required at the village school. They were generally obliged to commit to memory a certain portion of the Dictionary and English Grammar, each day; and by hearing them read it aloud frequently, for that purpose, as my memory was better than theirs (perhaps rendered by necessity), I learned the task much sooner than they, and frequently heard them repeat it.[18]

Browne learned language systematically, rather than denominationally, painstakingly building up her vocabulary from a store of references that enabled her to interpret new words contextually, aided by friends' explanations. Browne's account of her own education emphasised how the world may be known and represented in language without the necessity of direct visual perception of objects. The sense of hearing was particularly important for Browne, who listened acutely and noted her superior memorising skills. In terms that we find echoed in Collins's novel, blindness in fact set her at an advantage, for her memory was 'better', perhaps by 'necessity', than her sighted peers, and she began to overtake them in language acquisition. Browne reminds us of Edmund Burke's earlier realisation that the auditory, rather than the visual, is of central importance in the subject's ability to grasp and communicate concepts in language, as I discussed in the first chapter. Indeed, Browne's editor of *The Star of Atteghei* urges her reader to read Browne's poetry before her biography, and only 'with the music in his ear of some of these beautiful little poems' to turn to 'the touching account of these impeding circumstances amid which has welled up this fountain of natural song'.[19] He thus emphasises the musical quality of her writing. Yet Browne's capacity to fully understand concepts and ideas ostensibly relating to sight (such as colour) was questioned by many of her nineteenth-century readers. Browne's readers speculated on the truthfulness of her descriptions of visual concepts without direct experience. The tendency to privilege the visual in language, which Burke argued against in his *Enquiry*, remained strong.

In his mid-century study of deafness and blindness, John Kitto's lengthy analysis of Browne's narrative poem 'The Star of Atteghei' emphasised moments of aesthetic failure in its construction of visual scenes. Whilst broadly complimentary ('it would require very close inspection to discover that the author is blind'), Kitto's discussion is marked by an underlying scepticism as to Browne's ability to fully know certain scenes that she describes. Kitto presumes that where a word picture is 'perfect' it is 'probably copied from the poetry or prose of Scott'.[20] He pores over examples of her poetry, eager to find some 'new ideas respecting visual objects by one who is blind'.[21] His critical analysis of her work is confined mainly to identifying instances in which her poetic images break down when 'she does not appear to have had an idea' of a thing, such as shadow.[22] Browne's poetic writing is critically analysed in terms of the gap between visual sign and signified, as Kitto locates textual meaning in the body of 'The Blind Poetess'. Browne's novel draws on a visual framework even more sharply in its attempt to define and describe the life of its fictional narrator. The blinding and suicide of the female love interest is a tragically driven interrogation of Browne's own status as blind writer.

## Blindness as Metaphor in Browne's Fictional Autobiography

*My Share of the World* turns on the relationship between sight and representation. Browne calls upon certain conventions of literary autobiographies to create an intricate network of visual relations in the text. Situated against this network of visual relations, Browne inscribes herself in the text through the creation of a blind(ed) female character, Lucy. The complex gender politics underline the novel's anxiety in relation to the embodied self. Unusually for a Victorian novel penned by a woman writer, Browne constructs a fictional male narrator, Frederic Favoursham, to narrate events. Browne's authorial identity is thus split between a (feminised) male narrator, who looks at and observes the world, and a beautiful woman figured firstly as the object of the male gaze and secondly as a tragic suicide.

The novel, published in three volumes, outlines the fortunes of the fictional autobiographer, Frederic Favoursham.[23] Favoursham is the son of an abandoned mother living in Manchester, who is sent to live with relatives at the age of 14, at which point he receives training as a portrait artist. After leaving this situation, he tries out various jobs such as teaching, phrenology and journalism, without ever establishing a firm career. As a young man he falls in love with Lucy Rose, who ultimately marries George Fenton, a relative of Frederic and an industrialist. Frederic eventually stands as the heir of a distant relative's fortune, Mr Rollinson. Ultimately, Frederic doesn't actually *do* anything in his life apart from write this autobiography, the narrator admitting at the novel's close that 'as none of these modes of passing the time accorded with my inclinations, I have taken my own way, and done nothing, except write this story, and collect materials for better ones' (*MSW*, III: 288). In his lack of career and purposiveness, Frederic is feminised, capable only of acting out his masculinity.

The novel opens on a remembered scene, with the older Frederic looking back on his younger self. The narrator opens his autobiography with the reflection that 'the starting point of one's memory seems to me the true beginning of life. Mine is a low back parlour, about twelve feet square, with a worn and washed out look in all its furniture, a very small fire in the grate, a shop of all-wares seen through a half-open door, and a sound of heavy rain at the window' (*MSW*, I: 1). Memory here is unambiguously associated with recalling visual images. Further, the narrator recollects:

> There is a subjugated-looking young woman sewing hard in the corner, and seated on the floor at her feet a very little boy, whom I did not see, but he

> had on a newly-torn pinafore; with three oyster-shells in it – his name was Frederic Favoursham – and he has lived to be the writer of the present story. (*MSW*, I: I)

Tellingly, the narrator cannot see himself, although he constructs himself as a visual image by revealing details of his dress and his place in the room. The narrative oscillates between the desire to limit vision to this 'very little boy' seated on the floor, with his restricted view, and the urge to capture a wider, omniscient vision. Frederic, who attaches sight to knowledge, remembers the image in heightened visual terms:

> The absorbed look of every face in that room, whether speakers or listeners may have engraved the scene on my recollection, – where it stands distinct and unattached, in the fashion of first-remembered things. All around it is a blank, broken by half memories of falls, frights, and great surprises ... by and bye, however, the look-out becomes clearer, and the ground more firm. I know the tall sharp-faced pair to be my aunt Grizzle and my uncle Gurney ... I know the subjugated young woman to be my loving mother. (*MSW*, I: 2)

The novel echoes with allusions to preceding models of literary autobiography – not least *David Copperfield*, as the manner in which David's history is told relies heavily upon vision, as I traced in the previous chapter. This association between vision and the self is also expressed in Frederick's early, and unsuccessful, training as a portrait painter. Portraiture forms part of a critique of the relationship between the authoring and writing of the text, as that relationship is repeatedly grounded on visual self-representation. The association between vision and self-representation draws Browne into the text, as her literary fame rests partly on her reputation as a blind writer. Such instances positively bear out Browne's systematic employment of language in which objects and actions associated with vision may be conceptually, if not sensorially, known. Strangely however, the way in which she approaches blindness through the character of Lucy suggests that in conceptualising vision and the gaze, Browne is symbolically reduced by it.

Lucy's portrait is taken at the same time as she is introduced to the reader. During her life and after her death, this image is circulated between her grandfather, husband and Frederic. Frederic notes that 'George bought it at the sale of the Rosebank furniture. I bought it at the sale of his, and somebody will, doubtless, buy it at the sale of mine. It represents Lucy as she looked then, standing under a rose tree on the lawn' (*MSW*, I: 115). In the novel's romantic plot, Lucy's visual image is fixed early on; the degeneration of her own sight prevents her from seeing this likeness of herself.

In Dinah Craik's *Olive* (1850), the vain Sybilla Rothesay is blinded in part to critique an aesthetic system in which women exist to be looked at, as passive objects. Lucy's blinding also acts as a mute reminder of her own passivity in the network of gazes surrounding her.

Lucy begins to lose her sight towards the novel's close. Although ostensibly the result of a cold, both Frederic and her grandfather attribute Lucy's blindness to anxiety brought on by the failure of her husband's business enterprises, and his harsh attitude towards her. Her blindness is thus linked to her psychological state, and suggested to be either the cause of her suicide, or a symptom of the mental illness that leads to it. Frederic and her husband dramatically argue as to the cause of her blindness, with Frederic believing that a consultation with a London oculist will lead to a cure. George argues instead that this will be a pointless waste of his working hours:

> 'Dr. Dixon tells me, and you see, yourself, there is nothing wrong with her eyes.'
>
> 'Dr. Dixon's a quack,' said I, 'if he says any such thing; trouble and vexation may impair the nerves of sight, while the outward organs remain perfect, and that I fear is her case'. (*MSW*, III: 178)

The connection between Lucy's psychological state and her vision associates blindness with an anxiety of self-identity in the text's visual system, and exemplifies what David Bolt, in a discussion of mourning, describes as 'the most disturbing element of the metanarrative of blindness' – the cultural belief that death is equal or preferable to being blind.[24]

As Lucy begins to lose her sight she is advised by her husband's doctor to avoid reading and writing, 'for Dr Dixon, whom George thought the cleverest man in Lancashire, had told her there was nothing so trying to the eyes as white paper. He said the less she read the better; and George talked of locking up her desk and bookcase' (*MSW*, III: 116). Poignantly, as her sight fails, Lucy's writing also breaks down, an inversion of the authorial self inscribed in the text:

> His [George's] mention of Lucy had grown less every letter; but he was sure if anybody could benefit her it was Dr Dixon. She had written rarely, and then only a line or two enclosing something for Harry. Latterly, there was a queer uncertainty about her writing, and the latest note was by Mary Anne Fenton, in her name. (*MSW*, III: 166)

The reference to the 'queer uncertainty' of Lucy's writing emphasises the uncanny nature of this description, as a blind writer imagines someone writing blind, and eventually writing with an amanuensis. Browne herself relied upon a sighted hand to record her narration (John Kitto describes how Browne employed her sister as an amanuensis).[25] In this image of a woman dictating to her amanuensis, the gendered codes of writing in the Victorian period (in which the woman bears language for the man) are disrupted.

Lucy takes to wearing spectacles as her sight worsens and Frederic tells us:

> Her sight was worse than I had heard or imagined; the soft violet eyes which had … lit up many an after dream, were still bright and tender as the evenings of May, but the fountain of sight, which no remedy could reach and no microscope examine, was losing life and power, and bringing down on her the night that knows no morning. Her spirit was withering in the fall of that great darkness; I knew it by the hopeless look which had settled on her face …
>
> 'Frederic, my sight is not so good as it used to be, but I think your hair is darker, and,' … (*MSW*, III: 175–6)

Although Frederic futilely attempts to agitate George into seeking a cure for her blindness, her loss of vision ascribes to Lucy the role of passive and silent victim, outside of the bounds of both medical and narrative recovery. In her suicide note, both her failing vision and tears erase her own account of her death:

> On the table beside the empty phial we found a written paper, beginning, 'Dear grandfather, forgive me, and lay me beside my poor mother'. The writing which followed could not be read, from the uncertainty of the hand, and the heavy tears which had fallen and blotted it. (*MSW*, III: 263)

Lucy's blindness and despair both combine to erase her writing, and silence Lucy's attempt to tell her story and record her wishes. She is cast in the role of a passive, mute object at the novel's close, unable to author her final trace. The terms with which psychoanalyst Jacques Lacan problematises the gaze through his reading of Merleau-Ponty's writing on the visible and invisible are particularly apposite here. Describing the 'limits that we encounter in the experience of the visible', Lacan suggests that the gaze is 'presented' to us 'only in the form of a strange contingency' and as 'the thrust of our experience, namely, the lack that constitutes castration anxiety'. Distinguishing between the eye and the gaze, Lacan – like Merleau-Ponty – is uneasy about a subjectivity formed fully in the scopic field.[26]

The stultifying effect of the gaze in Browne's novel emerges, however, in the way in which it draws attention to the unfunctioning eye of the writer (the castration anxiety *is* blindness). Anxiously probing the experience of the visible, Browne is unable to embody blindness.

As I discussed in Chapter 4, the nineteenth-century blind campaigner Mrs Hippolyte van Landeghem called for a shift in understanding of the nature of blindness through greater dialogue with actual blind people and recognition of their capabilities and needs. She used biography to demonstrate blind people's achievements in the past and present, identifying Frances Browne as a contemporary role model:

> Her poems are well known; and in the vigorous pages of her two novels, *My Share of the World*, and *The Castle-ford Case*, we may look in vain for that weakness of ideas which generally marks those blind whom ignorance or selfishness dooms to move, to suffer, and to die, without having lived.[27]

Yet Browne herself perpetuates a negative image of blindness, in associating it with Lucy's melancholy and despair, and making it part of her novel's more tragic drive.

Whilst Browne's readers may have recognised traces of the author in the figure of Lucy, Browne, the author, both resists and fears the debilitating effects of blindness which she draws in the novel. In reinforcing a structure in the novel that associates subjectivity with vision, her own embodied experience as a blind woman is – like Lucy's suicide note – erased. In a novel written a few years later, Wilkie Collins presents to his audience a blind girl with a similar first name: Lucilla Finch. Her name, as Samuel Lyndon Gladden points out, associates her blindness with imprisonment ('Lucilla' is the Latin diminutive for sight, and 'Finch' represents the songbird that can confine itself to its cage).[28] Collins returns us to the speculative problem of Molyneux's question and raises a fresh set of questions for its depiction in literature: what would happen if a person born blind were made to see? Collins does not just focus on this to emphasise points about sight; instead, he demonstrates a marked preoccupation with the actual condition and experience of blindness, and the psychological consequences that might accompany the restoration of sight.

## Wilkie Collins's *Poor Miss Finch* and Embodying Blindness

Collins had already explored the relationship between the novel and sensory impairment in his third and fourth novels, *Hide and Seek* (1854) (deafness) and *The Dead Secret* (1857) (blindness). In *Hide and Seek*, he draws upon John Kitto's previously mentioned two-volume *The Lost Senses* (1845) in his characterisation of the deaf mute Madonna. Speculating on whether or not there has been a successful depiction of deafness and muteness in literature, he describes the problems that he encountered when he attempted such a depiction himself:

> When the idea first occurred to me of representing the character of a 'Deaf Mute' as literally as possible according to nature, I found the difficulty of getting at tangible and reliable materials to work from, much greater than I had anticipated; so much greater, indeed, that I believe my design must have been abandoned, if a lucky chance had not thrown in my way Dr Kitto's delightful little book, *The Lost Senses*.[29]

Collins writes of how he found the 'authority' for Madonna's character in this text (Kitto was himself deaf and includes his own experience of hearing loss, which Collins describes as an 'interesting and touching narrative').[30] Collins recognises that an interdisciplinary approach best suits his purpose of depicting deafness credibly, opening up a range of 'tangible and reliable materials' beyond the limited representations found in the literary tradition. Kitto's book, the second volume of which has blindness as its theme, also influences both his construction of Leonard Frankland in *The Dead Secret* and Lucilla in *Poor Miss Finch*. Collins's note to *Hide and Seek* indicates that he understands the novelist to have a responsibility to construct a tangible reality in their fictions, correlative to the world in which they live. This is re-emphasised in the preface to *Poor Miss Finch*, where he reveals how he has 'carefully gathered the information necessary to the execution of this purpose from competent authorities of all sorts. Whenever 'Lucilla' acts or speaks in these pages, with reference to her blindness, she is doing or saying what persons afflicted as she is have done or said before her (*PMF*, xxxix). One of these persons may have been, via Kitto, Frances Browne.

*Poor Miss Finch* was categorised as a 'surgical and medical novel' by an unsigned reviewer for the *Saturday Review*, who noted how Collins departs from other literary writers who have 'idealised' blindness 'gracefully'. Before its publication as a three-volume novel by Richard Bentley in early 1872, it was first serialised in *Cassell's Magazine* between October 1871 and March 1872. The popular demand for domestic medical dramas at this time by *Cassell's* readers is suggested by the magazine's next leading serialised novel, Hesba Stratton's *The Doctor's Dilemma*. However, *Poor Miss Finch* was not well-received when first published (one reviewer perplexedly asked, 'what is the aim of this story? That the blind should marry the dark-blue?'), and has continued to suffer from critical neglect.[31] The reviewer for the *Saturday Review* alerts us to some of the ambivalent and hostile reactions to the novel, as he feels uncertain whether Collins can live up to his claim of representing a blind person 'as she would really act and speak', for 'we do not see how a story based on circumstances purely fictitious can prove anything'.[32] Collins's blending of fact and fiction does, however, suggest the ways in which the (N)ovel offers a space in which to test and probe the truth claims of textual authority, as events in *Poor Miss Finch* are frequently constructed through textual sources that are open to misinterpretation, or indeed misrepresentation. Language is the primary mechanism for transmitting knowledge to Lucilla, but it can be used to deceive, and to 'cover up what can be seen'.[33]

Using a strategy familiar to his readers – the inserted journal entry – Collins, through Pratolungo, allows Lucilla to 'tell the story of her life at Ramsgate, herself … Variety, freshness, and reality – I believe I shall secure them all three by following this plan' (*PMF*, 322). The entry is, however, marked by Pratolungo's revisions, and Lucilla's blindness at the novel's close means that it is Pratolungo, rather than Lucilla, who must make sense of the textual material (journals, letters) to construct the story. Again, the novel is ambivalent as to where textual authority resides: in Lucilla's autobiographical journal entry, or in Pratolungo's narrative, which itself edits and annotates Lucilla's voice? This multi-narrative strategy is used effectively in other Collins novels, such as *The Woman in White* (1860) and *The Moonstone* (1868), to demonstrate that self is not integral, but contradictory and unstable, dependent upon the position of who interprets it. In her classic study of the relationship between sensation fiction and newly emerging bourgeois domestic spaces, which, she argues, turns on anxieties of concealed identity, disguise and secrecy, Jenny Bourne Taylor emphasises that such anxieties often centre on the problem of what is seen and how it is interpreted.[34] A metaphoric blindness underlies sensation fiction more generally, as power is negotiated through who sees; weakness is often figured as being a passive object to the gaze. This is certainly borne out in Collins's first sensation novel, *The Dead Secret* (1857), in which Leonard Frankland's blindness both heightens the drama – which turns on the problem of familial recognition and the search for a hidden object – and the narrative drive of the text, as his wife, Rosamond, must narrate and describe events to him. Whilst such issues continue to inform Collins's revisiting of blindness in *Poor Miss Finch*, other aspects of the sensation genre – particularly its interest in embodiment – temper the way in which power is distributed through the visual.

Lucilla is a passive object of a system of narrative gazes: both of the narrator and of the other characters who subject her to deception. For example, Pratolungo records how she spies on Lucilla, such as on one of the first meetings she has with Oscar. Sheltered by a Venetian blind, Oscar's back is to Pratolungo, but Lucilla stands facing her: Pratolungo records, with some shame, how she 'peeped in' on the scene (*PMF*, 36). Yet more complexly, Lucilla's blindness renders her, to some degree, a free subject. For instance, when she meets Oscar, instead of her blindness 'making her nervous in the presence of a man unknown to her … it made her fearless' (*PMF*, 37). Lucilla, freed from consciousness of the scrutinising stare of others, possesses a certain social liberty. Again, however, shifting perspectives complicate interpretation of crucial statements about Lucilla's self and identity. The novel seems to cast her as an object of pity – she is 'called … compassionately' 'poor' Miss Finch by the 'simple people' of the South Downs who 'added their word of pity to her name' (*PMF*, 13). Madame Pratolungo repeats this construction of her, referring to her 'poor, dim, sightless eyes' (*PMF*, 14). Whilst acknowledging her beauty, intelligence and independent spirit, Pratolungo continues to emphasise Lucilla's difference from the sighted:

> The minds of the blind are, by cruel necessity, forced inward on themselves. They live apart from us – ah, how hopelessly far apart! – in their own dark sphere, of which we know nothing. What relief could come to Lucilla from the world outside? None! (*PMF*, 33)

However, in a radical subversion of the marriage plots of *Jane Eyre* and *Aurora Leigh*, at the novel's end Lucilla exclaims: 'thank God, I am blind' (*PMF*, 417). She explains that although she has lost sight, she has gained 'happiness': ' "My life lives in my love. And my love lives in my blindness" ' (*PMF*, 418). Whilst deciding not to restore her sight may demonstrate her desire to be passive to Oscar, it is more an active decision taken to return her to a tactile world in which she feels integrated. This is a point Martha Stoddard Holmes perceptively notes in her reading of the novel within the context of nineteenth-century 'marital melodramas', featuring disabled women and marriage plots. Noting the disturbing and transgressive nature of the 'century's most radical novel about blindness and sexuality', Holmes argues that 'Collins scrambles the codes of melodrama and disability'.[35] Holmes convincingly details the ways in which Collins's portrayal of Lucilla powerfully critiques contemporary discourses of blindness, disability and reproduction, demonstrating how it overturns fears about the hereditary nature of disability, as well as resisting the 'correct' (ablebodied) attributes for maternal figures.[36] However, her reading does not address the implications of the novel's preoccupation with blueness, colour and race, nor the unstable masculine identities represented in the twins (as Gladden's study does) and the way this complicates our understanding of Lucilla's decision to return to blindness. Oscar's feminisation, and Lucilla's desire for him as feminised, disrupt the heteronormative fulfilment Holmes identifies in the novel ('blindness and blueness notwithstanding, the most sensational thing about this novel may be how conventional a heroine Lucilla Finch finally is').[37] Resolutions, typically with Collins, are not what they seem, as Lucilla does not want to 'see [Oscar] disfigured as he is now', thus refusing to learn visual difference (*PMF*, 417). The racial prejudices she held as a blind person, explored in more detail below, are not fully dismantled.

Indeed, ambiguities around gender identity and its relation to blindness permeate the novel. We see in the theme of the male's disfigurement contrasted with female beauty echoes of the 'Beauty and the Beast' myth. Naomi Schor, reading 'Beauty and the Beast' through the lens of the metaphorical weight of blindness in nineteenth- and twentieth- century French, British and American culture outlines the way in which Beauty's blindness within the story underwrites two potent and complementary myths of misogyny: firstly, that women should be seen rather than see; secondly, that men have an inner beauty to be revealed despite their outer monstrous appearance.[38] Seemingly, the conclusion to *Poor Miss Finch* supports such a reading, as Lucilla, described as 'the Dresden Madonna' by Nugent (*PMF*, 141), marries the disfigured Oscar. However, whilst the Beauty and the Beast myth is certainly recalled in the triangulated love story of Lucilla, Oscar and Nugent, the fluid gender identities and unstable visual systems rewrite the story somewhat. Oscar *becomes* monstrous; inverting the parable of the Beauty and the Beast, he is not restored to beauty after marrying Lucilla, who has already rejected his perfect double, Nugent. Whilst in her rejection of Nugent as male beauty, Lucilla goes some way towards learning that outer vision/inner goodness are not a correlative binary, she still elects to be blind rather than confront Oscar's disfigurement.

Oscar, as the Beast, is feminised from the start and Lucilla's attraction to him, as Gladden's study emphasises, is not grounded on traditional heterosexual desire. Pratolungo continually emphasises his girlishness, and our first impressions of him, through her eyes, are of a nervous character with his 'colour coming and going like the colour of a young girl' (*PMF*, 37). Oscar's unstable gender identity is also played out through the visual, as he fears the castrating effect of the gaze and seeks to assert control over it. The false accusation of murder made against him before his arrival at Dimchurch makes Oscar the object of the gaze; in his helplessness to control or discipline the stares of others, he fears its castrating effect. Explaining his acute nervousness to Pratolungo when he first meets her, he asks her: '"Have *you* been stared at by hundreds of cruel eyes?"' (*PMF*, 40). Strangely, Pratolungo later imagines 'startling pictures' of Oscar with a blue face 'as a Medusa's head too terrible to be contemplated by mortal eyes' (*PMF*, 121). Monstrously feminised, he becomes the castrating gaze himself, as the visual disturbs the gender identities at play in the novel.

The sensational romance plot is also an indicator of the discursive space Collins's novel shares with medical and psychological studies of sight restoration to the long-term blind, and it sets up an emotional crisis common to all of these narratives. Absorbing in his novel what we might term 'the medical gaze', Collins develops a mode of clinical realism (anticipating the strategies of naturalist fiction of the fin-de-siècle). Scholars working on the intersection of medicine and literature in nineteenth-century culture (including Janis Caldwell, Lawrence Rothfield and Sally Shuttleworth) have traced the new ways of looking that develop alongside the professionalisation of medicine (understanding this in terms of a power exchange, whereby the clinician gains power over the patient), and the traffic between medical and literary discourse. These scholars build on Foucault's work in *The Birth of the Clinic*, in which he describes the disciplinary gaze of early clinicians as they sought to see, name and classify the newly emerging layers of the body – to penetrate the secrets of the visible. In Lawrence Rothfield's discussion of Flaubert's realism, we recognise aspects of Collins's own construction of his literary project, albeit problematised by Collins's multi-narrative framework. Rothfield describes how the 'medical point of view' is also that of the realist, in 'its immanent power to penetrate and know the embodied self it treats'.[39]

Recognising in the medical gaze an interiorised model of selfhood which lays the foundations for the later Freudian theory of subjectivity, Sally Shuttleworth's important study of the exchange between Charlotte Brontë's fiction and Victorian psychological discourse describes how 'supreme interpretative authority' resides in the 'figure of the doctor who enshrines his judgments within the hallowed domain of science'. Moreover, this gaze is masculine, as 'male science … unveils female nature, piercing through her outer layers to reveal her hidden secrets'.[40] More recently, Janis Caldwell has questioned the validity of the 'medical gaze', as inherited from Foucault, as a model for understanding the relationship between the clinic and literature in early nineteenth-century British literature. Dealing with primarily pre-Darwinian medical culture, Caldwell argues that Foucault's model (turning on the 'void' left by the death of the 'gods') does not hold because of the sustained natural theological leanings of early British medicine.[41] Disruptions to Foucault's model are also at work in *Poor Miss Finch* as, by making medical discourse one of several competing discourses of the blind subject in a multi-narrative novel, the text does not end up endorsing the medical gaze: rather, it competes for authority with the testimony of the blind subject herself. Rather than simply repurposing information from scientific treatises, Collins's novel invites us to consider the literary strategies employed by them.

## Vision and Touch: Narrating Sight Restoration, from Cheselden to Merleau-Ponty

Although they inspired much philosophical debate and captured the nineteenth-century cultural imagination, in actual fact cases of sight restoration to people with long-term blindness were relatively rare.[42] However, Elisabeth Gitter notes that the stage soon picked up on the dramatic richness of Cheselden's operation, with French and British melodramas of the early nineteenth century often casting an oculist in the role of saviour to a blind girl's sight.[43] The questions that intrigued philosophers and surgeons were simplified somewhat, recycling spiritual stories of sight restoration, as the moment of (perfect) sight restoration usually occurred as a miraculous conclusion to the end of the play. Blindness as a condition from birth was likewise rare, as statistics from the 1871 census returns indicate. A report on training for the blind, quoting the census returns, notes that 'the Blind' in the Metropolis were stated to be '2,890 in number, of whom 292 … were under the age of 15; 991 … were over 15 and under 50; and 1,607 … were above 50. Of these only 1 in 12 were returned as born blind.'[44] Collins assigns his heroine a rarer and more sensational type of blindness than, for example, Elizabeth Gaskell does in *Mary Barton* (1848), in which the needleworker Margaret Jennings loses her sight as a result of poor working conditions.

There was a paradigmatic shift in nineteenth-century diagnostic practice from patients' narratives to the physical exam.[45] In medical studies of sight restoration for the long-term blind there is still, however, strong emphasis on narrative and testimony. This is in part because sight restoration poses a problem to the ophthalmologist, in the co-mingling of psychological and physiological factors. Newly exposed to sight, patients re-order what the structure of the visible world might be and thus turn the medical gaze back on ophthalmologists.[46] Such an intermixture is by necessity reflected in the form of *Poor Miss Finch*, as clinical observation is framed by the storytelling narrative. Herr Grosse, the ophthalmologist who treats Lucilla, is in part a stock comic character, with his Germanic interpretation of English phrases, his rotundness and his predilection for Pratolungo's home-made mayonnaise. However, the diagnosis of Lucilla's blindness and description of her operation and recovery led some readers to believe that he was in fact a real ophthalmologist. Collins had to add a preface to the second edition, reminding his readers of Grosse's fictional status:

> The German oculist – 'Herr Grosse' – has impressed himself so strongly as a real personage on the minds of some of my readers afflicted with blindness, or suffering from diseases of the eye, that I have received several written applications requesting me to communicate his present address to readers desirous of consulting him! (*PMF*, xl)

This preface provides us with a glimpse of the blind and visually impaired readers of Collins's novel, some of whom appeared to have read the novel in part as factual. Through Pratolungo's observation, we witness Grosse's clinical examination of Lucilla's eyes and prognosis for them, in which the medical touch is figured as violent. Pratolungo narrates:

> As a short-sighted man, he had necessarily excellent eyes for all objects which were sufficiently near to him. He bent forward, with his face close to Lucilla's, and parted her eyelids alternately with his finger and thumb; peering attentively, first into one eye, then into the other … He took a magnifying glass out of his waistcoat pocket … Then the examination – so cruelly grotesque in itself, so terribly serious in the issues which it involved – resumed its course: Herr Grosse glaring at his patient through his magnifying glass. (*PMF*, 194–5)

Through this invasive examination, in which Grosse does not simply look at his patient but more violently glares, he establishes that Lucilla has some visual perception – she can distinguish between day and night. Grosse says to her, ' "if you can see as much as that, you are not properly blind at all" ' (*PMF*, 195). With this statement he echoes Cheselden, who argued that in the case of cataract, people are 'never so blind … but that they can discern day from night', as light is let in 'obliquely through the aqueous humour, or the anterior surface of the chrystalline', likening it to the perception of a healthy eye through a glass of broken jelly.[47] Medicine itself turns on hypothesis and counter-hypothesis, and its dramatic nature is embodied in Collins's novel through the introduction of Dr Sebright (his name clearly suggestive of good vision), who Pratolungo suggests should consult with Grosse on Lucilla's case (and who indeed advises contrarily to Grosse).

We do not see the operation itself; rather, Collins ends the first part with Lucilla 'deftly fingering' the 'horrid instruments' before the operation, and opens the second part between six and seven weeks later, at the end of Lucilla's 'imprisonment' (*PMF*, 231, 233). Instead, the emphasis is on Lucilla learning to use her sight, and the emotional impact this has on her. Lucilla is confused and disorientated by her initial experience of sight, and Grosse puts her through a series of tests to establish her new visual perception of space and shape. When asked to walk to Pratolungo, on the other side of the room, she becomes confused after three steps, unable to understand why she is still a distance away. ' "I saw her here," she said, pointing down to the spot on which she was standing ... "I see her now – and I don't know where she is! She is so near, I feel as if she touched my eyes" ' (*PMF*, 297). This reminds us of Berkeley's belief in *An Essay Towards a New Theory of Vision* that, upon restoration of vision to the man born blind, 'the Sun and Stars, the remotest Objects as well as the nearer wou'd all seem to be in his Eye, or rather in his Mind'.[48] Lucilla, not wanting to appear a 'helpless fool', as she later describes herself, closes her eyes to walk to Pratolungo (*PMF*, 300). Attitudes towards sight and touch are, however, complex and contradictory in the novel. Lucilla's love for Oscar at first compels her to attempt to regain her sight, as she explains passionately to Pratolungo:

> "If you were blind ... you would not willingly delay by a single hour the time when you might see ... It is like death to be sitting here blind, and to know that a man is within a few hours' reach of me who can give me my sight!" (*PMF*, 210)

Swiftly after this, however, she reprimands Pratolungo by asserting, ' "I set my touch, my dear, against your eyes, as much the most trustworthy, and much the most intelligent sense of the two" ' (*PMF*, 220). The novel sustainedly explores the different ways in which touch and sight negotiate (and compete) in the subject's experience of the world, and the relationship between the different senses and language. Lucilla's contradictory attitude towards sight and touch is grounded in the investigations by Enlightenment philosophers including Locke, Berkeley and Diderot into the relationship between sensory perception and knowledge.

Collins's novel also shared ground with other disciplines that were emerging in the nineteenth century, notably psychology and phenomenology, which similarly investigate the cognitive and ontological implications of the relationship between touch and sight. Marius von Senden argued that language is poor in words drawn from the tactile sphere, and that blind people have to use words from sighted teachers, so 'that the blind man finds no means of expressing many of the finer shades of his tactual experience within the vocabulary provided for him; he therefore has to rely, for better or worse, on words which in turn evoke impressions in the sighted that are by no means associated with these words in the blind man's experience and are not so intended when he uses them'.[49] Significantly, Von Senden talks of the difficulty of 'penetrating the secrets of the tactual world of the blind', a description which resonates with the narrative strategies of sensation genre. The subjects who we might question and whose secrets we might thus penetrate are 'those people who have successfully had experience of both the blind and the sighted man's world'.[50]

Twentieth-century phenomenology, in particular the writings of Maurice Merleau-Ponty, developed a new language of feeling and perception outside of the visual. Significantly, Merleau-Ponty borrowed extensively from Von Senden's study in his chapter 'Sense Experience' in *Phenomenology of Perception*. Von Senden's study concludes that 'by tactual perception alone the patient is unable to acquire an awareness of space', as this is 'solely dependent on visual perception'.[51] Merleau-Ponty, however, answering Von Senden, argues that the experiences of people blind from birth and operated upon for cataracts have 'never proved, and could never prove, that for them space begins with sight'.[52] Collocating Diderot's observations about the simultaneity of perception afforded by touch with Descartes' analogies between sight and touch in his defence of geometrical vision, Merleau-Ponty refigures the blind man's stick. Striving towards a more embodied account of the relationship between the perceiving subject and the world, he argues that the stick is not an external object of perception, as Descartes conceives it to be; rather, it is 'an instrument with which he perceives. It is a bodily auxiliary, an extension of the bodily synthesis.'[53] Sympathetic here to a technology which integrates with the body and acquires perceptual agency, Merleau-Ponty nevertheless alerts us to the instability of the individual's experience of space, and the limits of its expression as an empirical category. Opening up the relationship between touch and space, he argues:

> All senses are spatial if they are to give access to some form or other of being, if, that is, they are senses at all … Empiricism could not find facts to refute this deduction. If for example we desire to show that the sense of touch is not spatial by itself, if we try, in cases of real or psychic blindness, to discover a pure tactile experience, and to prove that its articulation owes nothing to space, these experimental proofs presuppose what they are

> meant to establish. How are we to know in fact whether blindness and psychic blindness have abstracted from the patient's experience the merely 'visual data', and whether they have not also affected the structure of his tactile experience?[54]

Merleau-Ponty criticises empirical experiments into sense perception that assume that a blind person's tactile experience is equivalent to a sighted person's, with the visual data merely abstracted. Rather, the experience of blindness and visual impairment may also affect the experience of touch. Further, answering to and refuting Von Senden's thesis about sight and space, Merleau-Ponty restores the possibility of a tactile *field*. Although arguing that sight and touch do not correlate, this does not rule out 'the idea of a tactile space'; far from it: 'the facts prove on the contrary that there is a space so strictly tactile that its articulations do not and never will stand in a relationship of synonymity with those of visual space'.[55] The blind person's subjectivity is re-imagined, as a new relationship between touch and the phenomenal world comes into play.

Whilst *Poor Miss Finch* focuses on the way in which Lucilla touches and negotiates space, Collins also grapples with the limitations of language that Lucilla might face in attempting to describe her tactile world. In one important passage, Lucilla describes how she perceives space and shape superiorly to the sighted. She laments that the 'stretching out of *these* [her arms] to an enormous and unheard-of length' is impossible:

> 'That is what I should have liked! ... I could find out better what was going on at a distance with my hands, than you could with your eyes and your telescopes. What doubts I might set at rest for instance about the planetary system, among the people who can see, if I could only stretch out far enough to touch the stars.' (*PMF*, 220)

Although Lucilla does not have an accurate perception of extension, touch allows her an intimate knowledge of the objects she handles, one that is not dependent on external conditions, such as light. Echoing the question of whether a blind person has a tactual concept of space equivalent to the visual found in the philosophical and medical texts on blindness (Catherine Peters observes the similarity between this and a passage from Diderot's *Essay on Blindness*),[56] this passage demonstrates how Collins was at pains to present to his reader an accurate account of blindness, and the debates in which it was situated.

Lucilla likens her tactual ability to sight, as she uses touch to gain knowledge of the appearance of things, notably people's faces (on first meeting Pratolungo she asks her, '"may I see you, in *my* way? May I touch your face?"' (*PMF*, 14)). Echoing Diderot, Oscar believes that Lucilla has '"eyes in the ends of her fingers"' (*PMF*, 35). In a dramatic scene, which also emphasises the text's sometimes punitive treatment of Lucilla, she is put to the test to detect the difference between Oscar and his identical brother, Nugent, by touching their faces. Although she is confused at first, and laughed at by Nugent when she mistakes him for Oscar (she 'angrily' steps away from him at this (*PMF*, 145)), she then reframes the test to suit her own abilities. She says that she wants to try again, '"not in your way"' but '"in a way of my own that has just come into my head"' (*PMF*, 146). By taking both of their hands into hers, she can accurately distinguish one from the other, demonstrating the accuracy of her emotional perception. When asked to explain how she can tell the difference, she is 'unwilling, or unable, to reply to that question plainly'. With this refusal, we are reminded of Von Senden's caution of the limited vocabulary for tactual experience: Lucilla simply says, '"something in me answers to one of them and not to the other"' (*PMF*, 147). Here hands, as the appendages through which we touch and feel the world, function as an index of the self.[57]

In focusing more on Lucilla's abilities whilst blind, Collins echoes certain other narratives of famous born-blind people restored to sight, such as Wardrop's and Dugald Stewart's famous descriptions of the blind and deaf boy James Mitchell, whose vision was significantly improved by the extraction of a cataract in his left eye.[58] Recounting the experience and behaviour of this active and intelligent boy, seemingly to prove his fitness for the operation, Wardrop conveys to us the fullness of his blind and deaf world. Mitchell appeared to have some visual perceptivity, as he responded to 'bright and dazzling colours' before the operation.[59] However, he 'derived little, if any, assistance from his eyes, as organs of vision', and Wardrop highlights Mitchell's independence and success in negotiating his environment, and interacting with the world around him.[60] He 'appeared to know his relations and intimate friends, by smelling them very slightly', likewise recognising strangers this way; he was also able to do so 'at a considerable distance from the object'.[61] Wardrop writes that 'perhaps the most striking feature of the Boy's mind, was his avidity and curiosity to become acquainted with the different objects around him'.[62] Wardrop's narrative reminds us of the fuller phenomenological qualities of objects in the boy's excitement of the phenomenal world: 'he seemed to select and show a preference to particular *forms*, *smells*, and other *qualities* of bodies'.[63]

Bodily blindness is at points conflated with metaphorical blindness in Collins's novel. This is most apparent in the contentious issue of Lucilla's perception of colour, which indicates an underlying preoccupation with issues of race and nationality in the novel. This resonates with the colonial narrative of *The Moonstone* (1868), which tapped into Britain's imperial anxieties following the Indian Mutiny of 1857. Collins frames this imperialist narrative through a debate on colour perception that we find in discourses on blindness in the eighteenth and nineteenth centuries (and which themselves reflect implicitly racist ideas). This debate hinged on whether a blind person could distinguish synaesthetically different colours through touch,[64] and whether there was a natural antipathy towards certain colours (notably dark) in blind people restored to sight. Although when they first meet, Lucilla likes Pratolungo from the touch of her face, she recoils from touching her purple dress, shaking her fingers 'as if something had hurt them'. She then asks Pratolungo not to wear dark colours, saying, '"I have my own blind horror of anything that is dark'" (*PMF*, 14). With this statement, Collins seems to rework an account provided by Kitto of a blind woman, whose blindness was described in the *Philosophical Transactions* of 1758, and whose touch and sense of smell 'became so exquisitely sensitive, that it is affirmed she would discover the different colours of silks and flannels'. He recounts an episode in which a relative of the lady, wearing an apron embroidered with silk of different colours, asked her if she could tell her what colour it was: 'after applying her fingers attentively to the figures of the embroidery, she replied that it was red, blue, and green'.[65] In his chapter on 'Blind Poets', Kitto, discussing the poet Blacklock, describes 'one of the most wonderful circumstances related of the attainments of the blind – namely, the power which some of them are alleged to have possessed of distinguishing colours by the touch'.[66] Blacklock's biographer, Spence, recorded his apparent ability to apply the names of colours to different objects with exact propriety, suggesting both that he had a tactual appreciation of colour and that his use of colours in his poems correlated with a real engagement with them as phenomenal qualities. Kitto suggests that this may be because 'the very same variety in the disposition of the parts in the surfaces of objects which makes them reflect different rays of light to the eye may make them feel as differently to the exquisite touch of the blind'. Blind people, possessing a 'new sort of vocabulary ...' of the tactual qualities of things, restore materiality to an object's coloured surface.[67]

Cheselden had first suggested that there may be a natural antipathy towards colour in his description of his patient's reaction to a black woman:

> Now scarlet he thought the most beautiful of all colours ... whereas the first time he saw black, it gave him great uneasiness, yet after a little time he was

> reconciled to it; but some months after, seeing by accident a negro woman, he was struck with great horror at the sight.[68]

This passage emphasises that the gaze is *white*; those with coloured bodies such as the 'negro woman' of Cheselden's account and the 'Hindoo' of Lucilla's imagination are the object of a white, imperialist scrutiny (something Oscar dreads, as, with his face dyed blue, he threatens to become, according to Pratolungo, 'an object of horror' to everyone who sees him (*PMF*, 118)).[69] Significantly, this part of Cheselden's theory helps to shape Western Romantic aesthetic theory, as Burke drew from Cheselden's account in his discussion of darkness as a category for the sublime. His narrative appears to prove that 'blackness and darkness are in some degree painful by their natural operation, independent of any associations whatsoever'. In this section, 'Darkness Terrible in Its Own Nature', medical evidence is used to support the text's implicit racist claims. Burke reveals how 'Mr Chesdelden has given us a very curious story' in his narrative of a 'particularly observing and sensible' boy couched for a cataract, who expresses 'great uneasiness' at the first sight of black.[70] For Burke, this supports the idea that dread of dark colours is somehow natural, as the boy's reaction does not appear to arise from association. Collins also borrows from Cheselden in emphasising Lucilla's aversion to dark colours, and dark-skinned people, subverting the debate as it is Lucilla's *idea* of black before she regains her sight that is of interest. This is at stake in her admittedly 'unreasonable' horror of her aunt's Indian friend, whom she imagines 'as a kind of monster in human form' (*PMF*, 118). Testing attitudes towards colour, Lucilla uncomfortably suggests that such an antipathy, expressed as a racist reaction, is somehow innate. However, narrated as it is from the perspective of a 'curious foreign woman', the authorial presence disassociates itself from Lucilla's racist prejudices. Dr Sebright, the English ophthalmologist, says that aversion towards dark colours is 'a common antipathy' in his experience of blind people, as blindness has its '"mysterious moral influence"' (*PMF*, 223). Kitto touches on this in his description of Laura Bridgman, when he notes that 'like other blind persons, she forms an idea (vague of course) about colours; she thinks that black is a dirty colour', whilst another blind person says that 'black is rough, while white is smooth'.[71] Lucilla's antipathy is rather more fierce than vague, and belongs to a moral and intellectual blindness, an untested ignorance. This is emphasised as the scientific interpretative scheme breaks down: Sebright argues that '"we can observe it, but we can't explain it"'. He argues that it is 'incurable', except on one condition – the recovery of sight (*PMF*, 223–4).

Collins's depiction of Lucilla's varying emotional attitude towards sight accords with the more detailed case studies into the restoration of sight to the long-term blind. Von Senden early recognised that 'unless the intellectual and mental attitudes are exceptionally favourable, as for instance in Wardrop, Franz, Latta I and others, the process of learning to see almost always represents a long struggle, calling for great patience and endurance'.[72] In the twentieth century, Richard Langton Gregory and Jean G. Wallace's story of 'SB', effectively blind from birth but who regained his sight after two operations aged 52, tragically demonstrated Von Senden's observation. Although SB made some progress with his new sense, the dislocation he felt, and loss of identity as a *blind* man, caused him great mental stress and aggravated other illnesses, and he died within two years of the operation. Gregory and Wallace concluded: 'we have ascertained that vision, although it may prove genuinely useful to the man long blind, is at the same time a potential source of grievous hurt'.[73] Lucilla describes the times when she had sight as the unhappiest she has experienced; whilst this is in part due to her imprisonment by the false Oscar, the melodramatic plot serves to heighten and exaggerate a more realistic psychological anxiety, as Lucilla experiences a sense of bereavement upon gaining vision. Poignantly, she hopes that she will become used to her 'new self', expressing a sense of radical dislocation common to cases of blind people restored to sight. Lucilla expresses what Albert Valvo terms the 'motivation crisis', the depression which follows the initial shock of surgery. She tells Grosse:

> "The restoration of my sight … has made a new being of me. In gaining the sense of seeing, have I lost the sense of feeling which I had when I was blind? … I want to know if I shall ever enjoy … the happy days … when I was an object of pity, and when all the people spoke of me as Poor Miss Finch". (*PMF*, 362)

Although Lucilla has always been fiercely independent, this longing to be an 'object of pity' echoes a concern of others whose sight has been restored; because of people's prejudices about blindness, strangers and even family are surprised and impressed by a blind person's performance of everyday tasks (such as negotiating travel). Alberto Valvo quotes one of his patients, who reflected, 'I had to die as a blind person to be reborn as a seeing person'.[74]

Unlike in the stage melodramas, Grosse is not Lucilla's saviour; instead, Collins assumes that role by controversially returning her to blindness, as he has 'written this book expressly to show that happiness can exist independently of bodily affliction'.[75] Collins displays an acute sensitivity towards the integrity of the disabled or differently abled body, which we can see throughout his fiction. Validating Lucilla's desire to return to blindness, he accepts and promotes the condition of blindness as part of her identity. As he has Madame Pratolungo conclude: 'Her life was a happy one. Bear this in mind – and don't forget that your conditions of happiness need not necessarily be her conditions also' (*PMF*, 424). Although the happy marriage plot is undercut by anxieties about race, Lucilla's experience of the world as blind woman is finally validated.

## Conclusion

This chapter has explored the ways in which cultural discourses of blindness help shape the outcomes of two fictional blind heroines in sharply contrasting ways. Frances Browne's character Lucy becomes increasingly depressed as her eyesight fails and she eventually commits suicide, whereas Wilkie Collins's Lucilla Finch fears losing her identity as a blind person with the surgical restoration of her sight. Collins's novel, intent on rewriting stereotypical depictions of blindness, engages with a range of philosophic, educational and medical ideas concerning visual impairment at this point in the nineteenth century. Powerfully, he repurposes debates which called attention to blind people's sensory ability – particularly tactile ability – to emphasise how a blind person might find more happiness in their experience of sightlessness, than through its medical cure. In its articulation of Lucilla's embodied selfhood, which sets out how she knows and navigates the world through her fingertips as well as through a whole-body spatial awareness, the novel constructs a phenomenology of blindness.

Browne's portrayal perpetuates a model of blindness as tragedy, which is all the more ironic given her own status as a successful writer and long-term blind person. Yet Browne's contemporary critical reception, as I have charted here, also displayed ambivalence as to the true success of some portions of her literary output, as critics, writing in the tradition of *ut pictura poesis*, struggled to accept that Browne could accurately construct language describing the visual quality of things, with no memory of sight. Browne's novel *My Share of the World* is itself highly visual, privileging sight in both the narrative structure and descriptive style (past and present scenes are filtered through the narrator Frederic Favoursham's visual perspective), as well as in its interest in the visual arts through the depiction of activities such as portrait painting. This valorising of the visual mode curtails the possibilities for a character with visual impairments, much as critics cautioned the value of Browne's literary output. It is strangely in this fictional work by a blind author, then, that the negative cultural associations between blindness and language we have traced in other literary works find so tragic a conclusion.

The next chapter examines a novel which, similarly to *My Share of the World*, perpetuates a problematic link between blindness and tragedy: George Gissing's *New Grub Street*. Whereas Browne tragically framed blindness as a limiting condition in a society that valorises sight as the primary mode for knowing the self, Gissing's rendering of blindness derives its tragic force explicitly from anxieties concerning the mechanised nature of literature. Gissing's construction of blindness as disability reveals the limits and possibilities of and for literary form, as the body of the writer, automaton-like, cannot continue to produce whilst impaired.

CHAPTER 8

# *Blindness, Writing, and the Failure of the Imagination in Gissing's* New Grub Street

A central scene in George Gissing's *New Grub Street* (1891) is the blinding of the writer Alfred Yule, followed swiftly by his decline into poverty and death. *Blindness and Writing* opened with a portrait of a blind beggar by John Thomas Smith that dramatised a changing social concern with the relationship between blindness and literacy at the start of the nineteenth century. Towards the close of my book, I show how Gissing's novel continued to probe this relationship at the century's end. Smith, a middle-class observer, was troubled by the status of the blind person in a society that privileged the ability to access written text as a visible form. Gissing directs this fear, embodied in Smith's figure of the blind beggar, towards the figure of the writer, as Yule faces the prospect of poverty with the failure of his eyesight. In the context of a novel that exhaustively explores the cultural and economic forms of literature, blindness is framed clearly as a disability. Yet it is not so much the condition of blindness that is the driver of Yule's tragedy, as it is the failure of writing to flourish outside of material constraints. So whilst Yule's sight loss has a thickly material embodiment, both in its citing of medical knowledge and in its stultifying effects upon his literary career, it also functions metonymically, as a biting criticism of the damaging effects of the market, which has impaired the body of nineteenth-century literature. Gissing's voice is by no means the only one negotiating the meaning of blindness at this point: H. G. Wells later imagines a very different scene, in which a race of people adapted to blindness are favoured in the struggle for survival in 'The Country of the Blind' (1904). However, Gissing's exploration of the relationship between blindness and writing in *New Grub Street* is an emphatic articulation of the ways in which writing is tied to the working body of the writer, and in particular to his or her sensory capacity. At the end of the nineteenth century, it offers a detailed meditation on the way in which blindness both opens and closes the imagination posited at the origin of writing, taking us back to the 'blind cavern' of Wordsworth's poetic project.

*New Grub Street* registers a deep pessimism about the mechanisation of literature in the Victorian literary marketplace, in which there is now little room for the imagination. Tropes, metaphors and scenes of writing construct and thicken the metafictional frame of the novel, and Gissing writes his autobiography into the text (for example, much of Gissing's composition process of *New Grub Street* mirrors that of his character Edwin Reardon's stunted attempts to write his novel).[1] Writing and literature in *New Grub Street* are no longer situated within Romantic-era debates of creative transcendence, but rather within Marxist and Darwinian analyses of production and competition. Paper – as both commodity and capital (via the profits of John Yule's paper factory and stationery firm) – controls the social and romantic relations in the novel. Furthermore, Gissing draws attention to the evolutionary competition between different literary products, which struggle for survival in an over-saturated environment (the 'market' greedily consumes flippant journalistic pieces but has lost its appetite for the three-decker novel). Biological and economic models compete then in Gissing's model of literature: writing is conceptualised as organic, but defined by market forces, with those writers and genres capable of adapting surviving, and those unable to do so degenerating. Jasper Milvain, for example, recognises that, at the end of the century, 'the struggle for existence among books is nowadays as severe as among men' (*NGS*, 493). In such an environment, idealist novelists like Reardon 'sink down' (*NGS*, 229) whilst the new type of literary man, embodied in Jasper Milvain, ascends. Margot Stafford argues that both Alfred Yule and Edwin Reardon 'have modelled their careers on literary men who are a dying breed in late Victorian Grub Street'.[2] Milvain is the mouthpiece for this hybridised Darwinian/capitalist view of literature, as he pronounces that Edwin Reardon is 'the old type of unpractical artist; I am the literary man of 1882. He won't make concessions, or rather, he can't make them; he can't supply the market … Literature nowadays is a trade. Putting aside men of genius, who may succeed by mere cosmic force, your successful man of letters is your skilful tradesman' (*NGS*, 38). 'Type' alerts us to the complexity of ideas here at an etymological level, as it is a biological marker of species and organism and it reminds us of the stuff of the writer's trade – print. This etymological linking subtly encloses literature in a mode where medium is everything, where there is no meaning other than the consumption of machine-produced print, and where genius can only succeed, as Gissing's Milvain would have it, by 'mere cosmic force'.

Within this context, many of the diverse relations between blindness and writing discussed in this book cohere in the blinding of the 'battered man of letters', Alfred Yule (*NGS*, 49). Described as belonging to a 'past age' (*NGS*, 123), Yule struggles to hold his place in the changeable environment of New Grub Street. However, it is unclear whether Yule's decline is attributable to evolutionary factors, as Margot Stafford understands it (for example, because he is not interesting enough to give the public what it wants), or whether he is actually a subject of fate, enmeshed in a providential framework that rules against him. At one point we are told of his 'quarrel with destiny' (*NGS*, 311), and initially upon being diagnosed blind, we are told:

> Among all the strugglers for existence who rushed this way and that, Alfred Yule felt himself a man chosen for fate's heaviest infliction. He never questioned the accuracy of the stranger's judgment, and he hoped for no mitigation of the doom it threatened. His life was over – and wasted. (*NGS*, 446)

Yule is tormented by the will's impotence, and by his lack of subjective agency. These conflicting frames are crucial in our investigation of the significance of Yule's blindness in the novel, shaped as it is by changing social and medical ideas.

Yule's realisation that his fears about his eye troubles are grounded comes after an argument with his daughter Marian, when on a walk: 'he noticed that the objects at which he looked had a blurred appearance … he took up a scrap of newspaper that lay on the stall; he could read it, but one of his eyes was certainly weaker than the other; trying to see with that one alone, he found that everything became misty' (*NGS*, 441–2). An overbearing father, jealous of Marian's financial independence from an inheritance, and opposed to her proposed marriage to Milvain, Yule is symbolically aligned with mythical figures of blindness, including Lear and Oedipus. Yet he also places a wavering faith in medical authority to cure his encroaching blindness: he tells Marian that she can research cataracts in the British Museum if she wants to find out more about their diagnosis and cure (*NGS*, 460); and at a moment of crisis, he also meets former surgeon Victor Duke (who has fallen on hard times). Duke takes Yule to his poor rooms and diagnoses him with cataract, applying a 'catoptric test'.

Catoptric refers to the phenomenon of reflected light, and this test for cataracts involved holding a candle to the patient's eyes: in a healthy eye, three images are discernible. One or more of these images will be missing in an eye with cataract.[3] From this test, Duke diagnoses a cataract behind the lens of the right eye. The surgeon also guesses that Yule is a literary man, after he tells him he uses his eyes 'fourteen hours a day' (*NGS*, 445).

The diagnosis is made with old science, as Duke explicitly urges Yule to seek a more 'competent man', as 'science has advanced rapidly since the day when I was a student; I am only able to assure you of the existence of the disease'. Although the more precise instrument for diagnosing cataract, the ophthalmoscope, had been in existence for some time by this point, this older form of diagnosis fits in with the degeneration narrative at work with Yule's character, indicating how his condition will be beyond modern medical intervention. The effect of the diagnosis on Yule is immediate, and described as a fatal 'crushing blow'; 'his thoughts were such as if actual blindness had really fallen upon him' (*NGS*, 446). He later goes to see a more prominent oculist; again, the intersection of a mythic, or providential framework, with the medical and social, produces conflict in the portrayal of blindness. Whilst it fits into Yule's conception of himself as a maligned subject of fortune's wheel, he also tries to draw on medical progress to resist this fate. However, defeated again as the operation fails, he slips into the social construction of blind person as disabled, unable to participate in the labour market.

Although we are not told what procedure surgeons follow in attempting to remove the cataract, Yule has to wait for the cataract to progress before he can be operated on. During this period, he reduces his reading to a few hours a day, reading only 'large type'; the 'whiteness' of the cataract becomes a visible marker of his blindness (*NGS*, 511). Despite Yule remaining hopeful we are told:

> When the fitting moment arrived, Alfred Yule underwent an operation for cataract, and it was believed at first that the result would be favourable. This hope had but short duration; though the utmost prudence was exercised, evil symptoms declared themselves, and in a few months' time all prospect of restoring his vision was at an end. Anxiety, then the fatal assurance, undermined his health; with blindness, there fell upon him the debility of premature old age. (*NGS*, 542)

Yule fears that he will be fit only for the workhouse and indeed his family position becomes 'desperate' after the failure of his operation. He understands blindness to be a disability, preventing him from writing, and from working. Yule is the negative realisation of the speculative fear of blindness that haunts many of the texts discussed in this book; there is no transcendental genius of imagination or intellect that can overcome an impaired human body. However, in the text itself, we hear echoes of other literary voices, which open up an imaginary space of blindness. Although Yule's death emphasises the poverty to which blindness has driven him, it also echoes Milton's *Paradise Lost.* Milvain describes how Yule has 'died in the country somewhere, blind and fallen on evil days, poor old fellow'. The speaker in Book VII of *Paradise Lost* appeals to the Muses at the start of this book, recounting: 'More safe I Sing with mortal voice, unchang'd / To hoarse or mute, though fall'n on evil days, / On evil days though fall'n, and evil tongues; / In darkness'.[4] Partly referring to Milton's own blindness, this literary echo reminds us that, unlike Milton, who authored his greatest works after the loss of sight, the writer who loses his sight in late-Victorian capitalist society is disabled by social and material conditions. The spaces and structures that facilitated Milton's imagination, in which blindness offers the supreme conditions for undistracted, original composition, have been erased by pressures caused by the burgeoning marketplace of literature. The imagination is invoked throughout the novel, but sits uneasily alongside what Gissing identifies as a new mechanistic environment for literature. Although Yule has read vastly – his memory is like a 'literary cyclopaedia' (*NGS*, 69) – without vision his penmanship is at an end.

What space is there, then, for the imagination in this text? Visionary moments do rupture the claustrophobic, gloomy fog that Gissing repeatedly associates with London in the text (and which also acts as a metaphor for blindness, or limited vision). Reardon's haunting descriptions of Greece, which torment Biffen, are strange scenes of 'an ideal world that was not deceitful … which seems to me … beyond the human sphere, bathed in diviner light'. His account of a sunset at Athens is more consciously poetic, as he says to Biffen how 'the sun itself sank into the open patch of sky and shot glory in every direction, broadening beams smote upwards over the dark clouds and made them a lurid yellow[;] over black Salamis, lay delicate strips of pale blue – indescribably pale and delicate' (*NGS*, 406–7). Here, the writing becomes momentarily visionary and imaginative. However, such poetic language is associated with the voice, rather than with writing: it is an instance of reported speech, not literature (these are the images Reardon cannot write), although of course Reardon's voice is substantiated as print in Gissing's novel. The imagination has moved to the edges of the text; it is a centripetal force that acts on the novel from the outside.

Yule's blinding puts an end to his writing but, intriguingly, it is the publication of an earlier essay, 'On Imagination as a National Characteristic', that precipitates a crisis from which his career never fully recovers. One speculates that this essay, described by the narrator as 'rather pretentious and long-winded but far from worthless', would have assessed both Milton and the Romantic-era poets and theories of imagination. Although Yule has always had 'an unhappy trick of exciting the hostility of men who were most likely to be useful to him', in the 'great quarrel' of 1873, the younger Clement Fadge (who has previously reviewed for Yule's paper *The Balance*) attacks his former editor's essay with an 'exquisite virulence'. Yule's 'savage assault' on Fadge in *The Balance* is miscalculated, and throws 'ridicule upon the heavy, conscientious man' and 'ended in the disappearance of Yule's struggling paper, and the establishment on a firm basis of Fadge's reputation' (*NGS*, 126). Yule's attempt to deal with the imagination results in his worst career humiliation: his creative faculties have been diminished by the critical review industry in which he works. As Marian despairs over the literary machine she is trapped in, questioning 'what was the use and purpose of such a life as she was condemned to lead', 'exhausting herself in the manufacture of printed stuff which no one even pretended to be more than a commodity for the day's market', she asks:

> To write – was not that the joy and the privilege of one who had an urgent message for the world? Her father, she knew well, had no such message; he had abandoned all thought of original production, and only wrote about writing. (*NGS*, 137–8)

The free indirect style here blends Marian's thoughts with the narrator's. Yet it also aligns Gissing with Yule, as we might question to what extent this metafictional novel, which seems to write only of writing, can be called an 'original production'. What place does Gissing's novel take in the 'day's market'? Imitating Yule, Gissing, the writer of *New Grub Street*, is aligned with a figure of blindness.

Marian has acted as Yule's amanuensis since the age of 12, and Yule, a tyrannical figure towards his wife and daughter, is highly dependent on her assistance. Whilst Yule writes about the national status of the imagination, it is Marian who recognises the dearth of original writing, and longs for a creative re-engagement with the world – significantly by giving up writing, as she would 'throw away her pen with joy but for the need of earning money' (*NGS*, 138). Strangely, this parallels John Yule's loathing of literary production, which he would like to see 'abolished'. He promotes instead 'muscular manliness' above the emasculating profession of writing (which feminises men by turning them into 'weak, flabby creatures, with ruined eyes and dyspeptic stomachs' (*NGS*, 49, 54)). If, as Catherine Maxwell argues, castration is the necessary mark of poethood for the male poet, in *New Grub Street* writing itself becomes the act of castration as the pen becomes a figure of feminine endlessness, of dissipated energy that struggles to inscribe new marks. Marian recognises how her own self is constrained by the pointless and regressive acts of research and writing demanded of her by her father. Despite her assistance, Yule is convinced that his blindness will irrevocably damage not only his career, but his very identity. Commenting on his insurance, he tells Marian:

> But that is no provision for possible disablement. If I could no longer earn money with my pen, what would become of me? (*NGS*, 347)

Yule anticipates here that blindness, as a disablement, will emasculate him and reduce him to dependency. However, whilst he has managed to make a living from his writing, the failure of his own imagination has already taken place: the symbolic currency of 'the pen' no longer clearly standing for masculine virility.

## Conclusion

The contemporary social meanings of blindness as disability in an industrial age powerfully combine with the mythic fear of blindness as punishment in the novel. Gissing recognises the visionary status of blindness as a literary trope, not least in his invocations of Milton. However, he overwrites both this possibility for blindness signalling the beginning of imaginary writing and the possibility of an encounter with text outside of vision. '"Before long I shall certainly be disabled from earning my livelihood by literature"': Yule cannot adapt to the condition of blindness, despite the coincidence of his blindness with the consolidation of embossed writing systems (*NGS*, 459). That his blindness is a tragedy, because it is a disability, allows us to understand the nature of the anxieties around the mechanical, reductively material state of writing that Gissing identifies in this novel. In my epilogue, I question how Gissing's novel functions as a riposte to the episodes of blind literary culture I have considered throughout this book, and consider how it marks a regressive moment for the potential of blind people's writing practices.

# *Epilogue*

In concluding my book, I return to George Gissing's novel *New Grub Street*, considered in the previous chapter, to question how it functions as a riposte to the other episodes of blind literary culture I have analysed. *Blindness and Writing* has shown some of the rich and flourishing ways in which blind and visually impaired people sought to take control of public discourse and policy concerning blindness, actions which frequently sprang from the contentious issue of literacy. Indeed the action of Gissing's novel, set in the early 1880s, is coterminous with other socially progressive episodes in the development of blind people's education and literacy, including the founding of the National Library for the Blind in 1882, which stocked primarily braille-print books and marked a shift towards greater standardisation and increased choice of textual material for visually impaired readers. A Royal Commission on blindness followed in 1885, established following the campaigning efforts of several blind figures including the Liberal MP Henry Fawcett and Thomas Rhodes Armitage. The Commission secured important provisions for blind people's education and welfare, signalling a widespread desire to promote and raise standards. Despite these indications of progressive attitudes towards blind people's literacy, Gissing's novel at the century's close displays, as David Bolt puts it, an 'ocularcentric ontology': a deep anxiety as to the potential for writing and literature to flourish outside of the regime of the eye.[1] It simultaneously signals, despite the range of testimonies and evidence from blind people detailing their skills and learning that I have drawn attention to throughout this book, a cultural suppression of blind people's intellectual agency. The ease with which blindness is invoked as a form of tragic 'disablement' for a writer – against the grain of the contemporary contexts for blind people's literacy – is perhaps indicative of the process of historical erasure that has resulted in the latter narrative being largely forgotten. In this epilogue, I evaluate how *Blindness and Writing* functions as a riposte to Gissing's practice of cultural forgetting.

As I described in the introduction, disability studies has tended to identify advocacy movements and its attendant literary genres (notably biography and autobiography) as largely contemporary, springing from the disability rights movement of the 1960s. Yet in the nineteenth century, there were numerous people, including William Hanks Levy, John Bird and Hippolyte van Landeghem, who demanded that the condition of blindness be defined *by* blind and visually impaired people. In narrating their experiences and agitating for change, they were both a visible and audible part of nineteenth-century public discourse; yet they have been largely forgotten, indicative of the erasure at work in Gissing's novel. One of the aims of *Blindness and Writing* has been to reanimate the historical record and challenge this cultural suppression, through using the twentieth- and twenty-first-century tools of cultural phenomenology and disability studies. My examination of key areas of blind people's involvement in literacy and literary culture – notably embossed literature and autobiographical and biographical form – has shown surprising and important counter-narratives to accounts of nineteenth-century culture as hegemonically ocularcentric. My study has demonstrated that, despite varying degrees of sighted prejudice, blind people did seek and gain control over both their social education and their cultural representation. This suggests that the mid-nineteenth century was a period of flux for the experience of visual impairment, with possibilities opening out for more positive modes of blind identity, whilst other possibilities were shut down within the structures of an increasingly capitalist and industrialist society. Crucially, however, my focus has been on the relationship between blindness and literary form, examining how blindness assumed new meanings through its relationship to literacy, which in turn produced new forms of experience for people with visual impairments.

*Blindness and Writing* has focused attention then on how fluctuating meanings of blindness shaped its representation in fictional form. Gissing's depiction of blindness marks a complex riposte to the other authors I have considered in this book, who variously aligned blindness with literary writing both creatively and critically. In their contradictory handling of the boundary between sight and blindness, writers such as Dickens, Charlotte Brontë and Elizabeth Barrett Browning resisted portraying blindness as a disability. Drawing on their experiences of blindness and interactions with blind people, they privileged the relationship between blindness and the imagination, recognising it as a condition that facilitated description and narration; and found in blindness new modes of experiencing the world through touch and sound. Yet paradoxically they also feared the ways in which it emphasised the material nature of literary production, and raised questions about the nature of the literary sign outside of visual perception. Within the rapidly expanding print economy of the nineteenth century, blindness raised particular anxieties concerning the ways in which subjects produced and consumed text, by pointing to the ways in which language was a material – rather than ideal – entity, contingent upon the interrelation of body and text. These fears come full circle in Gissing's novel, which critiques the dwindling status of the imagination in modern literary work and pessimistically registers how literature has become aggressively materialist in substance. *New Grub Street* plays through the uncertainties and anxieties over the place of the imagination in literature, embodied in the figure of Alfred Yule. Blindness is the end of writing for Yule, and the factor that materially reduces him and his family, because writing cannot transcend mechanistic and automatous processes. Gissing, in mourning the disappearance of the imagination, closes down the possibilities for blindness as a condition for knowing, and writing, the world.

Perhaps significantly, of all the writers I have considered, Gissing evidences the least direct engagement with the lived experience of blindness. Yet one of the concerns of this book has been to show how the binary between sighted and blind comes under pressure through personal involvement with, or experience of, visual impairment. In such instances, blindness, far from signalling the end of writing, creates the sensory conditions in which new writing can flourish; from Jane moving from the visual to the verbal in *Jane Eyre* (mirroring Charlotte Brontë's creative progression in Gaskell's biography) to David's first storytelling in the dark in *David Copperfield*. The literary works I have considered also engage with contemporary discourses on raised print systems and tactile perception to imagine the material form of writing in new, multisensory ways, alert to the possibilities for touch as a mode through which the world may be known, as Collins's *Poor Miss Finch* perhaps articulates most strongly. As such, they offer complex constructions of visual impairment as both a significant theme and method of literary creativity. In other words, the new writing practices associated with blind people did not simply prompt anxiety in the wider cultural sphere; they also offered possibilities for new and creative imaginings of the material text.

Despite this, I have also detailed how more recent critical interpretations which focus on the metaphoric or symbolic meanings of blindness – particularly psychoanalytically informed approaches – have tended to produce readings of visual disability as lack, reinforcing the fictional stereotypes propagated by authors such as Gissing. This has been exemplified in feminist readings of the trope of blindness in nineteenth-century women's writing which equate blindness with castration. Problematically, such readings have relied on disability metaphors to express anxiety about women's inability to claim parity with men, without sufficient attention to the ways in which this further marginalises people with disabilities, as scholars such as David Mitchell and Sharon Snyder have argued.[2] The phenomenological approach I have adopted throughout this book – attending to the embodied experience of blindness as well as its material contexts – certainly redresses this tendency, and considers the dialectic between material and metaphorical meanings of visual impairment. Nineteenth-century blind spokespeople were as alert to the material effects that negative literary representations of blindness could have on their lives as Mitchell and Snyder are writing in the early twenty-first century. And, in response to feminist criticism, whilst blindness pointed to the ways in which writing practices were materially gendered – for example, women were associated with the transcription, rather than origination, of words – I also show how engagement with and disruption of these practices had creative and generative potential for writers such as Elizabeth Barrett Browning and Charlotte Brontë.

My approach has yielded two further important critical results. Firstly, it contributes towards and extends recent debates in nineteenth-century studies that have challenged Victorian culture as visually oriented. Exploring the experiences and interactions of blind people and literature opens up the multisensory nature of nineteenth-century culture, which increasingly valued the haptic as a mode of engaging with the world. Relatedly, these findings complicate the dis/abled binary that many disability studies scholars have identified in nineteenth-century representations of blindness, largely as I undermine readings of the period as straightforwardly ocularcentric. I point instead to a more entangled relationship between sight, blindness and ability than has hitherto been acknowledged.

Yet this is not to ignore the numerous contradictions and instabilities that marked cultural debates, discussions and representations of blind people's writing practices. Nineteenth-century audiences weren't always entirely sure how to make up their minds about visual impairment, often to the great frustration of blind commentators themselves, who criticised the patronising and fearful attitudes they encountered. *Blindness and Writing* has sought to impress the range of attitudes and perspectives at work, whilst assessing the impact and effect that cultural constructions of visual impairment had on the lives of blind people. The lonely death of Yule has its counterparts in other earlier fictional examples I have considered here, including the suicide of Frances Browne's heroine Lucy after losing her sight. A successful blind writer – Browne – is unable to imagine a character living a full and happy life without sight, in the context of a novel which privileges visual modes of representation. Browne's depiction of Lucy suggests the amount of cultural work that was required in order to challenge the 'pernicious' practices of literary authors in their stereotyped and pitiable constructions of blind characters.[3] In these instances, then, blindness is culturally constructed as a disability. Whilst literature offers a space for the exploration of the overlapping nature of sight and vision, the conclusions of several of the blind characters discussed throughout this book – who either are returned to some degree of sight (Edward Rochester, Esther Summerson) or die (Lucy Rose, Alfred Yule) – are indicative of how these novels helped to uphold an ableist reality (certainly, they could not fully valorise a disabled reality). Yet though Wilkie Collins claimed Lucilla Finch's uniqueness in being a composite portrait of real blind people, *Blindness and Writing* has shown the consistent weaving of blind people's experience into their fictional counterparts. In so doing, it has drawn attention to the changing and sometimes-privileged roles that blind people assumed in literary discourse. Perhaps, then, the imperative now is that critical readings of nineteenth-century disability representations must be grounded in their material and embodied contexts, which help impress and recall – rather than illuminate – the competing experiences and claims of bodily and sensory experience replete in the cultural record. Such a critical practice, it is hoped, may help challenge our own cultural assumptions about bodies and ability.

# *Notes*

## Introduction

1 Published in John Thomas Smith, *Vagabondia; or, anecdotes of Mendicant Wanderers through the Streets of London* (London, 1817), p. 29.

2 For a historical overview of the figure of the blind beggar in medieval and early modern societies, see Moshe Barasch, *Blindness: The History of a Mental Image in Western Thought* (London: Routledge, 2001), pp. 92–102; 116–20.

3 Mara Mills, 'The Co-Construction of Blindness and Reading', published in German translation in *Disability trouble: Ästhetick und Bildpolitik bei Helen Keller*, ed. by Ulrike Bergermann (Berline: b_books, 2013), pp. 195–204 (p. 195).

4 William R. Paulson, *Enlightenment, Romanticism, and the Blind in France* (Princeton, NJ: Princeton University Press, 1987), p. 5. Kate Flint, *The Victorians and the Visual Imagination* (Cambridge: Cambridge University Press, 2000); Mary Klages, *Woeful Afflictions: Disability and Sentimentality in Victorian America* (Philadelphia: University of Pennsylvania Press, 1999).

5 Jennifer Esmail, *Reading Victorian Deafness: Signs and Sounds in Victorian Literature and Culture* (Ohio: Ohio University Press, 2013), p. 5.

6 Ibid., p. 4.

7 Kate Flint, for example, in *The Victorians and the Visual Imagination* lucidly demonstrates how the trope of blindness allowed visual artists to reflect on the limits of their craft, and also charts how writers and artists deployed blindness to meditate on the nature of inner vision and the imagination.

8 Jacques Derrida, *Memoirs of the Blind: The Self-Portrait and Other Ruins*, trans. by Pascale-Anne Brault and Michael Naas (Chicago, IL: University of Chicago Press, 1993), p. 2.

9 Ibid., p. 45.

10 In particular, Catherine Maxwell's *Bearing Blindness: The Female Sublime from Milton to Swinburne* (Manchester: Manchester University Press, 2001) and Edward Larrissy's study on blindness and Romantic-era literature, *The Blind and Blindness in Literature of the Romantic Period* (Edinburgh: Edinburgh University Press, 2007).

11 David Bolt, *The Metanarrative of Blindness: A Re-Reading of Twentieth-Century Anglophone Writing* (Ann Arbor: University of Michigan Press, 2014), pp. 8–9; 15.
12 Ibid., p. 10.
13 For example, the *Disability Studies Quarterly* journal was founded in 1980 (originally titled the *Disability Newsletter*).
14 According to the UK Disabled People's Council, 'impairment' is a medically classified biophysiological condition. See Colin Barnes and Geof Mercer, *Exploring Disability*, 2nd edn (Cambridge: Polity Press, 2010), p. 11 and pp. 14–42, for a fuller discussion of issues around terminology and competing models and approaches towards disability. See also Shelley Tremain, 'Foucault, Governmentality, and Critical Disability Theory', in *Foucault and the Government of Disability*, ed. by Shelley Tremain (Ann Arbor: University of Michigan Press, 2005), pp. 1–26.
15 Martha Stoddard Holmes, *Fictions of Affliction: Physical Disability in Victorian Culture* (Ann Arbor: University of Michigan Press, 2004), p. 116.
16 He argued that 'beggary, of late, particularly for the last six years, had become so dreadful in London, that the more active interference of the legislature was deemed absolutely necessary' (*Vagabondiana*, p. v).
17 Douglas Baynton, 'Disability and the Justification of Inequality in American History', in Paul K. Longmore and Lauri Umansky, eds., *The New Disability History: American Perspectives* (New York and London: New York University Press, 2001), pp. 33–57 (p. 35). See also Rosemarie Garland-Thomson, *Staring: How We Look* (Oxford: Oxford University Press, 2009), pp. 30–32.
18 Baynton, p. 52. See also Rosemarie Garland-Thomson's influential study *Extraordinary Bodies: Figuring Physical Disability in American Culture and Literature* (New York: Columbia University Press, 1997).
19 Lennard J. Davis, 'Constructing Normalcy: The Bell Curve, the Novel, and the Invention of the Disabled Body in the Nineteenth Century', in *Enforcing Normalcy: Disability, Deafness, and the Body* (London: Verso, 1995), pp. 23–49 (pp. 26–7; p. 41).
20 See, in particular, Garland-Thomson, *Extraordinary Bodies*; and 'The Beauty and the Freak', in Susan Crutchfield and Marcy Epstein, eds., *Points of Contact: Disability, Art and Culture* (Ann Arbor: University of Michigan Press, 2000), pp. 181–96.
21 The concretisation of literary and cultural disability studies has come with the founding of an important journal series in 2007, the *Journal of Literary & Cultural Disability Studies* (initially titled the *Journal of Literary Disability Studies*). The general editor, David Bolt, described how the journal was founded in response to a series of absences: notably that, despite disability's ubiquitous presence in literary works, it was 'too frequently absent in literary criticism' ('Introduction', *Journal of Literary Disability Studies*, 1:1 (2007), i–vi (p. i)). The journal has contributed towards the increasing theorisation of disability in literary criticism. Important studies exploring the relationship between literary form and disability include: G. Thomas Couser, *Recovering Bodies: Illness,*

*Disability, and Life Writing* (Wisconsin: University of Wisconsin Press, 1997); Lennard J. Davis, *Bending Over Backwards; Disability, Dismodernism, and Other Difficult Positions* (New York: New York University Press, 2002); G. L. Albrecht, Katherine D. Seelman and M. Bury, eds., *Handbook of Disability Studies* (Thousand Oaks, CA: Sage, 2001); Lennard J. Davis, ed., *The Disability Studies Reader*, 2nd edn (New York and Oxford: Routledge, 2006); Tanya Titchkosky, *Reading and Writing Disability Differently: The Textured Life of Embodiment* (Toronto: University of Toronto Press, 2007). For more focused discussions of disability and Victorian literature, see, for example: Holmes, *Fictions of Affliction*; David Bolt, Julia Miele Rodas and Elizabeth J. Donaldson, eds., *The Madwoman and the Blindman: Jane Eyre, Discourse, Disability* (Columbus: Ohio State University Press, 2012); Esmail, *Reading Victorian Deafness*; Karen Bourrier, *The Measure of Manliness: Disability and Masculinity in the Mid-Victorian Novel* (Ann Arbor: University of Michigan Press, 2015).

22 D. T. Mitchell and S. L. Snyder, *Narrative Prosthesis: Disability and the Dependencies of Discourse* (Ann Arbor: University of Michigan Press, 2001), pp. 9; 8.

23 Ibid., p. 6.

24 Ibid., pp. 6, 47.

25 Ibid., p. 51.

26 Ibid., pp. 17, 21.

27 Ibid., p. 164.

28 See, for example, contributions to Bolt, Rodas and Donaldson, *The Madwoman and the Blindman.*

29 Garland-Thomson, *Extraordinary Bodies*, pp. 15–16.

30 Phenomenology has been deployed as a tool for understanding and writing about bodily and sensory difference in the field of disability studies. See, for example, Lisa Deidrich, 'Breaking Down: A Phenomenology of Disability', *Literature & Medicine*, 20:2 (2001), 209–30; William A. Cohen, *Embodied: Victorian Literature and the Senses* (Minneapolis, University of Minnesota Press, 2009), p. 24.

31 Georgina Kleege, 'Introduction: Blindness and Literature', *Journal of Literary & Cultural Disability Studies*, 3:2 (2009), 113–14 (p. 113).

32 Tory Vandeventer Perman, 'Refiguring Disability: Deviance, Blinding, and the Supernatural in Thomas Chestre's *Sir Launfal*', *Journal of Literary & Cultural Disability Studies*, 3:2 (2009), 131–46 (p. 144).

33 Dawne McCance, 'Introduction', *Mosaic: A Journal for the Interdisciplinary Study of Literature*, 46:3 (2013), v–x (p. viii).

34 H. Peter Steeves, 'Gone Missing', *Mosaic: A Journal for the Interdisciplinary Study of Literature*, 46:3 (2013), 1–26 (p. 23).

35 Mark Paterson, '"Looking on darkness, which the blind do see": Blindness, Empathy, and Feeling Seeing', *Mosaic: A Journal for the Interdisciplinary Study of Literature*, 46:3 (2013), 159–77 (pp. 160, 175).

36 Vanessa Warne, '"So that the sense of touch may supply the want of sight": Blind Reading and Nineteenth-Century Print Culture', in *Media,*

*Technology, and Literature in the Nineteenth Century: Image, Sound, Touch*, ed. by Colette Colligan and Margaret Linley (Farnham: Ashgate, 2011), pp. 43–64 (p. 44).

37 Maren Linett, 'Blindness and Intimacy in Early Twentieth-Century Literature', *Mosaic: A Journal for the Interdisciplinary Study of Literature*, 46:3 (2013), 27–42 (pp. 27–8).

38 Christopher Tilley, *Metaphor and Material Culture* (Blackwell: Oxford, 1999), p. xiv.

39 Ibid., p. 37.

40 Mitchell and Snyder, p. 48.

41 Ibid., pp. 58–60.

42 Bolt, *Metanarrative of Blindness*, p. 12.

43 James Wilson, *Autobiography of the Blind James Wilson, Author of 'The Lives of Useful Blind'; with a Preliminary Essay On his Life, Character, and Writings, As Well as on the Present State of the Blind* ed. by John Bird (London: Ward & Lock, 1856), p. xlvi.

44 For a discussion of the role of language in shaping popular conceptions of and associations with blindness, including common sayings such as 'blind rage' and 'the blind leading the blind', see Julia Miele Rodas, 'On Blindness', *Journal of Literary & Cultural Disability Studies*, 3:2 (2009), 115–30.

45 Paulson, p. 201.

46 Charles Dickens, *Barnaby Rudge: A Tale of the Riots of 'Eighty*, ed. by John Bowen (Harmondsworth: Penguin, 2003), p. 377.

47 John Bowen, *Other Dickens: Pickwick to Chuzzlewit* (Oxford: Oxford University Press, 2000), p. 170.

48 Ibid., p. 176.

49 Nicholas Mirzoeff, *Bodyscape: Art, Modernity and the Ideal Figure* (London and New York: Routledge, 1995), pp. 38.

50 Bolt, *Metanarrative of Blindness*, p. 16.

51 Bolt also includes a discussion of the ways in which twentieth-century literature continued broadly to homogenise 'the blind' (Ibid., p. 23).

52 Tanya Titchkosky, 'Cultural Maps: Which Way to Disability', in Mairian Corker and Tom Shakespeare, eds., *Disability/Postmodernity: Embodying Disability Theory* (New York and London: Continuum, 2002), pp. 101–11 (p. 104).

## 1 Writing Blindness, from Vision to Touch

1 James Gall, *A First Book for Teaching the Art of Reading to The Blind; A Short Statement of the Principles of the Art of Printing, as here Applied to the Sense of Touch* (Edinburgh: James Gall, 1827), p. 14.

2 Jan Eric Olsén, 'Vicariates of the Eye: Blindness, Sense Substitution, and Writing Devices in the Nineteenth Century', *Mosaic: A Journal for the Interdisciplinary Study of Literature*, 46:3 (2013), 75–91 (p. 76).

3 Ferdinand de Saussure, *Course in General Linguistics*, 2nd edn, ed. by Charles Bally and Albert Sechehaye in collaboration with Albert Reidlinger, trans. by Wade Baskin (Glasgow: Fontana/Collins, 1960; reprt 1974).

4 Paulson, pp. 12–13.
5 Rodas, p. 116.
6 John Ruskin, *Sesame and Lilies* in *The Works of John Ruskin*, ed. by E. T. Cook and Alexander Wedderburn (London: George Allen, 1903–12), vol. XVIII, 5–192 (p. 64) (second emphasis mine).
7 Walter J. Ong, *Orality and Literacy: The Technologizing of the Word* (London: Methuen, 1982; reprt 1985), pp. 117–23.
8 Gerard Curtis, *Visual Words: Art and the Material Book in Victorian England* (Aldershot: Ashgate, 1999).
9 Ibid., pp. 1, 4.
10 Ibid., p. 16.
11 Alenka Zupancic, 'Philosophers' Blind Man's Buff', in *Gaze and Voice as Love Objects*, ed. by Renata Salecl and Slavoj Žižek (Durham: Duke University Press, 1996), pp. 32–58 (p. 38).
12 George Berkeley, *An Essay Towards a New Theory of Vision* (Dublin: 1709), sections LV–LVI.
13 Ibid., section XCVI.
14 Margaret Atherton, *Berkeley's Revolution in Vision* (Ithaca, NY: Cornell University Press, 1990), pp. 196–7.
15 Samuel Bailey, *Review of Berkeley's Theory of Vision, Designed to show the Unsoundness of that Celebrated Speculation* (London: 1842). In terms of Berkeley's influence on other thinkers, Bailey lists Adam Smith; Etienne Bonnot de Condillac, 'Essay on the Origin of Human Knowledge' (1746); John Stuart Mill, *Analysis of the Phenomena of the Human Mind* (1829); and William Whewell, *Philosophy of the Inductive Sciences* (1840).
16 J. S. Mill's review of Bailey, *London and Westminster Review*, 38 (July–October 1842), pp. 319–36.
17 Ibid., pp. 320, 322, 325.
18 Bailey, p. 168.
19 Mill, p. 322.
20 Ibid.
21 Georgina Kleege, 'Blindness and Visual Culture: An Eye-Witness Account', *Journal of Visual Culture*, 4:2 (2005), 179–90 (pp. 180, 189).
22 Denis Diderot, *An Essay on Blindness, in a Letter to a Person of Distinction*, 3rd edn (London: J. Barker, 1750), pp. 51–2.
23 Jeffrey Mehlman, *Cataract: A Study in Diderot* (Middletown, CT: Wesleyan University Press, 1979), p. 8.
24 Barasch, p. 33.
25 Ibid., p. 151.
26 Edmund Burke, *A Philosophical Enquiry into the Origin of our Ideas of the Sublime and Beautiful*, ed. by Adam Phillips (Oxford: Oxford University Press, 1990), p. 149.
27 Ibid., p. 152.
28 Ibid., p. 153.

29 For a fuller discussion of contemporary discussions of how Blacklock was able to construct visual ideas without experience of sight, see Larrissy, pp. 14–19.
30 Burke, pp. 154–5.
31 Larrissy, p. 2.
32 See particularly David Howes, 'Scent, Sound and Synaesthesia: Intersensoriality and Material Culture Theory', in Christopher Tilley, Webb Keane, Susanne Küchler, Michael Rowlands and Patricia Spyer, eds., *Handbook of Material Culture* (London: Sage, 2006), pp. 161–72; Elizabeth Edwards, *Raw History: Photographs, Anthropology and Museums* (Oxford: Berg, 2001) and 'Thinking Photography beyond the Visual?', in *Photography: Theoretical Snapshots*, ed. by J. J. Long, Andrea Noble and Edward Welch (Abingdon: Routledge, 2009), pp. 31–48.
33 Christopher Tilley, 'Theoretical Perspectives', in *Handbook of Material Culture*, ed. by Christopher Tilley, Webb Keane, Susanne Küchler, Michael Rowlands and Patricia Spyer (London: Sage, 2006), pp. 7–11 (p. 8).
34 Ong, pp. 71–4.
35 This relationship shifted again in the twentieth century. In his account of the history of the UK's Talking Book service, Matthew Rubery has recently traced how those involved in rehabilitation of soldiers blinded in the First World War made use of advancements in sound-recording technology such as gramophones to produce audio texts for blind readers. These gained in popularity with both blind soldiers and citizens throughout the twentieth century, and were used both solely and as a complement to other reading formats such as braille. 'From Shell Shock to Shellac: The Great War, Blindness, and Britain's Talking Book Library', *Twentieth Century British History* (first published online: 7 May 2014), doi: 10.1093/tcbh/hwu017, 25pp.
36 N. Katherine Hayles, *My Mother was a Computer: Digital Subjects and Literary Texts* (Chicago, IL: University of Chicago Press, 2005), p. 102.
37 These are the three categories that comprise investigation of the history of the book as identified by Roger Chartier in his influential study *The Order of Books: Readers, Authors, and Libraries in Europe between the Fourteenth and Eighteenth Centuries*, trans. by Lydia G. Cochrane (Stanford, CA: Stanford University Press, 1994).
38 Christopher Flint, *The Appearance of Print in Eighteenth-Century Fiction* (Cambridge: Cambridge University Press, 2011); Christina Lupton, *Knowing Books: The Consciousness of Mediation in Eighteenth-Century Britain* (Philadelphia: University of Pennsylvania Press, 2012).
39 Lyn Pykett provides an early survey of Victorian material culture studies, including a discussion of the importance of Marxist critical theory to interpretations of nineteenth-century commodity culture, as well as its limits as a methodological approach: 'The Material Turn in Victorian Studies', *Literature Compass*, 1 (2004), 1–5. See also Elaine Freedgood, *The Idea in Things: Fugitive Meaning in the Victorian Novel* (Chicago, IL: University of Chicago Press, 2006). Freedgood's influential work examines objects which readers are usually

encouraged to overlook in three Victorian novels, detailing how these things (for example, mahogany furniture in *Jane Eyre*) can be connected to disturbing narratives – of imperialism and slavery – that the novels' symbolic systems fail to register explicitly. Her approach draws on Bill Brown's important work on 'thing theory', which marked an attempt to break with the Cartesian binary pitting subject against object, instead reappraising the thingness of objects asking: how is the (human) subject affected when objects assert themselves as things, for example when they no longer work? Bill Brown, 'Thing Theory', *Critical Inquiry*, 28:1 (2001), 1–22. For further engagement with the theoretical issues Brown's and Freedgood's work brings to bear on Victorian Studies, see also Victoria Mills, 'Introduction', as well as the essays which form part of a special issue on 'Victorian Fiction and the Material Imagination', in *19: Interdisciplinary Studies in the Long Nineteenth Century*, 6 (2008) www.19.bbk.ac.uk.

40 Leah Price, *How to Do Things with Books in Victorian Britain* (Princeton, NJ: Princeton University Press, 2012), pp. 7–8.

41 Ibid., pp. 5–6.

42 Andrew Piper, *Book was There: Reading in Electronic Times* (Chicago, IL: University of Chicago Press, 2012). See in particular pp. 1–23.

43 Maurice Merleau-Ponty, *Phenomenology of Perception*, trans. by Colin Smith (Abingdon: Routledge, 2002), p. x. Originally published in French as *Phénomènologie de la perception* in 1945.

44 Isobel Armstrong, 'Victorian Studies and Cultural Studies: A False Dichotomy', *Victorian Literature and Culture*, 27:2 (1999), 513–16 (p. 515).

45 See also Steven Connor, 'Making an Issue of Cultural Phenomenology', in *Critical Quarterly*, 42:1 (2000), special issue ed. by Steven Connor and David Trotter, 2–7; and 'CP: or, a Few Don'ts by a Cultural Phenomenologist', *Parallax*, 5:2 (1999), 17–31.

46 Martin Jay, 'Sartre, Merleau-Ponty, and the Search for a New Ontology of Sight', in *Modernity and the Hegemony of Vision*, ed. by David Michael Levin (Berkeley: University of California Press, 1993), pp. 143–85 (p. 165).

47 Merleau-Ponty, *Phenomenology of Perception*, p. 253.

48 Ibid., p. 259.

49 See Cohen, *Embodied*, p. 17, for a further discussion of Merleau-Ponty's 'haptic visuality' in relation to nineteenth-century literary culture.

50 Maurice Merleau-Ponty, 'The Intertwining – the Chiasm', in *The Visible and the Invisible*, ed. by Claude Lefort, trans. by Alphonso Lingis (Evanston, IL: Northwestern University Press, 1968), pp. 130–55 (p. 143).

51 Ibid., p. 133.

52 'Haptic, adj. (and n.)', *OED Online*, www.oed.com.

53 Heather Tilley, 'Introduction: The Victorian Tactile Imagination', *19: Interdisciplinary Studies in the Long Nineteenth* Century, 19 (2014), pp. 11–13, www.19.bbk.ac.uk.

54 Alexander Bain, *The Senses and the Intellect* (London: John W. Parker and Son, 1855), p. 346.

55 For example, the physiologist William B. Carpenter described how blind people learned to diminish the size of embossed font they read, until, with sufficient practice, they could 'read a type not much larger than that of an ordinary large-print Bible' (*Principles of General and Comparative Physiology, Intended as an introduction to the study of human physiology, and as a guide to the philosophical pursuit of natural history*, 5th edn (London: John Churchill, 1855; first published 1841), p. 690).
56 Jonathan Crary, *Techniques of the Observer: On Vision and Modernity in the Nineteenth Century*, 7th edn (Cambridge, MA: The MIT Press, 1996) p. 70.
57 Ibid., p. 95–6.
58 See in particular Nancy Armstrong, *Fiction in the Age of Photography: The Legacy of British Realism* (Cambridge, MA: Harvard University Press, 1999); Carol T. Christ and John O'Jordan, *Victorian Literature and the Victorian Visual Imagination* (Berkeley: University of California Press, 1995).
59 Armstrong, pp. 7, 76.
60 Curtis, pp. 12–13; pp. 187, 189–90.
61 Luisa Calè and Patrizia di Bello, 'Introduction: Nineteenth-Century Objects and Beholders', in Luisa Calè and Patrizia di Bello, eds., *Illustrations, Optics and Objects in Nineteenth-Century Literary and Visual Cultures* (Basingstoke: Palgrave Macmillan, 2010), pp. 1–21 (p. 4).
62 Hilary Fraser, 'Foreword', in Luisa Calè and Patrizia di Bello, eds., *Illustrations, Optics and Objects in Nineteenth-Century Literary and Visual Cultures* (Basingstoke: Palgrave Macmillan, 2010), pp. ix–xv (p. ix).
63 Cohen, *Embodied*, p. 23.
64 George Eliot, *Romola* (1862–3), ed. by Dorothea Barrett (Harmondsworth: Penguin, 2005), p. 51.
65 George Eliot, *Middlemarch*, ed. by W. J. Harvey (Harmondsworth: Penguin, 1965; reprt 1994), pp. 88–90.
66 Ibid., p. 408.
67 Mitchell and Snyder, p. 2.
68 Maxwell, p. 5.
69 Harold Bloom, *The Anxiety of Influence: A Theory of Poetry* (Oxford: Oxford University Press, 1973), p. 78.
70 Maxwell, p. 6.
71 Calè and di Bello, 'Introduction', p. 4.
72 Artists including Henry Fuseli, George Romney and Eugène Delacroix had visited this theme in their paintings. Whilst Fawcett's colleague Sir Charles Dilke commissioned the portrait as an individual portrait of Henry, it was Brown's decision to paint a double body portrait, outlining to the artist F. G. Stephens how 'a group might be made of them full of character and pathos'. Letter from Ford Madox Brown to F. G. Stephens, 21 January 1872 (British Library, Add.MS.43909, fol. 246).
73 For details of this and further context to the painting, see Mary Bennett, *Ford Madox Brown: A Catalogue Raisonné*, vol. 1 (New Haven, CT: Yale University Press, 2010), pp. 398–9.

## 2 The Materiality of Blindness in Wordsworth's Imagination

1 Notes dictated by Wordsworth to Isabella Fenwick, 1842–3, in *Shorter Poems, 1807–1820 by William Wordsworth*, ed. by Carl H. Ketcham (Ithaca, NY: Cornell University Press, 1989), p. 542.

2 I use the term 'ophthalmia' throughout this chapter in the interests of historical accuracy. Occasionally, for variety or when describing more contemporary clinical understandings of the condition, I use 'trachoma'.

3 Most recently, for example, Edward Larrissy has comprehensively documented the episodes of blindness in Wordsworth's writing as border states, whereby the terms of blindness and insight signal the limits between self and other, the latter being a historical conditioning also encompassing the past self. He shows convincingly how Wordsworth's thought is characteristically 'modelled on the idea of compensatory enhancement of aural sensitivity in the blind'. Whilst he acknowledges that there is 'sometimes an autobiographical element at play' in Wordsworth's references to blindness after 1805, the impact of the trachoma is not a focus of Larrissy's discussion. Larrissy, p. 103.

4 For example, Jeffrey Baker explores how deafness and blindness in Wordsworth's writings are invoked to explore the limits of faith. 'The Deaf Man and the Blind Man', *Critical Survey*, 8:3 (1996), 259–69.

5 Romanticists have traditionally focused on the visionary nature of Romantic-era poetry and philosophy, in which blindness upholds the binary between inner and outer vision. See, for example: M. H. Abrams, *The Mirror and the Lamp: Romantic Theory and the Critical Tradition* (New York: Oxford University Press, 1953); Harold Bloom, 'The Internalisation of Quest Romance', in *The Ringers in the Towers: Studies in Romantic Tradition* (Chicago, IL: University of Chicago Press, 1971), pp. 12–35.

6 Maurice Merleau-Ponty, 'Eye and Mind', in *The Merleau-Ponty Aesthetics Reader: Philosophy and Painting*, ed. by Galen A. Johnson (Evanston, IL: Northwestern University Press, 1993), pp. 121–49 (pp. 135–6).

7 This resonates with Alan Richardson's consideration of Wordsworth's 'embodied approach to language', in which he stresses how the poet recognised the advantages as well as limitations of embodied communication. This is in the context of an investigation into the relationship between literature and Romantic-era physiological theories of mind, in which Richardson gives weight to Wordsworth's knowledge of the 'new materialism' promulgated by figures such as Jonathan Hartley and Erasmus Darwin in the 1790s. Whilst questioning the critical implications of Wordsworth's lack of a sense of smell, he does not, however, take into account the effect of the poet's visual impairment. *British Romanticism and the Science of the Mind* (Cambridge: Cambridge University Press, 2001), pp. xiii, 9–16, 71.

8 Elizabeth Dolan, *Seeing Suffering in Women's Literature of the Romantic Era* (Aldershot: Ashgate, 2008), p. 2.

9 Julius Hirschberg, *The History of Ophthalmology*, trans. by Frederick C. Blodi, 11 vols. (Bonn: 1987), vol. VIII a, p. 25. Trachoma, a bacterial infection, remains one of the most common causes of blindness in the developing world today,

despite being easily treatable with antibiotics, as Khalid F. Tabbara argues in 'Blinding Trachoma: The Forgotten Problem', online version of *British Journal of Ophthalmology*, 85 (2001), 1397–9, http://bjo.bmj.com/cgi/content/full/85/12/1397.

10 John Stevenson, *On the Morbid Sensibility of the Eye, Commonly Called Weakness of Sight* (London: Samuel Highley, 1810), pp. 1–2. See also John Vetch, 'Of the British Army', in his *A Practical Treatise on the Diseases of the Eye* (London: G and W. B. Whittaker, 1820), pp. 175–237, for an account of the origins of the epidemic in the British army's campaign in Egypt, 1801.

11 Luke Davidson, 'Identities Ascertained: British Ophthalmology in the First Half of the Nineteenth Century', *Social History of Medicine*, 9:3 (1996), 313–33, p. 313.

12 Michel Foucault, *The Birth of the Clinic: An Archaeology of Medical Perception*, 2nd edn (London: Tavistock, 1973; reprt 1975) (first published in France as *Naissance de la Clinique*, 1963), pp. x and 55.

13 Dolan, p. 5.

14 James Wardrop, *Essays on the Morbid Anatomy of the Eye* (Edinburgh: George Ramsay, 1808), pp. vi–vii.

15 Hirschberg, vol. VIII a, p. 9.

16 Janis Caldwell, *Literature and Medicine in Nineteenth-Century Britain: From Mary Shelley to George Eliot* (Cambridge: Cambridge University Press, 2004), pp. 1–2.

17 Dolan, p. 50.

18 On 24 August 1804, Dorothy Wordsworth wrote to Lady Beaumont, 'I have got a disorder in my eyes, I do not know whether it is occasioned by being disturbed in my rest of late, or if it be the same disease I am told has of late been common all over England,' in William Wordsworth, *The Letters of William and Dorothy Wordsworth*, ed. by E. D. Selincourt, rev. by Chester L. Shaver, Mary Moorman and Alan G. Hill, 2nd edn, 8 vols. (Oxford: Clarendon Press, 1967–88), vol. 1, p. 496. Despite Wordsworth's later attribution of the illness to overexertion, as described in the epigraph to this chapter, the disease would most likely have been spread to him from contact with another sufferer.

19 Further severe attacks took place in 1810, 1816, 1820, 1823, 1826, 1829, 1831, 1832, 1833, 1837 and 1845.

20 Dorothy Wordsworth to Charles Lloyd, 30 May 1820, unpublished letter, collection of the Wordsworth Trust (ref. 2003.48.151).

21 Sara Hutchinson to John Monkhouse, 12 December 1825, unpublished letter, collection of the Wordsworth Trust (ref. WLMS Hutchinson/1/6/6).

22 Wardrop, *Essays*, pp. xxi–xxiii.

23 Sara Hutchinson to Edward Quillinan, *The Letters of Sara Hutchinson, from 1800 to 1835*, ed. by Kathleen Coburn (London: Routledge, 1954), p. 329.

24 Dorothy Wordsworth to Miss Laing, 23 January 1827, unpublished letter, collection of the Wordsworth Trust (ref. DWLMS 15/15).

25 Tabbara (p. 1399) notes that the first effective therapeutic modality using copper sulphate sticks was described by early Egyptians.

26 Vetch, p. 79.
27 Sara Coleridge to Elizabeth Wardell, 13 April 1829, unpublished letter, collection of the Wordsworth Trust (ref. WLMS A/Coleridge, Sara/23).
28 Stephen Gill, *William Wordsworth: A Life* (Oxford: Oxford University Press, 1990), p. 468, n. 135.
29 December 24, 1666. Quoted in C. S. Flick, *A Gross of Green Spectacles* (London: Hatton Press, 1951), p. 15.
30 Oliver Goldsmith, *The Vicar of Wakefield: A Tale Supposed to be Written by Himself* (1766), ed. by Arthur Friedman (London: Oxford University Press, 1974), p. 61.
31 First published in *Bentley's Miscellany*, 4 (September 1838), 209–27. This reference is from Charles Dickens, *Sketches by Boz and Other Early Papers, 1833–39*, ed. by Michael Slater (London: J. M. Dent, 1994), p. 546.
32 Vetch, pp. 16–17.
33 Georg Joseph Beer, *The Art of Preserving the Sight Unimpaired to an Extreme Old Age; and of Re-establishing and Strengthening it When it is Become Weak* (London: Henry Colburn, 1813), pp. 178–9.
34 William Kitchener, *The Economy of the Eyes: Precepts for the Improvement and Preservation of the Sight* (London: Hurst, Robinson & Co., 1824), pp. 91–2.
35 Stevenson, *Morbid Sensibility of the Eye*, p. 103.
36 Ibid., p. 32.
37 Dora Wordsworth to Christopher Wordsworth, cousin, 12 April 1829, unpublished letter, collection of the Wordsworth Trust (ref. WLL/Wordsworth, Dora/1/19).
38 Dora Wordsworth to Christopher Wordsworth, 5 May 1833, unpublished letter, collection of the Wordsworth Trust (ref. WLL/Wordsworth, Dora/1/53).
39 Quoted in Juliet Barker, *Wordsworth: A Life* (Harmondsworth: Penguin, 2000), p. 434.
40 Dora Wordsworth to her cousins, 5 October 1837, unpublished letter, collection of the Wordsworth Trust (ref. WLL/Wordsworth, Dora/1/67).
41 Vetch, p. 5.
42 William Wordsworth, *The Thirteen-Book Prelude*, ed. by Mark Reed, 2 vols. (Ithaca, NY: Cornell University Press, 1991), vol.t 1, book XIII, lines 171–81. This passage is taken from Reed's reading text prepared from the two fair copy manuscripts, A and B, of Wordsworth's first major iteration of the *Prelude* in its 13 book form, dated between 1804 and 1805 (the AB-Stage Reading text). Unless otherwise stated, all subsequent references are from this version of the poem and will be given in the main body of the text.
43 Cited in Geoffrey H. Hartman, 'Diction and Defense', in *The Unremarkable Wordsworth* (London: Methuen, 1987), pp. 120–28 (p. 123).
44 Dorothy Wordsworth to Frances Merewether, 13 September 1831, in Wordsworth, *The Letters of William and Dorothy Wordsworth*, vol. v, p. 430.
45 Sara Hutchinson, letter for William Wordsworth to Edward Quillinan, 10 July 1832, in Wordsworth, *Letters of William and Dorothy Wordsworth*, vol. v, p. 540.

46 Judith Pascoe, *Romantic Theatricality: Gender, Poetry and Spectatorship* (Ithaca, NY: Cornell University Press, 1997), p. 200.
47 Ibid., pp. 203–4.
48 Moreover, as Lucy Newlyn notes, *The Prelude* clearly borrowed from Milton's *Paradise Lost* in structure as well as echoing some of its themes. Lucy Newlyn, Paradise Lost *and the Romantic Reader* (Oxford: Clarendon Press, 1993), pp. 24–5.
49 Pascoe, p. 200.
50 William Wordsworth to Susanna Wordsworth (in Dora Wordsworth's hand), 21 October 1839, in Wordsworth, *The Letters of William and Dorothy Wordsworth*, vol. VI, pp. 728–9.
51 Paul de Man, 'Autobiography as De-Facement', in *The Rhetoric of Romanticism* (New York: Columbia University Press, 1984), pp. 67–82 (pp. 73–4).
52 Paul de Man, 'The Rhetoric of Blindness: Jacques Derrida's Reading of Rousseau', in *Blindness and Insight: Essays in the Rhetoric of Contemporary Criticism*, 2nd edn (London: Routledge, 1983; reprt 2005), p. 137.
53 See the notes in William Wordsworth, *The Borderers by William Wordsworth*, ed. by Robert Osborn (Ithaca, NY: Cornell University Press, 1982), for dates on composition. Osborn corrects Wordsworth's dating of the play to 1795–6 to 1796–7 (p. 3). Osborn publishes the two versions as parallel texts. Hereafter referred to in the main body of the text, with version date provided. Wordsworth changed some characters' names in the later version: in these instances, both names are given.
54 William Wordsworth, *Poems, Chiefly of Early and Late Years; including 'The Borderers, a Tragedy'* (London: Edward Moxon, 1842), p. 243.
55 Blake Reeve, *Romantic Tragedies: The Dark Employments of Wordsworth, Coleridge, and Shelley* (Cambridge: Cambridge University Press, 2011), p. 13.
56 Ibid., p. 22.
57 See Robert Osborn's discussion of textual revision process in Wordsworth, *The Borderers*, p. 446.
58 'A Little Onward Lend Thy Guiding Hand', in William Wordsworth, *Shorter Poems, 1807–1820 by William Wordsworth*, ed. by Carl H. Ketcham (Ithaca, NY: Cornell University Press, 1989), pp. 223–5. All subsequent references are from this edition and line numbers are given in the main body of the text.
59 See note to poem, Wordsworth, *Shorter Poems*, p. 223.
60 Hartman, p.125.
61 Wordsworth, *Shorter Poems*, note to p. 224.
62 For an overview of the Victorians' cultural inheritance of Wordsworth, see Stephen Gill, *Wordsworth and the Victorians* (Oxford: Oxford University Press, 2001).
63 For a survey of the complex compositional and revisionary process of *The Prelude*, see the introductions to the Cornell editions of the poem's early and later versions: firstly, Wordsworth, *The Thirteen-Book Prelude*, vol. I, pp. 1–89. Editor Mark Reed provides reading texts based on the two fair copy manuscripts (A and B) dated from around 1804 to 1805, as well as MS. C, the

'incomplete, often unreliable, but principal new manuscript of 1818–20' (vol. II, p. 5). Secondly, William Wordsworth, *The Fourteen-Book Prelude*, ed. by W. J. B. Owen (Ithaca, NY: Cornell University Press, 1985). Owen, contesting the accuracy of the first printed edition from 1850, and the MS. E on which it was based, argues for using MS. D (dating from 1832) as the final reading text that Wordsworth himself had most confidently authorised.

64 Quoted in Rei Terada, 'Phenomenality and dissatisfaction in Coleridge's Notebooks', *Studies in Romanticism*, 43 (2004), 257–81 (p. 281).

65 Bloom, 'Visionary Cinema of Romantic Poetry', in *The Ringers in the Towers*, pp. 37–52 (p. 40).

66 Luisa Calè, *Fuseli's Milton Gallery: 'Turning Readers into Spectators'* (Oxford: Clarendon Press, 2006), pp. 108–9.

67 Ibid., pp. 107–9.

68 For example, John Stevenson's treatises, published between 1810 and 1834, use Miltonic language as a framing device, quoting passages from *Paradise Lost* on the frontispieces and dropping in quotes throughout the texts.

69 This also follows a custom, as Lucy Newlyn reminds us in her study of Milton's reception by romantic readers, to read poetry biographically (Paradise Lost *and the Romantic Reader*, p. 29).

70 This reference to dithyrambic verse is deleted in subsequent revisions.

71 Similarly, Neil Hertz argues that descriptions of London summon up a 'different order of experience from what we think of as characteristically Wordsworthian' as they resist the phenomenological reading that seems appropriate elsewhere in the poem, a reading attuned to 'seeing and gazing, listening, remembering, feeling' ('The Notion of Blockage in the Literature of the Sublime', in *The End of the Line: Essays on Psychoanalysis and the Sublime* (New York: Columbia University Press, 1985), pp. 40–60 (p. 56)).

72 Ibid., p. 57.

73 John Thomas Smith, *Vagabondiana*, p. v.

74 This corresponds with Neil Hertz's suggestion that book VII turns particularly on the difference between seeing and reading. Hertz, 'The Notion of Blockage in the Literature of the Sublime', p. 58.

75 Ibid., pp. 59–60.

76 See Wordsworth, *The Thirteen-Book Prelude*, vol. I, pp. 19, 41, 54, for the most authoritative account of the compositional process of book VII. Mark Reed argues that it is highly likely Wordsworth drafted book VII during the course of spring 1804.

77 See Ibid., p. 314 (for a dating of MS. X), and pp. 348–9 for the transcript of the first entry of this passage in William's hand.

78 See Wordsworth, *The Thirteen-Book Prelude*, vol. II, transcription of MS. X, p. 348.

79 Ibid., pp. 354–5.

80 See Wordsworth, *The Fourteen-Book Prelude*, pp. 3–5. Editor W. J. B. Owen rejects MS. E as copy for his reading text, as he argues that it was 'carelessly and mechanically written, especially in the sections (books 1–7) written by

Dora Wordsworth; the copying was evidently done without the poet's supervision'. There is, however, little alteration between this passage in MS. D and the 1850 printed version: see pp. 154 and 798–9 for facsimiles and transcriptions of the related MS. D section.

81 This revision to MS. A is made in Mary's hand. For a detailed account of the ways in which Reed identifies and displays later revisions to base AB copy, see Wordsworth, *The Fourteen-Book Prelude*, vol. II, p. 483.

82 See Wordsworth, *The Thirteen-Book Prelude*, vol. II, pp. 724–5, for a transcription of the passage, lines 610–23. Reed notes here that the majority of the revisions made to MS. A here are D stage.

83 Gill, *Wordsworth: A Life*, p. 191.

84 See note to lines 615–25 of the transcription of MS. A, in Wordsworth, *The Thirteen-Book Prelude*, vol. II, p. 725.

85 For a discussion of some of the constraints of the Cornell editions of *The Prelude*, see Jerome McGann, *Radiant Textuality: Literature After the World Wide Web* (Basingstoke: Palgrave, 2001), pp. 67–8.

86 As Reed notes, the poet experienced a severe and prolonged episode of eye inflammation between September 1819 and early 1820, which prohibited study and halted revisions to MSS. A and B. By January 1820, Wordsworth was again able to work on the revisions by daylight. Wordsworth, *The Thirteen-Book Prelude*, vol. I, pp. 68–9.

87 Larrissy, pp. 128–9.

### 3 'A Literature for the Blind'

1 Jeffrey A. Auerbach, *The Great Exhibition of 1851: A Nation on Display* (New Haven, CT: Yale University Press, 1999), p.91.

2 *Annual Report for the London Society for Teaching the Blind to Read*, 13 (1851), p. 10.

3 *Annual Report for the London Society for Teaching the Blind to Read*, 14 (1852), p. 10.

4 Auerbach, p. 111.

5 'Paper, Printing, and Bookbinding', Class 17, *Official Illustrated Catalogue to the Great Exhibition of 1851*, 4 vols. (London: Spicer & Clowes, 1851), vol. II, 536–52 (p. 536).

6 Edmund C. Johnson, *Tangible Typography: or, How the Blind Read* (London, 1853), p. 7.

7 Charles Tomlinson, ed., *Cyclopaedia of Useful Arts and Manufactures, Mechanical and Chemical, Manufactures, Mining, and Engineering*, 4 vols. (London: George Virtue & Co., 1854), vol. IV, p. 502.

8 Warne, p. 44.

9 Tomlinson, *Cyclopaedia of Useful Arts and Manufactures*, vol. IV, p. 503.

10 Valentin Haüy, 'Essay on the Education of the Blind', translated from the French and published in *Poems by the Late Reverend Dr. Thomas Blacklock; Together with an Essay on the Education of the Blind. To which is Prefixed a New*

*Account of the Life and Writings of the Author* (Edinburgh: Chapman and Co., 1793), pp. 217–62 (p. 229).

11 Haüy, pp. 217, viii.

12 Gall, *First Book*, p. 8.

13 Ibid., p. 8.

14 Ibid., p. 4.

15 John Alston, *Narrative of the Progress of Printing for the Blind at the Glasgow Institution* (Glasgow, 1838).

16 John Alston, *First Specimen of Printing for the Use of the Blind, Made in Glasgow by the Asylum for the Blind, Oct 21, 1836* (Glasgow, 1836).

17 Charles Baker, 'The Origin and Progress of the Art of Printing for the Blind', *Scottish Christian Herald*, 114 (May 5 1838), p. 1.

18 Esmail, p. 4. Esmail's study of the changing status of signed language in Victorian culture also reveals similar anxieties from hearing communities over its 'primitive' nature. She details the tensions that developed between deaf communities and oralists over the right to use signed languages, the increased suppression of which amounted to a form of 'cultural "genocide"' (p. 3; see also pp. 16, 22–68). Whilst I am cautious about drawing simplistic parallels between debates concerning signed languages and raised print systems, blind communities did seem more successful in advocating for a writing system that differed from the seeing alphabet. This raises important questions concerning the ways in which disabilities were hierarchised in nineteenth-century culture.

19 Warne, p. 56.

20 James Hatley Frere, *A Letter to Lord Wharncliffe, in reply to the allegations made by the London Society for teaching the blind to read, against the Phonetic method of instruction* (London: W. H. Dalton, 1843), p. 11.

21 Ibid., p. 10.

22 Ibid., p. 21.

23 Saussure, p. 16.

24 Ibid., p. 23.

25 Ibid., p. 30.

26 James Gall, *A Historical Sketch of the Origin and Progress of Literature for the Blind: and Practical Hints and Recommendations as to their Education. With an Appendix Containing Directions for Teaching Reading and writing to the Blind, With and Without a Regular Teacher* (Edinburgh: James Gall, 1834), p. 8.

27 T. M. Lucas, *Instructions for Teaching the Blind to Read with the Britannic or Universal Alphabet, and Embossing their Lessons &c* (Bristol: Philip Rose and Son, 1837), pp. 12–13.

28 Ibid., pp. 17–18.

29 Ibid., p. 53.

30 Warne, p. 45.

31 Carpenter, p. 691. Carpenter's evidencing of blind people's tactile processes forms part of his theorising on the distinction between the working of tactile and muscular elements of the touch sense.

32 W. Hanks Levy, *Blindness and the Blind; or, a treatise on the science of typhlology* (London: Chapman and Hall, 1872), p. vii. Levy had for several years used

a Foucault frame to emboss notes, and corresponded with blind colleagues, including Bessie Gilbert, using tactile messages.

33 Ibid., p. 111.
34 Ibid., p. 111.
35 Ibid., p. 113.
36 Ibid., p. 124–5.
37 Gall, *Origin and Progress*, p. 129.
38 Gall, *First Book*, p. 3.
39 Lucas, *Instructions*, p. iv.
40 Ibid., p. iv.
41 Ibid., p.12.
42 The quantity of paper annually manufactured in England had all but doubled between 1834 and 1850 to 132,675 lb, prompting a fall in its cost from 36s in 1801 to less than half that sum in 1843. See 'Paper, Printing, and Bookbinding', Class 17, in *Official Illustrated Catalogue to the Great Exhibition*, vol. II, p. 536.
43 Gall, *First Book*, p. 7.
44 For a discussion of the BFBS's effect on the book trade in wider nineteenth-century culture, see Leslie Howsam, *Cheap Bibles: Nineteenth-Century Publishing and the British and Foreign Bible Society* (Cambridge: Cambridge University Press, 1991), p. xiii.
45 Doreen M. Rosman, *Evangelicals and Culture* (Aldershot: Gregg Revivals, 1984), p. 7.
46 Ibid., p. 23.
47 *Magazine for the Blind* (London: Simpkin, Marshall & Co.; York: Joseph Moxon, 1839–41), pp. 1, 4.
48 Gall, *Origin and Progress*, pp. 12–13.
49 *Annual Report for the London Society for Teaching the Blind to Read*, 1 (London, 1839), pp. 13–14. By the 1860s, the IBVS was focusing on the efforts to educate blind people in embossed type, detailing in 1866 how 70 of its members were learning Frere's system of embossed type based on phonetic principles (*Annual Report for the Indigent Blind Visiting Society*, 31 (1866), p. 6).
50 Howsam, p. 3.
51 [?John Alston], *Statements of the Education, Employments and Internal Arrangements, Adopted at the Asylum for the Blind, Glasgow; With a Short Account of its Founder, and General Observations Applicable to Similar Institutions (with Lithographic Illustrations)*, 10th edn (Glasgow: John Smith, 1846), p. 51.
52 Ibid.
53 Johnson, *Tangible Typography*, p. 1 (emphasis mine).
54 Testimonials were often reproduced in the annual reports for different reading embossing societies. The names here are drawn from the *Fifth Annual Report of the Fund for Embossing Books for the Blind, by William Moon, of the Improved System of Reading* (Brighton: William Moon, 1853), pp. 6–7.
55 Ibid., p. 6, emphasis in the original.
56 As the historian Gordon Philips notes, it is very difficult to get quantitative data relating to the rates at which blind and partially sighted people took up

reading in the embossed systems available. *The Blind in British Society: Charity, State and Community, c. 1780–1930* (Aldershot: Ashgate, 2004), pp. 226–7.

57 Frances Martin, *Elizabeth Gilbert and Her Work for the Blind* (London: Macmillan and Co., 1887), pp. 77–8.

58 Cathy Kudlick, 'Disability History: Why We Need Another "Other"', *The American Historical Review*, 108:3 (June 2003), 763–93 (p. 789).

59 Vanessa Warne links these displays with the more troubling scenes of blind people street-reading for financial gain reported on by commentators such as Andrew Halliday in Henry Mayhew's series *London Labour and the London Poor* (Warne, pp. 57–9).

60 Looking back at earlier census records, we find Emma Mollard in 1851, aged three. Young Emma has already been newly counted as one of Britain's blind. She is one of four children, with the mother, Emma Mollard, noted as head of the family, working as a laundress. Emma Mollard is still listed as a pupil in the Birmingham Institution's fortieth annual report (1887–8), where she is, at 39, the eldest of the 35 female pupils; and forty-second annual report (1889–90), where she is again the eldest of 44 female pupils. These annual reports also detail those pupils dismissed for want of ability or capacity to learn.

61 *First Report of the Institution for the Blind, no. 113 Broad Street, Birmingham* (1848), pp. 4–5.

62 Reported to Royal Commission, and cited by Phillips, p. 223.

63 John Bird, Letter to the Editor, *The Social Science Review*, vol. 11, no. 51 (30 May 1863), 364–5 (p. 365).

64 John Bird, *Contributions to Social Pathology. Sections I & II. The Blind and the Deaf and Dumb*, 2nd edn (London: Ward and Lock, 1862), p. 56.

65 Bird, Letter to *The Social Science Review*, p. 364. The reviewer of his book had registered dismay at the 'anger and bitterness' displayed in his book which had 'better not have been expressed'. Unknown reviewer, 'Review of *Social Pathology – The Blind, Deaf, and Dumb*, by John Bird', *The Social Science Review*, vol. 11, no. 50 (23 May 1863), p. 336.

66 In Alfred Payne, *The Education of the Blind and the Deaf and Dumb; A Lecture, Delivered December 9th, 1862* (Manchester: John Phillips, 1862), p. 12 (emphasis mine).

67 Gordon Phillips suggests 'it seems reasonable to propose' that by time of the Royal Commission only one in two of blind adults could read (p. 227).

68 Johnson, *Tangible Typography*, pp. 8–9.

69 G. A. Hughes, *The Punctiuncular Stenographic System of Embossing, by Which the Blind of All Nations Will be Able to Emboss for themselves on Any Paper without the Use of Type, and to Attain a Perfect Knowledge in Reading, Arithmetic etc., with Unpredicted Faculty* (London: Published by the author, 1843), pp. iii–iv.

70 G. A. Hughes, *An explanation of the Embossed Systems, adopted in the United Kingdom for educating the Blind; including music, thorough bass and musical writing for the sightless* (London: 1848), p. 4 (emphasis mine).

71 Bird, *Social Pathology*, p. 21. Bird's statement coincided with an international conference on blindness which was held in France between 1862 and 1863. Here, the Earl of Shaftesbury proposed a pan-European government enquiry into the condition of blind, deaf and mute communities, as well as a call for educating the blind in tactile alphabets on a wider scale.
72 'Blind Leaders of the Blind' (unknown author), *All the Year Round* (7 May 1870), pp. 550–52.
73 Ibid.
74 Armitage, born in 1824, had trained as a doctor but retired from medicine in the 1850s due to his failing sight. He was a member of the Indigent Blind Visiting Society's committee from 1866 to 1868, after which, in 1868, he formed the British and Foreign Society for Improving the Embossed Literature of the Blind, later altered to the British and Foreign Blind Association for Promoting the Education and Employment of the Blind.
75 Thomas Rhodes Armitage, *The Education and Employment of the Blind. What it has been, is, and ought to be* (London: British & Foreign Blind Association, 1871), p. 14.
76 Ibid., p. 13.
77 Ibid., p. 12.
78 Braille died in 1852 before his system was used more widely – indeed, before his own institution began to employ it. Throughout this chapter I use 'Braille' to refer to the person of Louis Braille, and 'braille' to refer to the raised script.
79 A growing preference for systems based on symbolic rather than Roman systems is evidenced by Mansfield Turner and William Harris in their 1871 compendium, which distributed forms to institutions and societies for blind people throughout the country. *A Guide to the Institutions and Charities for the Blind in the United Kingdom, together with lists of books and appliances for their use, A Catalogue of Books published upon the subject of the Blind, and A List of Foreign Institutions, etc*, 2nd edn (London: Robert Hardwicke, 1871).
80 *Annual Report of the Indigent Blind Visiting Society*, 35 (1870), p. 4.
81 *Annual Report of the Indigent Blind Visiting Society*, 36 (1871), pp. 10–11.
82 Mary G. Thomas, *N. I. B. Biographies: Thomas Rhodes Armitage* (London: National Institute for the Blind, 1952), p. 10.
83 Levy, *Blindness*, p. 119.
84 Armitage, pp. 17–18.
85 William Moon, *Light for the Blind: A History of the Origin and Success of Moon's System of Reading (Embossed in Various Languages) for the Blind* (London: Longmans & Co., 1873).
86 Olsén, p. 79.
87 Armitage, pp. 20–22.
88 Levy, *Blindness*, p. 131.
89 David E. Wellbery, foreword to Friedrich A. Kittler, *Discourse Networks 1800/1900*, trans. by Michael Metteer, with Chris Cullens (Stanford, CA: Stanford University Press, 1987), p. xiv.
90 Kittler, *Discourse Networks*, p. 231.

91 Friedrich A. Kittler, *Gramophone, Film, Typewriter*, trans. by Geoffrey Winthrop-Young and Michael Wutz, 2nd edn. (Stanford, CA: Stanford University Press, 1986; reprt 1999), p. 189.
92 Darren Wershler-Henry, *'The Iron Whim': A History of Typewriting* (Ithaca, NY: Cornell University Press, 2007), pp. 47–51. Wershler-Henry mistakenly attributes the typograph to G. A. Hughes, although it was in fact invented by William Hughes, director of Henshaw's Institution for the Blind in Manchester.
93 Gall, *Origin and Progress*, pp. 383–8. Other examples include Wedgwood's noctograph (inscription on carbon paper).
94 This is within the context of a discussion of Nietzsche's brief experiment with a writing ball in 1881, which marked a 'turning point in the organisation of discourse' by releasing reading from the productive continuation of reading that it had been in 1800 (Kittler, *Discourse Networks*, pp. 191–5).
95 Thomas Anderson, *Observations on the Employment, Education, and Habits of the Blind; with a Comparative View of the Benefits of the Asylum and School Systems* (London: Simpkin, Marshall & Co, 1837), p. 74.
96 Martin Heidegger, *Parmenides*, trans. by André Schuwer and Richard Rojewicz (Bloomington: Indiana University Press, 1998), p. 81.
97 See the exhibition and learning resource I curated at the Peltz Gallery, Birkbeck, in 2013, *Touching the Book: Embossed Literature for Blind People in the Nineteenth Century*, http://blogs.bbk.ac.uk/touchingthebook/.

## 4 Memoirs of the Blind

1 Klages, p. 148.
2 Ibid., p. 147.
3 Couser, *Recovering Bodies*, pp. 4–5.
4 Ronald J. Ferguson, *We Know Who We Are: A History of the Blind in Challenging Educational and Socially Constructed Policies: A Study in Policy Archaeology* (San Francisco, CA: Caddo Gap Press, 2001), p. xii.
5 Ibid., pp. 58–9.
6 Couser, 'Disability, Life Narrative, and Representation', *PMLA* (2005), 602–6 (p. 604).
7 Ibid., p. 604.
8 Couser, 'Signs of Life: Deafness and Personal Narrative', in *Recovering Bodies: Illness, Disability, and Life Writing* (Wisconsin: University of Wisconsin Press, 1997), pp. 221–87 (pp. 226–30).
9 Bird, *Social Pathology*, p. 6.
10 James Wilson, *Biography of the Blind, Including the Lives of All Those, from Homer down to the Present Day, who have Distinguished themselves, as Poets, Philosophers, Artists, &c., &c., By James Wilson who has been Blind from his Infancy* (Belfast: Lyons, 1821). Subsequent editions appeared in 1833, 1842 and 1856. Wilson also published his autobiography in 1825. The re-issuing of *Biography of the Blind* indicates both its popularity (Southey seemingly read

it in 1834, according to John Bird in his edited *Autobiography of the Blind James Wilson, Author of 'The Lives of Useful Blind'; with a Preliminary Essay On his Life, Character, and Writings, As Well as on the Present State of the Blind* (London: Ward & Lock, 1856), p. 5) and its expansive nature – each edition included new biographies of past and present blind figures.

11 Ibid., p. vi.

12 Bird in Wilson, *Autobiography*, p. xlvi. Bird defended both Dickens's and Edward Bulwer Lytton's portrayals of blindness, however, claiming that no one has 'so thoroughly conceived and described the objectless state of vacuity in which we exist and move and the consequent depression it produces on the mind, as the author of ... the blind girl's song in *The Last Days of Pompeii*' (p. xlvi).

13 James Wilson, *The Life of James Wilson, Blind from His Infancy, Author of Original Poems* (Limerick: R. P. Canter, 1825), pp. 70–71.

14 Ibid., pp. 70–71.

15 Ibid., p. 15.

16 Ibid., p. 15.

17 Ibid., pp. 18–19.

18 Ibid., p. 21.

19 Ibid., pp. 29–30.

20 Wilson, *Biography*, p. 321.

21 Ibid., pp. 37–8.

22 Alexander Beecroft, 'Blindness and Literacy in the Lives of Homer', *Classical Quarterly*, 61:1 (2011), pp. 1–18.

23 Wilson, *Biography*, p. 41.

24 The works that Wilson cites are Robert Wood, 'An Essay on the Original Genius and Writings of Homer' (1775); Richard Cumberland, *The Observer: Being a Collection of Moral, Literary and Familiar* (1785); the *Encyclopaedia Britannica*; and Lemprière's *Classical Dictionary*.

25 Ibid., p. 40.

26 Ibid., p. 41.

27 Beecroft, pp. 2–3, 4.

28 Wilson, *Biography*, p. 54.

29 James Holman, frontispiece to *The Narrative of a Journey, Undertaken in the Years 1819, 1820, & 1821, Through France, Italy, Savoy, Switzerland, Parts of Germany Bordering the Rhine, Holland, and the Netherlands; Comprising Incidents that Occurred to the Author, who has long Suffered Under a Total Deprivation of Sight; With Various Points of Information collected on his Tour* (London: F. C. and J. Rivington, 1822); Unknown author, 'Blind Leaders of the Blind'.

30 Joseph Dennie [Oliver Oldschool], *The Port-folio*, I (Philadelphia, 1806). The American man of letters Joseph Dennie published this work under the pseudonym Oliver Oldschool. In my discussion, I attribute quotations to Joseph Dennie and page numbers to Wilson's 1821 edition.

31 Ibid., p. 77.

32 Ibid., p. 95.
33 Ibid., p. 95.
34 Thomas Reid, *An Inquiry into the Human Mind: On the Principles of Common Sense* (4th edn, 1785), ed. by Derek R. Brookes (Edinburgh: Edinburgh University Press, 1997), pp. 78–9.
35 Dennie [Oldschool], p. 96.
36 Ibid., p. 96.
37 Ibid., p. 98.
38 These poems were published in the *Belfast Chronicle* in 1811.
39 Wilson, *Life*, pp. 35–6.
40 Ibid., p. 36.
41 Ibid., p. 37.
42 Bird in Wilson, *Autobiography*, p. xlvii.
43 Edmund H. White, *Blindness; a Discursive Poem in Five Cantos. Composed in Total Blindness* (London: James Martin, 1856), p. vii.
44 Bird in Wilson, *Autobiography*, p. viii.
45 Ibid., p. viii.
46 White, p. viii.
47 John Kitto, *The Lost Senses: Deafness and Blindness*, 2 vols. (Edinburgh: William Oliphant & Co., 1845), vol. II, pp. 111–12.
48 William Wordsworth, 'Lines Written a Few Miles Above Tintern Abbey', in *Lyrical Ballads, and Other Poems, 1797–1800*, ed. by James Butler and Karen Green (Ithaca, NY: Cornell University Press, 1992), pp. 116–20 (p. 119, line 107).
49 White, p. 17.
50 Ibid., pp. 17–18.
51 Ibid., p. 18.
52 White, p. ix.
53 Ibid., p. 64.
54 Charles Dickens, *American Notes*, ed. by Patricia Ingham (London: Penguin, 2004), p. 64.
55 White, p. x.
56 Ibid., p. xvi.
57 Bird in Wilson, *Autobiography*, p. xi.
58 Bird wrote that 'few people, as they pass an individual blind man or woman of their acquaintance, imagine that there are in the United Kingdom 30, 000 so imprisoned' (Bird in Wilson, *Autobiography*, p. x); Van Landeghem titled her treatises *Charity Misapplied. When Restored to Society after having been immured for several years in exile schools … the blind, and the deaf and the dumb are found to be incapable of self-support. Why? The question considered and answered* (London, 1864) and *Exile and Home: The Advantages of Social Education for the Blind* (London, 1865).
59 Bird in Wilson, *Autobiography* p. x.
60 Ibid., p. x.
61 Ibid., p. xi.

62 Ibid., p. xii (original emphasis).
63 Ibid., p. ix.
64 Ibid., p. xviii.
65 Ibid., p. xviii.
66 Ibid., p. xiii.
67 Ibid., p. xiii.
68 Ibid., p. xiv.
69 Ibid., p. xviii.
70 Ibid., p. xxxiii.
71 Ibid., p. xiv.
72 Ibid., p. xxiv.
73 Ibid., pp. xlii–xliii.
74 Van Landeghem, *Charity Misapplied*, pp. 3–4.
75 Ibid., pp. 11–12.
76 'Training for the Blind', p. 8.
77 Van Landeghem, *Charity Misapplied*, p. 42.
78 Van Landeghem, *Exile and Home*, pp. iii–iv.
79 Ibid., p. vi.
80 Levy, *Blindness*, p. 278.
81 Levy, *Blindness*, p. 145–6.
82 Kleege, *Blind Rage: Letters to Helen Keller* (Washington, DC: Gallaudet University Press, 2006), p. 1. In *Blind Rage*, Kleege examines her own feelings of resentment towards the popular image of Helen Keller as a 'symbol of human fortitude in the face of adversity' (ix), which shifts through her consideration of Keller's autobiographical writings, and Kleege's realisation that Keller's personal and emotional life were more complex than official biographies could signal.
83 Martin, p. vii.
84 Ibid., p. 87.
85 Anderson, p. 78.
86 Ibid., p. 80.
87 Garland-Thomson, *Staring*, pp. 38, 44, 187.
88 Martin, p. 87.
89 Robert Lowe, 'Autobiographical Fragment', in A. Patchett Martin, in *Life and Letters of the Right Honourable Robert Lowe, Viscount Sherbrooke*, 2 vols. (London: Longman, Green, and Co., 1893), vol. 1, 3–44. The fragment was only published after his death by his first biographer, A. Patchett Martin.
90 Ibid., p. 5.
91 Ibid., p. 3.
92 Ibid., p. 44.
93 Lowe notes that whilst he was never able to 'understand the use of keeping accounts or keeping a journal', and that he kept no correspondence, he felt compelled to write a record of his life after pressure from friends, and from his own sense that 'a narrative of the very great difficulties with which I have had to contend' would be of use to a wider public (Ibid., pp. 3–4). His biographer,

Martin, recounts that Lowe made no attempt to reproduce the concluding portion of the memoir, which was lost in the post, and argues that this evidences his lack of interest in the project (Ibid., p. 44).

## 5 Blindness, Gender and Autobiography

1 Lennard J. Davis, 'Seeing the Object as in Itself it Really Is', in *The Madwoman and the Blindman*, ed. by Bolt, Rodas and Donaldson, pp. ix–xii (p. xi).
2 David Bolt, Julia Miele Rodas and Elizabeth J. Donaldson, 'Introduction: The Madwoman and the Blindman', in Bolt, Rodas and Donaldson, *The Madwoman and the Blindman*, pp. 1–9.
3 Ibid., p. 2.
4 Hélène Cixous, 'Writing Blind', in *Stigmata* (London: Routledge, 1998; reprt 2005), pp. 184–203 (p. 198). Cixous's framing of her account of myopia within the concept of stigmata is particularly apposite, given that early cultural disability studies developed from theoretical and philosophical work on stigma, which recognised how all human differences may be stigmatised to reflect the value judgements of the dominant group. For a discussion of the relationship between stigma and disability studies, including the contribution of sociologist Erving Goffman's *Stigma: Notes on the Management of Spoiled Identity* (1963), see Bolt, *Metanarrative of Blindness*, pp. 4–5.
5 Ibid., p. 185.
6 Ibid., p. 186.
7 Heather Glen, *Charlotte Brontë: The Imagination in History* (Oxford: Oxford University Press, 2002), p. 125.
8 Charlotte Brontë, *Jane Eyre: An Autobiography* (1847), ed. by Margaret Smith, 3rd edn (Oxford: Oxford University Press, 1969; reprt 2000), p. 447. Hereafter referred to as *JE* in the main body of the text; all subsequent page numbers are taken from this edition.
9 See Gilbert and Gubar, pp. 48–9.
10 The complex defines the relationship between child and father as one of anxiety and neurosis, in which the father plays 'the part of a dreaded enemy to the sexual interests of childhood. The punishment which he threatened is castration, or its substitute, blinding' (Sigmund Freud, 'Totem and Taboo' (1913), in *The Standard Edition of the Complete Psychological Works of Sigmund Freud*, trans. and ed. by James Strachey, 23 vols. (London: Hogarth Press, 1955), vol. XIII, pp. 1–161 (pp. 129–30)).
11 Gilbert and Gubar, p. 368.
12 Margaret Rose Torrell, 'From India-Rubber Back to Flesh: A Reevaluation of Male Embodiment in *Jane Eyre*', in *The Madwoman and the Blindman*, ed. by Bolt, Rodas and Donaldson, pp. 71–90 (pp. 71–7).
13 Essaka Joshua, '"I Began to See": Biblical Models of Disability in *Jane Eyre*', in *The Madwoman and the Blindman*, ed. by Bolt, Rodas and Donaldson, pp. 111–28 (pp. 114–15).

14 Bolt, Rodas and Donaldson, 'Introduction', in *The Madwoman and the Blindman*, p. 2.
15 Ibid., p. 4.
16 David Bolt, 'The Blindman in the Classic: Feminisms, Ocularcentrism and Charlotte Brontë's *Jane Eyre*', *Textual Practice*, 22:2 (2008), 269–89 (p. 271).
17 Ibid., p. 271.
18 Indeed, 'The Blindman in the Classic' was foundational to the collection of essays edited by David Bolt, Julia Miele Rodas and Elizabeth J. Donaldson on *Jane Eyre* in 2012, cited throughout this chapter, and several contributors responded to the provocations of Bolt's original argument. Whilst a revised version of the essay is reproduced in that volume, I quote from the original essay, as did other contributors to the volume who engaged with Bolt's argument.
19 Notably Lennard Davis's influential argument, cited earlier, that the novel developed as a genre in the nineteenth century as part of a co-operative effort to shore up the normal body; and David Mitchell and Sharon L. Snyder's concept of disability as a form of narrative prosthesis (Susannah B. Mintz, 'Illness, Disability, and Recognition in *Jane Eyre*', in *The Madwoman and the Blindman*, ed. by Bolt, Rodas and Donaldson, pp. 129–49 (pp. 130, 146).
20 Mintz, p. 130.
21 Ibid., p. 131.
22 Ibid., pp. 147–8.
23 Elizabeth Gaskell, *The Life of Charlotte Brontë* (1857), ed. by Elisabeth Jay (Harmondsworth: Penguin, 1997), p. 111. Hereafter referred to in the main body of the text as *LCB*; all subsequent page numbers are taken from this edition.
24 Cohen, *Embodied*, p. 62.
25 As Susannah B. Mintz points out, in response to critics such as Bolt who have argued convincingly for the 'unequal dynamics inherent in Jane's staring at Rochester in his blindness, we might remember that Jane has been staring at Rochester all along' (Mintz, p. 147).
26 Garland-Thomson, *Staring*, p. 10.
27 See Christopher Gabbard, 'From Custodial Care to Caring Labour: the Discourse of Who Cares in *Jane Eyre*', in *The Madwoman and the Blindman*, ed. by Bolt, Rodas and Donaldson, pp. 91–110 (pp. 103–4, 110).
28 Martha Stoddard Holmes, 'Visions of Rochester: Screening Desire and Disability in *Jane Eyre*', in *The Madwoman and the Blindman*, ed. by Bolt, Rodas and Donaldson, pp. 150–74 (p. 154); Torrell, pp. 86–8.
29 Linett, p. 27. Linett uses Rochester as a prime example in her discussion.
30 Torrell, p. 90.
31 Cohen, *Embodied*, p. 63.
32 Bolt, 'The Blindman', p. 285.
33 Charlotte Brontë to Ellen Nussey, 26 August [1846], in Charlotte Brontë, *The Letters of Charlotte Brontë, with a Selection of Letters by Family and Friends*, ed. by Margaret Smith, 2 vols. (Oxford: Clarendon Press, 2000), vol. 1, p. 494.

34 In the first decades of the nineteenth century, the treatment of cataracts, through either couching or extraction, was subject to some debate. The traditional method of couching involved piercing the eye with a sharp instrument, and pushing the opaque cataract lens away from its supports, allowing light to enter the eye through the pupil (but vision would be unfocused as there was no lens). As the cataract lens was only pushed away, not removed, it could move back upwards. More specialised surgeons, with enhanced anatomical knowledge of the eye, began practising extraction (where the lens was removed entirely) in the early nineteenth century: the technique had been introduced in France in the mid-eighteenth century.
35 This is on pp. 226–7 of the Brontë family copy in the Brontë Parsonage Museum, catalogue number bb210.
36 Sally Shuttleworth, *Charlotte Brontë and Victorian Psychology* (Cambridge: Cambridge University Press, 1996), p. 6.
37 Ibid., p. 18.
38 Ibid., p. 27.
39 Caldwell, p. 97.
40 Thomas J. Graham, *Modern Domestic Medicine: A Popular Treatise* (London: Simpkin & Marshall, 1826), p. 227.
41 John Stevenson, *On the Morbid Sensibility of the Eye, Commonly Called Weakness of Sight* (London: Samuel Highley, 1810), p. 32. In his discussion of the costs of reading, Simon Eliot details how the expense of domestic lighting impacted on reading practices by restricting the availability of light in middle-class households until the invention of the more affordable paraffin lamp in the 1860s ('"Never Mind the Value, What about the Price?" Or, How Much Did "Marmion" Cost St. John Rivers?', *Nineteenth-Century Literature*, 56 (2001), 160–97 (p. 170)).
42 Elsie B. Michie, *Outside the Pale: Cultural Exclusion, Gender Difference, and the Victorian Woman Writer* (Ithaca, NY: Cornell University Press, 1993), p. 2.
43 Charlotte Brontë to Ellen Nussey, 13 June 1845, Brontë, *Letters of Charlotte Brontë*, vol. 1, p. 397.
44 Juliet Barker, *The Brontës* (London: Phoenix Press, 1995; reprt 2001), p. 505.
45 See the chapter 'Milton's Bogey: Patriarchal Poetry and Women Readers', in Gilbert and Gubar, pp. 187–212.
46 Maxwell, pp. 5–6.
47 Anna K. Nardo, *George Eliot's Dialogue with John Milton* (Columbia: University of Missouri Press, 2003), p. 23.
48 Ibid., p. 26.
49 Ibid., p. 35.
50 Quoted in the introduction to Gaskell, *The Life of Charlotte Brontë*, p. xxii.
51 Wardrop, *Essays*, pp. 90–91.
52 Charlotte Brontë to Monsieur Heger, quoted by Elizabeth Gaskell from a series of letters between 24 July 1844 and 18 November 1845, in Brontë, *The Life of Charlotte Brontë*, pp. 207–8.
53 Barker, *The Brontës*, p. 441.

54 De Man, 'The Rhetoric of Blindness', p. 106.
55 Ibid., p. 137.
56 Naomi Schor, 'Blindness as Metaphor', *differences: A Journal of Feminist Cultural Studies*, 11 (1999), 76–105 (p. 81).
57 Deirdre David, *Intellectual Women and Victorian Patriarchy: Harriet Martineau, Elizabeth Barrett Browning, George Eliot* (Basingstoke: Macmillan Press, 1987), p. 128.
58 Elizabeth Barrett Browning, *An Elizabeth Barrett Browning Concordance*, compiled by Gladys W. Hudson, 4 vols. (Detroit: Gale Research, 1973), vol. III, *Aurora Leigh*. The concordance lists 144 references to eyes in the poem.
59 Elizabeth Barrett Browning, *Aurora Leigh* (1857), in *Aurora Leigh and Other Poems*, ed. by John Robert Glorney Bolton and Julia Bolton Holloway (Harmondsworth: Penguin, 1995), pp. 1–308 (book 5: lines 183–7). Hereafter referred to in the main body of the text as *AL*; all subsequent book and line references are taken from this edition.
60 Elizabeth Barrett Browning, 'An Essay on Mind' (1826), with other poems, in *The Complete Works of Elizabeth Barrett Browning*, ed. by Charlotte Porter and Helen A. Clarke, 6 vols. (New York: Thomas Y. Crowell, 1900), vol. I, pp. 55–99 (p. 58). Hereafter referred to in the main body of the text as *EM*; all subsequent book and line numbers are taken from this edition.
61 Kate Flint, p. 89.
62 Elizabeth Barrett Browning to Cornelius Matthews, July 17 [1844], in Elizabeth Barrett Browning, *The Brownings' Correspondence*, ed. by Philip Kelley and Scott Lewis, 14 vols. (Winfield: Wedgestone Press, 1982–98), vol. IX, p. 52.
63 Hugh Stuart Boyd, 'Written When Afflicted by Weak Sight', in *Select Poems of Synesius and Gregory Nazianzen; translated from the Greek* (London: F. C. and J. Rivington, 1814), p. 87.
64 Elizabeth Barrett Browning, *Elizabeth Barrett to Mr Boyd: Unpublished Letters of Elizabeth Barrett Browning to Hugh Stuart Boyd*, ed. by Barbara P. McCarthy (London: John Murray, 1955), p. xxi.
65 Elizabeth Barrett Browning to Hugh Stuart Boyd, 6 June 1828, in ibid., p. 47.
66 Elizabeth Barrett Browning to Hugh Stuart Boyd, Monday [1832], in ibid., p. 165. This was around the time that Boyd was due to leave Malvern at the expiration of his and his wife's lease of Ruby Cottage – Barbara McCarthy records that Elizabeth grew hysterical over the potential separation (p. xxvii).
67 Elizabeth Barrett Browning to Hugh Stuart Boyd, [1832], in ibid., p. 180.
68 See Elizabeth's letter to Robert Browning, 17 August 1846, in Barrett Browning, *The Brownings' Correspondence*, vol. XIII, p. 264.
69 Elizabeth Barrett Browning to Hugh Stuart Boyd, Florence, 26 May [1847], in ibid., pp. 285–6.
70 Elizabeth Barrett Browning, 'Hugh Stuart Boyd: His Blindness' (1850), in *Aurora Leigh and Other Poems*, ed. by Bolton and Holloway, p. 376.
71 Elizabeth Barrett Browning, 'Hugh Stuart Boyd: Legacies' (1850), in *Aurora Leigh and Other Poems*, ed. by Bolton and Holloway, p. 376.

72 Elizabeth Barrett to Robert Browning, 20 March 1845, in Barrett Browning, *The Brownings' Correspondence*, vol. x, p. 133.
73 Elizabeth Barrett Browning to Robert Browning, 15 July 1846, in *The Brownings' Correspondence*, vol. xiii, p. 163.
74 Elizabeth Barrett Browning to Mrs Jameson, 26 December 1856, in Elizabeth Barrett Browning, *The Letters of Elizabeth Barrett Browning*, ed. by Frederic G. Kenyon, 2 vols. (London: Smith, Elder & Co., 1897), vol. ii, pp. 245–6.
75 David, p. 136.
76 Angela Leighton, *Elizabeth Barrett Browning* (Brighton: The Harvester Press, 1986), p. 22.
77 Quoted in Leighton, p. 31.
78 Sigmund Freud, 'Some Psychical Consequences of the Anatomical Distinction between the Sexes' (1925), in *The Standard Edition of the Complete Psychological Works*, vol. xix, pp. 243–58 (p. 253).
79 Ibid., p. 256.
80 Ibid., pp. 256–7.
81 Dina Mulock Craik, *Olive* (1850), ed. by Cora Kaplan (Oxford: Oxford University Press, 1999), p. 23. Subsequent page references are taken from this edition and are given in the main body of the text.
82 Slavoj Žižek, '"I Hear You with My Eyes"; or, The Invisible Master', in *Gaze and Voice as Love Objects*, ed. by Renata Salecl and Slavoj Žižek (Durham: Duke University Press, 1996), pp. 90–128 (p. 94).
83 Schor, 'Blindness as Metaphor.'
84 Rochester's partial regaining of sight is interpreted by some critics as a reassertion of normalcy after his blindness (for example, Elizabeth J. Donaldson, 'The Corpus of the Madwoman', in *The Madwoman and the Blindman*, ed. by Bolt, Rodas and Donaldson, pp. 11–32 (p. 11)).
85 'Inscient, adj.[1] and adj.[2]', *OED Online*, www.oed.com.

### 6 Writing Blindness

1 Charles Dickens, *The Pickwick Papers* (1836–7), ed. by Mark Wormald (London: Penguin, 2003), p. 15. Whilst Dickens's fiction had appeared in print earlier with *Sketches by Boz* (1836), it was *Pickwick* that launched him to fame.
2 Ibid., p. 20.
3 Charles Dickens, *Dombey and Son* (1848), ed. by Andrew Sanders (London: Penguin, 2002), p. 702.
4 Bowen, p. 5.
5 For a discussion of ghosts in Dickens, see Luke Thurston, *Literary Ghosts from the Victorians to Modernism* (London: Routledge, 2012), pp. 11–33 (p. 22).
6 Gavin Edwards, 'Dickens, Illiteracy, and "Writin' Large"', *English*, 61 (2012), 27–49. Edwards focuses particularly on *Bleak House*, *Great Expectations*, *Our Mutual Friend* and *Dr Marigold's Prescriptions*.
7 I have written elsewhere on the function of vision and blindness in Dickens's *Christmas Books*, which encompass the period between the publication

of *American Notes* and *David Copperfield*: Heather Tilley, 'Sentiment and Vision in Charles Dickens's *A Christmas Carol* and *The Cricket on the Hearth*', *19: Interdisciplinary Studies in the Long Nineteenth Century*, special issue *Rethinking Victorian Sentimentality*, 4 (2007), www.19.bbk.ac.uk.

8 Linda M. Shires, 'Literary Careers, Death, and the Body Politics of *David Copperfield*', in *Dickens Refigured: Bodies, Desires, and Other Histories*, ed. by John Schad (Manchester: Manchester University Press, 1996), pp. 117–35 (p. 121).

9 Dickens, *American Notes*, p. 38. Hereafter referred to as *AN* in the main body of the text; all subsequent page numbers are taken from this edition.

10 In Chapter 3, I detail how the term 'arbitrary' was used by educators and inventors of tactile alphabetic systems for blind people to describe those departing from the standard Roman alphabet. Howe, in his discussions of Laura, uses the term 'arbitrary' in reference to all alphabetic sign systems.

11 Heather Tilley, 'The Sentimental Touch: Dickens's *Old Curiosity Shop* and the Feeling Reader', *Journal of Victorian Culture*, 16:1 (2011), 226–41.

12 Elisabeth Gitter, 'The Blind Daughter in Charles Dickens's *Cricket on the Hearth*', *SEL: Studies in English Literature, 1500–1900*, 39 (1999), 675–89 (p. 678).

13 Ibid., p.679.

14 Ibid., p. 683.

15 Laura Mulvey, 'Visual Pleasure and Narrative Cinema', in *Visual and Other Pleasures* (Basingstoke: Macmillan, 1989), pp. 14–28 (p. 15).

16 Charles Dickens, *David Copperfield* (1849–50), ed. by Jeremy Tambling (London: Penguin, 1996; reprt 2004), p. 25. Hereafter referred to in the main body of the text as *DC*; all subsequent book and line numbers are taken from this edition.

17 Gareth Cordery, 'Foucault, Dickens and *David Copperfield*', *Victorian Literature and Culture*, 26:1 (1998), 71–86 (p. 80). Cordery draws most significantly from Foucault's *History of Sexuality* and *Discipline and Punish* (1977) as well as from D. A. Miller, *The Novel and the Police* (1988).

18 Audrey Jaffe, *Vanishing Points: Dickens, Narrative, and the Subject of Omniscience* (Berkeley: University of California Press, 1991), p. 20.

19 Michael Hollington, 'Dickens, the City, and the Five Senses', *AUMLA*, 113 (2010), 29–38; Cohen, *Embodied*, pp. 27–40.

20 'Charles Dickens and *David Copperfield*' (unsigned review), *Fraser's Magazine*, December 1850, xlii, 698–710, in Philip Collins, ed., *Charles Dickens: The Critical Heritage*, (London: Routledge, 1971), p. 246.

21 Ibid., p. 246.

22 John Forster, *The Life of Charles Dickens*, 3 vols. (London: Chapman & Hall, 1872), vol. 1, p. 8.

23 This borrows from De Man's analysis of the critical strategies of Binswanger and Blanchot. De Man, 'The Rhetoric of Blindness", p. 105.

24 Forster, p. 8.

25 Ibid., p. 2.

26 Ibid., pp. 20–21.
27 Ibid., pp. 28–9.
28 Alan P. Barr, 'Mourning Becomes David: Loss and the Victorian Restoration of Young Copperfield', *Dickens Quarterly*, 24:2 (2007), 63–79 (p. 63).
29 Ibid., pp. 63–4.
30 Jeremy Tambling, 'Introduction', in Dickens, *David Copperfield*, pp. xi–xxxix (pp. xx–xxi).
31 Tambling suggests that the description of David in Switzerland in chapter 58, 'Absence', not only evokes Dickens's trip to Switzerland in 1846, but also 'encapsulates Wordsworthian echoes': for example *Prelude*, VI, 'Cambridge and the Alps' (Tambling, notes to Dickens, *David Copperfield*, p. 972). A further passage in which David describes the 'awful solitudes' of the Alps, where he finds 'sublimity and wonder in the dread heights and precipices' (820–21), borrows explicitly from *The Prelude*, in the speaker's description of the 'awful *solitude*' of Chartreuse (*Prelude* (1850), VI, line 419.
32 Wordsworth, 'Lines written a few miles above Tintern Abbey', in *Lyrical Ballads, and Other Poems*, lines 157–8. Line numbers hereafter are given in the text.
33 Cordery, p. 78.
34 Leah Price has compellingly detailed how *David Copperfield* is permeated with references to the material cultures of writing, such as David's acquirement of stenography. Leah Price and Pamela Thurschwell, 'Stenographic Masculinity', in *Literary Secretaries/Secretarial Culture*, ed. by Price and Thurschwell (Aldershot: Ashgate, 2005), pp. 32–47 (p. 32).
35 For a discussion of the relationship between Dickens's own early career as a court reporter and his development as a novelist, see Robert Douglas-Fairhurst, *Becoming Dickens: The Invention of a Novelist* (Cambridge, MA: Harvard University Press, 2011), pp. 69–80.
36 Bowen, p. 8.
37 Ibid., p. 9.
38 Ibid., p. 9.
39 Forster, p. 6.
40 Bowen, p. 8.
41 J. Hillis Miller, 'Introduction', in Charles Dickens, *Bleak House*, ed. by Norman Page (Harmondsworth: Penguin, 1971), pp. 11–34 (p. 11). *Bleak House* is hereafter referred to as *BH* in the main body of the text; all subsequent page numbers are taken from this edition.
42 In a discussion of the chapter in which this passage appears, 'Jo's Will', which charts Jo's determination to produce a will, Gavin Edwards points out that whilst Jo may not be able to attach meaning to the 'mysterious symbols', he understands that meaning is generated from the relative size of printed letters and words (Edwards, p. 33).
43 John Forster, for example, criticised the narrative structure, stating that Esther's supposed ignorance of 'the good qualities in herself she is naively

revealing in the story, was a difficult enterprise, full of hazard in any case, not worth success, and certainly not successful'. *The Life of Charles Dickens*, vol. III, p. 20.

44 Marcia Renee Goodman, '"I'll Follow the Other": Tracing the (M)other in *Bleak House*', *Dickens Studies Annual*, 19 (1990), 147–67, pp. 147, 150.

45 J. Hillis Miller, 'Introduction', pp. 13 and 20.

46 Suzanne Graver, 'Writing in a "Womanly Way" and the Double Vision of *Bleak House*', *Dickens Quarterly*, 4:1 (1987), 3–15 (pp. 12–13).

47 Ibid., p. 3.

48 Dickens, *Dombey and Son*, p. 702.

49 Christine L. Corton, *London Fog: The Biography* (Cambridge, MA: Belknap Press of Harvard University Press, 2015), p. 58.

50 Ibid., pp. 59–61.

51 See Bolt, 'The Blindman', pp. 269–89.

52 John Cunningham Saunders, *A Treatise on Some Practical Points Relating to the Diseases of the Eye: To Which is Added, A Short Account of the Author's Life, and his Method of Curing the Congenital Cataract, by His Friend and Colleague, J.R. Farre* (London: Longman, Hurst, Rees, Orme, and Brown, 1811), p. 135.

53 On combination of cataract and amaurosis, see Saunders, *Treatise*, pp. 115–30; for an early pathological description see Vetch, *Practical Treatise*, pp. 133–47. By 1840, some ophthalmologists were arguing that the term was too broad to encompass a specific pathological condition; for example, James J. Adams noted that he would use the term 'in accordance with its true meaning, by signifying, simply, a dim or darkened sight, without implying any organic disease of the optic nerve' (*A New Operation for the Cure of Amaurosis, Impaired Vision, and Shortsightedness* (London: John Churchill, 1840), pp. 10–11).

54 Vetch, pp. 136–7.

55 Ibid., p. 116.

56 See, for example, Christine van Boheemen-Saaf, who argues that not only does smallpox relate on a symbolic level to the unbridled sexuality of Esther's parents, but it is also a disease which leaves pockmarks on the face, 'suggesting the "wound" of castration of non-phallic origin'. ('"The Universe Makes an Indifferent Parent": *Bleak House* and the Victorian Family Romance', in *Interpreting Lacan*, ed. by Joseph H. Smith and William Kerrigan (New Haven, CT: Yale University Press, 1983), pp. 225–57 (pp. 245–6)). In her analysis of *Bleak House*, Helen Michie, drawing on Elaine Scarry's terminology that pain is constitutive of the making or unmaking of self, argues powerfully that, for Dickens, the process of making and unmaking is foregrounded in the illnesses of his heroines ('"Who is this in Pain?": Scarring, Disfigurement, and Female Identity in *Bleak House* and *Our Mutual Friend*', *NOVEL: A Forum on Fiction*, 22:2 (1989), 199–212 (p. 199)).

57 For an overview of the history and treatment of the disease, see F. Fenner, D. A. Henderson, I. Arita, Z. Ježek and I. D. Ladnyi, eds., *Smallpox and Its Eradication* (Geneva: World Health Organisation, 1988).

58 Alfred Collinson, *Smallpox and Vaccination Historically and Medically Considered: An Inquiry into the Causes of the Recent Increase of Smallpox, and the Means for its Prevention* (London: Hatchard and Co, 1860), pp. 49–53.
59 The Compulsory Act of 1853 provided that every child should be vaccinated within four months of its birth. The failure to provide a public officer to enforce the Act meant that approaches to vaccination were still haphazard.
60 On 12 May 1850, shortly before a meeting of the Metropolitan Sanitary Association, Dickens wrote to Henry Austin, another of its members as well as Secretary of the General Board of Health: 'I am sincerely anxious to serve the cause and am doing it all the good I can, by side-blows in the Household Words.' Charles Dickens, *The Pilgrim Edition: The Letters of Charles Dickens. Volume Six: 1850–1852*, ed. by Graham Storey, Kathleen Tillotson and Nina Burgis (Oxford: Clarendon Press, 1988), pp. 98–9. According to John Drew, Hazel Mackenzie, and Ben Winyard, there were over 20 articles on sanitary reform in the first semester of *Household Words*, and there was 'no doubt that at this point public health and sanitary reform was the most pressing social issue covered by the journal'. *Dickens Journal Online*, www.djo.org.uk/indexes/volumes/1850-volume-i.html#_ftn38.
61 For a discussion of the novel's radical politics, see Sally Ledger, *Dickens and the Popular Radical Imagination* (Cambridge: Cambridge University Press, 2007), pp. 193–208.
62 After contact with a person infected with the virus, the virus would remain dormant for eight to twelve days before the sufferer experienced symptoms including headache, nausea and eruptions on the skin. See Sheldon Watts, *Epidemics and History: Disease, Power and Imperialism* (New Haven and London: Yale University Press, 1997), p. 86.
63 Lawrence Rothfield, *Vital Signs: Medical Realism in Nineteenth-Century Fiction* (Princeton, NJ: University of Princeton Press, 1992), p. 7.
64 Fenner, Henderson, Arita, Zežek and Ladnyi, p. 231.
65 See, for example, D. A. Miller's important study of the way in which *Bleak House* represents the police in both content and form, thus ideologically policing the reader. He identifies how vision and surveillance are crucial to the emergence of the detective in the figure of Inspector Bucket (see the chapter 'Discipline in Different Voices: Bureaucracy, Police, Family, and *Bleak House*', in *The Novel and the Police* (Berkeley: University of California Press, 1988), pp. 58–106 (p. 79).
66 Damaged eyes, perhaps even more than her scarred face, would write Esther out of normative dictates of sexual attractiveness and the nineteenth-century marriage plot. See Bolt, *Metanarrative of Blindness*, pp. 57, 66; Holmes, *Fictions of Affliction*, p. 7.
67 Harriet Martineau, 'Blindness', *Household Words*, vol. IX (17 June 1854), 421–5 (p. 421–2).
68 Ibid., p. 424. Martineau distances herself from the exhibition of blind readers, noting: 'we do not relish such addresses and public hymn-singing (we mean by a body of sufferers exhibiting themselves to raise money, by means of their privations and devotions together)', p. 424.

69 Ibid.
70 Ibid., p. 425.
71 Martineau's article followed on from an article published on the same topic the previous year, in which the author George Dodd similarly endorsed the selection of a system that could be understood 'by persons possessing ordinary eyesight'. 'Books for the Blind', *Household Words*, vol. VII (2 July 1853), 421–4 (p. 424).
72 For a discussion of queer family formation in Dickens's fiction, see Holly Furneaux, *Queer Dickens: Erotics, Families, Masculinities* (Oxford: Oxford University Press, 2009), pp. 107–40.

### 7 Embodying Blindness in the Victorian Novel

1 Frances Browne, *The Star of Atteghei; The Vision of Schartz; and Other Poems* (London: Edward Moxon, 1844); *My Share of the World*, 3 vols. (London: Hurst & Blackett, 1861) (hereafter referred to in the main body of the text as *MSW*; all subsequent volume and page numbers are taken from this edition).
2 See the editor's preface to Browne, *The Star of Atteghei*, pp. vii–xxii; see Frances Browne's listing in *The Wellesley Index to Victorian Periodicals, 1824–1906*, ed. by Walter E. Houghton, 5 vols. (Toronto: University of Toronto Press; London: Routledge & Kegan Paul, 1966–79), vol. V, p. 110.
3 Wilkie Collins, *Poor Miss Finch* (1872), ed. by Catherine Peters (Oxford: Oxford University Press, 1995; reprt 2000), p. xxxix. Hereafter referred to in the main body of the text as *PMF*; all subsequent page numbers are taken from this edition.
4 Armstrong, p. 7.
5 Kate Flint, p. 70.
6 Cohen, *Embodied*, pp. 13–14.
7 Ibid., p. 16.
8 See Merleau-Ponty, *Phenomenology of Perception*, pp. 252–60. Marius von Senden's study *Space and Sight: The Perception of Space and Shape in the Congenitally Blind Before and After Operation*, trans. by Peter Heath (London: Methuen & Co., 1960).
9 Browne was the main original poetry contributor to the *Athenaeum* between 1841 and 1854, with up to 12 new poems published a year at the height of her popularity in the early to mid-1840s; see notices for new novels in the *Athenaeum* between 23 February and 30 March 1861.
10 'The Life and Writings of Miss Browne, the Blind Poetess', *Dublin Review*, 34 (December 1844), 517–60 (p. 545).
11 Ibid., p. 519.
12 Marguerite Gardiner (Countess of Blessington), footnote to 'The First', by Frances Browne, in *The Keepsake*, ed. by Marguerite Gardiner, the Countess of Blessington (1844), pp. 110–11.
13 Elizabeth Barrett Browning to John Kenyon, [London], 29 October 1844, in Barrett Browning, *The Brownings' Correspondence*, vol. IX, pp. 203–4.
14 'The Life and Writings of Miss Browne', p. 546.

15 *Ibid.*, pp. 550–51.
16 Paulson, pp. 12–13.
17 'The Life and Writings of Miss Browne', pp. 532–7.
18 Browne, *Star of Atteghei*, pp. ix–x.
19 'Editor's introduction' in ibid., p. vii.
20 Kitto, vol. II, pp. 161–2.
21 Ibid., p. 168.
22 Ibid., p. 163.
23 Although it is suggested in Browne's entry in *Nineteenth-Century Women Poets* that the book is an autobiography, it is in fact a novel (see 'Frances Browne', in Isobel Armstrong and Joseph Bristow, with Cath Sharrock, eds., *Nineteenth-Century Women Poets* (Oxford: Clarendon Press, 1998), pp. 356–8).
24 Bolt, *Metanarrative of Blindness*, pp. 113–14.
25 Kitto, vol. II, p. 159.
26 Jacques Lacan, *The Four Fundamental Concepts of Psycho-Analysis*, trans. by Alan Sheridan (London: Penguin, 1973; reprt 1994), pp. 72–3. For a fuller discussion of Lacan's splitting of the eye and gaze, and critique of ocularcentrism, see Martin Jay, *Downcast Eyes: The Denigration of Vision in Twentieth-Century French Thought* (Berkeley: University of California Press, 1994), pp. 360–70.
27 Van Landeghem, *Charity Misapplied*, pp. 42–3.
28 Samuel Lyndon Gladden, 'Spectacular Deceptions: Closets, Secrets, and Identity in Wilkie Collins's *Poor Miss Finch*', *Victorian Literature and Culture*, 33 (2005), 467–86 (p. 469).
29 Wilkie Collins, *Hide and Seek* (1854), ed. by Catherine Peters (Oxford: Oxford University Press, 1999), p. 431.
30 Ibid.
31 Unsigned review, *Nation* (7 March 1872), xiv, 158–9, in Wilkie Collins, *Wilkie Collins: The Critical Heritage*, ed. by Norman Page (London: Routledge & Kegan Paul, 1974), p. 199. Interestingly, Collins formed the idea for this after Dickens had a similar affliction from taking silver nitrate to treat a skin disorder (Gladden, p. 473).
32 Unsigned review, *Saturday Review*, 2 March 1872, xxxiii, 282–3, in Collins, *Critical Heritage*, pp. 196–7.
33 Gladden, pp. 479–80.
34 Jenny Bourne Taylor, *The Secret Theatre of Home: Wilkie Collins, Sensation Narrative and Nineteenth-Century Psychology* (London: Routledge, 1988) p. 11.
35 Holmes, *Fictions of Affliction*, p. 7.
36 Ibid., p. 75.
37 Ibid., p. 89.
38 Schor, p. 88.
39 Rothfield, p. 85.
40 Shuttleworth, pp. 9–10.
41 Caldwell, pp. 6–7.
42 After Cheselden, there were only 50 more cases up to the 1960s (Richard Langton Gregory and Jean G. Wallace, *Recovery from Early Blindness: A Case Study* (Cambridge: W. Heffer & Sons, 1963), p. 2).

43 Gitter, 'The Blind Daughter', p. 677.
44 Charity Organisation Society, 'Training of the Blind', *Report of Special Committee of the Charity Organisation Society*, presented to the Council 21 February 1876 (London: Longman, Green & Co., 1876), p. 5.
45 See '*Middlemarch* and the Medical Case Report: The Patient's Narrative and the Physical Exam', in Caldwell, pp. 143–70, for an overview of changing diagnostic practice in the nineteenth century.
46 Gregory and Wallace, Alberto Valvo, and Oliver Sacks all note the importance of interviewing patients at all stages of the sight restoration process to determine the success of the operation, both physically and psychologically (Alberto Valvo, *Sight Restoration after Long-Term Blindness: The Problems and Behaviour Patterns of Visual Rehabilitation* (New York: American Foundation for the Blind, 1971); Oliver Sacks, 'To See and Not See', in *An Anthropologist on Mars: Seven Paradoxical Tales* (London: Picador, 1995), pp. 102–44).
47 William Cheselden, 'An Account of Some Observations made by a young Gentleman, who was born blind, or lost his sight so early, that he had no Remembrance of ever having seen, and was couch'd between 13 and 14 years of age', *Philosophical Transactions*, 25 (1728), 447–50, p. 447.
48 Berkeley, section XLI.
49 Von Senden, p. 22.
50 Ibid., pp. 42–3.
51 Ibid., p. 309.
52 Merleau-Ponty, *Phenomenology of Perception*, p. 222.
53 Ibid., p. 152.
54 Ibid., p. 217.
55 Ibid., p. 223.
56 In Collins, *Poor Miss Finch*, p. 431.
57 For a brief but suggestive reading of the cultural coding of hands in the Victorian period see William A. Cohen, 'Manual Conduct in *Great Expectations*', in *Sex Scandal: The Private Parts of Victorian Fiction* (Durham, NC: Duke University Press, 1996), pp. 27–72 (pp. 33–5).
58 John Kitto's chapter on Mitchell quotes a paper read by Dugald Stewart before the Royal Society of Edinburgh in 1812, as well as drawing on Wardrop's account (Kitto, 'James Mitchell', in *The Lost Senses*).
59 James Wardrop, *History of James Mitchell, a Boy Born Blind and Deaf, with An Account of the Operation Performed for the Recovery of His Sight* (London: John Murray, 1813), p. 3.
60 Ibid., p. 6.
61 Ibid., pp. 10–11.
62 Ibid., p. 14.
63 Ibid., p. 21 (my emphasis).
64 This was posed as a question in the first issue of the *Magazine for the Blind* and returned to throughout the magazine's run (the author notes that 'it is the opinion of Dr Klein [of Vienna], Dr Zeune & others, who have long been accustomed to blind persons, that they cannot [distinguish different colours by touch]'), 1 (1839), p. 36.

65 Kitto, vol. I, pp. 78–9.
66 Kitto, vol. II, pp. 139–40.
67 Ibid., p. 141.
68 Cheselden, 'An Account of Some Observations', p. 447.
69 For an overview of the critical field of the 'white gaze' see, for example, Frantz Fanton, *Black Skin, White Masks* (1952), trans. by Richard Philcox (New York: Grove Press, 2007); Gail Chiang-Liang Low, *White Skins/ Black Masks: Representation and Colonialism* (London: Routledge, 1995); Mary Louise Pratt, *Imperial Eyes: Travel Writing and Transculturation* (London: Routledge, 2002).
70 Burke, p. 131.
71 Kitto, vol. II, p. 67.
72 Von Senden, pp. 168–9.
73 Gregory and Wallace, p. 40. See also Valvo, pp. 22, 28.
74 Valvo, p. 4.
75 Letter to Arthur Locker, 18 January 1872, quoted by Peters, in the introduction to Collins, *Poor Miss Finch* (p. xiv).

## 8 Blindness, Writing, and the Failure of the Imagination in Gissing's *New Grub Street*

1 Bernard Bergonzi, 'Introduction', in George Gissing, *New Grub Street* (1891), ed. by Bergonzi (London: Penguin, 1985), p. 10. Hereafter referred to in the main body of the text as *NGS*; all subsequent page numbers are taken from this edition.
2 Margot Stafford, 'Keeping One's Own Counsel: Authorship, Literary Advice and *New Grub Street*', *The Gissing Journal*, 37:2 (2001), 1–18 (p. 12).
3 For a description of the test, see Henry H. Smith, *The Principles and Practice of Surgery, Embracing Minor and Operative Surgery*, 2 vols. (Philadelphia: J. B. Lippincourt, 1863), pp. 112–13.
4 John Milton, *Paradise Lost*, ed. by Christopher Ricks (London: Penguin, 1968), vol. VII, lines 24–7 (p. 158).

## Epilogue

1 David Bolt, 'Aesthetic Blindness: Symbolism, Realism, and Reality', *Mosaic: A Journal for the Interdisciplinary Study of Literature*, 46:3 (2013), 93–108 (p. 103).
2 Mitchell and Snyder, p. 2.
3 Bird, *Autobiography*, p. xlvi.

# *Bibliography*

## PRIMARY SOURCES


Adams, James J., *A New Operation for the Cure of Amaurosis, Impaired Vision, and Shortsightedness* (London: John Churchill, 1840)

*Practical Observations on Ectropium, or Eversion of the Eyelids, with the Description of a New Operation for the Cure of that Disease; on the Modes of Forming An Artificial Pupil, and On Cataract* (London: J. Callow, 1812)

Alston, John, *First Specimen of Printing for the Use of the Blind, Made in Glasgow by the Asylum for the Blind, Oct 21, 1836* (Glasgow: 1836)

*Narrative of the Progress of Printing for the Blind at the Glasgow Institution* (Glasgow, 1838)

[?Alston, John], *Statements of the Education, Employments and Internal Arrangements, Adopted at the Asylum for the Blind, Glasgow; With a Short Account of its Founder, and General Observations Applicable to Similar Institutions (with Lithographic Illustrations)*, 10th edn (Glasgow: John Smith, 1846)

Anderson, Thomas, *Observations on the Employment, Education, and Habits of the Blind; with a Comparative View of the Benefits of the Asylum and School Systems* (London: Simpkin, Marshall, & Co, 1837)

*Annual Report for the Indigent Blind Visiting Society*, 31–46 (1866–81)

*Annual Report for the London Society for Teaching the Blind to Read*, 136 (London, 1839–71)

Armitage, Thomas Rhodes, *The Education and Employment of the Blind. What it has been, is, and ought to be* (London: British & Foreign Blind Association, 1871)

Bailey, Samuel, *Review of Berkeley's Theory of Vision, Designed to show the Unsoundness of that Celebrated Speculation* (London: 1842)

Bain, Alexander, *The Senses and the Intellect* (London: John W. Parker and Son, 1855)

Baker, Charles, 'The Origin and Progress of the Art of Printing for the Blind', *Scottish Christian Herald*, 114 (May 5 1838)

Beer, Georg Joseph, *The Art of Preserving the Sight Unimpaired to an Extreme Old Age; and of Re-establishing and Strengthening it When it is Become Weak* (London: Henry Colburn, 1813)

Berkeley, George, *The Theory of Vision, or Visual Language … Vindicated and Explained* (London: J. Tonson, 1733)

*An Essay Towards a New Theory of Vision* (Dublin: 1709)

Bird, John, *Contributions to Social Pathology. Sections* I *&* II. *The Blind and the Deaf and Dumb*, 2nd edn (London: Ward and Lock, 1862)

Letter to the Editor, *The Social Science Review*, vol. II, no. 51 (30 May 1863), 364–5

'Blind Leaders of the Blind' (unknown author), *All the Year Round*, 7 May 1870 (pp. 550–52)

Birmingham Institution for the Blind, *First Report of the Institution for the Blind*, no. 113 Broad Street, Birmingham (1848)

Boyd, Hugh Stuart, 'Written when Afflicted by Weak Sight', in *Select Poems of Synesius and Gregory Nazianzen; translated from the Greek* (London: F. C. & J. Rivington, 1814)

Brontë, Charlotte, *Jane Eyre: An Autobiography* (1847), ed. by Margaret Smith, 3rd edn (Oxford: Oxford University Press, 1969, reprt 2000)

*The Letters of Charlotte Brontë, with a Selection of Letters by Family and Friends*, ed. by Margaret Smith, 2 vols. (Oxford: Clarendon Press, 2000)

Browne, Frances, *The Castleford Case*, 3 vols. (London: Hurst & Blackett, 1862)

'The First', in *The Keepsake*, ed. by Marguerite Gardiner, the Countess of Blessington (1844), pp. 110–11

*My Share of the World*, 3 vols. (London: Hurst & Blackett, 1861)

*The Star of Atteghei; The Vision of Schartz; and Other Poems* (London: Edward Moxon, 1844)

Browning, Elizabeth Barrett, *Aurora Leigh* (1857), in *Aurora Leigh and Other Poems*, ed. by John Robert Glorney Bolton and Julia Bolton Holloway (Harmondsworth: Penguin, 1995), pp. 1–308

*The Brownings' Correspondence*, ed. by Philip Kelley and Scott Lewis, 14 vols. (Winfield, KS: Wedgestone Press, 1982–98)

*An Elizabeth Barrett Browning Concordance*, compiled by Gladys W. Hudson, 4 vols. (Detroit, MI: Gale Research, 1973)

*Elizabeth Barrett to Mr Boyd: Unpublished Letters of Elizabeth Barrett Browning to Hugh Stuart Boyd*, ed. by Barbara P. McCarthy (London: John Murray, 1955)

'An Essay on Mind' (1826), with other poems, in *The Complete Works of Elizabeth Barrett Browning*, ed. by Charlotte Porter and Helen A. Clarke, 6 vols. (New York: Thomas Y. Crowell, 1900), vol. I, pp. 55–99

'Hugh Stuart Boyd: His Blindness' (1850), in *Aurora Leigh and Other Poems*, ed. by Bolton and Holloway, p. 376

'Hugh Stuart Boyd: Legacies' (1850), in *Aurora Leigh and Other Poems*, ed. by Bolton and Holloway, p. 376

*The Letters of Elizabeth Barrett Browning*, ed. by Frederic G. Kenyon, 2 vols. (London: Smith, Elder & Co., 1897), vol. II, pp. 245–6

Burke, Edmund, *A Philosophical Enquiry into the Origin of our Ideas of the Sublime and Beautiful*, ed. by Adam Phillips (Oxford: Oxford University Press, 1990)

Carpenter, William B., *Principles of General and Comparative Physiology, Intended as an introduction to the study of human physiology, and as a guide to the philosophical pursuit of natural history*, 5th edn (London: John Churchill, 1855; first published 1841)

Charity Organisation Society, 'Training of the Blind: Report of a Special Committee of the Charity Organisation Society' (London: Longman, Green and Co., 1876)

'Charles Dickens and *David Copperfield*' (unsigned review), *Fraser's Magazine*, December 1850, xlii, 698–710

Cheselden, William, 'An Account of Some Observations made by a young Gentleman, who was born blind, or lost his sight so early, that he had no Remembrance of ever having seen, and was couch'd between 13 and 14 years of age', *Philosophical Transactions*, 25 (1728), 447–50

Collins, Wilkie, *The Dead Secret* (1857), ed. by Ira B. Nadel (Oxford: Oxford University Press, 1997)

*Hide and Seek* (1854), ed. by Catherine Peters (Oxford: Oxford University Press, 1999)

*The Moonstone* (1868), ed. by John Sutherland (Oxford: Oxford University Press, 1999)

*Poor Miss Finch* (1872), ed. by Catherine Peters (Oxford: Oxford University Press, 1995, reprt 2000)

*Wilkie Collins: The Critical Heritage*, ed. by Norman Page (London: Routledge & Kegan Paul, 1974)

Collinson, Alfred, *Smallpox and Vaccination Historically and Medically Considered: An Inquiry into the Causes of the Recent Increase of Smallpox, and the Means for its Prevention* (London: Hatchard and Co, 1860)

Craik, Dinah Mulock, *Olive* (1850), ed. by Cora Kaplan (Oxford: Oxford University Press, 1999)

Dennie, Joseph [Oliver Oldschool], *The Port-folio*, I (Philadelphia, PA, 1806)

Dickens, Charles, *American Notes* (1842), ed. by Patricia Ingham (London: Penguin, 2004)

*Barnaby Rudge: A Tale of the Riots of 'Eighty* (1841), ed. by John Bowen (Harmondsworth: Penguin, 2003)

*The Cricket on the Hearth* (1845), in *Christmas Books: Including 'A Christmas Carol'*, ed. by Ruth Glancy (Oxford: Oxford University Press, 1988), pp. 183–278

*David Copperfield* (1849–50), ed. by Jeremy Tambling (London: Penguin, 1996, reprt 2004)

*Dombey and Son* (1848), ed. by Andrew Sanders (London: Penguin, 2002)

*The Pilgrim Edition: The Letters of Charles Dickens. Volume Six: 1850–1852*, ed. by Graham Storey, Kathleen Tillotson and Nina Burgis (Oxford: Clarendon Press, 1988)

*The Old Curiosity Shop* (1840–41), ed. by Norman Page (London: Penguin, 2000)

*The Pickwick Papers* (1836–7), ed. by Mark Wormald (London: Penguin, 2003)

*Sketches by Boz and Other Early Papers, 1833–39*, ed. by Michael Slater (London: J. M. Dent, 1994)

Diderot, Denis, *An Essay on Blindness, in a Letter to a Person of Distinction*, 3rd edn (London: J. Barker, 1750)

Dodd, George, 'Books for the Blind', *Household Words*, vol. VII (2 July 1853), 421–4

Eliot, George, *Middlemarch* (1872), ed. by W. J. Harvey (London: Penguin, 1965, reprt 1994)

*Romola* (1862–3), ed. by Dorothea Barrett (Harmondsworth: Penguin, 2005)

*Fifth Annual Report of the Fund for Embossing Books for the Blind, by William Moon, of the Improved System of Reading* (Brighton: William Moon, 1853)

Forster, John, *The Life of Charles Dickens*, 3 vols. (London: Chapman & Hall, 1872)

Frere, James Hartley, *A Letter to Lord Wharncliffe, in reply to the allegations made by the London Society for teaching the blind to read, against the Phonetic method of instruction* (London: W. H. Dalton, 1843)

Gall, James, *A First Book for Teaching the Art of Reading to The Blind; A Short Statement of the Principles of the Art of Printing, as here Applied to the Sense of Touch* (Edinburgh: James Gall, 1827)

*A Historical Sketch of the Origin and Progress of Literature for the Blind: and Practical Hints and Recommendations as to their Education. With an Appendix Containing Directions for Teaching Reading and Writing to the Blind, With and Without a Regular Teacher* (Edinburgh: James Gall, 1834)

Gardiner, Marguerite (Countess of Blessington), footnote to 'The First', by Frances Browne, in *The Keepsake*, ed. by Marguerite Gardiner, the Countess of Blessington (1844), pp. 110–11

Gaskell, Elizabeth, *The Life of Charlotte Brontë* (1857), ed. by Elisabeth Jay (Harmondsworth: Penguin, 1997)

*Mary Barton* (1848) (London: Penguin, 1994)

Gissing, George, *New Grub Street* (1891), ed. by Bernard Bergonzi (London: Penguin, 1985)

Goldsmith, Oliver, *The Vicar of Wakefield: A Tale Supposed to be Written by Himself* (1766), ed. by Arthur Friedman (London: Oxford University Press, 1974)

Graham, Thomas J., *Modern Domestic Medicine: A Popular Treatise* (London: Simpkin & Marshall, 1826)

Haüy, Valentin, 'Essay on the Education of the Blind', translated from the French and published in *Poems by the Late Reverend Dr. Thomas Blacklock; Together with an Essay on the Education of the Blind. To which is Prefixed a New Account of the Life and Writings of the Author* (Edinburgh: Chapman and Co., 1793), pp. 217–62

Hayley, William, *The Life of Milton, in Three Parts, to Which are Added, Conjectures on the Origin of Paradise Lost: with an Appendix* (Dublin: William Porter, 1797)

Holman, James, *The Narrative of a Journey, Undertaken in the Years 1819, 1820, & 1821, Through France, Italy, Savoy, Switzerland, Parts of Germany Bordering the Rhine, Holland, and the Netherlands; Comprising Incidents that Occurred to the Author, who has Long Suffered Under a Total Deprivation of Sight; With Various Points of Information collected on his Tour* (London: F. C. and J. Rivington, 1822)

Hughes, G. A., *An explanation of the Embossed Systems, adopted in the United Kingdom for educating the Blind; including music, thorough bass and musical writing for the sightless* (London: 1848)

*The Punctiuncular Stenographic System of Embossing, by Which the Blind of All Nations Will be Able to Emboss for themselves on Any Paper without the Use of Type, and to Attain a Perfect Knowledge in Reading, Arithmetic etc., with Unpredicted Faculty* (London: Published by the author, 1843)

Hutchinson, Sara, *The Letters of Sara Hutchinson, from 1800 to 1835*, ed. by Kathleen Coburn (London: Routledge, 1954)

Johnson, Edmund C., *Annuities to the Blind* (London: Henry Roberts, 1876)

*Tangible Typography: or, How the Blind Read* (London, 1853)

Kitchener, William, *The Economy of the Eyes: Precepts for the Improvement and Preservation of the Sight* (London: Hurst, Robinson & Co., 1824)

Kitto, John, *The Lost Senses: Deafness and Blindness*, 2 vols. (Edinburgh: William Oliphant & Co., 1845)

Levy, W. Hanks, *Blindness and the Blind; or, a treatise on the science of typhlology* (London: Chapman and Hall, 1872)

'The Life and Writings of Miss Browne, the Blind Poetess', *Dublin Review*, 34 (December 1844), 517–60

Locke, John, *An Essay Concerning Human Understanding* (1690), ed. by Roger Woolhouse (London: Penguin, 1997)

Lowe, Robert, 'Autobiographical Fragment', in A. Patchett Martin, *Life and Letters of the Right Honourable Robert Lowe, Viscount Sherbrooke*, 2 vols. (London: Longman, Green, and Co., 1893), vol. I, 3–44.

Lucas, T. M., *Instructions for Teaching the Blind to Read with the Britannic or Universal Alphabet, and Embossing their Lessons &c* (Bristol: Philip Rose and Son, 1837)

*Magazine for the Blind* (London: Simpkin, Marshall & Co.; York: Joseph Moxon, 1839–41)

Martin, Frances, *Elizabeth Gilbert and Her Work for the Blind* (London: Macmillan and Co., 1887)

Martineau, Harriet, 'Blindness', *Household Words*, vol. IX (17 June 1854), 421–5

Mill, J. S., 'Review of Samuel Bailey's *Review of Berkeley's Theory of Vision, Designed to show the Unsoundness of that Celebrated Speculation*', *London and Westminster Review*, 38 (July–October 1842), pp. 319–36

Milton, John, *Paradise Lost*, ed. by Christopher Ricks (London: Penguin, 1968)

Moon, William, *Light for the Blind: A History of the Origin and Success of Moon's System of Reading (Embossed in Various Languages) for the Blind* (London: Longmans & Co., 1873)

'Paper, Printing, and Bookbinding', Class 17, *Official Illustrated Catalogue to the Great Exhibition of 1851*, 4 vols. (London: Spicer & Clowes, 1851), vol. II, 536–52

Payne, Alfred, *The Education of the Blind and the Deaf and Dumb; A Lecture, Delivered December 9th, 1862* (Manchester: John Phillips, 1862)

Reid, Thomas, *An Inquiry into the Human Mind: On the Principles of Common Sense* (4th edn, 1785), ed. by Derek R. Brookes (Edinburgh: Edinburgh University Press, 1997)

Ruskin, John, *Sesames and Lilies* (1865), in *The Works of John Ruskin*, ed. by E. T. Cook and Alexander Wedderburn (London: George Allen, 1903–12), vol. xviii, 5–192

Saunders, John Cunningham, *A Treatise on Some Practical Points Relating to the Diseases of the Eye: To Which is Added, A Short Account of the Author's Life, and his Method of Curing the Congenital Cataract, by His Friend and Colleague, J.R. Farre* (London: Longman, Hurst, Rees, Orme, & Brown, 1811)

Smith, Henry H., *The Principles and Practice of Surgery, Embracing Minor and Operative Surgery*, 2 vols. (Philadelphia: J. B. Lippincourt, 1863)

Smith, John Thomas, *Vagabondia; or, anecdotes of Mendicant Wanderers through the Streets of London* (London, 1817)

Stevenson, John, *On the Morbid Sensibility of the Eye, Commonly Called Weakness of Sight* (London: Samuel Highley, 1810)

Tomlinson, Charles, ed., *Cyclopaedia of Useful Arts and Manufactures, Mechanical and Chemical, Manufactures, Mining, and Engineering*, 4 vols. (London: George Virtue & Co., 1854)

Turner, Mansfield, and William Harris, *A Guide to the Institutions and Charities for the Blind in the United Kingdom, together with lists of books and appliances for their use, A catalogue of books published upon the subject of the Blind, and A List of Foreign Institutions, etc*, 2nd edn (London: Robert Hardwicke, 1871)

van Landeghem, Hyppolite, *Charity Misapplied. When Restored to Society after having been immured for several years in exile schools … the blind, and the deaf and the dumb are found to be incapable of self-support. Why? The question considered and answered* (London: 1864)

*Exile and Home: The Advantages of Social Education for the Blind* (London, 1865)

Vetch, John, *A Practical Treatise on the Diseases of the Eye* (London: G. and W. B. Whittaker, 1820)

Wardrop, James, *Essays on the Morbid Anatomy of the Eye* (Edinburgh: George Ramsay, 1808)

*History of James Mitchell, a Boy Born Blind and Deaf, with An Account of the Operation Performed for the Recovery of His Sight* (London: John Murray, 1813)

White, Edmund H., *Blindness; a Discursive Poem in Five Cantos. Composed in Total Blindness* (London: James Martin, 1856)

Wilson, James, *Autobiography of the Blind James Wilson, Author of 'The Lives of Useful Blind'; with a Preliminary Essay On his Life, Character, and Writings, As Well as on the Present State of the Blind*, ed. by John Bird (London: Ward & Lock, 1856)

*Biography of the Blind, Including the Lives of All Those, from Homer down to the Present Day, who have Distinguished themselves, as Poets, Philosophers, Artists, &c., &c., By James Wilson who has been Blind from his Infancy* (Belfast: Lyons, 1821; reissued as new editions in 1833, 1842 and 1856)

*The Life of James Wilson, Blind from His Infancy, Author of Original Poems* (Limerick: R. P. Canter, 1825)

Wordsworth, William, *The Borderers by William Wordsworth*, ed. by Robert Osborn, (Ithaca, NY: Cornell University Press, 1982)

*The Fourteen-Book Prelude*, ed. by W. J. B. Owen (Ithaca, NY: Cornell University Press, 1985)

*The Letters of William and Dorothy Wordsworth*, ed. by E. D. Selincourt, rev. by Chester L. Shaver, Mary Moorman and Alan G. Hill, 2nd edn, 8 vols. (Oxford: Clarendon Press, 1967–88)

*Lyrical Ballads, and Other Poems, 1797–1800*, ed. by James Butler and Karen Green (Ithaca, NY: Cornell University Press, 1992)

*Poems, Chiefly of Early and Late Years; including The Borderers, a Tragedy* (London: Edward Moxon, 1842)

*Shorter Poems, 1807–1820 by William Wordsworth*, ed. by Carl H. Ketcham (Ithaca, NY: Cornell University Press, 1989)

*The Thirteen-Book Prelude*, ed. by Mark Reed, 2 vols. (Ithaca, NY: Cornell University Press, 1991)

## SECONDARY SOURCES

Abrams, M. H., *The Mirror and the Lamp: Romantic Theory and the Critical Tradition* (New York: Oxford University Press, 1953)

Albrecht, G. L., Katherine D. Seelman and M. Bury, eds., *Handbook of Disability Studies* (Thousand Oaks, CA: Sage, 2001)

Armstrong, Isobel, and Joseph Bristow, with Cath Sharrock, eds., *Nineteenth-Century Women Poets*(Oxford: Clarendon Press, 1998)

'Victorian Studies and Cultural Studies: A False Dichotomy', *Victorian Literature and Culture*, 27:2 (1999), 513–16

Armstrong, Nancy, *Fiction in the Age of Photography: The Legacy of British Realism* (Cambridge, MA: Harvard University Press, 1999)

Atherton, Margaret, *Berkeley's Revolution in Vision* (Ithaca, NY: Cornell University Press, 1990)

Auerbach, Jeffrey A., *The Great Exhibition of 1851: A Nation on Display* (New Haven, CT: Yale University Press, 1999)

Baker, Jeffrey, 'The Deaf Man and the Blind Man', *Critical Survey*, 8:3 (1996), 259–69

Barasch, Moshe, *Blindness: The History of a Mental Image in Western Thought* (Routledge: London, 2001)

Barker, Juliet, *The Brontës* (London: Phoenix Press, 1995; reprt 2001)

*Wordsworth: A Life* (Harmondsworth: Penguin, 2000)

Barnes, Colin, and Geof Mercer, *Exploring Disability*, 2nd edn (Cambridge: Polity Press, 2010)

Barr, Alan P., 'Mourning Becomes David: Loss and the Victorian Restoration of Young Copperfield', *Dickens Quarterly*, 24:2 (2007), 63–79

Baynton, Douglas, 'Disability and the Justification of Inequality in American History', in Paul K. Longmore and Lauri Umansky, eds., *The New Disability*

*History: American Perspectives* (New York and London: New York University Press, 2001), pp. 33–57

Beecroft, Alexander, 'Blindness and Literacy in the Lives of Homer', *Classical Quarterly*, 61:1 (2011), pp. 1–18

Bennett, Mary, *Ford Madox Brown: A Catalogue Raisonné*, vol. 1 (New Haven, CT: Yale University Press, 2010)

Bloom, Harold, *The Anxiety of Influence: A Theory of Poetry* (Oxford: Oxford University Press, 1973)

*The Ringers in the Towers: Studies in Romantic Tradition* (Chicago, IL: University of Chicago Press, 1971)

Bolt, David, 'Aesthetic Blindness: Symbolism, Realism, and Reality', *Mosaic: A Journal for the Interdisciplinary Study of Literature*, 46:3 (2013), 93–108

'The Blindman in the Classic: Feminisms, Ocularcentrism and Charlotte Brontë's *Jane Eyre*', *Textual Practice*, 22:2 (2008), 269–89

'Introduction', *Journal of Literary Disability Studies*, 1:1 (2007), i–vi

*The Metanarrative of Blindness: A Re-Reading of Twentieth-Century Anglophone Writing* (Ann Arbor: University of Michigan Press, 2014)

Bolt, David, Julia Miele Rodas, and Elizabeth J. Donaldson, eds., *The Madwoman and the Blindman: Jane Eyre, Discourse, Disability* (Columbus: Ohio State University Press, 2012)

Bourrier, Karen, *The Measure of Manliness: Disability and Masculinity in the Mid-Victorian Novel* (Ann Arbor: University of Michigan Press, 2015)

Bowen, John, *Other Dickens: Pickwick to Chuzzlewit* (Oxford: Oxford University Press, 2000)

Brown, Bill, 'Thing Theory', *Critical Inquiry*, 28:1, 'Things' (2001), 1–22

Caldwell, Janice, *Literature and Medicine in Nineteenth-Century Britain: From Mary Shelley to George Eliot* (Cambridge: Cambridge University Press, 2004)

Calè, Luisa, *Fuseli's Milton Gallery: 'Turning Readers into Spectators'* (Oxford: Clarendon Press, 2006)

Calè, Luisa, and Patrizia di Bello, eds., *Illustrations, Optics and Objects in Nineteenth-Century Literary and Visual Cultures* (Basingstoke: Palgrave Macmillan, 2010)

'Introduction: Nineteenth-Century Objects and Beholders', in *Illustrations, Optics and Objects*, ed. by Luisa Calè and Patrizia di Bello, pp. 1–21

Chartier, Roger, *The Order of Books: Readers, Authors, and Libraries in Europe between the Fourteenth and Eighteenth Centuries*, trans. by Lydia G. Cochrane (Stanford, CA: Stanford University Press, 1994)

Christ, Carol T., and John O'Jordan, *Victorian Literature and the Victorian Visual Imagination* (Berkeley: University of California Press, 1995)

Cixous, Hélène, 'Writing Blind', in *Stigmata* (London: Routledge, 1998; reprt 2005), pp. 184–203

Cohen, William A., *Embodied: Victorian Literature and the Senses* (Minneapolis: University of Minnesota Press, 2009)

*Sex Scandal: the Private Parts of Victorian Fiction* (Durham, NC: Duke University Press, 1996)

Collins, Philip, ed., *Charles Dickens: The Critical Heritage* (London: Routledge, 1971)

Connor, Steven, 'CP: or, a Few Don'ts by a Cultural Phenomenologist', *Parallax*, 5:2 (1999), 17–31

'Making an Issue of Cultural Phenomenology', in *Critical Quarterly*, 42:1 (2000), special issue ed. by Steven Connor and David Trotter, 2–7

Cordery, Gareth, 'Foucault, Dickens and *David Copperfield*', *Victorian Literature and Culture*, 26:1 (1998), 71–86

Corton, Christine L., *London Fog: The Biography* (Cambridge, MA: Belknap Press of Harvard University Press, 2015)

Couser, G. Thomas, 'Disability, Life Narrative, and Representation', *PMLA* (2005), 602–6

*Recovering Bodies: Illness, Disability, and Life Writing* (Madison: University of Wisconsin Press, 1997)

Crary, Jonathan, *Techniques of the Observer: On Vision and Modernity in the Nineteenth Century*, 7th edn (Cambridge, MA: The MIT Press, 1996)

Curtis, Gerard, *Visual Words: Art and the Material Book in Victorian England* (Aldershot: Ashgate, 1999)

David, Deirdre, *Intellectual Women and Victorian Patriarchy: Harriet Martineau, Elizabeth Barrett Browning, George Eliot* (Basingstoke: Macmillan Press, 1987)

Davidson, Luke, 'Identities Ascertained: British Ophthalmology in the First Half of the Nineteenth Century', *Social History of Medicine*, 9:3 (1996), 313–33

Davis, Lennard J., *Bending Over Backwards; Disability, Dismodernism, and Other Difficult Positions* (New York: New York University Press, 2002)

ed., *The Disability Studies Reader*, 2nd edn (New York and Oxford: Routledge, 2006)

*Enforcing Normalcy: Disability, Deafness, and the Body* (London: Verso, 1995)

'Seeing the Object as in Itself it Really Is', in *The Madwoman and the Blindman*, ed. by Bolt, Rodas and Donaldson, pp. ix–xii

De Man, Paul, *Blindness and Insight: Essays in the Rhetoric of Contemporary Criticism*, 2nd edn (London: Routledge, 1983; reprt 2005)

*The Rhetoric of Romanticism* (New York: Columbia University Press, 1984)

Derrida, Jacques, *Memoirs of the Blind: the Self-Portrait and Other Ruins*, trans. by Pascale-Anne Brault and Michael Naas (Chicago, IL: University of Chicago Press, 1993)

Diedrich, Lisa, 'Breaking Down: A Phenomenology of Disability', *Literature & Medicine*, 20:2 (2001), 209–30

Dolan, Elizabeth A., *Seeing Suffering in Women's Literature of the Romantic Era* (Aldershot: Ashgate, 2008)

Donaldson, Elizabeth J., 'The Corpus of the Madwoman', in *The Madwoman and the Blindman*, ed. by Bolt, Rodas and Donaldson, pp. 11–32

Douglas-Fairhurst, Robert, *Becoming Dickens: The Invention of a Novelist* (Cambridge, MA: Harvard University Press, 2011)

Edwards, Elizabeth, *Raw History: Photographs, Anthropology and Museums* (Oxford: Berg, 2001)

'Thinking Photography beyond the Visual?', in *Photography: Theoretical Snapshots*, ed. by J. J. Long, Andrea Noble and Edward Welch (Abingdon: Routledge, 2009), pp. 31–48

Edwards, Gavin, 'Dickens, Illiteracy, and "Writin' Large"', *English*, 61 (2012), 27–49

Eliot, Simon, '"Never Mind the Value, What about the Price?" Or, How Much Did "Marmion" Cost St. John Rivers?', *Nineteenth-Century Literature*, 56 (2001), 160–97

Esmail, Jennifer, *Reading Victorian Deafness: Signs and Sounds in Victorian Literature and Culture* (Athens: Ohio University Press, 2013)

Fanton, Frantz, *Black Skin, White Masks* (1952), trans. by Richard Philcox (New York: Grove Press, 2007)

Fenner, F., D. A. Henderson, I. Arita, Z. Ježek and I.D. Ladnyi, eds., *Smallpox and Its Eradication* (Geneva: World Health Organisation, 1988)

Ferguson, Ronald J., *We Know Who We Are: A History of the Blind in Challenging Educational and Socially Constructed Policies: A Study in Policy Archaeology* (San Francisco, CA: Caddo Gap Press, 2001)

Flick, C. S., *A Gross of Green Spectacles* (London: Hatton Press, 1951)

Flint, Christopher, *The Appearance of Print in Eighteenth-Century Fiction* (Cambridge: Cambridge University Press, 2011)

Flint, Kate, *The Victorians and the Visual Imagination* (Cambridge: Cambridge University Press, 2000)

Foucault, Michel, *The Birth of the Clinic: An Archaeology of Medical Perception*, 2nd edn (London: Tavistock, 1973; reprt 1975) (first published in France as *Naissance de la Clinique*, 1963)

*Discipline and Punish: The Birth of the Prison*, trans. by Alan Sheridan (London: Penguin, 1977, reprt 1991) (first published in France as *Surveiller et Punir: Naissance de la Prison*, 1975)

Fraser, Hilary, 'Foreword', in *Illustrations, Optics and Objects*, ed. by Calè and di Bello, pp. ix–xv

Freedgood, Elaine, *The Idea in Things: Fugitive Meaning in the Victorian Novel* (Chicago, IL: University of Chicago Press, 2006)

Freud, Sigmund, 'Some Psychical Consequences of the Anatomical Distinction between the Sexes' (1925), in *The Standard Edition of the Complete Psychological Works of Sigmund Freud* trans. and ed. by James Strachey, 23 vols. (London: Hogarth Press, 1955), vol. XIX, pp. 243–58

'Totem and Taboo' (1913), in *Standard Edition of the Complete Psychological Works*, trans. and ed. by Strachey, vol. XIII, pp. 1–161

Furneaux, Holly, *Queer Dickens: Erotics, Families, Masculinities* (Oxford: Oxford University Press, 2009)

Gabbard, Christopher, 'From Custodial Care to Caring Labour: the Discourse of Who Cares in *Jane Eyre*', in *The Madwoman and the Blindman*, ed. by Bolt, Rodas and Donaldson, pp. 91–110

Garland-Thomson, Rosemarie, 'The Beauty and the Freak', in Susan Crutchfield and Marcy Epstein, eds., *Points of Contact: Disability, Art and Culture* (Ann Arbor: University of Michigan Press, 2000), pp. 181–96

*Extraordinary Bodies: Figuring Physical Disability in American Culture and Literature* (New York: Columbia University Press, 1997)

*Staring: How We Look* (Oxford: Oxford University Press, 2009)

Gilbert, Sandra, and Susan Gubar, *The Madwoman in the Attic: The Woman Writer and the Nineteenth-Century Literary Imagination*, 2nd edn (New Haven, CT: Yale University Press, 1979; reprt 2000)

Gill, Stephen, *William Wordsworth: A Life* (Oxford: Oxford University Press, 1990)

*Wordsworth and the Victorians* (Oxford: Oxford University Press, 2001)

Gitter, Elisabeth, 'The Blind Daughter in Charles Dickens's *Cricket on the Hearth*', *SEL: Studies in English Literature, 1500–1900*, 39 (1999), 675–89

Gladden, Samuel Lyndon, 'Spectacular Deceptions: Closets, Secrets, and Identity in Wilkie Collins's *Poor Miss Finch*', *Victorian Literature and Culture*, 33 (2005), 467–86

Glen, Heather, *Charlotte Brontë: The Imagination in History* (Oxford: Oxford University Press, 2002)

Goodman, Marcia Renee, '"I'll Follow the Other": Tracing the (M)other in Bleak House, *Dickens Studies Annual*, 19 (1990), 147–67

Graver, Suzanne, 'Writing in a "Womanly Way" and the Double Vision of *Bleak House*', *Dickens Quarterly*, 4:1 (1987), 3–15

Gregory, Richard Langton, and Jean G. Wallace, *Recovery from Early Blindness: A Case Study* (Cambridge: W. Heffer & Sons, 1963)

Hartman, Geoffrey H., 'Diction and Defense', in *The Unremarkable Wordsworth* (London: Methuen, 1987)

Hayles, N. Katherine, *My Mother was a Computer: Digital Subjects and Literary Texts* (Chicago, IL: University of Chicago Press, 2005)

Heidegger, Martin, *Parmenides*, trans. by André Schuwer and Richard Rojewicz (Bloomington: Indiana University Press, 1998)

Hertz, Neil, 'The Notion of Blockage in the Literature of the Sublime', in *The End of the Line: Essays on Psychoanalysis and the Sublime* (New York: Columbia University Press, 1985), pp. 40–60

Hirschberg, Julius, *The History of Ophthalmology*, trans. by Frederick C. Blodi, 11 vols. (Bonn: 1987)

Holmes, Martha Stoddard, *Fictions of Affliction: Physical Disability in Victorian Culture* (Ann Arbor: University of Michigan Press, 2004)

'Visions of Rochester: Screening Desire and Disability in *Jane Eyre*', in *The Madwoman and the Blindman*, ed. by Bolt, Rodas and Donaldson, pp. 150–74

Hollington, Michael, 'Dickens, the City, and the Five Senses', *AUMLA*, 113 (2010), 29–38

Houghton, Walter E., ed., *The Wellesley Index to Victorian Periodicals, 1824–1906*, 5 vols. (Toronto: University of Toronto Press; London: Routledge & Kegan Paul, 1966–79)

Howes, David, 'Scent, Sound and Synaesthesia: Intersensoriality and Material Culture Theory', in *Handbook of Material Culture*, ed. by Christopher Tilley, Webb Keane, Susanne Küchler, Michael Rowlands and Patricia Spye (London: Sage, 2006), pp. 161–72

Howsam, Leslie, *Cheap Bibles: Nineteenth-Century Publishing and the British and Foreign Bible Society* (Cambridge: Cambridge University Press, 1991)

Jaffe, Audrey, *Vanishing Points: Dickens, Narrative, and the Subject of Omniscience* (Berkeley: University of California Press, 1991)

Jay, Martin, *Downcast Eyes: The Denigration of Vision in Twentieth-Century French Thought* (Berkeley: University of California Press, 1994)

'Sartre, Merleau-Ponty, and the Search for a New Ontology of Sight', in *Modernity and the Hegemony of Vision*, ed. by David Michael Levin (Berkeley: University of California Press, 1993), pp. 143–85

Joshua, Essaka, '"I Began to See": Biblical Models of Disability in *Jane Eyre*', in *The Madwoman and the Blindman*, ed. by Bolt, Rodas and Donaldson, pp. 111–28

Kittler, Friedrich A., *Discourse Networks 1800/1900*, trans. by Michael Metteer, with Chris Cullens (Stanford, CA: Stanford University Press, 1987)

*Gramophone, Film, Typewriter*, trans. by Geoffrey Winthrop-Young and Michael Wutz, 2nd edn (Stanford, CA: Stanford University Press, 1986; reprt 1999)

Klages, Mary, *Woeful Afflictions: Disability and Sentimentality in Victorian America* (Philadelphia: University of Pennsylvania Press, 1999)

Kleege, Georgina, *Blind Rage: Letters to Helen Keller* (Washington, DC: Gallaudet University Press, 2006)

'Blindness and Visual Culture: An Eye-Witness Account', *Journal of Visual Culture* 4:2 (2005), 179–90

'Introduction: Blindness and Literature', *Journal of Literary & Cultural Disability Studies*, 3:2 (2009), 113–114

Kudlick, Cathy, 'Disability History: Why We Need Another "Other"', *The American Historical Review*, 108:3 (June 2003), 763–93

Lacan, Jacques, *The Four Fundamental Concepts of Psycho-Analysis*, trans. by Alan Sheridan (London: Penguin, 1973; reprt 1994)

Larrissy, Edward, *The Blind and Blindness in Literature of the Romantic Period* (Edinburgh: Edinburgh University Press, 2007)

Ledger, Sally, *Dickens and the Popular Radical Imagination* (Cambridge: Cambridge University Press, 2007)

Leighton, Angela, *Elizabeth Barrett Browning* (Brighton: The Harvester Press, 1986)

Linett, Maren, 'Blindness and Intimacy in Early Twentieth-Century Literature', *Mosaic: A Journal for the Interdisciplinary Study of Literature*, 46:3 (2013), 27–42

Low, Gail Chiang-Liang, *White Skins/Black Masks: Representation and Colonialism* (London: Routledge, 1995)

Lupton, Christina, *Knowing Books: The Consciousness of Mediation in Eighteenth-Century Britain* (Philadelphia: University of Pennsylvania Press, 2012)

Maxwell, Catherine, *Bearing Blindness: The Female Sublime from Milton to Swinburne* (Manchester: Manchester University Press, 2001)

McCance, Dawne, 'Introduction', *Mosaic: A Journal for the Interdisciplinary Study of Literature*, 46:3 (2013), v–x

Mehlman, Jeffrey, *Cataract: A Study in Diderot* (Middletown, CT: Wesleyan University Press, 1979)

Merleau-Ponty, Maurice, 'Eye and Mind', in *The Merleau-Ponty Aesthetics Reader: Philosophy and Painting*, ed. by Galen A. Johnson (Evanston, IL: Northwestern University Press, 1993), pp. 121–49

'The Intertwining – the Chiasm', in *The Visible and the Invisible*, ed. by Claude Lefort, trans. by Alphonso Lingis (Evanston, IL: Northwestern University Press, 1968), pp. 130–55

*Phenomenology of Perception*, trans. Colin Smith, 9th edn (translated from the French *Phenomenologie de la Perception*, first pub. London, Routledge: 1962; reprt 2003)

McGann, Jerome, *Radiant Textuality: Literature After the World Wide Web* (Basingstoke: Palgrave, 2001)

Michie, Helen, '"Who is this in Pain?": Scarring, Disfigurement, and Female Identity in *Bleak House* and *Our Mutual Friend*', *NOVEL: A Forum on Fiction*, 22:2 (1989), 199–212

Miller, D. A., *The Novel and the Police* (Berkeley: University of California Press, 1988)

Miller, J. Hillis, 'Introduction', in Charles Dickens, *Bleak House*, ed. by Norman Page (Harmondsworth: Penguin, 1971), pp. 11–34

Mills, Mara, 'The Co-Construction of Blindness and Reading', published in German translation in *Disability trouble: Ästhetick und Bildpolitik bei Helen Keller*, ed. by Ulrike Bergermann (Berline: b_books, 2013), pp. 195–204

Mills, Victoria, ed., 'Victorian Fiction and the Material Imagination', in *19: Interdisciplinary Studies in the Long Nineteenth Century*, 6 (2008) www.19.bbk.ac.uk/index.php/19/issue/view/69 [Accessed 1 March 2013]

Mintz, Susannah B., 'Illness, Disability, and Recognition in *Jane Eyre*', in *The Madwoman and the Blindman*, ed. by Bolt, Rodas and Donaldson, pp. 129–49

Mirzoeff, Nicholas, *Bodyscape: Art, Modernity and the Ideal Figure* (London and New York: Routledge, 1995)

Mitchell, D. T. and Snyder, S. L., *Narrative Prosthesis: Disability and the Dependencies of Discourse* (Ann Arbor: University of Michigan Press, 2001)

Mitchie, Elsie B., *Outside the Pale: Cultural Exclusion, Gender Difference, and the Victorian Woman Writer* (Ithaca, NY: Cornell University Press, 1993)

Mulvey, Laura, 'Visual Pleasure and Narrative Cinema', in *Visual and Other Pleasures* (Basingstoke: Macmillan, 1989), pp. 14–28

Nardo, Anna K., *George Eliot's Dialogue with John Milton* (Columbia: University of Missouri Press, 2003)

Newlyn, Lucy, Paradise Lost *and the Romantic Reader* (Oxford: Clarendon Press, 1993)

Olsén, Jan Eric, 'Vicariates of the Eye: Blindness, Sense Substitution, and Writing Devices in the Nineteenth Century', *Mosaic: A Journal for the Interdisciplinary Study of Literature*, 46:3 (2013), 75–91

Ong, Walter J., *Orality and Literacy: The Technologizing of the Word* (London: Methuen, 1982; reprt 1985)

Pascoe, Judith, *Romantic Theatricality: Gender, Poetry and Spectatorship* (Ithaca, NY: Cornell University Press, 1997)

Paterson, Mark, '"Looking on darkness, which the blind do see": Blindness, Empathy, and Feeling Seeing', *Mosaic: A Journal for the Interdisciplinary Study of Literature*, 46:3 (2013), 159–77

Paulson, William R., *Enlightenment, Romanticism, and the Blind in France* (Princeton, NJ: Princeton University Press, 1987)

Perman, Tory Vandeventer, 'Refiguring Disability: Deviance, Blinding, and the Supernatural in Thomas Chestre's *Sir Launfal*', *Journal of Literary & Cultural Disability Studies*, 3:2 (2009), 131–46

Phillips, Gordon, *The Blind in British Society: Charity, State and Community, c. 1780–1930* (Aldershot: Ashgate, 2004)

Piper, Andrew, *Book was There: Reading in Electronic Times* (Chicago, IL: University of Chicago Press, 2012)

Pratt, Mary Louise, *Imperial Eyes: Travel Writing and Transculturation* (London: Routledge, 2002)

Price, Leah, *How to Do Things with Books in Victorian Britain* (Princeton, NJ: Princeton University Press, 2012)

Price, Leah, and Pamela Thurschwell, 'Stenographic Masculinity', in *Literary Secretaries/ Secretarial Culture*, ed. by Price and Thurschwell, pp. 32–47

Pykett, Lyn, 'The Material Turn in Victorian Studies', *Literature Compass*, 1 (2004), 1–5

Reeve, Blake, *Romantic Tragedies: The Dark Employments of Wordsworth, Coleridge, and Shelley* (Cambridge: Cambridge University Press, 2011)

Richardson, Alan, *British Romanticism and the Science of the Mind* (Cambridge: Cambridge University Press, 2001)

Rodas, Julia Miele, 'On Blindness', *Journal of Literary & Cultural Disability Studies*, 3:2 (2009), 115–30

Rosman, Doreen M., *Evangelicals and Culture* (Aldershot: Gregg Revivals, 1984)

Rothfield, Lawrence, *Vital Signs: Medical Realism in Nineteenth-Century Fiction* (Princeton, NJ: University of Princeton Press, 1992)

Rubery, Matthew, 'From Shell Shock to Shellac: The Great War, Blindness, and Britain's Talking Book Library', *Twentieth Century British History* (first published online: 7 May 2014), doi: 10.1093/tcbh/hwu017, 25pp

Sacks, Oliver, 'To See and Not See', in *An Anthropologist on Mars: Seven Paradoxical Tales* (London: Picador, 1995), pp. 102–44

Saussure, Ferdinand de, *Course in General Linguistics*, 2nd edn, ed. by Charles Bally and Albert Sechehaye in collaboration with Albert Reidlinger, trans. by Wade Baskin (Glasgow: Fontana/Collins, 1960; reprt 1974)

Schor, Naomi, 'Blindness as Metaphor', *differences: A Journal of Feminist Cultural Studies*, 11 (1999), 76–105

Shires, Linda M., 'Literary Careers, Death, and the Body Politics of *David Copperfield*', in *Dickens Refigured: Bodies, Desires, and Other Histories*, ed. by John Schad (Manchester: Manchester University Press, 1996), pp. 117–35

Shuttleworth, Sally, *Charlotte Brontë and Victorian Psychology* (Cambridge: Cambridge University Press, 1996)

Stafford, Margot, 'Keeping One's Own Counsel: Authorship, Literary Advice and *New Grub Street*', *The Gissing Journal*, 37:2 (2001), 1–18

Steeves, H. Peter, 'Gone Missing', *Mosaic: A Journal for the Interdisciplinary Study of Literature*, 46:3 (2013), 1–26

Tabbara, Khalid F., 'Blinding Trachoma: The Forgotten Problem', online version of *British Journal of Ophthalmology*, 85 (2001), 1397–9, http://bjo.bmj.com/cgi/content/full/85/12/1397 [accessed 20 December 2006]

Taylor, Jenny Bourne, *The Secret Theatre of Home: Wilkie Collins, Sensation Narrative and Nineteenth-Century Psychology* (London: Routledge, 1988)

Terada, Rei, 'Phenomenality and dissatisfaction in Coleridge's Notebooks', *Studies in Romanticism*, 43 (2004), 257–81

Thomas, Mary G., *N. I. B. Biographies: Thomas Rhodes Armitage* (London: National Institute for the Blind, 1952)

Thurston, Luke, *Literary Ghosts from the Victorians to Modernism* (London: Routledge, 2012)

Tilley, Christopher, 'Theoretical Perspectives', in *Handbook of Material Culture*, ed. by Christopher Tilley, Webb Keane, Susanne Küchler, Michael Rowlands and Patricia Spye (London: Sage, 2006), pp. 7–11

*Metaphor and Material Culture* (Blackwell: Oxford, 1999)

Tilley, Heather, 'Introduction: The Victorian Tactile Imagination', *19: Interdisciplinary Studies in the Long Nineteenth Century*, 19 (2014)

'Sentiment and Vision in Charles Dickens's *A Christmas Carol* and *The Cricket on the Hearth*', *19: Interdisciplinary Studies in the Long Nineteenth Century*, special issue *Rethinking Victorian Sentimentality*, 4 (2007) www.19.bbk.ac.uk

'The Sentimental Touch: Dickens's *Old Curiosity Shop* and the Feeling Reader', *Journal of Victorian Culture*, 16:1 (2011), 226–41

Titchkosky, Tanya, *Reading and Writing Disability Differently: The Textured Life of Embodiment* (Toronto: University of Toronto Press, 2007)

Torrell, Margaret Rose, 'From India-Rubber Back to Flesh: A Reevaluation of Male Embodiment in *Jane Eyre*', in *The Madwoman and the Blindman*, ed. by Bolt, Rodas and Donaldson, pp. 71–90

Tremain, Shelley, 'Foucault, Governmentality, and Critical Disability Theory', in *Foucault and the Government of Disability*, ed. by Shelley Tremain (Ann Arbor: University of Michigan Press, 2005), pp. 1–26.

Valvo, Alberto, *Sight Restoration after Long-Term Blindness: The Problems and Behaviour Patterns of Visual Rehabilitation* (New York: American Foundation for the Blind, 1971)

van Boheemen-Saaf, Christine, '"The Universe Makes an Indifferent Parent": *Bleak House* and the Victorian Family Romance', in *Interpreting Lacan*, ed. by Joseph H. Smith and William Kerrigan (New Haven, CT: Yale University Press, 1983), pp. 225–57

von Senden, Marius, *Space and Sight: The Perception of Space and Shape in the Congenitally Blind Before and After Operation*, trans. by Peter Heath (London: Methuen & Co., 1960)

Warne, Vanessa, '"So that the sense of touch may supply the want of sight": Blind Reading and Nineteenth-Century Print Culture', in *Media, Technology, and Literature in the Nineteenth Century: Image, Sound, Touch*, ed. by Colette Colligan and Margaret Linley (Farnham: Ashgate, 2011), pp. 43–64

Watts, Sheldon, *Epidemics and History: Disease, Power and Imperialism* (New Haven and London: Yale University Press, 1997)

Wershler-Henry, Darren, *'The Iron Whim': A History of Typewriting* (Ithaca, NY: Cornell University Press, 2007)

Žižek, Slavoj, '"I Hear You with My Eyes"; or, The Invisible Master', in *Gaze and Voice as Love Objects*, ed. by Renata Salecl and Slavoj Žižek (Durham: Duke University Press, 1996), pp. 90–128

Zupancic, Alenka, 'Philosophers' Blind Man's Buff', in *Gaze and Voice as Love Objects*, ed. by Renata Salecl and Slavoj Žižek (Durham: Duke University Press, 1996), pp. 32–58

# Index

*All the Year Round*, 90, *see also* Dickens, Charles
Alston, John, 75, 96
Anderson, Thomas, 94, 116–17
Armitage, Thomas Rhodes, 91, 237
  *Education and Employment of the Blind*, 91–93
asylums, 7
*Athenaeum*, 184
*Aurora Leigh*
  anxiety of woman writer, 145, 148–49
  Romney's blindness, 144–45, 148–50
  the maternal, 145–48
  similarity to *Jane Eyre*, 144–45, 148
  vision, 139

Bailey, Samuel, 25–26
Bain, Alexander, 34
Barrett Browning, Elizabeth, 184
  as blind writer, 143–44
  *Essay on Mind*, 139–40
  relationship with Hugh Stuart Boyd, 140–43
  relationship with Robert Browning, 142–44
Beecroft, Alexander, 102–3
Beer, Georg, 49
Berkeley, George, 24–26, 140, 199
Bichat, Marie François Xavier, 47
Bird, John, 99, 108, 111, 116
  as blind campaigner, 90
  critiques of blind education, 88–89, 111–13
  on James Wilson, 107–8, 112
  on literary depictions of blindness, 15, 100, 107
Birmingham Institution for the Blind, 87, 236
Blacklock, Thomas, 28–29, 73, 104, 203
*Bleak House* (Charles Dickens)
  blind writing practices, 179–80
  dual narrative, 173–74
  Esther as autobiographical, 173
  Esther's blindness, 178–79
  fog, 175–76
  smallpox, 176–78
  vision and power in novel, 179
'Blind Leaders of the Blind', 90–91
blindness
  autobiographical writings, 98–99, 115–16
  idealist models, 27
  as inner vision, 60
  literary critical theory, 10–11
  metanarrative of, 6, 14, 189
  as metaphor, 138, 169, 193
  relation to language, 22, 28–29
  as spiritual shortcoming, 81
  as tragedy, 190
  Victorian campaigners, 116, 215–16
Bloom, Harold, 37, 60
Bolt, David, 6, 14, 127
book
  materiality of, 5, 30–31
Bowen, John, 15–16, 152, 170–71
Boyd, Hugh Stuart, *see* Barrett Browning, Elizabeth: relationship with Hugh Stuart Boyd
Braille, Louis, 92, 237, *see also* raised print systems
braille (type), *see* raised print systems: braille
Bridgman, Laura, 204, *see also* Dickens, Charles, *American Notes*
Bristol Asylum for the Blind, 76
British and Foreign Bible Society, 80, 82
British and Foreign Society for Improving the Embossed Literature of the Blind, 86, 91
Brontë, Charlotte
  carer to Patrick Brontë, 131–34
  effect of visual impairment upon creative practice, 137–38
  opthalmology, 133
  shortsightedness, 136–37
Brontë, Patrick
  cataract operation, 132
  effect of cataract, 133–36
Brown, Ford Madox, 38–40

Browne, Frances, 182, 190
  fiction as autobiography, 191
  language acquisition, 185–86
  *My Share of the World*, 187–91
  *Star of Atteghei*, 185–86
Browning, Robert, *see* Barrett Browning, Elizabeth: relationship with Robert Browning
Burke, Edmund, 28–29, 60–61, 185–86, 204

Caldwell, Janis, 46, 196, 229
Calè, Luisa, 60–61
Carpenter, William B., 77–78, 227
cataract, 133, 175–76, 210, 244
  catoptric test, 210–11
Census, UK
  recording of disability, 87
Cheselden, William, 197, 203–4
Cixous, Hélène, 124–25
Cohen, William A., 33, 128–29, 183
Coleridge, Samuel Taylor, 60
Coleridge, Sarah, 48
Collins, Wilkie
  *The Dead Secret*, 192–93
  *Hide and Seek*, 191–92
Couser, G. Thomas, 98–99
Craik, Dinah
  *Olive*, 146–47, 189
Crary, Jonathan, 34–35
Crystal Palace, 70, *see also* Great Exhibition
cultural phenomenology
  relation to Victorian studies, 35
Curtis, Gerard, 22–23

*David Copperfield* (Charles Dickens), 188
  David as blind, 162–64, 167–68
  Dickens's autobiography, 164–65
  gender, 172
  intertextual resonances, 166–68
  material production of writing, 169–70
  touch, 164
  vision, 161–62
Davis, Lennard J., 8
De Man, Paul, 54–55, 138, 165
Dennie, Joseph [Oliver Olschool], 104–6
Descartes, Rene, 200
Dickens, Charles
  *American Notes*, 110, 154–58
  *Barnaby Rudge*, 15–16
  *Bentley's Miscellany*, 48–49
  *The Cricket on the Hearth*, 158–60
  *Dombey and Son*, 152
  literacy, 152–53, 156–57, 172–73
  *Old Curiosity Shop* (embossed), 158
  *The Pickwick Papers*, 152–53
  public health campaigns, 176–77
Diderot, Denis, 27–28, 77
disability
  embodiment, 5–6
  naturalisation of, 17–18
  social model, 221
disability studies
  cultural form, 8–9
  emergence of, 6–7
  relation to Victorian novel, 9, 12–13, 243
Dolan, Elizabeth, 43, 46, 228

Edinburgh Asylum for the Blind, 94, 116
*Edinburgh Medical and Surgical Journal*, 45
Edwards, Elizabeth, 30
Edwards, Gavin, 153, 246
Eliot, George
  *Middlemarch*, 36–37, 142
  *Romola*, 35–36
empiricism, 24
Esmail, Jennifer, 2–4, 75
evangelicalism, 80–81
eye glasses, coloured, 48–49
eye injury
  caused by literary pursuits, 50

Fawcett, Henry, 38–40
Fawcett, Millicent Garrett, 38–40
Ferguson, Ronald J., 98
finger alphabet, 157
Flint, Christopher, 30
Flint, Kate, 220
Forster, John
  *Life of Charles Dickens*, 164, 170
Foucault, Michel, 44, 229
Freud, Sigmund, 145, *see also* Oedipus complex

Gall, James, 21, 74, 79–81, 96
Garland-Thomson, Rosemarie, 9, 117, 129
Gaskell, Elizabeth
  *Life of Charlotte Brontë*, 128, 135–38
  *Mary Barton*, 197
gaze, the, 160, 190–91, 195–97, 204
gender politics of writing, 37, 190
General Association for the Welfare of the Blind, 78
Gilbert, Elizabeth ('Bessie'), 78, 84–85
  biography, 116, 117
Gilbert, Sandra and Susan Gubar, 126
Gill, Stephen, 67
Gillies, Margaret, 53, *see also* Wordsworth, William
Gissing, George, *see New Grub Street*

Glasgow Asylum for the Blind, 82
glaucoma, 175–76
Goldsmith, Oliver, 48
Great Exhibition, *see also* Crystal Palace
  display of blind literary technologies, 70–71
  *Official Catalogue*, 71

haptic, 34
Hartman, Geoffrey, 57
Haüy, Valentin, 72–73
Hayles, N. Katherine, 30
Hayley, William, 135
Hertz, Neil, 63, 65
Holmes, Martha Stoddard, 7, 194–95
Homer, 102–3
Howe, Samuel Gridley, 154, 156, 158
Howes, David, 30
Hutchinson, Sara, 46–48
hypothetical blind man, 24, 26–27

idealism, 24
Indigent Blind Visiting Society, 81, 92, 110
Institute for Blind Youth in Paris, 73, 92

*Jane Eyre* (Charlotte Brontë)
  blindness as generative of narrative, 128–30
  disability studies, 123, 124, 126–30
  feminist theory, 126
  privileging of vision, 125
  Rochester modelled on Patrick Brontë, 131, 136
  touch, 130–31
Jay, Martin, 32
Johnson, Edmund C., 71, 84, 89, 92

Kittler, Friedrich, 93–94
Kitto, John
  *The Lost Senses*, 109, 186, 192, 202–4
Klages, Mary, 97
Kleege, Georgina, 10, 26, 115, 222
Kudlick, Cathy, 85, 236

Lacan, Jacques, 190
language
  as ableist, 17
  as multisensory, 28–30
  as visual, 7, 21–23, 25–26, 105–6, 180, 185
Larrissy, Edward, 29, 228
Lessing, Gotthold Ephraim, 60–61
Levy, William Hanks, 70, 92, 116–17
  *Blindness and the Blind*, 115
literacy, 2–4
Locke, John, 24, 139
London Society for Teaching the Blind to Read, 70, 76, 81, 86
Lowe, Robert (Viscount Sherbrooke), 117–18
Lucas, T. M., 76, *see also* raised print systems
Lupton, Christina, 30

*Magazine for the Blind*, 81
material culture studies, 29–30
  relation to Victorian studies, 226
Maxwell, Catherine, 29
medical gaze, *see* gaze, the
Merleau-Ponty, Maurice
  'The Intertwining – the Chiasm', 33
metaphor
  materiality of, 14
Mill, John Stuart, 25–26
Millais, John Everett, 69
Miller, D. A., 250
Miller, J. Hillis, 172, 248
Milton, John
  anxiety of influence on female writers, 133–35
  influence on blind writers, 109–10
  influence of blindness on aesthetic discourse, 61
  as model for literary characters, 36–37
  ophthalmologic diagnoses of blindness, 61
  *Paradise Lost*, 103–4, 211–12
  *Samson Agonistes*, 56–57
  visual representations of, 39–40, 53
Mintz, Susannah B., 127–28
Mitchell, David and Sharon L. Snyder, 8–9, 14, 37
*Modern Domestic Medicine* (Thomas John Graham), 132
Molyneux's problem, 24, 27, 34–35
Mulvey, Laura, 158–60
myopia, *see* shortsightedness

Napoleonic wars, 64, 69
narrative prosthesis, 8–9, 243
National Library for the Blind, 215
*New Grub Street* (George Gissing), 208
  blindness as disability, 211
  blindness as tragedy, 210, 215
  imagination, 211–13
  literary marketplace, 209
  literary production, 213–14
  Yule's blindness, 210–12
New Poor Law, 7

ocularcentrism, 16, 118, 181, 215–16
Oedipus complex, 16, 126, 145–46
Olsén, Jan Eric, 21, 223
Ong, Walter, 23, 30
ophthalmia, *see* trachoma
ophthalmology, 5, 44–46

Pascoe, Judith, 53
Paulson, William, 22
Perkins Institution, Boston, 154
phenomenology, 14, 31–32, 222
*Poor Miss Finch* (Wilkie Collins), 182–83
  contemporary reviews, 192–93
  gender identity, 194–96
  Lucilla's blindness, 194, 201–2, 205–6
  narrative technique, 193
  Preface, 192
  racial debates, 202–4
  sight restoration, 197–99, 205
  touch, 199
*Prelude* (William Wordsworth), 51, 166
  anxieties about literacy, 63–64
  the blind beggar, 64–69
  depictions of London (book VII), 63–64
  drafting and revision process, 231
  as sensory text, 62–63, 68
  treatment of vision, 59–60
Price, Leah, 248

raised print systems, 71–72
  Alston type, 74–75
  Boston line type, 79, 158
  braille, 91–92
  criticisms by blind campaigners, 89–90
  cultural influence, 170
  Curry, Harriet, 85–86
  debates over format, 72, 74–76
  early history, 72–73
  Frere type, 79
  Fry type, 74
  Gall type, 79
  Hughes's dotted type, 90
  limited evidence, 88
  limited reading material, 82–84
  Lucas type, 76–77, 80, 85, 87
  material production of, 79–80, 82
  Mollard, Emma, 87–88
  Moon type, 82–84, 92–93
Reid, Thomas, 104–5
Richardson, Alan, 228
Rodas, Julia Miele, 22
Romantic materialism, 46
Rothfield, Lawrence, 177, 196, 250
Royal Commission on blindness (1885), 89, 215
Royal National Institute of Blind People, 85–87, *see also* British and Foreign Society for Improving the Embossed Literature of the Blind
Ruskin, John, 22

Saunders, John, 175
Saunderson, Nicholas, 28–29
Saussure, Ferdinand de, 76
senses, the
  hierarchies of, 4–5, 28
  substitution of, 21
Shelley, Mary
  *Frankenstein*, 46
Sherbrooke, Viscount, *see* Lowe, Robert
shortsightedness, 118, 125, 136–37, 144
Shuttleworth, Sally, 132–33, 196
sight restoration, 197–98, *see also Poor Miss Finch*
  Mitchell, James, 202
  psychological effect, 205
signed language, 234
*Sinnesvikariat, see* senses: substitution of
smallpox, 176–79
Smith, George, 81–82
Smith, John Thomas, 1–2, 18, 208
Sophocles
  *Oedipus at Colonus*, 57
Stevenson, John, 43, 49
Strand, Paul, 69

Tilley, Christopher, 14, 30, 223
Titchkosky, Tanya, 17–18
Tomlinson, Charles, 71–72, 233
touch, tactility, 33, 77–79, 201–2
trachoma, 41, 43–44, 46, 102, 140
'Training for the Blind' report, 1876, 113

*ut pictura poesis*, 29, 105

van Landeghem, Mrs Hippolyte, 111, 113–15, 191
Vetch, John, 49, 175
von Senden, Marius, 199–201, 205

Wardrop, James, 44, 202
Warne, Vanessa, 75, 77
Weber, Ernst Heinrich, 77
Wells, H. G., 208
White, Edmund, 108–10
Wilson, James
  *Biography of the Blind*, 99–106
  legacy, 112, 115
  *Life*, 101, 106
  poetry, 106–7
Wordsworth, Dora, 50–51
Wordsworth, Dorothy, 52, 66
Wordsworth, Mary, 53, 66
Wordsworth, William
  'A little onward lend thy guiding hand', 56–58
  anxieties about eyesight and literary career, 41, 50–51, 58
  experience of trachoma, 46–47, 65

'Lines Written a Few Miles above Tintern Abbey', 109, 167–68
literary critical interpretations of blindness, 228
Margaret Gillies portrait, 53
*The Borderers*, 55–56
treatments for trachoma, 48
use of amanuenses, 52–53, 56, 66, 233
writing technologies for blind people, 93–94
braille frame, 93
cultural anxieties, 95
Gall's typhlograph, 94
Nietzsche's writing ball, 238
William Hughes's typograph, 93–94

CAMBRIDGE STUDIES IN NINETEENTH-CENTURY LITERATURE AND CULTURE

*General Editor*
Gillian Beer, University of Cambridge

*Titles published*

1. *The Sickroom in Victorian Fiction: The Art of Being Ill*
Miriam Bailin, Washington University

2. *Muscular Christianity: Embodying the Victorian Age*
Edited by Donald E. Hall, California State University, Northridge

3. *Victorian Masculinities: Manhood and Masculine Poetics in Early Victorian Literature and Art*
Herbert Sussman, Northeastern University, Boston

4. *Byron and the Victorians*
Andrew Elfenbein, University of Minnesota

5. *Literature in the Marketplace: Nineteenth-Century British Publishing and the Circulation of Books*
Edited by John O. Jordan, University of California, Santa Cruz and Robert L. Patten, Rice University, Houston

6. *Victorian Photography, Painting and Poetry*
Lindsay Smith, University of Sussex

7. *Charlotte Brontë and Victorian Psychology*
Sally Shuttleworth, University of Sheffield

8. *The Gothic Body: Sexuality, Materialism and Degeneration at the Fin de Siècle*
Kelly Hurley, University of Colorado at Boulder

9. *Rereading Walter Pater*
William F. Shuter, Eastern Michigan University

10. *Remaking Queen Victoria*
Edited by Margaret Homans, Yale University and Adrienne Munich, State University of New York, Stony Brook

11. *Disease, Desire, and the Body in Victorian Women's Popular Novels*
Pamela K. Gilbert, University of Florida

12. *Realism, Representation, and the Arts in Nineteenth-Century Literature*
Alison Byerly, Middlebury College, Vermont

13. *Literary Culture and the Pacific*
Vanessa Smith, University of Sydney

14. *Professional Domesticity in the Victorian Novel Women, Work and Home*
Monica F. Cohen

15. *Victorian Renovations of the Novel: Narrative Annexes and the Boundaries of Representation*
Suzanne Keen, Washington and Lee University, Virginia

16. *Actresses on the Victorian Stage: Feminine Performance and the Galatea Myth*
Gail Marshall, University of Leeds

17. *Death and the Mother from Dickens to Freud: Victorian Fiction and the Anxiety of Origin*
Carolyn Dever, Vanderbilt University, Tennessee

18. *Ancestry and Narrative in Nineteenth-Century British Literature: Blood Relations from Edgeworth to Hardy*
Sophie Gilmartin, Royal Holloway, University of London

19. *Dickens, Novel Reading, and the Victorian Popular Theatre*
Deborah Vlock

20. *After Dickens: Reading, Adaptation and Performance*
John Glavin, Georgetown University, Washington D C

21. *Victorian Women Writers and the Woman Question*
Edited by Nicola Diane Thompson, Kingston University, London

22. *Rhythm and Will in Victorian Poetry*
Matthew Campbell, University of Sheffield

23. *Gender, Race, and the Writing of Empire: Public Discourse and the Boer War*
Paula M. Krebs, Wheaton College, Massachusetts

24. *Ruskin's God*
Michael Wheeler, University of Southampton

25. *Dickens and the Daughter of the House*
Hilary M. Schor, University of Southern California

26. *Detective Fiction and the Rise of Forensic Science*
Ronald R. Thomas, Trinity College, Hartford, Connecticut

27. *Testimony and Advocacy in Victorian Law, Literature, and Theology*
Jan-Melissa Schramm, Trinity Hall, Cambridge

28. *Victorian Writing about Risk: Imagining a Safe England in a Dangerous World*
Elaine Freedgood, University of Pennsylvania

29. *Physiognomy and the Meaning of Expression in Nineteenth-Century Culture*
Lucy Hartley, University of Southampton

30. *The Victorian Parlour: A Cultural Study*
Thad Logan, Rice University, Houston

31. *Aestheticism and Sexual Parody 1840–1940*
Dennis Denisoff, Ryerson University, Toronto

32. *Literature, Technology and Magical Thinking, 1880–1920*
Pamela Thurschwell, University College London

33. *Fairies in Nineteenth-Century Art and Literature*
Nicola Bown, Birkbeck, University of London

34. *George Eliot and the British Empire*
Nancy Henry, The State University of New York, Binghamton

35. *Women's Poetry and Religion in Victorian England: Jewish Identity and Christian Culture*
Cynthia Scheinberg, Mills College, California

36. *Victorian Literature and the Anorexic Body*
Anna Krugovoy Silver, Mercer University, Georgia

37. *Eavesdropping in the Novel from Austen to Proust*
Ann Gaylin, Yale University

38. *Missionary Writing and Empire, 1800–1860*
Anna Johnston, University of Tasmania

39. *London and the Culture of Homosexuality, 1885–1914*
Matt Cook, Keele University

40. *Fiction, Famine, and the Rise of Economics in Victorian Britain and Ireland*
Gordon Bigelow, Rhodes College, Tennessee

41. *Gender and the Victorian Periodical*
Hilary Fraser, Birkbeck, University of London
Judith Johnston and Stephanie Green,
University of Western Australia

42. *The Victorian Supernatural*
Edited by Nicola Bown, Birkbeck College, London
Carolyn Burdett, London Metropolitan University
and Pamela Thurschwell, University College London

43. *The Indian Mutiny and the British Imagination*
Gautam Chakravarty, University of Delhi

44. *The Revolution in Popular Literature: Print, Politics and the People*
Ian Haywood, Roehampton University of Surrey

45. *Science in the Nineteenth-Century Periodical: Reading the Magazine of Nature*
Geoffrey Cantor, University of Leeds
Gowan Dawson, University of Leicester
Graeme Gooday, University of Leeds

Richard Noakes, University of Cambridge
Sally Shuttleworth, University of Sheffield
and Jonathan R. Topham, University of Leeds

46. *Literature and Medicine in Nineteenth-Century Britain from Mary Shelley to George Eliot*
Janis McLarren Caldwell, Wake Forest University

47. *The Child Writer from Austen to Woolf*
Edited by Christine Alexander, University of New South Wales
and Juliet Mcmaster, University of Alberta

48. *From Dickens to Dracula: Gothic, Economics, and Victorian Fiction*
Gail Turley Houston, University of New Mexico

49. *Voice and the Victorian Storyteller*
Ivan Kreilkamp, University of Indiana

50. *Charles Darwin and Victorian Visual Culture*
Jonathan Smith, University of Michigan-Dearborn

51. *Catholicism, Sexual Deviance, and Victorian Gothic Culture*
Patrick R. O'Malley, Georgetown University

52. *Epic and Empire in Nineteenth-Century Britain*
Simon Dentith, University of Gloucestershire

53. *Victorian Honeymoons: Journeys to the Conjugal*
Helena Michie, Rice University

54. *The Jewess in Nineteenth-Century British Literary Culture*
Nadia Valman, University of Southampton

55. *Ireland, India and Nationalism in Nineteenth-Century Literature*
Julia Wright, Dalhousie University

56. *Dickens and the Popular Radical Imagination*
Sally Ledger, Birkbeck, University of London

57. *Darwin, Literature and Victorian Respectability*
Gowan Dawson, University of Leicester

58. *'Michael Field': Poetry, Aestheticism and the Fin de Siècle*
Marion Thain, University of Birmingham

59. *Colonies, Cults and Evolution: Literature, Science and Culture in Nineteenth-Century Writing*
David Amigoni, Keele University

60. *Realism, Photography and Nineteenth-Century Fiction*
Daniel A. Novak, Lousiana State University

61. *Caribbean Culture and British Fiction in the Atlantic World, 1780–1870*
Tim Watson, University of Miami

62. *The Poetry of Chartism: Aesthetics, Politics, History*
Michael Sanders, University of Manchester

63. *Literature and Dance in Nineteenth-Century Britain: Jane Austen to the New Woman*
Cheryl Wilson, Indiana University

64. *Shakespeare and Victorian Women*
Gail Marshall, Oxford Brookes University

65. *The Tragi-Comedy of Victorian Fatherhood*
Valerie Sanders, University of Hull

66. *Darwin and the Memory of the Human: Evolution, Savages, and South America*
Cannon Schmitt, University of Toronto

67. *From Sketch to Novel: The Development of Victorian Fiction*
Amanpal Garcha, Ohio State University

68. *The Crimean War and the British Imagination*
Stefanie Markovits, Yale University

69. *Shock, Memory and the Unconscious in Victorian Fiction*
Jill L. Matus, University of Toronto

70. *Sensation and Modernity in the 1860s*
Nicholas Daly, University College Dublin

71. *Ghost-Seers, Detectives, and Spiritualists: Theories of Vision in Victorian Literature and Science*
Srdjan Smajić, Furman University

72. *Satire in an Age of Realism*
Aaron Matz, Scripps College, California

73. *Thinking About Other People in Nineteenth-Century British Writing*
Adela Pinch, University of Michigan

74. *Tuberculosis and the Victorian Literary Imagination*
Katherine Byrne, University of Ulster, Coleraine

75. *Urban Realism and the Cosmopolitan Imagination in the Nineteenth Century: Visible City, Invisible World*
Tanya Agathocleous, Hunter College, City University of New York

76. *Women, Literature, and the Domesticated Landscape: England's Disciples of Flora, 1780–1870*
Judith W. Page, University of Florida
Elise L. Smith, Millsaps College, Mississippi

77. *Time and the Moment in Victorian Literature and Society*
Sue Zemka, University of Colorado

78. *Popular Fiction and Brain Science in the Late Nineteenth Century*
Anne Stiles, Washington State University

79. *Picturing Reform in Victorian Britain*
Janice Carlisle, Yale University

80. *Atonement and Self-Sacrifice in Nineteenth-Century Narrative*
Jan-Melissa Schramm, University of Cambridge

81. *The Silver Fork Novel: Fashionable Fiction in the Age of Reform*
Edward Copeland, Pomona College, California

82. *Oscar Wilde and Ancient Greece*
Iain Ross, Colchester Royal Grammar School

83. *The Poetry of Victorian Scientists: Style, Science and Nonsense*
Daniel Brown, University of Southampton

84. *Moral Authority, Men of Science, and the Victorian Novel*
Anne Dewitt, Princeton Writing Program

85. *China and the Victorian Imagination: Empires Entwined*
Ross G. Forman, University of Warwick

86. *Dickens's Style*
Daniel Tyler, University of Oxford

87. *The Formation of the Victorian Literary Profession*
Richard Salmon, University of Leeds

88. *Before George Eliot: Marian Evans and the Periodical Press*
Fionnuala Dillane, University College Dublin

89. *The Victorian Novel and the Space of Art: Fictional Form on Display*
Dehn Gilmore, California Institute of Technology

90. *George Eliot and Money: Economics, Ethics and Literature*
Dermot Coleman, Independent Scholar

91. *Masculinity and the New Imperialism: Rewriting Manhood in British Popular Literature, 1870–1914*
Bradley Deane, University of Minnesota

92. *Evolution and Victorian Culture*
Edited by Bernard Lightman, York University, Toronto
and Bennett Zon, University of Durham

93. *Victorian Literature, Energy, and the Ecological Imagination*
Allen Macduffie, University of Texas, Austin

94. *Popular Literature, Authorship and the Occult in Late Victorian Britain*
Andrew McCann, Dartmouth College, New Hampshire

95. *Women Writing Art History in the Nineteenth Century: Looking Like a Woman*
Hilary Fraser Birkbeck, University of London

96. *Relics of Death in Victorian Literature and Culture*
Deborah Lutz, Long Island University, C. W. Post Campus

97. *The Demographic Imagination and the Nineteenth-Century City: Paris, London, New York*
Nicholas Daly, University College Dublin

98. *Dickens and the Business of Death*
Claire Wood, University of York

99. *Translation as Transformation in Victorian Poetry*
Annmarie Drury, Queens College, City University of New York

100. *The Bigamy Plot: Sensation and Convention in the Victorian Novel*
Maia Mcaleavey, Boston College, Massachusetts

101. *English Fiction and the Evolution of Language, 1850–1914*
Will Abberley, University of Oxford

102. *The Racial Hand in the Victorian Imagination*
Aviva Briefel, Bowdoin College, Maine

103. *Evolution and Imagination in Victorian Children's Literature*
Jessica Straley, University of Utah

104. *Writing Arctic Disaster: Authorship and Exploration*
Adriana Craciun, University of California, Riverside

105. *Science, Fiction, and the Fin-de-Siècle Periodical Press*
Will Tattersdill, University of Birmingham

106. *Democratising Beauty in Nineteenth-Century Britain: Art and the Politics of Public Life*
Lucy Hartley, University of Michigan

107. *Everyday Words and the Character of Prose in Nineteenth-Century Britain*
Jonathan Farina, Seton Hall University, New Jersey

108. *Gerard Manley Hopkins and the Poetry of Religious Experience*
Martin Dubois, University of Newcastle Upon Tyne

109. *Blindness and Writing: From Wordsworth to Gissing*
Heather Tilley, Birkbeck College, University of London